THEOLOGY
FROM THE BELLY
of THE WHALE

Frederick Herzog

THEOLOGY
FROM THE BELLY
of THE WHALE

A Frederick Herzog Reader

EDITED BY JOERG RIEGER

TRINITY PRESS INTERNATIONAL
Harrisburg, Pennsylvania

Trinity Press International, P.O. Box 1321, Harrisburg, PA 17105
Trinity Press International is a division of the Morehouse Group

Library of Congress Cataloging-in-Publication Data

Herzog, Frederick.
    Theology from the belly of the whale : a Frederick Herzog reader /
edited by Joerg Rieger.
        p. cm.
    Includes bibliographical references and index.
    ISBN 1-56338-265-2 (pbk. : alk. paper)
    1. Liberation theology. 2. Theology, Doctrinal.   I. Rieger,
Joerg. II. Title.
BT83.57.H46   1999
230′.0464 – dc21   99-26105

Printed in the United States of America

99   00   01   02   03   04   10   9   8   7   6   5   4   3   2   1

To our common Peruvian friends:
Rosanna Panizo,
Eric Torres and Ronda Lee-Torres,
Luis and Catty Reinoso,
Liselotte Schrader and her family,
and the children of the Aldea Infantil

So "in my soul" I kneel in the grass of the Dakota prairies that gave me birth. Today, knowing a little more of the "Trail of Tears" that led also through these prairies to Wounded Knee, I bury my head in the grass, incapable of tears. Looking up again, in my mind I see on the horizon toward the East the smoke of the ovens of Auschwitz. "Stony the road we trod, bitter the chastening rod, felt in the days when hope unborn had died." In small compass, this is my life — gutted yet not burned out, with "miles to go before I sleep." God all along is walking against the tyranny of mammon, superiority, and power while reinventing the American — nonviolently. "No statement, theological or otherwise, should be made that would not be credible in the presence of burning children" (Irving Greenberg).

— Frederick Herzog, "New Birth of Conscience"

Contents

PREFACE

The work of the late Frederick Herzog (1925–1995) takes a unique position in North American theology in the twentieth century. Presenting an alternative perspective on the major developments of the past four decades, Herzog introduces new voices and unique ways of doing theology that will continue to give direction to theology and the church well into the twenty-first century. Throughout his life Frederick Herzog tried to weave together academic work in theology and concrete struggles for liberation. Although he completed significant sections of his work, he was not able to finish it. This reader gives some color to the various strands of Herzog's life and work, and weaves them together to form a constructive vision for both theology and the church.

Herzog's work does not easily fit within established categories. As a systematic theologian he challenged his peers to expand the boundaries of the field by paying closer attention to what was happening in both church and world. As a teacher of the church he invited the churches to enter into a dialogue with theology that would be self-critical, constructive, and mutually empowering. Most important, however, he never stopped reminding both theology and church to listen to those who had been left out of the influential ranks of both: people at the margins, African Americans, Native Americans, women, poor people, and the poorest of the poor in Latin America and elsewhere. This is the common thread which holds his work and this reader together, symbolized by the image of the belly of the whale that Herzog chose for himself.

Listening to, and entering into solidarity with, people at the margins, Frederick Herzog became a bridge builder, forging connections and alliances without disregarding vital differences. His work, sparked by the encounter with the suffering of African Americans in the South, in touch with the plight of Latin Americans, women, and Native Americans, exemplifies the broad response to the crises of the modern world of a "theology from the belly of the whale." Herzog's work pulled together various strands not to imitate or supersede them, but to reform mainline theology and the church in the "First World," starting in North Carolina, with implications for North America and eventually even Europe.

The selection of texts in this volume takes the reader deep into Herzog's encounter with "belly of the whale" settings and their implications for theology and the church. It includes a number of unpublished pieces and translations of essays that have been available only in German. This selection also includes some of Herzog's last articles, which develop important new directions for the future, but have remained unpublished owing to his sudden death. Since many other important essays could not be included, this reader may serve as an invitation for further reading. The bibliography provides a virtually complete list of Herzog's books and essays.

For contemporary readers the lack of inclusive language in Herzog's early works is obvious. While I have made modest adjustment for consistency of spelling and other details in the essays included in this volume, I have not changed these idiosyncrasies as a sign that no theology is ever finished and that the task of theological reflection continues. The language of Herzog's later writings and lectures reflects his continuing efforts toward greater inclusivity.

Since Herzog never intended to found a specific theological school and resisted the theological enterprise where it would turn into a market of ideas, his work maintains a different kind of influence. For example, a volume that I edited recently (growing out of a session held in Herzog's memory at the American Academy of Religion in New Orleans, 1996) titled *Liberating the Future: God, Mammon, and Theology* (Minneapolis: Fortress Press, 1998) contains essays that, rather than giving eulogies, talk about the future of God's liberation in the twenty-first century. Herzog would not have wanted it any other way. The diverse list of contributors includes John B. Cobb, Jr., Gustavo Gutiérrez, M. Douglas Meeks, Jürgen Moltmann, Susan Thistlethwaite, Gayraud Wilmore, and myself. Covering the context of both Americas and Europe, the spirit of Herzog's work helped us to bring closer together our concerns for oppression along the lines of race, class, and gender.

Other publications that reflect the specific kind of impact Herzog had on theology and the church include *Theology and Corporate Conscience: Essays in Honor of Frederick Herzog,* edited by M. Douglas Meeks and Jürgen Moltmann (forthcoming). The *EKU-UCC Newsletter* 14, no. 1 (November 1996), published by the Wisconsin Synod of the United Church of Christ and edited by Frederick Trost, is dedicated to essays in memory of Frederick Herzog. Here some of the many anecdotes are told. Craig L. Nessan, *Orthopraxis or Heresy: The North American Theological Response to Latin American Liberation Theology* (Atlanta: Scholars Press, 1989), has dedicated a chapter to Herzog's work in relation to Latin American liberation theology. My own book, *Remember the Poor: The Theological Challenge of the Twenty-First Century* (Harrisburg, Pa.: Trinity Press International, 1998), develops new proposals for the theological role of people at the margins in light of the pioneering work of both Herzog and Gustavo Gutiérrez. Herzog's influence cannot be defined exclusively in light of new theological concepts and ideas, even though his work has been highly productive in this respect, but needs to be seen in the ways in which he still makes us think "on our feet," in the midst of life.

As editor of this volume I would like to express my gratitude first of all to Kristin Herzog, Frederick Herzog's wife and partner in theological dialogue, who supported this project in many ways. Her friendship, advice, and expertise have been invaluable. She has also done some of the translations, as has Mary Deasey

Collins, on the staff at Duke Divinity School. Peter McGuire, pastor of the South Davidson Charge of the United Methodist Church and former student of Herzog, deserves credit for suggesting the publication of a reader presenting Herzog's works, providing selected additions to the bibliography, a closer look at the unpublished sermons, assistance with gathering the permissions, and other support. His essay at the end of this volume looks at the work of Herzog from a pastor's perspective. I also want to thank Professors Gabriel Fackre, Stanley Hauerwas, Jürgen Moltmann, and Gayraud S. Wilmore for giving permission to publish letters Herzog addressed to them. Brian Minietta, one of my student assistants, has taken care of most of the retyping and editing of the original essays, and Ann Ralston, secretary to the faculty of Perkins School of Theology, Southern Methodist University, has done the rest. My work on this volume has been supported by a research and travel grant from Southern Methodist University. The vision and encouragement of Harold W. Rast, publisher of Trinity Press International, have made this volume possible.

JOERG RIEGER

Dallas, July 1998

Introduction

WHALING OUR WAY
INTO THE TWENTY-FIRST CENTURY

This volume contains a selection of essays, sermons, letters, and poems by a theologian who understood early on that modern theology had arrived at a crossroads. Already at a time when the clash of liberal and neoorthodox theology was still in full swing, Frederick Herzog began to develop alternative theological structures which led him to listen to the beat of a different drummer and to contribute one of the initial strands of liberation theology.

Today the question is whether theology is still able to make a difference in light of the challenges of the twenty-first century. At a time when many of us are beginning to realize that theology itself is in trouble, the work of Herzog is more relevant than ever. Throughout his writings he is broadening both our understanding of the challenges and hopes of the modern world, now dubbed postmodern, and our vision of theology.

Instead of narrowly focusing on a few select symptoms, like the crisis of interpretation that is now much discussed in intellectual circles, or the sometimes lamented, sometimes celebrated, loss of foundations, Herzog picks up a wider set of problems. Analyses of the structures of racism, recognized at the beginning of the civil rights struggle, of the structures of a globalizing economy which do not seem to benefit the vast masses of the poor, as well as analyses of the structures of oppression along the lines of gender, all point to the larger aspects of the crisis and direct our attention to structures which continue to determine much of our lives at the beginning of a new millennium.

Theology will make no significant progress unless its mandate is reconceived against this backdrop. If the deeper challenges of the present and the immense suffering of people at the margins of our world go unnoticed, theological reflection tends to become self-serving. No wonder the culture wars that are going on in church and theology today often quickly degenerate into mere smoke screens.

Theology and Life

It is a sign of hope that at present many theologians are becoming increasingly aware of the fact that theology is somehow connected to everyday life. More and more of us are no longer content with merely getting the doctrines right or devel-

oping ever more coherent theological systems. Looking beyond the tranquil halls
of academia, however tentatively, theology is starting to claim broader horizons.

Yet even where theology begins to hook up with life, our horizons often either
remain fairly narrow, determined by a certain self-centeredness, or they become
so broad that we will never discern the cracks and fissures of everyday life. Herzog's life and work provide a different model. In notes for a press release after
Herzog's death, his wife and partner in theological reflection, Kristin, put the
challenge in the following words: "His greatest concern was the embodiment of
academic insight in the messiness of daily living."

Theology "from the belly of the whale" is designed to uncover the hidden tensions and conflicts of everyday life, the full "messiness" of life that includes the
ghettoes, those forms of messiness that are made invisible by those who are better off and who often profit from them. The surprising insight is that tense and
oppressive situations in the bellies of whales and elsewhere provide new encounters with God, reminding us that throughout the history of Israel and the church
God has been at work where the pressure was greatest. In this way new horizons
and challenges for serious theological work are generated. Here theology is no
longer an attachment to life, whether as a stimulating conversation partner or
a stern moral guide, but is itself pulled into that messiness of living where God
is encountered in new ways. This approach puts things theological in a radically
different perspective, not only for those of us who often escape the messiness of
life at the margins, but also for those who are forced to live through it.

The development of Herzog's theology is instructive. While his work shows
deep familiarity with the tradition of the church and the theological state of the
art on both sides of the Atlantic, he did not develop its key themes primarily as a
response to other like-minded theologies or theologians. Much of his work took
shape in personal encounters with those who did not matter to theology or the
church, like sharecroppers in the fields of North Carolina, African Americans,
and poor people at home and in other parts of the world. For Herzog, all those
people had names. Familiar theological worlds were reconstructed, not first of all
in academic theological debates, but in personal encounters with people on the
underside of history, in what might be called "belly-of-the-whale settings."

These encounters, forcing theology to tackle some of the deepest elements
of its crisis, led to major new developments in theology. After almost a decade
of involvement in civil rights matters and with oppressed people, Herzog finally
began to understand when confronted with the martyrdom of Martin Luther
King, Jr.: "Here was not just the liberation process in the death of King, but
the theology of liberation."[1] Herzog was one of the first to understand that the
suffering of blacks had something to say to whites, and he was, as James Cone

---

1. Frederick Herzog, "Liberation and Process Theologies in the Church," *Prism* 5, no. 2 (Fall
1990): 61, included in this volume, as chapter 29. "I do not remember any significant step in that
process that was not related to the black church." Ibid.

noted in the seventies, the only white theologian who "has attempted to reorder theological priorities in the light of the oppression of black people."[2]

These dynamics were focused in the publication of one of the very first articles which introduced the term "liberation theology" in 1970.[3] Herzog soon found that others had picked up the term in their own settings. The liberation theologies of James Cone and Gustavo Gutiérrez were in the making at the same time; Rosemary Radford Ruether's book *Liberation Theology* followed a short time later. The different strands encountered each other only later, not without challenging and questioning each other.[4]

It is often overlooked that liberation theology did not develop out of one center, as a great idea that made its way from the top down. It developed in specific settings, independently but simultaneously, from the bottom up, where theology began to encounter not only the suffering but also the hope of the poor, African Americans, women, and others. And even though specific dates can be given, there is no use discussing who was "really first" in talking about a theology of liberation, since these theologies are not written as the brainchildren of intellectual heroes but in recognition of severe suffering and pressure in many shapes and forms.

Here a new form of theology emerges which finally breaks out of the modern fascination with the powers of the autonomous self, its claims to theological authority, and the heady thrill of individual authorship. Gustavo Gutiérrez has formulated the difference: "What we care about is not a matter of having 'our own theology,' the way the petit bourgeois used to dream of having 'their own house some day.' Such a dream does haunt the intellectual world."[5] Due to the fact that liberation theologies are done in close relation to history's nameless ones, it is no longer of primary importance whose name appears on articles and books. Herzog's work needs to be seen in this light, as a self-conscious move away from the stardom and soloist virtuosity that still counts in academia and the church.

---

2. James H. Cone, *God of the Oppressed* (Minneapolis: Seabury Press, 1975), 50, referring to Herzog's book *Liberation Theology*. See also James H. Cone, *Black Theology: A Documentary History, 1966–1979* (Maryknoll, N.Y.: Orbis Books, 1979), 138: "In his life and his writings, Herzog made it clear that Black Theology had something to say to White Theology which the latter dared not ignore if it wished to encounter the Word of God for our times. He suffered much isolation for his stand, because of the uncompromising way in which he stood his ground."

3. Frederick Herzog, "Theology of Liberation," *Continuum* 7, no. 4 (Winter 1970), included in this volume as chapter 9.

4. James H. Cone, *A Black Theology of Liberation*, 20th anniversary edition (Maryknoll, N.Y.: Orbis Books, 1990); Gustavo Gutiérrez, *Teología de la liberación: Perspectivas* (Lima: CEP, 1971), English translation: *A Theology of Liberation: History, Politics, and Salvation*, trans. and ed. Sister Caridad Inda and John Eagleson (Maryknoll, N.Y.: Orbis Books, 1973, 1988); Rosemary Radford Ruether, *Liberation Theology* (New York: Paulist Press, 1972). The first organized encounter of these various approaches took place in the Theology of the Americas Conference in Detroit in 1975. The emerging challenges and questions are recorded in *Theology in the Americas*, ed. Sergio Torres and John Eagleson (Maryknoll, N.Y.: Orbis Books, 1976).

5. Gustavo Gutiérrez, "The Historical Power of the Poor," in *The Power of the Poor in History* (Maryknoll, N.Y.: Orbis Books, 1983), 91.

The New Babylonian Captivity of the Church

In the encounter with God and others in oppressive and suffocating belly-of-the-whale settings, a new theological agenda gradually takes shape. Herzog envisioned a new era for theology and the church which he felt was already manifest in its humble beginnings precisely in places where those in charge would least expect it, on the underside of history.[6]

His hope was based on the trust that God is powerfully at work in ways that we often fail to recognize, because theologians and church people alike are often unable to read the signs of the times. The main problem, according to Herzog, is not God's revelation — God never played games of hide-and-seek anyway — but the fact that humanity tends to blind itself to what God is doing all along.[7] No real transformation can happen, therefore, without taking into account what, in the tradition of the Protestant Reformation, we might call the Babylonian captivity of the church today.

Herzog's work urges us to understand the captivity of the church and of theology in broad terms. While in the Reformation of the sixteenth century Martin Luther and others focused on the human being as enslaved by religious powers,[8] the modern era has produced the human being enslaved by politics. Political theologies in Europe and elsewhere have tried to address these structures. At present, however, another factor has gained prominence. Humanity defined in both religious and political terms is more and more replaced by humanity defined by economic structures. All of life, including religion and politics, is now captive to economic forces and trends. Even the current drive toward globalization is spurred mainly by economic interests. As a result, global corporations are gaining power over national governments. Many of their transactions cannot be regulated by national politics or law. Theology still needs to learn how to engage these structures.

Herzog believed that in contemporary North America theological reflection might find a clue in the dual heritage of North American Protestantism, which consists not only of the tradition of the Reformation but also of what he called the "tradition of liberation."[9] While we are still captive to controlling modes of

---

6. See Frederick Herzog, "Am Ende der Nachreformation: Zäsur in der amerikanischen Kirchengeschichte," *Evangelische Kommentare* 12, no. 9 (September 1979): 503–5. Herzog finds support for this hope in the work of church historians Sydney E. Ahlstrom and Robert T. Handy, who, in their own ways, have argued that North America finds itself at the end of a church historical period.

7. Already in his book *Liberation Theology: Liberation in the Light of the Fourth Gospel* (New York: Seabury Press, 1972), Herzog talks about God's "unconcealment." The relevant passages are included in this volume in chapter 12. See also Frederick Herzog, "Liberation Hermeneutic as Ideology Critique?" *Interpretation* 28, no. 4 (October 1974): 403, n. 51, and Herzog, "Responsible Theology?" in *Philosophy of Religion and Theology: 1974 Proceedings,* American Academy of Religion Section Papers, ed. James Wm. McClendon, Jr. (Missoula, Mont.: Scholars Press, 1974), 163–64.

8. Luther wrote a long treatise titled "The Babylonian Captivity of the Church." While he later recanted that treatise under pressure, he maintained his basic critique of the pope and the Roman Catholic Church.

9. In Herzog's own work, the traditions of the Reformation and of liberation come together in the hope for a genuine transformation of the church. A statement whose first draft he wrote, signed

religion in our churches (this is the primary concern of the Reformation tradition), the liberation tradition reminds us that theology and the churches are increasingly captive to the control of political and economic powers as well.

In his latest essays, some of which are included in this volume, Herzog has further developed the point that theology needs to pay closer attention to economic aspects of the contemporary scene. Instead of broad reflections on the relation of Christ and culture, for instance, the classic paradigm developed by H. Richard Niebuhr, Herzog's encounters with the poor in Peru, for instance (another belly-of-the-whale setting), trigger specific reflections on the relation of Christ and money.[10]

The goal of theological analysis of political and economic structures is not to politicize theology and the church, or to "economize" it, but to deal with the fact that everything is permeated by political and economic forces already. The trouble is that often we are hardly aware of what it is that controls us. In the United States, Herzog has argued, none of these powers has ever been challenged on a deeper level, an assessment that still rings true at the beginning of the twenty-first century.[11] Theology, even where it has developed certain critiques of the status quo in recent years, has yet to deal with the more specific aspects of the captivity of the church today.[12]

Herzog was convinced that the biggest challenge comes not from "broad reflection on books about the general cultural malaise or the promise of American culture," but from "specific analysis of the cities and towns in which we live in terms of their socio-political dynamics."[13] Since this comment was written, almost three more decades of general reflections by mainline theology have come and gone. The culture wars could not have taken place without them, and many heated debates about postmodernity have never really touched the ground. At the beginning of the twenty-first century we are perhaps finally at a stage where we can begin to take particular problems more seriously, not in order to promote parochialism, but in order to get in touch with actual places of suffering (did we ever really suffer because others label us "liberal" or "conservative,"

---

by thirty-nine theologians of the United Church of Christ, summarizes this hope: "Rooting ourselves in our traditions, especially the Liberation tradition and the Reformation tradition, we discover tremendous power for the future." The next sentence clarifies the challenge: "We have not listened enough to blacks, women, Native Americans, and others in our own ranks." *New Conversations* 8, no. 1 (Spring 1985): 2–3.

10. Some examples are provided in part 4 of this volume. See also Frederick Herzog, "Methodism, Missions, and Money," in *Doctrines and Discipline,* ed. Dennis M. Campbell, William B. Lawrence, and Russell E. Richey (Nashville: Abingdon Press, 1999).

11. See, for instance, Frederick Herzog, "Vernunft der Weisheit: Amerikanische Aufklärung im Licht kritischer Spiritualität," *Evangelische Kommentare* 18, no. 10 (October 1985): 551.

12. The impact of economic forces on theology, the church, and the world is addressed in *Liberating the Future: God, Mammon, and Theology,* ed. Joerg Rieger (Minneapolis: Fortress, 1998). The volume is dedicated to the memory of Frederick Herzog.

13. Frederick Herzog, "The Burden of Southern Theology: A Response," *Duke Divinity School Review* 38, no. 3 (Fall 1973): 157, n. 9.

"[post-]modern" or "traditional"?) and to develop better-informed visions of the broad picture.

Knowing full well that in theology we often leave it at taking "a few pot-shots in the dark," Herzog has sought to redirect theological attention to the silences of the church.[14] Theological reflection is not primarily an idealistic en-deavor, taking place at the level of ideal concepts, but an analytic one, tracing our captivity in order to get a clearer view for what God is doing all along.

Theology will need to cultivate what Herzog at one point calls "lab" settings, where listening to God is practiced in the context of listening to the "other," especially to people at the margins. Small groups woven together in mutual accountability provide the framework, combining action and reflection.[15] The traditional theological task of reflecting on the doctrines and the texts of the church does not become irrelevant but needs to be cultivated in this setting. As a result, doctrines are no longer metaphysical blueprints or conceptual propo-sitions to be put into praxis later, but "word-deeds," arising — as in the early church — out of praxis settings and feeding back into praxis.[16] This is the point of Herzog's final book, *God-Walk: Liberation Shaping Dogmatics.* Here he brings together the doctrinal teaching of the church and the "lab" setting of Christian praxis under the primacy of God's own praxis. I will come back to this issue later.

No transformation will take place without perceptive theological analyses. Unless we understand our dilemma, we will never be able to change it. Like few people in the field, Herzog has helped us understand where we are, start-ing at the local level. Many of his more specific analyses were not developed for publication but for local use. Full of references to local people and specific issues, they are examples of the need for precise understandings of our captivity at home. In these settings, an interdisciplinary perspective is no longer a matter of choice or intellectual affinity. Historical, political, and economic analyses are all part of the theological attempt to identify the difference God's justice makes in everyday life settings.[17]

---

14. Comments made in a lecture at Duke University, October 15, 1993. In this lecture Herzog claimed that "liberation theology is all about paying attention to the silences of the church."

15. Herzog used the image of the prophet Jonah in the belly of the whale for a brochure about prayer and contemplation groups at Duke Divinity School which emphasized an action-reflection model, creating what he calls a "lab" setting for better listening to God, to one another, and to the silences. A copy of it is reproduced in *Covenant Discipleship Quarterly* 1, no. 3 (April 1986): 5.

16. One of the later references to this issue can be found in Frederick Herzog, *God-Walk: Libera-tion Shaping Dogmatics* (Maryknoll, N.Y.: Orbis Books, 1988), 71: "In God-walk, Christian teachings are . . . word-deeds (metaphors), the *praxeis* of God, reflecting God's self-realization in history making conscience effective."

17. An unpublished piece titled "Toxic Injustice and the Integrity of God's Creation," for instance, written for a United Church of Christ Consultation in 1987 which included German participants, deals with the relation of race and ecology, starting at home. Herzog reports that people in black East Durham are more directly affected by ecological hazards than their white neighbors. In the larger picture, three out of every five African and Hispanic Americans live in communities with uncontrolled toxic waste sites. There is a close relation between toxic injustice and the sociopolitical system. Only a brief reference to this alarming trend is later included in the preface to *God-Walk,* xi–xii.

.

"Trialectical Theology"[18]

The challenge of so-called dialectical theology is well known. In settings where theology and the church are adapting to the dominant powers, the reminder of the difference between humanity and God, or God and world, can make a tremendous difference. In Germany such a process of adaptation had started long before Hitler's attempt to take over the church, but it became most visible during the Third Reich. At that time the confession of the sovereignty of God and the limits of humanity were courageous steps that had far-reaching implications. Here the theological affirmation of God's transcendence was not a matter of once again removing God from the world, but of disentangling God from the powers that be.

Stating that Jesus Christ "is the one Word of God which we have to hear and which we have to trust and obey in life and in death," the Barmen Declaration of 1934, drafted in large part by Karl Barth, one of the leading dialectical theologians and a teacher of Herzog, puts it this way: "We reject the false doctrine, as though the Church could and would have to acknowledge as a source of its proclamation, apart from and besides this one Word of God, still other events and powers, figures and truths, as God's revelation."[19] The recovery of the "Otherness" of God, God's independence from the powers that be, is one of the great theological lessons of the twentieth century and remains a challenge for any setting where God's name is invoked in order to justify the way things are.[20]

Nevertheless, from the perspective of the belly of the whale an important dimension is still missing. Is it possible to proclaim the Otherness of God without a certain amount of respect for the otherness of those who are different from us? This is a serious question at present when both progressive and conservative theologians are interested once more in notions of divine Otherness, one camp intrigued by the postmodern critiques of foundationalism and identity, the other by a more general concern to preserve respect for positions of authority and power. We need to develop new paradigms.

Herzog's work is instructive. He sensed early on that in a North American context the struggle to acknowledge God's Otherness and sovereignty made sense only in the context of real-life confrontations between black and white,

---

18. Herzog makes up this term, tongue in cheek, in a note to the dean of Duke Divinity School, Dennis M. Campbell, August 29, 1995, shortly before his death.

19. The Barmen Declaration, English translation in *Barth, Barmen and the Confessing Church Today*, ed. James Y. Holloway (Lewiston, N.Y.: Mellen Press, 1995), 5.

20. Here is, of course, another connection to the Reformation tradition. It is interesting to note that this is precisely the thing that Dietrich Bonhoeffer found missing in North American Protestantism. According to Bonhoeffer, this "Protestantism without Reformation" lacks a sense that God's work is the crisis of all human efforts, even of such well-meaning institutions as religion, the church, and ethics. God founded the church not on religion and ethics but on the person and work of Christ. Dietrich Bonhoeffer, "Protestantismus ohne Reformation," in *Gesammelte Schriften* (Munich: Kaiser, 1958), 1:354. Bonhoeffer acknowledges that there are certain exceptions like Reinhold Niebuhr's critique of liberalism, 350ff. In another context he talks about how he found the gospel alive in the black churches. Bonhoeffer, "Bericht über den Studienaufenthalt im Union Theological Seminary zu New York 1930/31," ibid., 96–98.

rich and poor, the powerful and the marginalized.[21] If the powerful are unable
to listen to the concerns of those without power, if whites are unable to respect
blacks, if the rich do not care about the poor, how would they be able to truly
respect and listen to God? If our approach to others is determined by relationships of power and control (even if well intentioned), how can we be so sure
that our approach to the wholly Other would be different?

Without respect for the human other, the reference to the divine Other can
easily become a cover-up. In other words, the same captivity of the church which
makes us unable to respond to the suffering of the human other also impedes
theological openness for the divine Other. No wonder Herzog paid close attention to any sign that the church might be rediscovering the other. One of
the first of these signs he found in the new attention given to the poor in the
document developed by the Latin American Bishops' Conference in Medellín
(1968).

In one of his last essays Herzog formulates the challenge in new ways: "What
the theologian needs most is to see God. Yet God will not be seen where the
divine can be controlled. The poor, as such, do not demonstrate God, and yet
they are the place for us to 'see' God. How can this be?" No doubt, this is a
description of one of the still little understood dynamics at work in theology
from belly-of-the-whale settings. Rather than giving an exhaustive explanation,
Herzog invites new thought by answering his own question with the observation
that "the poor cannot be controlled."[22] For those in positions of power, God will
be encountered only where we give up control in forging new relationships with,
and learning from, the powerless. In this process the poor do not need to be put,
or to put themselves, in the place of absolute theological authority (the constant
fear of modern theologians who sense that their own authority is under attack);
the poor simply open the way for new encounters with God, thus developing
new models of power and authority.[23]

---

21. Herzog explains his hesitation to transpose the insights of dialectical theology to North America: "One of the reasons why I felt that the time had not as yet come to relate American Protestant
thought to Barth was that the concept of heresy had been made completely innocuous in white theology." Frederick Herzog, "Reorientation in Theology: Listening to Black Theology," in *The Context
of Contemporary Theology: Essays in Honor of Paul Lehmann*, ed. Alexander J. McKelway and E. David
Willis (Atlanta: John Knox Press, 1974), 240, n. 6.

22. Frederick Herzog, "Athens, Berlin, and Lima," *Theology Today* 51, no. 2 (July 1994): 275.
In this essay Herzog addresses David Kelsey's claim that theology in the United States has a dual
heritage which needs to be negotiated. One is tied to the classic Greek notion of *paideia* (Kelsey
talks about Athens), based on the formation of persons and habits; the other is related to the German
concept of *Wissenschaft* (Kelsey talks about Berlin), focused on theory and technical reason. Herzog
suggests introducing a third element into the equation: Lima, Peru. "Lima reminds us that seeing
God is never direct, always indirect. *Paideia* (Athens) and *Wissenschaft* (Berlin) have to be brought
under the scrutiny of the vast encampments of the poor who are banging, as it were, at the doors of
our theological schools." Ibid., 276.

23. Theology from the underside ultimately leads beyond the dichotomy of the poor in positions
of absolute authority and power, and the poor as objects of charity, a dichotomy which still reflects
the two dominant camps of mainline theology. For an interpretation of the theological relevance of
these dynamics and an exploration of new models of authority and power, tied to the fact that even

In light of the fact that 45 percent of the potential Native American work-force are unemployed, Herzog determines the challenge to theology in the twenty-first century: "Only if we change ourselves in view of these 'invisible' people, will we become aware of the 'invisible God.' Here anchors our theological future."[24]

In this process, both the concerns for the relation of humanity and God, the "vertical" relationship emphasized by more traditional theological camps, and the concerns for the relation among human beings, the "horizontal" relationships emphasized by more liberal theological camps, are reconstructed. The binary relationships between self and other, or God and self, give way to ternary relationships which include self, other, and God. As we have seen, the "vertical" relationship between God and self can no longer be conceived without the ignored or oppressed other. But neither can the "horizontal" relationship of self and other be conceived without the divine Other. If God is indeed where we would least expect it, where the pain is, we can learn how to relate to each other differently. God's own encounter with those who suffer leads the way for relinquishing the control of the rich over the poor, men over women, white over black, Anglo over Hispanic, oppressors over oppressed, and so on. These new relationships, in turn, lead back to new encounters with the divine Other. It is a "trialectical" movement.

Some of these elements are part of an account which Herzog gives of the genesis of his own theology early on: "Liberation theology in the U.S. did not emerge because some people were looking in more kindly fashion on the poor, but because the poor were looking in more unkindly fashion on some people. In a new encounter with the Bible, the poor crossed the threshold of the theological consciousness. God's claim in the poor Christ was felt anew." The conclusion wraps it all up: "The experience was not triggered by the kindly sentiments of do-gooder white theologians. Rather, 'objective' claims made on us by God and by the poor on the margins of society turned us around."[25]

While the future of theology in North America is closely tied to the question whether or not the claim of the divine Other on all of life can still be identified, we are beginning to understand that we will not be able to move ahead without acknowledging the claim of the human other as well.

Building Bridges toward a Common Interest Theology

No doubt, the different voices arising out of belly-of-the-whale locations all around the world cannot be synchronized easily. Liberation theologies did not

---

the oppressed can never be completely controlled, see Joerg Rieger, *Remember the Poor: The Challenge to Theology in the Twenty-First Century* (Harrisburg, Pa.: Trinity Press International, 1998).

24. Frederick Herzog "New Birth of Conscience," *Theology Today* 53, no. 4 (January 1997): 483, also included in *Liberating the Future: God, Mammon, and Theology*, ed. Rieger.

25. Frederick Herzog, "Birth Pangs: Liberation Theology in North America," *Christian Century* (December 15, 1976): 1120.

emerge, as so many schools of theology still do, following a particular set of ideas or a few great theologians. Initially most liberation theologies, listening to the stories of marginalized people in specific settings, developed independently of each other.

Early on, Latin Americans understood, for instance, that large systemic structures of injustice could not be corrected by well-meaning efforts at development. Those larger structures are part of the theological crisis because they separate us not only from our neighbors but also from God. Feminist theologians have reminded us that there is still a discrepancy between the place of men and women in church and society, and womanist and *mujerista* theologians have refined that analysis. Theology is in crisis, they found, because it has not paid attention to God's walk with half of humanity. African American theologians realized that, long after slavery was abolished, their people were still not free. Asian and African theologians broadened the spectrum further.

This diversity has frequently been misunderstood. According to a widely accepted myth, liberation theologies are special interest theologies, at best relevant to specific groups of people, at worst just another outgrowth of postmodern pluralism. Yet this view forgets that liberation theologies did not develop according to the logic of the market. Their themes were located not in particular marketing niches but in areas of deep suffering and pressure that, while most strongly felt at the margins and the peripheries, affect also the centers and everything else as well. In addition, as the various liberation theologies soon found out, the different fault lines of oppression along the lines of class, gender, and race are connected in subtle ways.

Here a curious reversal takes place that has not yet reached the level of consciousness of mainline theology. Despite their claims to universality, the approaches developed in the centers of theology shape up as special interest theologies if they pay no attention to the deeper malaise which affects us all, oppressors and oppressed alike. We need to realize that, rather than addressing the special interests of one group only, the concern for those in the belly of the whale deals with an important part of reality which, even though often repressed and made invisible, affects us all. The apostle Paul, using a different metaphor, reminds us that "if one member suffers, all suffer together with it" (1 Cor. 12:26). No wonder Herzog at one time called this "common interest theology."[26]

Teaching and writing as a white male theologian in the southern United States, trained in the theological centers of Germany, Switzerland, and the United States, Herzog himself is a most unlikely participant in the liberation theology project. But he is proof that mainline theology can learn how to listen to the voices of the oppressed. His work is a witness to the fact that liberation

---

26. Frederick Herzog, "United Methodism in Agony," *Perkins Journal* 28, no. 1 (Fall 1974), reprinted in *Doctrine and Theology in the United Methodist Church*, ed. Thomas A. Langford (Nashville: Kingswood Books, 1991). The term is further developed in Joerg Rieger, "Developing a Common Interest Theology from the Underside," in *Liberating the Future: God, Mammon, and Theology*, ed. Rieger.

theology is relevant to all of theology. There is still hope that more theologians and members of the privileged classes will come to understand the new challenge for theology.

It is this solidarity with people on the underside that enabled Herzog to join in building new kinds of bridges. While bridges used to be built mostly at the level of those who share certain interests and some well-defined common denominators, the real challenge is to build bridges between those who are different. Yet the new types of bridges also differ from those built in our globalizing world that, while indeed connecting those who are different, often do not allow for traffic in both directions.[27]

In encounters with the suffering of African Americans in the South and with the plight of Latin Americans, women, and Native Americans, Herzog learned how to forge connections and alliances without disregarding vital differences.[28] Various strands of theological reflections in oppressive settings are pulled together, not in order to imitate or supersede them, but in order to reform mainline theology and the church in the so-called First World, starting in North Carolina, with implications for the Americas and eventually even Europe.

Herzog's final essays best exemplify these efforts (see part four). Here he explores ways to uncover and develop deeper connections between north and south in the Americas. He talks about a "common tradition" which would recognize existing asymmetries.[29] At a time when everybody in the field is talking about "globalization," he coins the term "mutualization." While the former term, now used in corporate boardrooms and seminaries alike, is based on economic processes, the latter term presupposes a different model. "Mutualization" suggests a two-way street between North and South, built in mutual accountability, that takes into account our repressed histories as well.[30] Such a relationship, of course, cannot be built in the abstract, in ideal terms. Herzog realized early on that in order to build bridges of mutuality, we need to take into account the pressures of our own situation: "Unless we in the U.S. pass through the needle's

---

27. This starts quite literally with permission to travel. At a time when U.S. citizens travel freely to Latin America, for instance, we grant travel visas only to a select group of Latin Americans. The traffic of profit is another drastic example of such one-way streets. What else would be the reason for First World corporations to relocate labor intensive manufacturing processes to Third World countries?

28. In *Liberating the Future: God, Mammon, and Theology,* ed. Rieger, his spirit has brought together the representatives of, and witnesses to, various strands of liberation theology once more.

29. See, for instance, "*Tradición Común* Shaping Christian Theology: Mutualization in Theological Education," included in this volume as chapter 35. Starting in 1987, Herzog took numerous trips to Peru, establishing relationships between churches in Peru and in North Carolina and between the Comunidad Bíblico-Teológica (CBT, the seminary of the Methodist Church of Peru in Lima) and Duke University. Herzog eventually taught a course at the CBT, but only after a number of years of listening.

30. Frederick Herzog, "A Theology for the Americas," *Christian Century* (July 13–20, 1994), review of Gustavo Gutiérrez, *Las Casas: In Search of the Poor of Jesus Christ,* 687: "North and South America have been kept apart for too long, and know too little of each other. It is time to realize the tradition the North shares with Latin American Catholicism and how this tradition shapes our destiny."

eye of the black, red, feminist, Chicano and other liberation experiences in the one America where we live, we will not enter the kingdom of liberation in *both* Americas."[31]

At the same time, Herzog also worked on the construction of bridges between the United States and Europe and, within Europe, between the east and west of the divided Germany.[32] As one of the main architects of full communion between the German Evangelical Church of the Union (EKU) and the United Church of Christ (UCC) in the United States, he combined the partnership among churches with other relationships, including the partnership between east and west in the Cold War.[33] While those latter relations meant a difficult diplomacy in cooperation with the EKU offices in East and West Berlin, they provided various outlets and openings for Christians in Communist East Germany that were not otherwise available.

In all of these relations, mutuality is key. Herzog hoped that the UCC would rediscover some of its theological roots in the German Reformation tradition and the EKU would be initiated into the liberation tradition. He worked hard to include African American UCC congregations in the relationship. Not surprisingly, it was Herzog who first introduced black theology to German theologians.[34] Highly familiar with Germany and the United States (Herzog held dual citizenship), he never forgot about the larger context. He was aware that the relations of two established churches in the North Atlantic could not be built without attention to global belly-of-the-whale settings. The tensions between a wealthy North and an impoverished South always remained part of the picture.[35]

Instead of building bridges on the lofty pillars of universals, the new types of bridges are kept closer to the murky waters where God is at work. Even established ecumenical relationships need to be reconstructed on this ground. When

---

31. Herzog, "Pre-Bicentennial U.S.A. in the Liberation Process," in *Theology in the Americas*, ed. Torres and Eagleson, 146.

32. Herzog taught at the University of Bonn in the summer for many years, dealing with German problems from a U.S. ecumenical point of view. See also his numerous articles published in German. From the seventies on, Herzog interpreted the cutting edge of the developments in North America to German readers as coeditor of the journal *Evangelische Kommentare*. In 1978 he established an exchange program between Bonn University and Duke University that is still active.

33. Common declarations of the churches include, for instance, a call in the eighties for the freeze of production, testing, and deployment of nuclear weapons. At the end of a common declaration titled "Swords into Plowshares" (unpublished) another bridge is built: "As Christians we join other religions in asking our government to reverse the nuclear arms race. We join especially Native American religions in appealing to justice for Creation — plants as well as animals. Give peace a chance."

34. His essay "Theology at the Crossroads," for instance (chapter 13 in this volume), was written in the context of a conversation between black theologians and white theologians of American and German descent.

35. Herzog's involvement at the level of the American Academy of Religion reflects all these commitments. He was cofounder, together with Letty Russell, of the liberation theology project which led to a broadening of the base for liberation theology in the United States, starting in 1974; a decade later there were over one hundred names on the membership list. He was also one of the leaders in a Euro-American studies seminar since 1987 which involved leading theologians of Europe and the Americas and was designed to bring both Americas and Europe closer together.

moving at the level of faith, and from faith to order (in the Faith and Order efforts of the World Council of Churches, for instance), the church is always in danger of circling around itself. In an essay written in the early stages of the relationship of EKU and UCC, Herzog summarizes the challenge of a fresh encounter with God's own mission: "God's Word clearly taught disenthralls us from our captivity to national chauvinism or private preoccupations. There is a world out there that needs our full attention. Struggling for justice and peace in facing the world's poor we forget ourselves and thus find ourselves as a people and as persons in new community."[36] This is truly *common* interest theology.

God-Walk Theology

The title of Herzog's last book, *God-Walk: Liberation Shaping Dogmatics*, is a summary of his work. Even a decade after its publication it continues to spark the imagination of many of my students, especially those who search for new ways of relating their theological training and Christian praxis. "We often grasp more about God on a walk than through a book," so reads the first sentence of *God-Walk*.[37] Theology is reshaped in walking together with God and "the least of these," from the bottom up.

God-Walk manifests a break with the conventions of the field. It reminds not only theologians but also preachers that God-talk cannot stand on its own, as a theory that is applied to praxis later. Nothing perhaps exemplifies the crisis of the conventional relation of theory and praxis better than the gap between Sunday and Monday. Theories that are not self-consciously rooted in specific praxis settings hardly ever feed back into faithful praxis, whether propounded in sermons or lectures. Such theories are irrelevant at best, but it is more likely that they are harmful, since they grow out of unreflected praxis settings. Pure theory does not exist. No wonder certain kinds of theory never lead to the desired kinds of praxis.

Yet God-walk does not replace God-talk. Theological reflection does not lose its critical edge. What changes is the type of critique that counts. By including the praxis setting into the process of reflection, theology can no longer pretend to pursue its business on neutral grounds, in the realm of theory alone. Theological critique now starts with a self-critical moment, as critical reflection on one's praxis setting which feeds back into the traditional theological task, the reflection on the teaching of the church. In this context, the doctrines of the church gain new significance for the life of the church. If doctrines are not the product of abstract speculation but grow out of self-critical theological reflection on the church's walk with God, what counts is the way they inspire the next stages of the walk.

---

36. Frederick Herzog, "What Does Full Communion Mean?" *EKU-UCC Newsletter* 1, no. 4 (November 1980): 5.

37. Herzog, *God-Walk*, xi.

Here the task of theology is no longer primarily the critique of the doctrines of the church in light of the questions of the modern world (as in more liberal theologies), nor is it simply the collection of, and commentary on, a selection of divine truths (as in more orthodox theologies). Theology becomes a lens that helps us to discern how our walk shapes up in light of God's own walk, exploring and reshaping the doctrines of the church in the process. Theology from the belly of the whale teaches the church as a whole what it might mean that, as God walks with the least and the last, "the true 'creeds' of today are bled out of the sufferings of the martyrs in the church of the oppressed."[38]

In this process, theology can once again make constructive contributions to the ongoing formation of Christian doctrine. This, according to Herzog, is of particular importance in the United States, where theological and doctrinal structures are not as clear-cut as elsewhere.[39] Yet the formation of Christian doctrine in a new spirit of mutual accountability with people at the margins does not aim at mere consensus. "How do we move from the search for a consensus church to becoming a *confessing* church?" As a confessing church in the twenty-first century, we need to understand that "every worship act is a political act." The teaching of the church never takes place completely outside the political and economic structures of the world.

The question is not whether or not the church should be political, but what its politics will be. Even the complete withdrawal from politics is a political move, a move that ultimately supports the way things are. While the church can never be reduced to being just another political player, Herzog proposes that "the powers and principalities of the age need to be confronted in the political act of worship in the *body* language of the Eucharist, manifesting a sociopolitical structure other than the world's, and in the body *language* of eucharistic preaching, clarifying that it is God's justice that lies at the core of the church's sociopolitical structure."[40]

In walking with God, the Eucharist becomes a focal point as the place where we meet a Christ who is still walking the streets, and where we become part of a community of diverse people whom he calls to the table, all drawn together

---

38. Frederick Herzog, "Reformation Today," *Christian Century* (October 27, 1982): 1079.

39. See Frederick Herzog, "Kirchengemeinschaft im Schmelztiegel — Anfang einer neuen Ökumene?" in *Kirchengemeinschaft im Schmelztiegel*, ed. Frederick Herzog and Reinhard Groscurth (Neukirchen-Vluyn: Neukirchener Verlag, 1989), 67. Explaining the North American situation to German readers, Herzog refers to Sidney E. Mead's observation that the great failure in North American Christianity is its lack of theological structure. The statement of the thirty-nine theologians of the United Church of Christ also talks about this problem: "Across the spectrum of opinion in the United Church of Christ there is a tendency for theological thought to be utilitarian, in the service of programmatic ends, without sustained, disciplined reflection on the present condition of the church. What is needed, we believe, is a sustained rethinking of our theological tradition (as reflected in the various traditions behind the United Church) to see how that tradition can be reappropriated in faithful and fresh ways as a discipline and resource for our life and faith." See *New Conversations* 8, no. 1 (Spring 1985): 2–3.

40. Frederick Herzog, "Why We Can't Wait," in *New Conversations*, 27–28. For a reminder that the church can never be reduced to politics see Herzog, *God-Walk*, 192.

by a common liturgy, the public reading of the Bible, and the elements of bread and wine, representing Christ's life as well as life's basic necessities, which are scarce for many people around the globe. In this eucharistic sharing with Christ and the people beside us we discover models for alternative forms of Christian community as well as for alternative political and economic structures.[41]

None of this would make much sense, of course, without a strong doctrine of the Holy Spirit. Without the Spirit, walking with God would become just another moral exercise for the elites, for those who feel that they can do whatever they put their minds to, rather than a matter of a new spirituality which empowers common people on the way. Without the Spirit, encounters with Christ would remain more or less encounters with the past. Instead of wondering, "What would Jesus do?" Herzog raises the question, "What is Jesus doing now?"[42] Without the Spirit, finally, encounters with people at the margins would more or less remain one-way streets, matters of charity, rather than opportunities for the transformation of self and places for new encounters with God. Not surprisingly Herzog himself saw in his book *God-Walk* the beginnings of a theology of the Holy Spirit. His next book was to have the title "Resistance Spirit."

This emphasis on the Spirit helps to account for one of the most important aspects of a theology from the belly of the whale. Herzog reports "the difficulty of being in the midst of empire and at the same time struggling to be at an absolute distance from it" as a factor that "keeps our walk — and thought — from being always steady." Situations of pressure demand a certain flexibility. But there is another factor which points to the need to keep things open: "Our leaps of thought are also brought on by our rejection of any hegemonic solution. Everything we do is in *via*, on the road.... The road is not preordained. That is why I try to avoid the words *must* or *should*. If we were not blind, we would see what is at the inside of history or the heart of creation."[43] Theology from the belly of the whale seeks to tie into the power of the Spirit without claiming absolute knowledge or control. It does not proceed by way of moralizing, according to a given set of norms. "There is not some goal we must reach, some

---

41. The Eucharist is a central theme in Herzog, *God-Walk*. See also "Full Communion and the Eucharist," included in this volume as chapter 31.

42. Herzog, *God-Walk*, xxiii: "This is the key question arising from this book." Critics often felt confused about what they saw as Herzog's "Pietism." Yet while Herzog was indeed interested in the heritage of Pietism, he would always argue for a critical piety: "On the American Continent pietism has been absorbed much too uncritically thus far. Our study of German Pietism seeks to make a contribution to the growth of a *critical* piety." This sentence concludes the introduction of a new edition and English translation of various pietist thinkers (Jean de Labadie, August Hermann Francke, Friedrich Christoph Oetinger) which Herzog was invited to prepare for the Library of Protestant Thought at Oxford University Press but which was never published because the project was discontinued after the first volumes. Both Jürgen Moltmann and M. Douglas Meeks have stressed Herzog's interest in Jean-Frédéric Oberlin. See Moltmann, *"In Memoriam," Evangelische Kommentare* (November 1995), English translation in *EKU-UCC Newsletter* 14, no. 1 (November 1996): 5, and Meeks, "The Way of Jesus, the Path of Discipleship," *EKU-UCC Newsletter* 14, no. 1 (November 1996): 7. See also Herzog's own account of Oberlin and the diaconic tradition in "Diakonia in Modern Times: Eighteenth–Twentieth Centuries," included in this volume as chapter 4.

43. Herzog, *God-Walk*, xxii.

rule we should follow. Instead, there is the innermost reality that God walks, and walks with us as we take the risk of walking."[44] Theology is constantly re-shaped on this walk, drawn into a process of widening its horizons in light of God's own walk.

Back to the Future

In recent years mainline theology has begun to add liberation theologies to its compendia. It may look as if theology from the belly of the whale has become part of the spectrum of accepted theological approaches. But there are still some basic questions that we need to ask ourselves.

First of all, in the midst of all kinds of theological turns, the turn to the self of modern theology, the turn to the divine Other of dialectical theology, and the postmodern turns to text and language, have we really taken seriously yet the challenge of the turn to the other? I am not talking about the rising stock of postmodern notions like otherness and difference. I am talking about actual people in oppressive belly-of-the-whale settings. Actions of charity, social activism, or what we often describe as the "prophetic task" of theology will not necessarily get us there. Charity today often works without much consideration of the other as person. Much of social activism is still driven by autonomous selves that do not need to act together with the other in order to function. And when we speak prophetically, we often tend to forget our own involvement in precisely those structures of injustice and oppression that we denounce.

The turn to the other starts not with well-meaning offers to help but with real encounters with the other that lead to questions like "Who put the other in place?" and "What is keeping her there?" The turn to the other will only be effective if it becomes a two-way street, if we learn to let ourselves be reshaped in relation to the other. We need to learn that the other is always *my* other. And we need to learn that there is no neutral ground, not even for prophets. The challenge is greatest for those of us in positions of power and privilege. But even people in belly-of-the-whale settings are not exempt. As Gustavo Gutiérrez has stated at various points, even the poor need to make an option for the poor. Furthermore, in addition to establishing new relations between self and other, we need to continue to create networks of solidarity among the various locations on the underside of history.

Second, in the midst of the constant temptation to correlate God with the way things are, how can we keep the view open for God's work? The apologetic enterprises of modern theology have not fared too well. We are beginning to understand that a God who fits into our frameworks can perhaps be presented to the logic of the modern world, but is becoming more and more irrelevant. Within this frame of mind one may still be able to make a case for religion and even the church, but who really needs a God who fits in? We will not find God where

---

44. Ibid., xxiii.

God can be controlled. The question of modern theology — "Is there a God?" — can only be addressed if we combine it with the question that arises today out of the screams of countless people on the underside of history: "Where is God?"

As a result, theology from the belly of the whale makes us turn the theodicy question that continues to fascinate modern theology back from its head to its feet. Rather than wondering "If there is a God, where does evil come from?" we begin with the question, "If this is evil, where does God enter the picture?" While the former question often deals with the notion of God in general and a priori terms which are the product of controlling theologies, the latter question opens the way to talk about God in specific settings, not unlike most of the biblical accounts. And while in the former question evil is often dealt with in equally abstract terms as God and often played down (since it has to fit in, for instance, with preconceived notions of God's omnipotence), the latter question not only has the potential to take evil more seriously but depends on a clear description of the specific forms of evil. Only if we address this question will it be worthwhile to continue doing theology in the twenty-first century.

The events of the twentieth century have taught us once more that talk about God acting in history can be dangerous. But it is not as if we would have much of a choice. If God is at work, theology cannot afford to bypass the issue. If God is not, why waste our time with theology? In this context theologies from the belly of the whale have taught us another important lesson. Perhaps talking about God's work as extension of the schemes of those in positions of power is not be the only option. Maybe claims for God's unflinching support of those in power are never on target, whether it be in the name of the Third Reich, in the name of the doctrine of Manifest Destiny, or even in the name of the church as a powerful institution. Already the Reformers sensed that something was wrong with a theology of glory.[45] People at the margins teach us that we do not necessarily need to identify God's work with the way things are, and that God is powerfully at work in unexpected and nontotalitarian ways under the sign of the cross and the crosses of today.

According to an old proverb, talk is cheap. God-talk can be cheap, too, as people at the margins continue to remind us. In the last few decades their voices have gotten louder and louder. All we need to do is listen. Theologies from the belly of the whale offer models for rooting God-talk in God-walk, thus pulling God-talk into the life-and-death issues of our time. The theological enterprise might once again pick up steam if it feeds back into the formation of a church that is not afraid to follow along with what God is doing in both church and world, and is ready to confess and live its faith in ways that take on the principalities and powers of our own time.

---

45. See Martin Luther's distinction between a theology of glory and a theology of the cross in the Heidelberg Disputation. *Luther: Early Theological Works*, Library of Christian Classics 16, ed. and trans. James Atkinson (Philadelphia: Westminster, 1962), 290ff.

The Structure of the Book

The four parts of this volume correspond to four stages in Herzog's work which build on each other. Early encounters with belly-of-the-whale settings pose new theological questions which are deepened along the way, setting the stage for constructive theological proposals. Out of these dialogues grow new paradigms which provide new directions for the future of theology, spirituality, and the church. In order to demonstrate the close connection of theology, spirituality, and the church, each of the four parts opens and closes with prayers, poems, or sermons.

The essays in the first part show what impact the encounters with people at the margins can have on mainline theological reflection. The collapse of theological language in the face of pain leads to new perspectives on both God and humanity. In this process the martyrdom of Martin Luther King, Jr., marks a turning point and opens up new theological vistas. Realizing that we cannot liberate ourselves, theology in North America needs to start over again with a deeper understanding of the role of mainline Christianity in the conflicts of our time and a new search for God's liberative power which creates new forms of solidarity with oppressed people.

In the encounter with the oppressed, Herzog develops specific proposals for a new way of doing theology which still bear the potential to revolutionize the field. The essays in the second part develop new relationships between God, self, and the other at the points where older relationships have broken down or are no longer functional. Here Christology becomes important. In Christ Godself joined humanity at the level of the nonpersons, and this divine act of solidarity opens the door for new encounters with God and neighbors. In Christ, personhood becomes a communal phenomenon. Yet community cannot be built without facing the existing asymmetries between those in power and those without power.

The essays of the third part are held together by the question how theology, in the midst of competing attempts to control its subject matter, might be able to keep the view open for what God is doing. A first step, according to Herzog, is to shift from theologizing about ideal concepts to analyzing what is actually going on. This leads to two questions which are not unrelated: What is actually happening in theology and the church today? And, what is God doing? If God deals with the pain of those who are pushed to the margins, theology and the church can no longer afford to avoid scrutinizing these contexts. Entering new worlds, theology becomes quite literally a matter of life and death.

The final part contains the latest works of Herzog, some of them unpublished due to his untimely death. Here Herzog works toward merging the different aspects of his work into a more comprehensive structure, extending the horizon of theology beyond the United States and Europe to Latin America in a search for mutual accountability, and developing practical models and plans for reshaping theological education and the church. Building blocks for Herzog's vision include an orientation in the work of the triune God, the formation of Christian communities, development of mutual accountability both in small groups and larger settings which maintain respect for diversity, and an understanding of theology as accountable teaching in which tradition is reshaped and further developed from the bottom up. Everything comes together at the Eucharist as the place where God's alternative economy is rooted.

The common thread which keeps those four parts together is Herzog's ongoing quest for what God is doing. "For this reason," he once wrote, "also a white theologian is enabled to do liberation theology. Perhaps on the lowest rung of the ladder. But woe unto me as a white if I do not witness to God's liberation!"[46] When I started thinking about a research project on his work, he made sure I would not get off on the wrong foot: "The question is not what kind of crazy ideas I had. Don't make it a psycho-history: I have seen the liberation thing 'riding on God's steam.'"[47]

Neither can the work of Frederick Herzog be understood in terms of a classical history-of-ideas approach. What got him thinking theologically was not primarily new theological ideas or concepts but new encounters with God in contexts of severe suffering and oppression. "Liberation theology begins as the poor begin to listen to each other before God. Liberation theology continues as we listen to the poor before God."[48]

---

46. Herzog, "Pre-Bicentennial U.S.A. in the Liberation Process," 166, n. 6.

47. Conversation April 12, 1992. See Joerg Rieger, "Approaches to the Real: Liberation Theology and Spirituality in Latin America and North America. A Comparison of the Works of Gustavo Gutiérrez and Frederick Herzog" (Ph.D. Dissertation, Duke University, 1994). See also Rieger, *Remember the Poor: The Theological Challenge of the Twenty-First Century.*

48. Herzog, *God-Walk*, xxii.

PART ONE

THE MAKING OF
A LIBERATION THEOLOGIAN

The essays included in this part give a sense of the impact of initial encounters with the acute pain and suffering of people at the margins of life on mainline theological reflection. Liberation theology, a term which imposes itself on Herzog and others independently of each other at the same time, does not grow out of idealistic dreams, political ideologies, or radical academic agendas. It begins with new encounters with God and neighbor in specific contexts where relations of paternalistic control are breaking down. Here otherwise lofty concepts such as ecumenicity, spirituality, and even the doctrine of God are reshaped from the bottom up. Ever since his call to Duke University in 1960, Herzog's work has been closely tied to a specific concern for the southern part of the United States. Subsequent efforts to rebuild national and international relationships are rooted in this context.

Opening a new chapter in the history of theology, liberation theology begins not with answers but with new questions. One of the first steps is an awareness of the failure of commonly accepted theological concepts — Herzog's writings of this period talk about the limits of spirituality, history, ontology, and the modern search for God — and the traumatic experience of a collapse of theological language.[1] Herzog formulates the challenge in this way: "Any theology today

---

1. In his first book, *Understanding God: The Key Issue in Present-Day Protestant Thought* (New York: Charles Scribner's Sons, 1966), Herzog argues that theology progresses not by promoting a safe haven on grounds of generally accepted historical or ontological frameworks, but by dealing with its historical and ontological impasse. While the awareness of the existence of things that transcend the human self is important, such awareness gets stuck in a complete lack of understanding (an "ontological aporia") without the interpretive framework of Jesus' history. At the same time, history as such does not reach all the way to God either (a "historical aporia"). Theology needs to start over where both aporiae come together in new encounters with the gospel and its subject matter, God, in specific settings of life which include the people at the margins mentioned in the preface to

that does not think through its questions relative to the agony of Vietnam, the plight of the sharecroppers, the riots of our cities, or even the ecstasy of the hippies, can lead to an equally meaningless theological narcissism."[2] Three decades later theological narcissism is still not extinct, and even contextual theologies often merely exchange one narcissism for another if they fail to touch on the life-and-death issues of the present.

The initial encounters with crisis situations help to keep the proposals modest. Theology can no longer pretend to have simple solutions or to set out to Christianize the social order, according to the famous motto of the Social Gospel movement. Contrary to a common misunderstanding, liberation theology is not first of all social ethics but rather the attempt to develop a new grasp of the teaching of the church, starting with new perspectives on God and humanity, closely tied to new readings of the biblical texts. Herzog credits African Americans with teaching him what he calls the "Bible-in-hand approach," a rereading of biblical texts from the perspective of "the other" which he did not learn from his theological teachers.[3] The later book *Liberation Theology* (see chapter 12 of this volume) will be just that: a rereading of the Bible in light of oppression and liberation.

On these grounds the horizon of theology is broadened. In a society where structures of power are all-pervasive but hardly noticed, theology needs to understand its own place: "The time has come to face some hard truths about ourselves."[4] Theology needs to pay attention to political structures, not because this would make its business more exciting or attractive, but because everything is politicized already. Mapping out power structures, theology can once more begin to understand the difference of God's power.

In the making of liberation theology, the martyrdom of Martin Luther King, Jr. opens up a new perspective. Realizing that we cannot liberate ourselves, theology needs to start over again with a deeper understanding of the role of mainline Christianity in the conflict and a new search for God's liberating power which creates new forms of solidarity with oppressed people. In all of this Herzog comes to understand more and more clearly that "the real question for whites is not, What should we do about black theology? It is rather, What are we going to do about white theology?"[5]

Understanding God. The theological task of the future will be to reshape those "doctrines felt as facts," or "the premises which are never mentioned" (171–72, n. 23). Due to a variety of circumstances it was not possible to reproduce parts of the book in this reader.

2. Frederick Herzog, "God, Evil, and Revolution," *Journal of Religious Thought* 25, no. 2 (Autumn–Winter 1968–69): 5.

3. "The poor with the Bible in their hands . . . taught us liberation theology in the South." Frederick Herzog, *Justice Church: The New Function of the Church in North American Christianity* (Maryknoll, N.Y.: Orbis Books, 1980), 3.

4. Frederick Herzog, "Black and White Together?" Included in this volume as chapter 5.

5. Frederick Herzog, "Liberation Hermeneutic as Ideology Critique?" *Interpretation* 28, no. 4 (October 1974): 388. To speak of "white theology" is to realize that theology as it is usually done brings in its own perspectival angle.

Already in these early stages, theology and spirituality are closely related. In retrospect, Herzog identifies a process of conversion or "mutation" taking place in these years, as an "encounter with the resurrection that did not have an antecedent."[6]

---

6. Author's interview with Frederick Herzog, April 12, 1992, in Durham, North Carolina.

– 1 –

LIBERATION HYMN

Herzog rarely published his poetry. On occasion he would present it in conversations or in the classroom. Friends would receive humorous birthday poems. Some verses were written for worship settings or as prayers. Nevertheless, his poetic writings provide helpful guides for reading his work. The condensed presentation of his most central concerns sparks curiosity and gives directions for our journey.

Here is the text for a hymn to the tune of one of the most famous battle hymns of the Reformation. Herzog talks about something that seems to have for the most part been banned from theological discourse since Luther: conflict. This gradual awakening to the tensions of the present, often covered up and repressed in the church, will lead to a fundamental reorientation of theology and new encounters with both God and neighbor.[1]

Tune: "A Mighty Fortress..."

A mighty conflict has arisen
Our unity dividing.
The black against the white is driven.
Fierce struggle is abiding.
And male and female fight
As we pray through the right
False peace is gone for sure.
God's pain we now endure
That brings true liberation.

God's peace is not an easy peace,
But spells harsh confrontation.
As searing pain and strife increase
Comes reconciliation.

Unpublished, 1970.

1. Kristin Herzog comments on the unusual phrase "pray through the right" that Herzog keeps in various editions of this text in the following way: "'Praying something through' meant for my husband always working something through intensively, or with spiritual commitment. The way I understand these lines is, 'while males and females are fighting, we are trying to work intensely on what we see as right or as demanded by God's justice.'"

The Cross in God's own heart
Is where we all will start
To learn our faith anew,
Finding in pain what's true:
Through suffering God is conquering.

How long had we forgot the truth
That God is conquering for us?
Doing our own thing proved uncouth,
Joining the crowd's loud chorus.
The Cross on Calvary
Rights all of history:
Since God is in the fray,
Justice is here to stay.
All humans will be equals.

Impelled by the amazing power
That bursts from Resurrection,
We know it's God's great mission hour
Off'ring us new direction
Through the oppressed and lost
At a tremendous cost.
Sent into sufferingkind
We all new meaning find,
Bearing each other's burdens.

– 2 –

PERILS OF ECUMENICITY?

*Throughout his career, Herzog was involved in the formation of ecumenical rela-
tionships at various levels, including the level of the World Council of Churches
(in 1963 he was a delegate to the Fourth World Conference on Faith and Order
of the World Council of Churches in Montreal, Canada). Yet while even today
such relationships are often built from the top down, starting with the negoti-
ations of professional theologians at the level of church doctrine, Herzog never
tired of exploring alternative approaches.*

*Here is an early proposal that calls for a grounding of ecumenical relation-
ships in the pressures of everyday life. In light of the tensions of the Cold War
(see his reference to Hungary) and the early stages of the conflict in the Middle
East, Herzog broadens the ecumenical horizon and sets the stage for an "awakening" to the real problems of our time. True ecumenicity which, through Christ,
includes all of humanity, can only be achieved if both personal piety and the
doctrinal mandates of orthodoxy are reshaped in these contexts. In this process
Herzog gradually uncovers the North American blind spots for those tensions
which exist at home.*

Recently I was reading in a Christian periodical an article on the perils of ecumenicity. There can be no doubt that ecumenicity has its perils. But then there
are perils to being a man, and it is especially perilous to be a Christian. It would
be greatly surprising if ecumenicity were not subject to the vices, weaknesses,
and temptations of man as an individual and of men engaged in the common
endeavor of living and making a living.

There is one peril of ecumenicity which is a peril to ecumenicity itself and
which is often overlooked. The danger is that the challenge of ecumenicity is
not taken seriously on the local level. Today ecumenicity means many things to
many people. The meaning of the word is often evasive and vague. There can be
little doubt, however, that it implies a worldwide concern of Christians for one
another. It is also almost equally well understood that *world*wide ecumenicity
is relevant to the world. Yet none of us lives in worldwide dimensions, even
though our responsibilities may go far beyond the local scene. Our really pressing

First published in *Mission House Seminary Bulletin* 3, no. 2 (December 1956): 7–9.

problems of life are still local, and ecumenicity can easily become an escape mechanism for those who would flee the pressing local problems of church and community and rest secure in the vague shadow land of worldwide dreams.

Some have felt this peril of ecumenicity and have begun to promote local ecumenicity which seems to be somewhat of a contradiction in itself. But the phrase, local ecumenicity, makes sense because it acknowledges the worldwide consequences of a single human act. Adam's sin! In a very definite way our sins are not merely sins against ourselves, but against the whole human race which has to bear the consequences, if not today then tomorrow or in ten years or in the next generation. Therefore, ecumenicity rightly understood teaches us how deeply we are involved in the woes and trials of the entire human race, how we are responsible for one another as men and altogether, without exception, our brother's keeper.

Here we must immediately think of the events of the past weeks in the Middle East and in Hungary. Christians often tend to simplify political and social issues. But simplifications at times have their virtue, too. What is the issue before the West? Perhaps there is more than one. But there can be no doubt that one important issue is whether or not the West is willing to accept the consequences of calling itself Christian. It must think through what it means that the large majority of the people in the West are claimed by the churches. Western society today is far from applying Christian ethics either directly or indirectly in any consistent way. But the conscience of the West is Christian. Nevertheless, the Christian whining over lack of courage to apply Christian principles is worse than the outright and consistent paganism of much of the East. In the West we must live for good or for ill with Christ or ostracize him from our personal and social life. According to the promise, to live with him works only for the good. The West can find that out by intensifying its study of Christ's significance for the social order.

The East presents a different problem, at least as regards the challenge which it presents to the West. Khrushchev recently told Western diplomats: History is for us (the Communists). We will bury you. (The West? The Capitalists? America?) His is the privilege of speaking as a pagan. He also speaks in the name of a pseudo-religious movement. Here the Christian must open his eyes and see clearly. After the burial of Jesus Christ it is no longer necessary that any man be offered up for the salvation of mankind. After his burial not a single Hungarian or a single Russian needs to be buried to save others. Furthermore, the Christian ought to know that history is not ruled by an ironclad law. Jesus Christ is the Lord of history, and *he* is for us, not history as such. History as such is not *for* any single person unless Jesus Christ is for him. And Jesus Christ died for all that every knee should bow. For that fact the cocky communist will someday also have to admit defeat: Thou hast conquered, meek Galilean! The Christian must not be ashamed to proclaim that communist history also is linked to the burial of Christ. It would be a great peril to ecumenicity if communism were denied its share in worldwide responsibility.

The world we live in has changed since the days of the apostles. They went out to conquer the then-known world in the name of the Lord. We today are aware of the entire inhabited globe. But in many respects our world, although covering the entire globe, is much smaller than the world of the apostles. The means of modern communication and travel have brought mankind a spatial closeness undreamed of in the days of the early church. Basically, however, we face the same problems when we think of guilt and salvation. In the world of our day we see their implications only in a more far-reaching way. We are not called merely to proclaim a message of salvation, but to work at the ordering of a society which is deeply influenced by the societal consequences of the proclamation of salvation throughout centuries of Christian expansion. Furthermore, our task is not merely to denounce the evils of a totalitarian system such as communism, but to assume responsibility for its origin in a context of thought which was at least partly Christian if only by name. Our unwillingness to do so would be a real peril to ecumenicity.

Personal piety does not suffice today, neither does stalwart promotion of orthodoxy or harping on the freedom of the individual soul. We need an awakening to the new facts of our age and a readiness to meet the need of our day. Mankind is one, and there is one Savior. Parties, social programs, and slogans cannot really help us experience the abundant life as we ought to. Only in focusing its thoughts on Christ will mankind be readied for a deeper experience of the mystery of human life. By developing a deep passion for the mystery of the Christ, the Church will find that greater hope which it needs to proclaim the Word in a world increasingly puzzled about its fate and its future. Ecumenicity would be greatly imperiled if the church would think that Christ had died only for the church. He died that all men should see how they belong together in sin and how salvation is for all the peoples. It is good to remember today, wherever we may live locally, how far-reaching our guilt is as well as our salvation. It is even better to live up to it locally with respect to its ecumenical implications. Thus, ecumenicity in the end must help us experience the dimensions of our Christian life more intensively. If this does not materialize we will have the worst peril of ecumenicity. Nevertheless, in any case it ought to be better to think of its challenge rather than its perils.

– 3 –

THE PERSONAL DEVOTIONAL LIFE; OR, CHAPEL IS NO SPIRITUAL BEAUTY PARLOR

For many years until his death Herzog taught a course titled "Prayer and Con-
templation," out of which grew small groups, grounded in a disciplined process
of action/reflection. Herzog insisted that "God-walk" needs to illumine and ini-
tiate "God-talk." This quest for new forms of spirituality is one of the common
threads that hold Herzog's work together. In this address (probably given to stu-
dents at Duke Divinity School), Herzog exposes common misunderstandings of
spirituality, leading him to reject that term for the moment.

How can we move beyond a kind of spiritual narcissism that was so preva-
lent in those days and that appears to be celebrating a comeback in North
American Protestantism today? Herzog suggests an alternative spirituality that
encompasses a whole new way of life, focused no longer on feeling our own spir-
itual pulse but on God's work. Here an opening is created for the broadening of
spirituality so that it will eventually be able to take into account the pain and
suffering in the life of all creation. While spirituality has often covered up conflict
and thus turned the church into a fool's paradise, the motto of Herzog's work
will be "struggle and contemplation."[1]

The story of our devotional life is for most of us one of failure. We know that
we fail in fulfilling our high calling as Christians. And so we pray in that familiar phrase: "We have left undone those things which we ought to have done,
and we have done those things which we ought not to have done." Many of
us would confess that it is in our devotional life where we fail most miserably.
Why? Most of us would answer: Because of its *irregularity*, its *shallowness*, and
its *perfunctoriness*. Some might even say: Why talk about it? *It only makes us feel*
more miserable....

There is the story of the pastor who wanted to visit a sick parishioner. At the
door the wife of this person met him. "You want to visit my husband?" "Yes."

Unpublished, mid-1960s.

1. Frederick Herzog, *God-Walk: Liberation Shaping Dogmatics* (Maryknoll, N.Y.: Orbis Books,
1988), 192; Frederick Herzog, "Birth Pangs: Liberation Theology in North America," *Christian*
Century (December 15, 1976): 1122.

"All right, but don't you talk to him about religion. He feels miserable enough already." Many of us react similarly when the subject of devotions is broached. Let's not talk about it, we feel miserable enough already.

Why talk about it? Because we might have a misconception of what devotions are. First, *devotions are not primarily a matter of regular or irregular outward observance.* Our Lord does not seem to have followed a very *rigid devotional* schedule. We read several times in the New Testament that Jesus withdrew to the wilderness or to a mountain to pray. But we do not get the impression that this was according to a *fixed pattern.* It says that he attended the synagogue, as his custom was, which, however, is a different matter, a matter of corporate worship. But no one would dare to say that therefore Jesus had a *barren* devotional life. He embodies for us what afterward Paul packed into that poignant phrase: *Pray constantly,* or *pray always* (1 Thess. 5:17). *Our Lord's life was his devotion.* His basic attitude was right. He always communed with God.

In the New Testament, if I see things rightly, the personal devotional life does not become a separate topic of special interest, except perhaps once in Acts 17:23, where Paul recounts his experience of walking through Athens to the Athenians, "I passed by, and beheld your *devotions....*" That's in the King James, and a poor translation at that. It reminds us, however, to look for the meaning of the root of the word "devotion." It means vow or sacrifice (*devotio*), even the sacrifice of one's own life. The root of the word leads us close to what Paul means when he says, "present your bodies as a *living sacrifice,* holy and acceptable to God, which is your spiritual worship" (Rom. 12:1).

This brings me to a second point. *Devotions are primarily a matter of the self-giving of one's life.* A devotional life is, by definition, a self-giving life. This is also what the life of Jesus teaches us. The goal of the devotional life is not "spirituality," a dubious and misleading term. Some fall into the danger of wanting to become disembodied spirits or specialists of spirituality. There is a spiritual narcissism which is just as bad as its secular counterpart. Those who fall in love with their spiritual image will spend too much of their time in spiritual beauty-culture, the improvement of their beautiful soul. Instead, remember Paul (as quoted above): "Present your *bodies...*" Paul does not say: "Lift up your *souls* for an hour every day in order to become more 'spiritual'!"

The goal of the devotional life is self-giving in communion. Only in the ongoing communion with those who commune with their Lord does devotional life take on concreteness. The communion lives by the reading and study of the Scriptures, prayer, praise, and witness. But the larger portion of the day we do not spend in worship together with the brethren. We are individuals and must be alone. Dietrich Bonhoeffer has said: "*Let him who cannot be in community beware of being alone.*" The point is, the private personal life of the Christian can only be a copy of what he does in the community as a whole: listening to God's Word, prayer, praise, and witness. Some will say: We have our own devotions, we need not "go to chapel." Beware: what does not happen in communion is not likely to happen when you are alone.

Significantly, Bonhoeffer turned the statement around in a second definition: *"Let him who cannot be alone beware of community."* We have to learn what it means to commune with God for ourselves. Too many rush into *togetherness* because they cannot stand themselves. In the end, *everyone of us must live his life alone before God,* must learn what it means to give his *self* to him.

It is the experience of the church that this is best done in the regular rhythm of Scripture reading and prayer, *listening* to God and *speaking* to God. The regularity and the repetition are partly an adjustment to human nature. Repetition makes for mastery of the subject. The master of the piano practices daily for hours. Why? He is a genius — can't he sit down at the piano and just play? But the matter of regularity is not merely a matter of habit formation. The Christian cannot cease to commune with God. Scripture reading and prayer are the most inexpendable means to continue in communion.

The main problem for me is to bring the two aspects I have been stressing together, the devotion of the entire life and the special devotional acts. I remember students — not here at Duke — talking to me about a professor: "You know he isn't much of a professor, but he has a strong spiritual life." This is just as wrong as the other comment: "He's quite a brain, but he hasn't heard of the Holy Spirit." Devotion is a matter of complete self-giving. A truly devotional Christian puts out quality work, whether as professor, minister, student, or garbage collector. A student cannot make up for his laziness by being *spiritual*, neither can a professor. But, on the other hand, *braininess* is not a substitute for devotion. There are many brainy people who are not devoted to anything.

Devotion is the commitment to a task with one's entire being. It may be that there is more devotion today among the poets, philosophers, diplomats, and the garbage collectors than among those who practice spiritual beauty-culture. Prayer is hard work, Scripture reading is hard work. An hour a day set aside for spiritual uplift may be wasted unless it is filled with hard work in study and concentration. So finally, *Christian devotion is our commitment to God's work with our entire being.*

– 4 –

Diakonia in Modern Times: Eighteenth–Twentieth Centuries

In this essay an important source in the formation of Herzog's approach to lib-eration theology can be identified: the rich heritage of the diaconic movement. At the core of the theological argument is the relation of worship and service, leitourgia and diakonia. Service is not based on moralistic appeals but on new encounters with God and neighbor.

In this context, the understanding of service, of diakonia, is reconstructed from the bottom up. Service is no longer what we often call an "outreach project," or a one-way street where the roles of benefactor and recipient are set in stone. Service in the new paradigm no longer refers to well-meaning hand-outs to the "less fortunate" but rather promotes new relationships in which the positions of receivers and recipients are reversed and real transformation happens.

The broadening of the notions of service and diakonia from private into public and political spheres which the essay describes, needs to be interpreted in light of this reversal. Herzog's future work provides further elaboration of the radical implications of this approach for theological reflection, the understanding of God and the church. In his essay "Humankind with a Human Face," included as chapter 33 of this book, he draws out the implications of the diaconic tradition for the twenty-first century.

The Isenheim Altar, until the late eighteenth century the center of the Antonite convent chapel at Isenheim in the Alsace,[1] in a unique way exemplifies the na-ture of Christian care for the sick and the poor. The Antonites, recognized as a brotherhood by Pope Urban II in 1095, were devoted to the care for the sick, especially the victims of the plague and syphilis epidemics. While receiving at Isenheim whatever medical attention was available at the time, the sick were

First published in *Service in Christ: Essays Presented to Karl Barth on His Eightieth Birthday*, ed. James I. McCord and T. H. L. Parker (London: Epworth Press, 1966), 135–50, © 1966 Epworth Press. Used by permission of Methodist Publishing House, 10 Ivatt Way, Peterborough PE3 7PG, England. This is an abbreviated version of the original essay.

1. When at the time of the French Revolution the Isenheim convent was dissolved and most of its furnishings were destroyed or disappeared, the altar was saved. Today it stands in the Unterlinden Museum at Colmar.

also brought to the chapel to sit or lie in front of the altar (probably completed in 1516) and to look at the paintings: "Participation in the liturgy could render the sufferer oblivious to the most terrible afflictions and enable a salutary germ of hope to spring up within him, stirring the other healing processes to life. Face to face with Christ crucified, hanging in dreadful isolation on the cross of shame, the ailing could forget their own sufferings, even the direst and most excruciating agony of mind and body."[2]

At Isenheim the care for the sick lay in the message of the paintings as well as in the hands of the religious. The biblical word that fits this type of care best is *diakonia*.[3] The term describes an act that shares in Christ's *diakonia*, in his servanthood most fully embodied on the cross.

Luke relates that Jesus thought of himself as *diakonos* (Luke 22:27).[4] The believer who seeks to follow him cannot but share in his care for the marginal figures of life. Its distinct characteristic is the fusion of care for the body with care for the soul.[5]

Lex Christi, Lex Orandi et Credendi

The Isenheim Altar testified to Christ's servanthood in a sanctuary. The witness of the paintings as well as the work of the religious was tied to *leitourgia*, the worship of the community. Jesus Christ himself rendered obedient service in terms of *leitourgia* before God. His work of mercy grew out of his worship of God. It was God's very being that informed his acts of mercy. Worship of God lies at the heart of *diakonia* and not moralistic perfectionism. Christ's *diakonia* qualifies Christian worship in a specific way. Learning to fulfill the *lex Christi,* "Bear one another's burdens and so fulfill the *law of Christ*" (Gal. 6:2), is the

---

2. Pierre Schmitt, *The Isenheim Altar* (Berne: Hallwag, 1960), 6; see Walter Nigg, *Maler des Ewigen* (Zurich and Stuttgart: Artemis, 1961), 45–54.

3. In the Greek *diakonia* covers waiting at the table, serving food, etc. See Hermann Wolfgang Beyer, "Diakonia," in *Theologisches Wörterbuch zum Neuen Testament,* Gerhard Kittel, ed. (Stuttgart: W. Kohlhammer, 1935), 2:81–93. Under the impact of the gospel such acts of menial service became expressions of the love of neighbor. See H. W. Surkau, "Armenpflege," in *Die Religion in Geschichte und Gegenwart,* 3d ed., ed. Kurt Galling (Tübingen: J. C. B. Mohr, 1957), 1:620.

4. The life and work of Jesus is the archetype of *diakonia.* The love of the Christian is grounded in his servant attitude. See H. Knittermeyer, "Diakonie," *Die Religion in Geschichte und Gegenwart,* 3d ed., Kurt Galling, ed. (Tübingen: J. C. B. Mohr, 1958), 2:162. See Heinz-Dietrich Wendland, "Christos Diakonos–Christos Doulos," in *Christos Diakonos* (Zurich: EVZ Verlag, 1962), 14: "The Son of man...serves in suffering. He is the servant of God who fulfils diakonia through his death."

5. Erich Beyreuther, *Geschichte der Diakonie und Inneren Mission in der Neuzeit* (Berlin: C. Z. U. Verlag, 1962), 12. See Arthur Rich, "Diakonie und Sozialstaat," in Beyreuther, *Geschichte der Diakonie,* 36. W. Schneemelcher, "Der diakonische Dienst in der alten Kirche," in Herbert Krimm, ed., *Das diakonische Amt der Kirche* (Stuttgart: Evangelisches Verlagswerk, 1953), 60f. A beautiful expression of the *wholeness of diaknoia* is related by J. C. van Dongen, "Die Diakonie in der reformierten Kirche der Niederlande," in Herbert Krimm, ed., *Das Diakonische Amt der Kirche im ökumenischen Bereich* (Stuttgart: Evangelisches Verlagswerk, 1960), 108. Ottho Gerhard Heldring, the pioneer of home missions in Holland, had a well dug for the poor population of a village when he read the story of the Samaritan woman (John 4): Christ can also quench another thirst!

heartbeat of Christian worship as well as of faith. The *lex orandi* is not of itself the *lex credendi*. Both are subject to the law of Christ.[6]

For the neighbor *diakonia* embodies a love that in *leitourgia* is received as God's love. Sharing completely in the mysterious love of God, it does not calculate whether the neighbor merits love. The basic question of *diakonia* is not whether the neighbor needs my love, but whether I am capable of sharing God's love.

With the discovery of the priesthood of all believers in the Reformation of the sixteenth century new vistas for understanding the Christian life opened up. In the gradual discovery of the diaconate of all believers the Reformation continued.[7] While the seventeenth century was still very much concerned with consolidating the reform of the church in systems of orthodoxy, the eighteenth century began to interpret the Reformation in new experiments of Christian living. Since then *diakonia* as a core concept of the Christian faith slowly moved across the consciousness-threshold of the church.

Diakonia in Education

Jean-Frédéric Oberlin (1740–1826) struggled to educate the people of his parish, that is, to lead them out of ignorance and poverty to a better day. In 1767, when Oberlin arrived in the Vosges mountain village of Waldersbach, some forty miles southwest of Strasbourg, most of his parishioners barely eked out a living. They spoke patois, a dialect neither French nor German, which isolated them even more in their mountain valleys. Oberlin realized that they could not be effectively helped by alms from the outside. They had to be able to stand on their own feet. Thus he began a great educational effort,[8] teaching them how to improve their soil,[9] how to raise better vegetables and build roads and bridges.[10] Central to his effort was the creation of schools. The education effort, however, was only part of the overall pastoral care of Oberlin. It was in terms of his comprehensive *diakonia* that he became influential in the church.[11]

---

6. For a more detailed examination of the relationship of worship and *diakonia* see my article, "The Montreal 'Crisis' of Faith and Order," *Theology and Life* 6, no. 4 (1963): 314ff.

7. Johann Hinrich Wichern's "Gutachten, die Diakonie und den Diakonat betreffend," in *Gesammelte Schriften* (Hamburg, 1902), 3:821–99, of 1856, is a milestone in this development. See also van Dongen, "Die Diakonie in der reformierten Kirche der Niederlande," 118.

8. Jean Paul Benoit, *J. F. Oberlin: pasteur d'hommes* (Strassbourg: Éditions Oberlin, 1955), 168, speaks of Oberlin as *pédagogue avant tout.* In Camille Leenhardt, *La vie de J. F. Oberlin* (Paris and Nancy: Berger, 1911), 33ff., the educational effort of Oberlin is considered first.

9. Karl Eduard Boch, *Das Steintal im Elsass: Eine geschichtliche Studie über die ehemalige Herrschaft Stein und deren Herren, sowie über die Entwicklung des gesamten Wirtschafts- und Geisteslebens im Steintal* (Strasbourg, 1914), 234.

10. Oberlin centered his *diakonia* in the improvement of his parish and rejected the suggestion that he build a diaconic institution. See Ernst Schering, *J. F. Oberlin: Sternstunde der Sozialpädagogik* (Bielefeld, 1959), 40, 46, 50.

11. See Johann Hinrich Wichern, *Die innere Mission der deutschen evangelischen Kirche* (Hamburg: Agentur des Rauhen Hauses, 1849), 143, 216.

Oberlin began his work in an age that was awakening to the need for education. In the sixteenth and seventeenth centuries in Europe hordes of beggars were roaming the countryside. The main Christian reaction had been almsgiving. In 1701 appeared a tract which is characteristic of the new approach of the eighteenth century: August Hermann Francke's *Segensvolle Fusstapfen des noch lebenden und waltendeden, liebreichen und getreuen Gottes.*[12] Francke (1663–1727) here describes the beginning of his educational effort with orphans and the children of the poor which grew into the so-called Franckesche Anstalten, leading from elementary school to college. A publishing house and a pharmacy were soon added. Both enterprises prospered and contributed major funds to the educational projects. At the time of Francke's death altogether twenty-five hundred students and personnel were associated with his schools. The responsibility for educating the poor had dawned on him as they came to the door of his parsonage to beg. "For some time I had bread distributed to them in front of the door. But soon I thought that this was a welcome opportunity to help the poor people in their souls through the Word of God."[13] Francke catechized them for about fifteen minutes. Seeing the need to instruct the children more extensively, he opened a school.

Francke already realized that poverty could not be overcome by almsgiving. It was also not a matter of merely getting the poor off the street. That had been attempted before in many quarters.[14] The time had come to try something new.[15] Man had to be equipped with knowledge. Understanding himself and his environment better, he could throw off the shackles of poverty. Elementary education as introduced by Francke quickly spread throughout Germany; princes and governments assumed responsibility. With one difference: education as public education was no longer tied to conversion![16]

The Emerging "Public Welfare" Concern

Pietism, of which Francke was an outstanding representative, had an individualist bent. Ironically, although aware of the failure of mere almsgiving, it generally continued it in a somewhat sublimated form. Instead of individuals, now a few

12. Translated into English by Anton Wilhelm Böhme under the title *Pietas Hallensis; or, an Abstract of the Marvellous Footsteps of Divine Providence,* 2d ed. (1707). See Erich Beyreuther, *August Hermann Francke* (Marburg: Verlag der Francke Buchhandlung, 1961), 199.

13. *Wahre und umständliche Nachricht von dem Waisen-hause, und übrigen Anstalten zu Glaucha vor Halle,* 3d ed. (1709), 2.

14. Francke had been especially impressed by what had been done in Dutch institutions. See Gerhard Uhlhorn, *Die christliche Liebestätigkeit* (Moers: Neukirchener Verlag, 1959), 608ff.

15. With special reference to the tons of gold expended on the poorhouses in Holland, Francke states that the Halle *Anstalten* are a much greater and more important work. See August Hermann Francke, *Der Grosse Aufsatz,* ed. Otto Podczeck (Berlin: Akademie Verlag, 1962), 41. Francke's self-confidence seems to be rooted in his conviction that *diakonia* in education can accomplish what mere almsgiving never could.

16. See Herbert Krimm, "Diakonie," in *Evangelisches Soziallexikon* (Stuttgart: Kreuz Verlag, 1954), 224: In Pietism "education and conversion were inseparable."

institutions were supported by a number of like-minded Christians. Pietism was unable to awaken the church as a whole to the needs of society, not to speak of providing leadership.[17] Soon the Enlightenment took its place as a formative influence.

As "the exodus of reason from its self-inflicted captivity" (Immanuel Kant) the Enlightenment continued to stress education as the best means to improve the human condition. But those who believed in the Enlightenment no longer based their ideals on the Christian faith. Man had become his own measure. Charity work now found two different expressions, one rooted in man's own capacities and the other in Christianity.[18] The feeling of a specific community responsibility for the sick, the poor, etc., emerged.[19] The church could still contribute benevolence funds. But leadership was not expected of it.

Even though communities began to take matters into their own hands, the earth did not become a paradise. Political and economic conditions kept the majority of the people poor. Wars and famines followed each other. In the famine of 1772–73 there were 150,000 dead in Kursachsen alone. Man had not learned as yet effectively to control his societal well-being. In the last part of the eighteenth century begging was again on the increase. In Cologne one counted 10,000 beggars among a population of 40,000. The intelligentsia found plenty of opportunities for discussing proper measures to improve the conditions of the poor. Programs and ideals, however, were not enough to wipe poverty off the face of the earth.[20]

Prefigurations of Later Developments

The care of the sick remained negligible in large parts of Europe in the eighteenth century. Even in a city like Hamburg, a community that prided itself in an awakened social conscience, two hospital patients still had to share the same bed. Untrained attendants reluctantly performed the necessary chores.

Already in the seventeenth century France's Vincent de Paul (1581–1660) in his *filles de la charité* had taken a big step toward a more thorough care for the sick. In the Middle Ages, although occasionally women had worked in this field, the male orders had been predominant. The Antonites are an example. De Paul gave women an independent place. No cloistered nuns, the *filles de la charité* were free to respond to need wherever it was found.[21] As early as 1652 three members went to Poland. But it was not before the beginning of the nineteenth

---

17. One must keep in mind, however, the long-range effect of Pietism: "Historical research sees in Puritanism the beginning of capitalism, in German Pietism the beginning of socialism" (Beyreuther, *Geschichte der Diakonie*, 41).

18. Uhlhorn, *Die christliche Liebestätigkeit*, 674.

19. Gerhard Noske, "Geschichtliche Voraussetzungen der heutigen Diakonie," in *Heutige Diakonie der evangelischen Kirche* (Berlin: Lettner Verlag, 1956), 10.

20. Uhlhorn, *Die christliche Liebestätigkeit*, 676ff.

21. For specific characteristics see Léonce Celier, *Les Filles de la Charité* (Paris: B. Grasset, 1929), 115ff.

century that they extended their work to Germany.[22] Two or three decades later the Protestant deaconess appeared on the scene.

Another example of the slow process in which the church became conscious of *diakonia* is the diaconic congregation. Jean-Frédéric Oberlin in the Ban-de-la-Roche came as close as any single individual in the eighteenth century to realizing local *diakonia*. Rejecting the suggestion of building an institution, a poorhouse or an orphanage, he spent his energies on the socioeconomic improvement of his parishioners as well as on their spiritual and intellectual growth. All efforts, such as the schools, the agricultural societies, and a type of bank where his parishioners could loan money, contributed to the growth of a diaconic congregation.[23] Only in the twentieth century, however, was the significance of the diaconic congregation more widely appreciated.

From *Diakonia* in Education to *Diakonia* in Social Service

An increase in knowledge meant an increase in man's capacity to master his environment. Education led to industrialization. One can often observe how the one directly works into the hands of the other. Upon Oberlin's initiative a Swiss entrepreneur, Jean-Luc Le Grand (1755–1825), built a factory in the Ban-de-la-Roche. Occasionally even the idea of founding a "Christian industry" was promoted. Two men, Philipp Matthäus Hahn (1739–90) and Gustav Albert Werner (1809–87), built factories in Germany on the principle of Christian cooperation between employer and employee. But their efforts stood outside the main current of the times. Both church and state in the eighteenth century had been unable to solve the problem of poverty. Inexorably the poor of the eighteenth became the proletariat of the nineteenth century. The victims of the anonymous forces creating the modern masses presented a new challenge for *diakonia*.

Industrialization on a large scale with its ensuing social blight hit England first. Robert Owen (1771–1858), co-owner of a cotton mill and thoroughly acquainted with the social conditions of the people, already in the early nineteenth century outlined a broad program of social reform.[24] His influence on the 1819 labor legislation, the First Factory Act, was considerable.[25]

---

22. *1660–1960 Monsieur Vincent vit encore: Sa survie par ses Filles de la Charité au long des siècles* (Paris, 1960), 27.

23. Oberlin was influenced by the Moravians, who began to establish themselves in the Alsace as early as 1735. By way of the Moravians, Oberlin was linked to the educational effort of the Halle *Anstalten*, whose product Nikolaus von Zinzendorf was. In Zinzendorf *diakonia* in education expanded into ecumenical *diakonia*. Important attempts at ecumenical *diakonia* are already found in August Hermann Francke. See Erich Beyreuther, "Ökumenische Diakonie im deutschen Protestantismus bis zum Beginn des 19. Jahrhunderts," in *Ökumenische Diakonie*, ed. Christian Berg (Berlin: Lettner Verlag, 1959), 43ff.

24. Robert Owen, *A New View of Society and Other Writings* (London and Toronto: J. M. Dent and Sons, 1927), xii.

25. When in 1818 Owen made a trip to France and other European countries he also paid a visit

Besides the new problems created by industrialization society still faced the old ones carried along from the past. While for some time in England great personalities continued to tackle the problems in a more individualistic manner,[26] the Germans began to launch concerted *diakonia* efforts — stimulated by the English pioneers.

The New Deacon

August Hermann Francke could still afford to wait for the poor to knock at his door. Johann Hinrich Wichern (1808–81), some hundred years later, in the slums of Hamburg, sought out the outcast child. In 1833 he founded in Hamburg the "Rauhe Haus," a home for vagrant boys in connection with a Sunday School enterprise brought into being under English influence.[27] Most of these boys had been running around in rags tied together with strings. Wichern even found children of a drunk who were drunk, too. Those he gathered he united in family-type groups of twelve to fourteen under the care of a "Bruder," an older brother, and educated them, combining theoretical with practical concerns, shoemaking, tailoring, baking, etc.

With Wichern's "Bruder" a new type of deacon originated. In 1839 Wichern founded a "Bruderhaus," an educational institution for deacons who would go into slums, jails, and other places where most pastors would not go and perhaps could not go without neglecting what they considered their foremost duties.[28] The general outlook of the church had not been geared to the social needs of the people. Even toward the end of the nineteenth century a professor for practical theology at the University of Berlin still advised his students not to make any calls. Too close a contact with the people would make the mantle of the prophet fall off their shoulders.[29]

In order to be fair one must recall the circumstances under which many pastors in Europe were working. At a time when Cincinnati, Ohio, was as large as Hamburg it counted 144 churches and chapels, while Hamburg had about a dozen.[30] At the same time the largest congregation in Berlin consisted of 89,000

---

to Oberlin. See Helene Simon, *Robert Owen: Sein Leben und seine Bedeutung für die Gegenwart* (Jena: G. Fischer, 1905), 144.

26. For a review of English *diakonia* discussions see Paul Philippi, *Christozentrische Diakonie* (Stuttgart: Evangelisches Verlagswerk, 1963), 22ff. As key work is cited J. S. Howson, *Deaconesses; or the Official Helps of Women in Parochial Work and in Charitable Institutions* (London: Longman, Green, Longman, and Roberts, 1862).

27. Uhlhorn, *Die christliche Liebestätigkeit*, 721. As regards English influence see also 731ff., 739ff., 755. Contacts between English and German Protestantism go back much farther. See Erich Beyreuther, *August Hermann Francke und die Anfänge der ökumenischen Bewegung* (Leipzig: Koehler and Amelang, 1957), 122.

28. As regards Wichern's hesitation to call the "brothers" deacons see Ernst Schering, *Erneuerung der Diakonie in einer veränderten Welt* (Bielfeld, 1958), 66f.

29. Günther Dehn, "Adolf Stöcker," *Zwischen den Zeiten*, no. 8 (1924): 26.

30. J. Wichern, *Das Rauhe Haus und die Arbeitsfelder des Rauhen Hauses* (Hamburg: Agentur des Rauhen Hauses, 1833), 90.

"souls" shepherded by five pastors. Wichern's deacons were supposed to bring change.

The New Deaconess

The very year Wichern founded the "Rauhe Haus" in Hamburg, in 1833, the first dismissed female prisoner entered the asylum of Theodor Fliedner (1800–1864) at Kaiserswerth am Rhein. Fliedner was pastor of a small struggling two-hundred-member congregation. In 1835 he organized a knitting school in order to give the unwanted woman, just dismissed from prison, something to do. In 1836 a kindergarten followed. The same year the school for female nurses was founded.

While Wichern's enterprise had brought forth the new deacon, Fliedner's produced the new deaconess.[31] In Fliedner's day the abominable conditions of the German hospitals had hardly improved over the eighteenth century. Usually two patients still had to share the same bed. If one patient died after 10 p.m., the other had to lie next to him until morning.[32] Understandably one preferred to be sick at home. Only the poor and lonely, those for whom no one could care at home, and occasionally journeymen were forced to choose these places of misery. Now Fliedner's deaconesses took over.[33] A new type of care for the sick began in Protestantism.[34]

The Limits of *Diakonia* in Social Service

Wichern expected the church to be concerned with the "whole" man, to save the people bodily as well as spiritually. He formulated the task as *innere Mission,* a type of "home mission" directed toward the church itself, an external and internal renewal of the German people who nominally at least were Christians. He recognized the responsibility of the bourgeoisie for the social dilemma and understood the proletarian plight, "but the new type of the proletarian as *socio-political element* who has nothing in common with the 'naturally' poor of all times did not

---

31. It was not completely without precedent for Fliedner. On his trip to Holland he had discovered deaconesses among the Mennonites, women who in the Mennonite congregations were responsible for the care of the poor. Fliedner refers to their work as an institution of primitive Christianity which ought to be imitated. Theodor Fliedner, *Collectenreise nach England* (Essen, 1831), 1:150ff. Another influence on Fliedner was an essay by the Protestant minister Friedrich Klönne, who discusses the possibility of reviving the work of the primitive Christian deaconess (published in Leipzig in 1820).

32. Uhlhorn, *Die christliche Liebestätigkeit,* 743.

33. Liselotte Katscher, *Geschichte der Krankenpflege* (Berlin: Christlicher Zeitschriften Verlag, n.d.), 53–73. It is noteworthy that Florence Nightingale received training in Kaiserswerth. A little of what Fliedner had received in England he could now return.

34. For a survey of Roman Catholic care for the poor, the sick, etc., in modern times see Joseph A. Fischer, "Die katholische Caritas in der Neuzeit," in Krimm, ed., *Das diakonische Amt der Kirche,* 388–432. Fliedner's relationship to Roman Catholic models is briefly examined in Theodor Schäfer, *Die Geschichte der weiblichen Diakonie* (Stuttgart, 1887), 299ff. and Uhlhorn, *Die christliche Liebestätigkeit,* 731.

enter his field of decision."[35] It was detrimental to his intention that he aligned himself with the state when in 1857 he became "Oberkirchenrat," an appointee of the Prussian church government.

Since the *innere Mission* stopped where for the rising proletariat the demands only began, the movement lost contact with the working class.[36] Too much alignment with the state meant too little critical distance to those responsible for the social dilemma. Since practice did not conform to theory in Wichern,[37] his revolutionary discovery that individual charity had to be broadened to a *diakonia* wrestling with the social structure had no effect on society. Wichern was afraid of revolutionary change and practically also took the attitude that "all revolutions are against the kingdom of God."[38] The fact that he had been a student of Friedrich Schleiermacher might explain part of his inability to attain a more radical understanding of the relationship of Christianity and culture.[39]

The limits of *diakonia* in social service of nineteenth-century Protestant Germany were especially revealed by two men, Adolf Stöcker (1835–1909) and Friedrich Naumann (1860–1919). Stöcker, since 1874 "Hofprediger" in Berlin (the "personal preacher" of the Kaiser), realized that Wichern's *innere Mission* offered no solution to the tough social problems.[40] He began to approach it in political terms and founded the Christian-Social Worker's Party. It failed miserably, however. To add insult to injury, the Kaiser dismissed the political preacher. Later in a famous telegram he declared: "Stöcker is finished. Christian-social is nonsense."[41]

The fact that Naumann founded a party without the word "Christian"[42] in its name did not keep it from failing likewise. Naumann realized that Christian-social politics was impossible. Jesus offered no basis for sociopolitical theory.

Both Stöcker and Naumann keenly saw the shortcomings of *diakonia* limited to social service. In a world of power struggle the Christian, if he wanted to get involved in the world, would also have to get involved in the power struggle. *Diakonia* in politics, "political *diakonia*,"[43] beyond *diakonia* in mere social service was inescapable. But since a political party did not seem a workable expression of *diakonia* in politics, what would be a more effective form? Was it not basically

---

35. Karl Kupisch, *Kirche und soziale Frage im 19. Jahrhundert* (Zurich, 1963), 17.

36. Ibid., 18ff.

37. See the examination of Wichern's theory in Heinz-Dietrich Wendland, *Der Begriff Christlich-sozial* (Cologne and Opladen: Westdeutscher Verlag, 1962), 15ff.

38. A famous word of Gottfried Menken, quoted in Emmanuel Hirsch, *Geschichte der neuern evangelischen Theologie* (Gütersloh: C. Bertelsmann, 1954), 5:96.

39. Uhlhorn, *Die christliche Liebestätigkeit*, 721.

40. Karl Kupisch, *Zwischen Idealismus und Massendemokratie: Eine Geschichte der evangelischen Kirche in Deutschland von 1815–1945* (Berlin: Lettner Verlag, 1955), 103.

41. Ibid., 109.

42. Dehn, "Adolf Stöcker," 43: "Naumann was able to do the liberating deed of giving up the predicate 'Christian' as description of his endeavors."

43. Helmuth Schreiner speaks of the "political *diakonia*" of Stöcker; see "Wichern, Löhe, und Stöcker," in Krimm, ed., *Das diakonische Amt der Kirche*, 348.

a matter of finding a form that would genuinely express the specific quality of *diakonia?* Stöcker and Naumann knew of no answer.

The Emerging Welfare State

While in Europe the "professional" deacon and deaconess proved only partial answers to pressing social needs, they did give the European discussion on *diakonia* in the last hundred years its peculiar slant. Some areas of the world did not develop a marked need for professionalized *diakonia.* The United States are the most striking example. The four deaconesses Fliedner personally brought to the Lutherans of Pittsburgh in 1849 were unable to enamor American women with the idea.[44] It was not before 1884, when seven deaconesses from Iserlohn (Westphalia) arrived in Philadelphia, that the deaconess became a more attractive professional option among the American Lutherans. Later the Evangelical Synod, the Episcopalians, and the Methodists also introduced deaconesses. But the overall situation did not call for professional *diakonia.*

It has been observed that the term *diakonia* is only today becoming more current in America, signalizing a more church-oriented interpretation of the social responsibility of the Christian.[45] Although *diakonia* did not become as professionalized in America as in Europe, the churches engaged in work that brought similar results. When in 1955 the National Council of Churches made a first national survey of the *diakonia* efforts in the churches cooperating in the council, it counted 2,783 health and welfare institutions. Of that number 18 percent were homes for old people, 14 percent neighborhood centers, and 10 percent establishments for children.[46] It is important to note in this context that of the total number of hospitals in the United States only one-sixteenth are Protestant whereas one-eighth are Roman Catholic.

For the development of *diakonia* in the United States the sharp separation of church and state has been beneficial. It kept church members from acting in terms of benevolence only. It was their obligation as citizens to be politically responsible for the marginal figures of life.[47] In the face of an increasingly brutal industrialization the obligation was too often forgotten. But the Social Gospel, most illuminatingly embodied in the figure of Walter Rauschenbusch (1861–1918), was characterized by its effective nurture of the social responsibility of the Christian as a citizen in an industrial society at least in some denominations.

---

44. Theodor Fliedner, *Nachricht über das Diakonissen-Werk in der christlichen Kirche, alter und neuer Zeit* (Kaiserwerth, 1856), 21.

45. E. Theodore Bachmann, "Diakonie in den Vereinigten Staaten," in Krimm, ed., *Das Diakonische Amt der Kirche im ökumenischen Bereich,* 171.

46. Ibid., 210. For a bibliography on *diakonia* in the United States see 218ff.

47. Johann Hinrich Wichern, *Die Behandlung der Verbrecher und der entlassenen Sträflinge* (Hamburg: Agentur des Rauhen Hauses, 1853), 10. American developments early in the nineteenth century already could serve as models for amelioration of conditions in Europe. Work in Boston influenced the founding of the *rheinisch-westfälische Gefängnisgesellschaft.*

One can easily understand why the United States as a whole did not know of a marked development from *diakonia* in education via *diakonia* in social service to a more political *diakonia*. A growing frontier nation at one and the same time faced a plurality of needs. Many of the American pioneer colleges were immediate expressions of *diakonia* in education. Simultaneously the new communities had to be structured socially and politically. One must also keep in mind that in the vast unpopulated spaces of the New World there were always new opportunities, so that the social needs were seldom as pressing as in Europe. Wherever such needs did make themselves felt, the multiplicity of the denominations worked against a common Christian approach. When in the thirties the Great Depression radically confronted the American for the first time with the modern social and political dilemmas, he built the welfare state, guided by the democratic vision. The economic homogenization of the West since World War II is perhaps the main reason for the emergence of the welfare state as ideal, if not as reality, in most parts of our hemisphere.

Because of the different socioeconomic development Christian thought in the United States did not regard *diakonia* as a master image. What Christians did not feel called upon to do externally in terms of social action they sought to manage internally under the guidance of the stewardship idea.[48] In view of the secularization of many of the activities of the church the desire recently has been expressed to reintroduce the challenge of genuine *diakonia*.[49]

Diakonia in Politics

The complex power structures developed by the state to provide for education[50] and social security[51] need constant surveillance and correction lest they become ends in themselves. In what form can *diakonia* share in this task? A recent test for finding an answer has been the struggle for civil rights in the United States.

One is tempted to list nonviolence, the technique of the sit-ins, as the most modern expression of *diakonia* in the political realm. But it is not a direct ex-

---

48. See Martin O. Dietrich, "Stewardship," in Krimm, ed., *Das diakonische Amt der Kirche*, 433–42. Little has as yet been done in serious theological comparison of *stewardship* and *diakonia*. The equation stewardship=*diakonia* is not as simple as some recent literature on the subject would have us believe. There are good reasons for seeing the term "stewardship" without a halo. See Gibson Winter, *The New Creation as Metropolis* (New York: Macmillan, 1963), 97: "Terms such as 'vocation' or 'stewardship' avoid ... basic questions. In fact, stewardship is little more than a fundraising 'gimmick' in most churches." One should read Dietrich's article in the light of Winter's critical remarks.

49. Bachmann, "Diakonie in den Vereinigten Staaten," 211.

50. Sheldom L. Rahn, "Neue Formen des Dienstes," in *Diakonie als ökumensiche Aufgabe II* (Berlin: Christlicher Zeitschriften Verlag, 1963), 45: "The time is past in which it was necessary for the church to be a pioneer, to organize most of the social, health and educational services."

51. Uhlhorn could already claim that the views about the task of the state had completely changed since the middle of the nineteenth century: "Until then one acted according to the principle *il mondo va da se* (the world runs by itself), now one cannot assign enough tasks to the state.... The care for the lower classes is part of it" (Uhlhorn, *Die christliche Liebestätigkeit*, 759). While in retrospect it appears that the state at the time did not assume enough responsibility or was not responsible in the right way, the change in attitude since the beginning of the eighteenth century is obvious.

pression of reconciling love.[52] Going beyond direct nonviolent action, *diakonia* in politics can attempt, however, to transform the societal structure.

An example is Fritz von Bodelschwingh's successful intervention for epileptics who had been condemned to euthanasia by measures of the Third Reich. Von Bodelschwingh was able to reach Adolf Hitler's personal physician, Dr. Brandt. No one else in Germany got through to the one truly responsible "and encountered him directly in a battle with his soul. Even in his final words at the Nuremberg trials before his execution Dr. Brandt . . . remembered: only one man had tried to stop him, Pastor von Bodelschwingh."[53] Von Bodelschwingh succeeded. Thirty thousand were saved from mercy killing. The whole program was called off.

Whether *diakonia* in the political realm immediately reaches the public limelight or not, it always leads to a clear confrontation of state and church. When during World War II the Netherlands was occupied by Germany, the deacons of the Dutch Reformed Church assumed the care for the politically persecuted, supplying food and providing secret refuge. Realizing what was happening, the Germans decreed that the elective office of the deacon should be eliminated. The Reformed Synod on July 17, 1941, resolved: "Whoever touches the diakonate interferes with what Christ has ordained as the task of the Church. He touches the cult of the Church."[54] Whoever lays hands on *diakonia* lays hands on worship! The Germans backed down. In taking *diakonia* seriously in a concrete political situation the church begins to grasp her very being.

The Theological Rediscovery of *Diakonia*

A remarkable change has taken place within the last two decades. Theology is beginning to learn that the basic structure of the church is diaconic. Proclamation, pastoral care, Christian education, church government and administration, stewardship, and charity work have diaconic character.[55] The language used in the ecumenical church to express this understanding may differ; the principal witness is the same.[56] This is due to at least two factors: the growing similarity of economic and cultural structures on every continent[57] and the breadth of ecumenical conversation.[58]

---

52. See William Robert Miller, *Nonviolence: A Christian Interpretation* (New York: Association Press, 1964), 177: "Nonviolence . . . is not love; nor is it a method for resolving conflict. It is a way of waging social conflict that is compatible with love. It does a minimum of damage and holds the door open to creative, constructive possibilities. But it has no intrinsic power to heal and to build anew. For this we must look beyond nonviolence to active, agapaic love and reconciliation."

53. Beyreuther, *Geschichte der Diakonie*, 203f.

54. Herbert Krimm, "Diakonie als Gestaltwerdung der Kirche," in *Christos Diakonos*, 62. See van Dongen, "Die Diakonie in der reformierten Kirche der Niederlande," 112ff.

55. Heinz-Dietrich Wendland, *Botschaft an die soziale Welt* (Hamburg: Furche Verlag, 1959), 254.

56. Winter, *The New Creation as Metropolis*, 150: "The notion of the servant Church owes much to . . . World Council discussions."

57. See Uhlhorn, *Die christliche Liebestätigkeit*, 767, 799f.

58. For *diakonia* this was crystallized at New Delhi. See W. A. Visser't Hooft, *The New Delhi Report* (London, 1962), 111.

Recent thinking on *diakonia* centers its understanding of the diaconic character of the church on Jesus as *the* deacon. Thus a "christocentric *diakonia*" is being developed.[59] In terms of the Protestant principle one author has expressed it in the words: *sola gratia, sola fide, solus Christus, sola Christi diakonia* (only through grace, only through faith, only through Christ, only through Christ's service).[60] The *sola Christi diakonia* implies that man's needs are ultimately met only by God's own intercession for man in Christ. Since the full manifestation of God's intercession still lies in the future, *diakonia* is directed toward the coming of God's kingdom. In *leitourgia* the Christian time and again is confronted with the eschatological dimension of his existence. Separated from *leitourgia, diakonia* would be the same as secular welfare work.[61]

Problems of definition are inevitable of which a few seem especially pressing: the relationship between the diaconic task of the church as a whole and the specific diaconic office, the difference between political *diakonia* and a more comprehensive societal *diakonia,* the unity between political or societal *diakonia* and other aspects of *diakonia,* the limitations of using such qualifications as political or societal, the difference between *diakonia* and mission, and the place of *diakonia* in the context of theology as a whole.

But the problems of definition are only secondary as compared with the significance of the great socioeconomic change in many parts of the world. What does it mean to live diaconically in the modern welfare state? Must *diakonia* conform to the social change? Or should it seek to transform the structure of society according to the gospel image of man and human community? New forms are sought that could transform the world.[62] In many areas of the West only preliminary spadework has been done for the creation of new forms.[63] Occasionally the desire is expressed to find new tasks for old forms, as may be the case with the Hospitallers, the Order of St. John, which goes as far back as the year 1099, the time of the Crusades.[64] More frequent is the demand for new forms of old tasks, as with the deaconesses.[65] The principal intention is to supplement the "saving" rescue mission *diakonia* of the past with a "formative" industrial mission *diakonia* for the new society.[66]

The frequent intermingling of *diakonia* and public welfare in the history of

---

59. Philippi, *Christozentrische Diakonie,* 227ff.

60. Schering, *Erneuerung der Diakonie in einer veränderten Welt,* 34.

61. Heinz-Dietrich Wendland, "Die dienende Kirche und das Diakonenamt," in Krimm, ed., *Das diakonische Amt der Kirche,* 443ff.

62. Rahn, "Neue Formen des Dienstes," 44–59.

63. Hans Christoph von Hase, "Die christliche Gemeinde und die gesetzliche Neuregelung der Jugend- und Sozialhilfe," in *Jahrbuch der Inneren Mission und des Hilfswerks der Evangelischen Kirche in Deutschland* (Stuttgart: Evangelisches Verlagswerk, 1963), 26.

64. In the same yearbook, ibid., 91–102, the essay on "Evangelische Ritterschaft in unserer Zeit." See especially 95: "Bridgebuilding toward Diakonia."

65. Friedrich Thiele, *Diakonissenhäuser im Umbruch der Zeit* (Stuttgart: Evangelisches Verlagswerk, 1963), 26ff.

66. See Eugen Gerstenmaier, " 'Wichern Zwei': Zum Verhältnis von Diakonie und Sozialpolitik," in Krimm, *Das Diakonische Amt der Kirche,* 501f.

the church and the replacement of large areas of *diakonia* work by public welfare forces theology to ask whether there is anything distinctive about *diakonia* that the state cannot offer.[67] Here theological reflection on *diakonia* joins the basic theological quest of our day. The recent stress on Jesus as the deacon points to the core of the contemporary theological concern: what is the distinctive characteristic of Jesus? The quest for new forms of *diakonia* is essentially the search for a form of life that can express the unique quality of Jesus' life — a form that man cannot produce by his own power.

The attempt of finding answers takes on ecumenical dimensions. Orthodox ecclesiology has an important contribution to make to the asking of the right questions.[68] The unusual interest in *diakonia* in Roman Catholicism of late promises to make a conversation on *diakonia* the cutting edge of the Roman Catholic-Protestant dialogue.[69]

Local *Diakonia*

In the ecumenical movement the trend toward local ecumenicity is paralleled by the emphasis on local *diakonia*.[70] It is very much part of the ecumenical concern for "all in each place."[71] It involves the fusion of the call to unity[72] with the call to service.[73] The new interest in local *diakonia* does not mean to suggest that diaconic congregations do not exist. But in terms of a comprehensive ecumenical concern new reflection is called for. What is the structure of the diaconic congregation? Does it need a professionally trained deacon? What is the place of the deaconess? Oberlin already hoped that laywomen could work as deaconesses in the local congregation, much as laymen were acting as deacons. The "professional" deacon and deaconess and the "lay" deacon and deaconess need not exclude each other as long as both are able to embody the unique dimension of the Christian life.

Drawing its strength from *leitourgia*,[74] *diakonia* must be related to the primordial structure of human existence. Too often the "rich" and "healthy" Christian has condescended in "diaconic paternalism" to the less fortunate — to improve

---

67. The question is already part of the ecumenical conversation. See Eugene C. Blake, "What Makes Christian Service Distinctive?" in *Consultation Digest* (World Council of Churches, 1962), 53–59.

68. See Iwan Pereswetow, "Zur Geschichte der karitativen Tätigkeit in der orthodoxen Ostkirche mit besonderer Berücksichtigung der russischen Kirche," in Krimm, ed., *Das diakonische Amt der Kirche*, 231ff.

69. From the growing literature we cite Karl Rahner and Herbert Vorgrimler, eds., *Diaconia in Christo* (Freiburg: Herder, 1962).

70. Hans Christoph von Hase, "Die Wiederentdeckung der dienenden Gemeinde," in *Diakonie der Gemeinde* (Berlin: Lettner Verlag, 1961), 15–43.

71. Rahn, "Neue Formen des Dienstes," 45.

72. Visser't Hooft, *The New Delhi Report*, 116.

73. Ibid., 111; P. C. Rodger and L. Vischer, eds., *The Fourth World Conference on Faith and Order* (London: SCM Press, 1964), 87ff.

74. Theodor Schober, *Gottesdienst und Diakonie* (Stuttgart: Calver Verlag, 1965), 9ff.

his condition, to make him feel good, or to convert him. As a result, the real point of *diakonia* has been missed. Primarily the poor and the sick person does not need me, but I need him. Is it not in the poor and sick that I meet Christ and in this encounter learn to love with the love of God? Is it not in the lowliness of the outcast that I am confronted with God's very being?

Christ? The love of God? God's very being? In the poor and the sick? In the outcast? *Diakonia* makes us ponder in action the mystery of the relationship between suffering and God. Words can only witness to the mystery, the way the words of John the Baptist witness on the Isenheim Altar — written near his large pointing finger: *illum oportet crescere, me autem minui* (he must increase, but I must decrease [John 3:30]).

BLACK AND WHITE TOGETHER?

In this essay Herzog talks about unexpected roadblocks at the end of a long process of theological and hermeneutical reflections of which his first book, Understanding God, *was a part.*

In the wake of a set of civil rights protests at Duke University which led to the occupation of the administration buildings by students of the Afro-American Society, Herzog begins to realize the full extent of the gap between black and white. In this context it is becoming ever clearer that even well-intentioned theological words are sucked into that gap and crash.

Not even the few white theologians who have supported the basic concerns of African Americans are off the hook. Listening to the voices of the other, new relationships need to be built on the honest recognition of differences. Rather than covering up the gaps, we need to develop new personal encounters that transform the power structures of racism which reach all the way into theological education and, ultimately, into the business of theology as well. As a result Herzog, together with AME Bishop Philip Cousin, introduced the Black Church Studies Program at Duke Divinity School, beginning in 1969.

It has been on my mind for some time that I had promised the *Duke Divinity School Review* a systematic theology piece on hermeneutic for the spring of 1969. After all the noise I have been making at Duke about hermeneutic for nearly a decade I probably should be one of the first to deliver a goodly stack of sheets on the subject for publication. But I will probably be the last one to turn in a contribution, and not a very lengthy one at that. Let me hasten to add that this does not reflect lack of concern for the total project so well prepared by Gene Tucker. It also does not mean that I have not made preparations for the writing of the article. But in the past six weeks since February 13, 1969, many of my theological words have broken into pieces. I have had to face unprecedented difficulties of communication, hermeneutical "hang-ups." I notice that others have had similar difficulties. At the core of my communication difficulties lies the realization that if people cannot understand one another, they certainly cannot understand some subject matter in common, say, the Bible. Understanding some common subject

First published in *Duke Divinity School Review* 34 (Spring 1969): 115–20.

matter in the event of understanding one another, this is what hermeneutic is all about. But here on Duke campus in the spring of 1969 we are further from understanding one another than at any time in my memory during the nearly ten years of my stay at this university. It may well be that it now merely became unconcealed how little we really understood one another before, when all was suffused in a glow of fellowship and friendly dialogue. But this insight is cold comfort when we need understanding *now.* Handwringing over the past will not help us on in the task of understanding. So where do we turn?

In preparation for this paper I read *The Pornography of Power* (Chicago, 1968) by Lionel Rubinoff, who in this book works with as clear a definition of herme‐ neutic as anyone I know of. At least he uses the word the way I have used it in my teaching and writing. His basic idea is as follows: "As opposed to 'causal' or 'scientific' analysis of behavior, which seeks primarily to *explain* partic‐ ular events by subsuming them under empirically verifiable laws, a hermeneutic analysis seeks rather to disclose the subjective significance or 'meaning' of human behavior.... As Sartre has argued, the substitution of *in order to* for *because* (or as a result of) is a matter of the utmost importance. It illustrates once again the difference between the phenomenological approach, which is essentially herme‐ neutic and which seeks to disclose the human significance of a phenomenon, and the naturalistic approach, which is essentially causal‐explanatory" (pp. 86f.). I find significant in this description of hermeneutic especially the emphasis on the role of the person. Hermeneutic is not a mere matter of taking apart a text and putting it back together again. It is a grasping of personhood, human or di‐ vine, often mediated through a text, but with the text always functioning as the medium that reveals personhood.

Systematic theology, as I understand it, evolves as a hermeneutic. It is def‐ initely a phenomenological approach to a particular subject matter. It cannot subsume its ultimate subject matter — God, Christ, and the Holy Spirit — under empirically verifiable general laws. It cannot strive for attaining objective sci‐ entific knowledge. What it must aim for is personal understanding. In order to arrive at this understanding there must first of all be a disclosure of the meaning of present human behavior, especially in the church. Where I teach theology — at Duke — some human behavior has become enigmatic and puzzling. System‐ atic theology must try to grasp the dynamics of this behavior as the matrix of its theological work. Underneath the antagonisms between black and white there must be some common human core that offers the basis for new understanding. Understanding is not found by brushing off the differences. It appears as one faces together some hard truths about one another. One must suffer through the differences together. The common solidarity of pain and suffering in the face of misunderstanding is probably the first stage through which we must pass in order that theological understanding may arise.

It may be that in new obedience to our common Lord, Jesus Christ, an over‐ riding reality may compel us to understand one another better. But we have mouthed so many theological phrases without probably ever really seeing each other that the demand of the hour is to take a new look at each other, so that we can engage in a hermeneutic of changing the conditions that made us move apart.

[I want to use the following ideas also in a different context with fellow students and colleagues. So if one of my readers finds in the pages of the *Review* what he has already read somewhere else, may he be undismayed: repetition is also the mother of understanding.]

I had initially planned on sharing these thoughts with the Concerned Students of Duke Divinity School [a spontaneous, unofficial organization which sprang into being immediately after the campus disturbance — Ed.]. But I had to be out of town during some of their meetings. The comments reflect several conversations I have had with black and white students in our midst (some of whom are now alumni) about the black-white tensions.

In one or two instances I got the impression that a black student simply felt crushed by the predominantly white setting of our Divinity School. Events following February 13 here on campus underscored the impression time and again.

One thing became clear to me over the past year: integration as such is no immediately effective solution to the race issue, also not in the Divinity School community.

The difficulty in terms of the educational process seems to be lodged in the fact that white Christianity has not identified with black history at any significant point. When the Reformation was developing in Europe, some of the blacks' ancestors were already being shipped across the Atlantic. When Friedrich Schleiermacher wrote his *Speeches on Religion*, black history in the United States was still slave history.

With what is the black to identify? Before he can identify with white church history he must identify with his own history. But he has no chance to study it in courses alongside white church history.

So in plunging into a white educational setting apparently a tremendous identity crisis develops for a large number of black students. What is more, the crisis is aggravated by the increasing stress on Black Power in the black community. A white seminary does not specifically discuss Black Power as a course topic, as little as black history or black culture.

As a consequence we have to face the question of what black students in white seminaries are trained for. A black alumnus said, "Remember, you are training people for jobs, not certificates." Does a black student who has been trained by Duke Divinity School still fit into the average black congregation?

In the encounter with the black student — I will never want to forget — we meet a unique struggle for personhood. It is not that the black does not acknowledge that the white also has a struggle for personhood to contend with. The issue seems to be whether there is any real outlet for discussing the special "hang-ups" of the black struggle. All counselors and professors are white.

Some blacks have the impression that there is race prejudice among both students and professors, the unconscious prejudice being even worse than the conscious.

One black student indicated that a professor (whose name he did not mention) told him at the very beginning of his studies that he should face up to the fact that this is Duke and that he could not expect to get the same high grades here that he got in his college. The student seemed rather perplexed about the well-meant advice.

As to social contacts, black students feel that they have hardly any social outlet at Duke. Black tables, etc., are demands that are simple corollaries of this lack of social outlet.

White girls occasionally chat with black students on campus, I was told. But when white boys come near, many of them prefer to move on.

Perception of situations depends on who we are. It is never absolutely objective. So we must deal with the one who perceives the situation and must take his word at face value.

All in all, we should probably make the race issue less central in our conversations. The whites have a responsibility here that may be overlooked most of the time. One black student said: "In seminary, I became an authority on race relations. And that is about all I became an authority in." Obviously the black student wants the white student to converse with him also about things other than race.

"It may be that we are hypersensitive right now as blacks," I was told. But the situation has to be faced by all as it is. The fact of the perception of the black-white antagonism is there. Said one black: "When I came to Duke, I knew Duke had accepted me. But had the white students accepted me?"

If I understand a little of what is being said right now, the struggle seems to be about personhood, human dignity. The black has to find his past — in order to know his personhood. He has to come to know also his present — in order to become a fuller person. So the comment of yet another student remains a judgment: "We get a middle-class, upper-class training at Duke Divinity School." The judgment should be obvious: we are more trained for status than for personhood.

Many of the new dilemmas we are facing are related to the increasing consciousness of being black. One black alumnus, who felt that at the beginning of integration at Duke these difficulties had not been as pressing, explained: "Just when the blacks were about getting what they wanted, they said: 'We don't want to be white.'"

There is at the same time the feeling that the white Divinity School community is taking integration too lightly. It does not struggle enough with the implications of integration for the whole person. A former black student summed up the issue: "Integration at the foot is just as bad as or worse than segregation at the side." If you are allowed into the same room, but the other person does not really see your face and acknowledge you as a person, segregation might still be the lesser of two evils.

I realize full well that the problems at Duke go far beyond reflections like the foregoing. Righting the wrongs of a slave society will take more time than a generation. Feeling guilty does not help at all. What we need to do is to work creatively at new models of better future relationships.

On the surface the turmoil of our university is centered in the right use of power, that is, in the possibility of the student's share in the power lodged in the academic structure. But as I try to look beyond the surface appearances, I begin to ask whether in the Christian context of the Divinity School we must not raise other issues as well. This context is never simply one of scrambling for power, prestige, and status. It also contains the criterion of truth that unconceals our foibles and stupidities. The time has come to face some hard truths about ourselves.

In order to give integration a Christian rationale some of us have been appealing to St. Paul's idea that in Christ there is neither Jew nor Greek. Accordingly, we have been claiming that in Christ there is neither white nor black. But in reality there is still very much black and white in Christ — white and black churches, for example. In our religious Pollyanna attitude we often fail to see that the hurts and wrongs of the exploitation of the blacks continue unabated, right in the midst of Christian people (as does the exploitation of whites, I know). Our black students often have families and friends who do not receive an ounce of benefit from our liberal opening up of the university to the blacks. The hurts and wrongs done to their loved ones and their people are ever before their eyes. Becoming color-blind — in which I have prided myself — easily can mean becoming blind to the savage struggle those of the other color are still caught in.

Just how much real charity we spend on the downtrodden or the outcast in our society, I do not know. There are still many who can only be reached by some charity, especially many physically handicapped. But many of us are merely *concerned* about the disadvantaged. And concern is not action. I was appalled to see how quickly the hustle and bustle of our concern during the 1968 vigil dissipated into doing nothing. Fine attitudes do not make any difference unless they are translated into changing wrongs. Political activity is the main possibility for introducing change. To be merely concerned is a sin against the Holy Spirit.

Finding a new sense of my "white sins" does not mean that I should look away when it comes to the faults of the other color. I am beginning to revolt more and more against making me conscious of the color of my skin as the cause of how sorry conditions are. I did not make the conditions. It does not help to make no distinctions between black and white. We need to see one another as persons, individuals who are responsible for their particular wrongs. There is a saying among some blacks that to the white all blacks look alike. The time has come to tell some blacks that apparently to them all whites look alike. With the present kind of attitude nobody will be the wiser in the long run.

For years many of us have been singing "We Shall Overcome." It came to express our civil rights theology. We should have known all along that it is poor theology. In any case, I am learning more and more that ultimately *we* will not overcome. God must overcome. We are messing things up. But God bears the cross of the present, of black and white alike. We have to open our eyes to what he can do to change our ways and the condition of society. God will overcome.

This does not mean that we should fold our hands and sit back and do nothing. To see what God can do to change our ways means to become more open to what is already happening in society. What begins to puzzle me more and more is the discrepancy between the kind of life we live as a Divinity School community and life as a whole, between the Divinity School culture and secular culture. On all sides we agree that the purpose of theological education is no longer simply and solely to train ministers for the local parish. The times are probably compelling us to see that the Divinity School is the place where a model community must be built, approximately also representing the ratio of the population segments of the area, so that those who are trained here can have a full experience in how the new community that is developing is being shaped and can become leaders who are able to share in the building of new community everywhere.

– 6 –

Let Us Still Praise Famous Men

In Herzog's office at Duke Divinity School there were no pictures of his great theological teachers. But there was a picture of William Edwards. The encounter with Edwards is one of the milestones in the development of a new outlook on theology. In this context the debate is shifted from charity and social service to self-critical solidarity. Theology and the church need to understand who they are and to change in light of actual encounters with the oppressed and suffering other.

Herzog was one of the few white theologians — if not the only one — willing to listen to some of the more radical challenges to the church by African American leaders like James Forman (the international affairs director of the Student Non-Violent Coordinating Committee), whose proclamation at Riverside Church in New York received national attention.

In the process he discovers that where theological words fall apart in the encounter with the reality of severe suffering, new theology begins to take shape. The encounters with the African American other lead to new encounters with the divine Other and, as Herzog's book Liberation Theology *will show, to new encounters with the Bible as well.*

I'll do what little I can in writing. Only it will be very little. I'm not capable of it; and if I were, you would not go near it at all. For if you did, you would hardly bear to live. —James Agee

In 1936, James Agee and the photographer Walker Evans traveled through the Deep South to produce a documentary series on the life of tenant farmers for *Fortune* magazine.[1] The series never appeared in *Fortune*. But four years later, in 1941, their expanded findings were published in book form under the title *Let Us Now Praise Famous Men*. In the main, their report was a description of the life of three tenant families with which they lived for altogether about six weeks. Those families and their descendants may long since have moved to the big cities. But the South is still dotted with countless cabins that often seem hardly inhabited.

First published in *Hannavee* 1 (April 1970): 4–6.

1. I shared this piece last year with a class in theology before the death of William Edwards on June 30, 1969. Since a number of Duke Divinity School students became personally acquainted with William Edwards, I am offering it for publication as a memorial tribute to a great man.

Who lives behind these pitiless paintless walls? Men — and women! — still to be praised.

I want to speak of only two at this time, Mr. and Mrs. William Edwards of Roanoke Rapids in the tidewater region of North Carolina. William Edwards, now age fifty-seven, had been a steam boiler fireman until 1954, when he became a paraplegic. By 1961 he was a bilateral amputee. An abscess developed, then kidney trouble. From 1961 to 1964 he was in and out of the hospital time and again. In the spring of 1965 he was able to pull out of the ten years of near paralysis. Now he was able to do a little "work" which he had been taught in the hospital by occupational therapy, making pot holders, belts, and the like. Never was illness completely banished. New operations interrupted the small measure of health he had finally found. But every time as soon as he had recovered some strength he took up loops, frame, and needle again and went back to "work." Keeping his arms and hands occupied gave his life new meaning and some hope.

Does society, does our government, provide any market for such "work"? Most certainly not. Friends and relatives, a women's exchange, a local store around Christmas and Easter, a small grade school boy, and a few students who learned about William Edwards, these have been his only "market."

Our Great Society has not as yet developed programs for the homebound. For a while we heard of Project Earning Power (P.E.P.) sponsored by the government and other agencies. It was hoped that it eventually could come to the aid of 2.5 million disabled Americans, so that they could at least eke out a living by the labor of their hands. Thus far it has turned out to be little more than an idealistic scheme unable to reach many people, except a few in two or three big cities where pilot projects had been launched.

Meanwhile, the Edwardses, after paying their regular medical bills, live on $88.62 a month, as best I have been able to ascertain. How much can a man take? How much deprivation, suffering, pain? And when one is black to boot?

Let us still praise famous men! I have never heard words of complaint from William Edwards. But I have seen hope and confidence and struggle. Does anyone expect him to protest? If a man is handicapped and has no leverage of power to make his protest stick, why protest? But I must protest.

My protest is that often in our society we offer a man just enough attention to make physical life prevail. But what a man might do with the little life he's got left, this question, while occasionally impinging on our calculations, has not triggered any great effort on our part. In our rich society we simply keep untold millions on a bare subsistence level.

I know, this is nothing much of news in a day when countless people are concerned with social change. What is still news is how the church relates to all this. For years we have been talking about the servant church. We have assumed that the church was relatively intact to be the servant. We felt society needed to be served, if not by paint brigades in dilapidated neighborhoods, at least by applying political pressure on the power structures. But many churches are power structures themselves or sanctioning agents of power structures. What do we say when it dawns on us that a theology student in summer fieldwork under the Duke Endowment can clear more money in three months than the Edwardses receive as a dole the whole year? Not to speak of the rich theology professor.

Let me make it quite clear that for me the whole issue is not one of bringing the poor, the fringe figures of society, up to middle-class standards. What is important to understand is that human beings must find enough wherewithal to live a decent life, to be able to occupy themselves fruitfully and to find meaning in their existence. It is a fact that in our kind of society *money* is a significant agent to make this possible.

When James Forman interrupted the worship service in Riverside Church on May 4 it seemed to many not very civil, but he made a point. The church has money to spare — everywhere. Could Riverside Church exist after giving 60 percent of its income from stocks and real estate to the National Black Economic Development Conference? Conscience will probably decide that before long. The idea that the church itself has to be put under political pressure will seem horrifying to many. But "the time has come for judgment to begin with the household of God" (1 Pet. 4:17). With all the emphasis on being the servant, the church forgot that Christ the servant also cleansed the temple. Today the temple needs to be cleansed again. The idea of reparation or restitution still has an awkward sound in our ears. But for what purpose is the church rich? We may not like what Forman said, but he has put a thorn into the flesh of the church: "Six million Jews were killed in Germany and Israel is still getting reparations. Fifty million blacks died in slavery and the black people have been paid nothing."

It is clear to me that, for example, descendants of those who died to free people from slavery might also ask for reparations on grounds of the same rationale. So we might enter into an endless circle of reparation demands that finally no one could settle. But what is at stake is basically how wealth is distributed in this country, and how the church "stacks up" in terms of its avowed ideals and its witness in action. Regardless of whether or not one feels that Forman was right in his action, the problem is that the church did not act *before* Forman did.

The church is now under attack from within the church. The servant church is under attack from the militant church. Also the servant church needs to be changed. The word now is not serve, but fight. "Fight the good fight with all thy might."

One candlestick on the altar is worth a month's bread. One cross dangling from the ceiling of the church is worth five years of doctor's bills. Let us still praise famous men! There is no rebuke on the face of the one who suffers. But his whole life is a rebuke to a church that put its pulpit and organ and stained glass first and hardened its heart to the suffering.

Our huckster heart will not change until we are able to *see* one human face that suffers. We have served on paper, or in magnanimous sit-ins. But we have not changed in our relationship to money.

Let us still praise famous men! We praise our neighbor best by refusing to deprive him of the possibility of living a decent life. As long as we are waxing rich while others wax poorer our theology will stay out of joint.

Can you understand how difficult it is these days to teach theology? For a long time theology has been oriented in the problem of "modern man." And so we have had all these theories about demythologizing, deliteralizing, etc. All along theology should have *oriented itself in suffering man*. My theological words break to pieces in the face of reality, also the demythologized words. They no longer fit. I know, a lot of people keep droning on with the old theological clichés. I do not hear them anymore. What I hear are Mrs. Edwards's words: "I'm getting afraid to go to town. I only go to town every two weeks now. We don't have the money for what we need anyway." And I, in a nice plush setting, am I supposed to explain that everything is all right with the world? "God's in his heaven, all's right with the world." It is not true. Very little is right with the world I know.

You don't understand what theology is unless you have looked in the face of suffering, unless you have become an atheist in the presence of pain. Then slowly you begin to grasp the sufferer's witness: "Though he slay me, yet will I trust him."

Let us still praise famous men! In finding them out, theology might still find a new beginning. Here theology will be confronted with its political responsibility liberating men in the clutches of society. Men are caught in the captivity of so much suffering because of wrong political decisions. The political dilemmas in which finally all of us are caught turn theology to a new focus in political theology.

GOD: BLACK OR WHITE?

*Modern theology, throughout its history, has dealt with the question of the exis-
tence of God. Even the theology of the death of God is still part of that debate.
At the end of the sixties Herzog discerns a new theological impulse, tied to the
question whether God is black or white. This question leads theology, in self-
critical fashion, back into the church. Who is the God that is still worshiped in
the churches? What if white American churches have, at least unconsciously,
made God into their own image?*

*Searching for ways out of the impasse of mainline theology and eager not to
repeat its mistakes in the new paradigm, Herzog redirects theological attention to
the interrelation of the voices of marginalized people, the constructive power of
the biblical word, and the shape of Jesus' ministry where life is most threatened.
Without playing off against each other white theology and black theology, theology needs to understand that God can hardly be grasped from a perspective of
privilege.*

*"Real otherness," including the otherness of God in Christ, can only be found
in the context of oppression. Rethinking all of theology in solidarity with people
at the margins is not only the challenge of theology in the seventies, as Herzog
initially thought; this remains one of the major challenges for the new millennium.*

*(The text printed in this reader reflects Herzog's own corrections of mistakes
of the original version.)*

The Upshot of the Debate about God in the Sixties

When I gets to heaven like you says I is, de good Lord hisself even He gwine to
make old Hark feel black- ... standin' befo' de golden throne. Dere He is, white
as snow, givin' me a lot of sweet talk and me feelin' like a *black-* ... angel. 'Cause
pretty soon I know his line, yas *suh!* Yas *suh*, pretty soon I can hear Him holler out:
"Hark! You dere, boy, Need some spick and span roun' de throne room. Hop to,
you black- ... scoundrel! Hop to wid de mop and de broom!"[1]

First published in *Review and Expositor* 67, no. 3 (Summer 1970): 299–313. The article also appeared
in the British journal *Fraternal*.

1. William Styron, *The Confessions of Nat Turner* (New York: Random House, 1967), 54.

When my book *Understanding God,* on the debate about God in the first half of the sixties, was published,[2] I did not anticipate the bang which would mark the end of this decade in theology. It certainly did not end on a whimper. At the end of the sixties the issue was not whether God was dead or alive, but whether he was black or white. William Styron, in *The Confessions of Nat Turner,* put the matter into words not easily forgotten: "Dere He is, white as snow...." Regardless of what one thinks of the white liberal Southerner putting these words on the lips of a black slave, Styron sensed the crucial issue that divides blacks and whites as regards God. For what kind of God is it in the first place we are talking about when we wonder whether he is dead?

To declare that God is dead is to say that there are some who have the experience of the absence of the white God. But this is not at all to say that God has expired. Instead of quickly accepting the death of God it is incumbent upon us to ask in what way the reality of God still functions in a church however nominally influenced by Christian maxims. Black theology is wondering whether the God declared dead by many jubilant or grieving whites was not merely the glorified sanctioner of white values and aspirations. From the perspective of the black Christian community the reality of God is not as easily debunked as a few white theologians claimed. What is more, black theology does not surrender the notion of God like the Black Muslims who have replaced God with Allah.[3] But it is good to keep in mind that extreme elements in the black community have also turned away from God, although in a peculiar way. James Baldwin characterizes this development in a few words: "God had come a long way from the desert — but then so had Allah, though in a very different direction. God, going north, and rising on the wings of power, had become white, and Allah, out of power, and on the dark side of Heaven, had become — for all practical purposes, anyway — black."[4] Baldwin feels God has turned white, which he relates to the growth of white power. Here lies the crucial issue that theology has not faced thus far.

Black theology has no interest in Allah. But it does wonder whether God, for all practical purposes anyway, isn't black. There is no reason why this should provoke immediate revulsion. The idea of a black God is not completely foreign to the American sensibility. Already back in 1930 Marc Connelly, in *The Green Pastures,* had a black God move across the stage, wondering as he reflected on the prophet Hosea: "Did he mean dat even God must suffer?"[5]

2. Frederick Herzog, *Understanding God: The Key Issue in Present-Day Protestant Thought* (New York: Charles Scribners Sons, 1966). Two years later I brought the debate up to date in "Die Gottesfrage in der heutigen amerikanischen Theologie," *Evangelische Theologie* 28, nos. 2–3 (February–March 1968): 129–53. In view of new developments, it seemed imperative not to cover old territory once more, but to turn to the most radical new challenge and to try to do justice to it in the space allowed.

3. The best account of the movement is C. Eric Lincoln, *The Black Muslims in America* (Boston: Beacon Press, 1961).

4. James Baldwin, *The Fire Next Time* (New York: Dell, 1964), 66.

5. Marc Connelly, *The Green Pastures* (New York: Holt, Rinehart and Winston, 1967 ed.), 172.

God in the Christian Community

The debate about the death of God was always on the sleazy side of things theological, since it operated on the assumption that we could talk about God on grounds of secularity and that one could decide on God's demise on grounds of secular criteria. God as primal cause, as explanatory principle for philosophical reflection, probably died as soon as the scientist thought of the universe as self-explanatory. But God as Lord of the Christian community is another matter. God as electing Israel for liberation in the Exodus event, God as choosing mankind for liberation in Jesus Christ, this is a factor that entered little into the ken of the death-of-God theologians as context of the debate.

We must take seriously the fact that secularity has invaded the church. We are not looking out from a safe bastion into the forays of secularity outside the walls trying to overcome the church. If ever the church was a bastion, today it is an occupied city. The occupier is in our midst. We are still free enough, however, to ask whether he has a right to determine what we may think. It is here that we must draw a line.

On these grounds I come into conflict with fellow theologians of whose attainments in contributing to a better understanding of the present theological situation I have no doubt. I am thinking here especially of Langdon Gilkey, who in his recent book on the debate about God describes the significance of the Christian community in this debate as follows:

> This upheaval, this radical questioning of the foundations of religious affirmation and so of theological language reflective of it, is now taking place *within* and not outside of the Church. Heretofore in this century, the radical questioning of religious beliefs was a characteristic of the secular world outside the Church.... In the present crisis, however, one finds not only concerned laymen wondering about the usage and meanings of religious language; even more one encounters younger clergy and theologians questioning whether it is any longer possible to speak intelligibly of God.[6]

While one must agree with what Gilkey states as a fact, he does not acknowledge the immediate significance of the radical questioning *within* the church as a *conflict of the church with itself.* Gilkey presupposes that world and church are

Probably the most radically formulated distinction between a black and a white God is found in Albert B. Cleage, Jr., *The Black Messiah* (New York: Sheed and Ward, 1969), 98: "Forget your white God.... Certainly God must be black if he created us in his own image." The distinction is not a new one for the black community. Preston N. Williams, "The Black Experience and Black Religion," *Theology Today* 26, no. 3 (October 1969), quotes Bishop Henry McNeal Turner (1834–1915): "*God is a Negro: Even the heathen in Africa believe that they are created in God's image*" (259; emphasis in original).

6. Langdon Gilkey, *Naming the Whirlwind* (Indianapolis: Bobbs-Merrill, 1969), 9. I would like to make it quite clear that in my view, in terms of scholarship and grasp of the history of the debate about God in the modern age, Gilkey's book is the outstanding contribution of the sixties to the debate. My critique of Gilkey does not reflect lack of appreciation of his achievement, but a fundamental difference in theological presuppositions.

talking about the same referend when they speak of God. So it makes little difference to him whether the struggle with God takes place outside the church or within the church. But this is becoming more and more questionable today.

As we said, it may well be that the idea of a Supreme Being called God in Western civilization has collapsed. Does this also mean that the God of the Christian community has died? The only problem is whether the Christian community is faithful and knows what it is appealing to when it uses the word "God." The nest of difficulties involved here is all wrapped up in a terse observation of Langdon Gilkey's: "One cannot begin, for example, with the presupposition of the presence of the Word of God, if one is asking the question of God.... That means (instead) starting as best one can on one's own at the level of concrete experience."[7] It is here that we today are immediately pressed for a decision. Are we to expect that some secular authority will *accredit* the foundations of what secularity doubts and even denies? The Christian community may be decreasing in numbers. It may be only a small remnant. But does this mean that it has no grounds of its own from which it emerges and must continue to emerge?

The appearance of black theology raises the question whether or not we are still able in the Christian community to recognize and acknowledge what in Christian terms might be meant when the word "God" is used in the Christian community. James H. Cone cuts through a lot of maze in the debate about God when he remarks:

> Some present-day theologians, like Hamilton and Altizer, taking their cue from Nietzsche and the present irrelevancy of the Church to modern man, have announced the death of God. It seems, however, that their chief mistake lies in their apparent identification of God's reality with the signed-up Christians. If we were to identify the work of God with the white church, then, like Altizer, we must "will the death of God with a passion of faith."[8]

The crucial issue before us in the seventies as to God is *how to acknowledge his reality in the Christian community.* It may just be that he is totally other from the God we have imaged — under the influence of secularity and the religious page in the Sunday papers.

What we are now facing is no longer general bull sessions about the reality of God, but a conflict of faith with unfaith within the Christian community. And that conflict can ultimately only be about the Bible, the most forgotten book in the church, and the God of this book. Has not the God of the white man, the white God, become more and more the sanctioner of exploitation, who uses his power to exalt the mighty on their thrones and to put down those of low degree, who fills the rich with good things and who sends the hungry away empty? Has not the white God become the trader writ large on the screen of the transcendent, a trader who assists the white man in putting the world under his heel? "Why are you knocking capitalism?" I was recently chastened by a fellow

---

7. Ibid., 11.
8. James H. Cone, *Black Theology and Black Power* (New York: Seabury Press, 1969), 71.

minister. "Why, God himself is a capitalist!" Do we need any more proof that we fashion God in our own image? Is God the Capitalist the God and Father of our Lord Jesus Christ? It may well be that our wealth and power have made us whites blind to seeing who God is. Whiteness is becoming a handicap in grasping the reality of God. The death of God was a white invention. We have not as yet grasped how much a handicap whiteness is in understanding what it means to be a man. In order not to focus too much on the black as counterpart of the white, let me appeal to a California Indian and how he sees the white man:

> When we Indians kill meat, we eat it all up. When we dig roots, we make little holes.... We shake down acorns and pine nuts. We don't chop down trees. We only use dead wood. But the white people plow up the ground, pull up the trees, kill everything. The tree says, "Don't. I am sore. Don't hurt me." But they chop it down and cut it up.... The Indians never hurt anything, but the white people destroy all. They blast rocks and scatter them on the ground. The rock says "Don't! You are hurting me." But the white people *pay* no attention.... Everywhere the white man has touched (the earth), it is sore.[9]

The significant point here is that this Indian sees the white man as exploiter. What kind of God-image does the exploiter have? It may be that whites are living with a sheer illusion of God. And those who are declaring God's death may be saying no more than that the God illusion of the white man, his glorified self-image, is dead. But from presuppositions such as Gilkey's it is impossible to face the problem of the reality of God *in the Christian community*. Black theology challenges white theology to ask to what extent whiteness has been transferred to God's very being.

Authority and Heresy

As soon as the issue is understood as a matter of an internal conflict of the Christian community about the God of the Bible the old question of authority appears again. Cone does not sidestep the issue: "To put it simply, Black Theology knows no authority more binding than the experience of oppression itself. This alone must be the ultimate authority in religious matters. Concretely, this means that Black Theology is not prepared to accept any doctrine of God, man, Christ, or Scripture which contradicts the black demand for freedom now."[10] Before one objects too vociferously to this view of authority, one should try to keep in mind that here a member of an oppressed community is speaking. We should not measure Cone's statement by an abstract concept of doctrinal purity. First of all it has to be heard as an *echo* of the white American Protestant view of authority. Its positive contribution lies in the fact that it makes it unmistakably clear that there still *is* a problem of authority.

---

9. Theodore Roszak, *The Making of a Counter Culture* (Garden City, N.Y.: Doubleday, 1969), 245.
10. Cone, *Black Theology and Black Power*, 103.

Today by and large white American Protestant theologians seem to argue that it does not make much of a difference where one begins to think theologically, just so one begins somewhere. Says John B. Cobb, Jr.:

> The starting point in earlier verbal formulations is not required. One's work is theology even if one ignores all earlier statements and begins only with the way things appear to him from that perspective which he acknowledges as given to him in some community of shared life and conviction.[11]

Cone's formulation of authority is only the black side of what many American theologians in recent years have all along been claiming about Christian maturity. What is sauce for the goose is sauce for the gander. The time has come to say that we can no longer work with private domains of authority predilections.

How does Christian thought come into being in the first place? If it is not by the originating Christian event, it cannot accredit itself as Christian. The question of authority today is not one of doctrinal orthodoxy, but of what *author*-izes us in our theological thinking, that is, of what brings our thinking into being. If for the white Cobb anything that happens to strike the fancy of "some community of shared life and conviction" can become authority, naturally the black Cone might just as well assume that for him the experience of oppression in the "shared life and conviction" of the black community can function as authority. It is difficult to describe the bankruptcy we have arrived at in American Protestant theology. And white theology has to take the blame. There are pitifully few points where it tries to witness to what true Christian authority might be.

Of course, as soon as one speaks of biblical authority in this country ugly memories raise their head. But why should we not be able to appreciate Christian authority without becoming biblicistic, fundamentalistic, or neoorthodox? Biblical authority does not have to imply a biblical system of thought that disregards the contemporary situation. That would be biblicistic. The question is to what extent the biblical Word has the *generating power* of truth in its focus in Jesus Christ. Any kind of fundamentalist conceptualization according to which we would have to prove the inerrancy of every word is also excluded. Obviously the Bible did not fall down from heaven. The authority we are pointing to is the *authorizing power* of truth in the biblical Word that can give man a new experience of God, an experience he otherwise could not have. Also eliminated is the neoorthodox view of the Bible according to which concepts like virgin birth, descent into hell, or ascension must become tenets of belief, just because they are mentioned in the Bible. The real question of biblical authority is fundamentally, whether the shape (gestalt) of Jesus' ministry can convey to us the reality of God in such a way that we are compelled to acknowledge it.

Black theology challenges the white theological establishment to think through once more its views of authority. If we cannot find a common focus

---

11. John B. Cobb, Jr., *A Christian Natural Theology* (Philadelphia: Westminster Press), 253.

in Jesus Christ, other "powers and principalities" will become authority for us. As a consequence we will be unable to experience Christian community. The experience of oppression as such can become as little *authority* for the Christian community as the white man's God, whether he is a White-headian philosophical construct or simply the Great White Father above. We need to rediscover the real source of Christian authority. Without a grasp of the living Word of Jesus Christ as authority, confronting us in the biblical witness, we will be unable to negotiate any claim we make upon each other or against each other.

The difficulty becomes focused in the new use of the concept of heresy. Cone is right in pointing to heresy in the white church: "White Christianity in America...was born in heresy."[12] He compares the present conflict in the church with that of the fourth century: "In our time, the issue of racism is analogous to the Arian controversy of the fourth century. Athanasius perceived quite clearly that if Arius's views were tolerated, Christianity would be lost. But few white churchmen have questioned whether racism was a similar denial of Jesus Christ."[13] If Cone's analysis is correct we have arrived at a theological situation in America which is similar to the one Karl Barth faced during the early thirties. Barth felt that we must take the *conflict of faith with unfaith in the church* more seriously than the irrelevance of faith to the unfaith of the world. We need to see that he was right in pointing to the possibility of heresy, "a conflict of faith with itself."[14] It is the unbelievably absentminded orientation of much of white American theology in apologetics as the programmatic principle of theology that keeps it from even noticing where the crux of the theological debate lies today. We should have the wisdom to drop apologetics as a program of negotiating with the secular in order to focus on the fundamental task of the church. Of course the church is not available to us everywhere as a self-critical community. But we must not be afraid to create such a community even if we must exist as a "remnant." Cone's accusation of heresy cannot be met except on grounds of biblical authority, that is, on grounds of what Jesus Christ as Lord still has to tell his church today. The whole question of the ground of Christian authority has to be faced with respect to this Lordship.

---

12. Cone, *Black Theology and Black Power*, 103.

13. Ibid., 73. It is impossible in this essay to discuss all the contributors to black theology. But I do wish to call attention to the significant book by Joseph R. Washington, Jr., *The Politics of God* (Boston: Beacon Press, 1967). Especially his discussion of racism (3–99) is "must" reading for anyone who wishes to understand how blacks today define this complex problem.

14. Karl Barth, *Church Dogmatics*, I/1 trans. Karl H. Kruger (Edinburgh: T. & T. Clark, 1936), 33. Karl Rahner, *Theological Investigations*, vol. 5 (Baltimore: Helicon Press, 1966), speaks of the conflict of faith with itself in somewhat different terms, but points very much in the same direction when he says: "The heretic...has enjoyed the gift of promised truth. In view of this experience, how could the heretic be guiltless in being incapable of distinguishing true from false Christianity? He is the most dangerous person of all: he combats the real and final truth of Christianity in the name of Christian truth itself" (470). For the ear of the liberal American the whole idea may sound harsh. But he will have to get used to it in the seventies as an inescapable theological issue.

Man's Judge

"What if the Divine Judge has retired from his bench, leaving all things in the hands of man? What then? Does evil for evil become mandatory?"[15] This question of Vincent Harding brings us to the major reason for raising the authority question. The white God is not a God of judgment. Permissiveness, if he is not considered dead, is his major characteristic. As long as man is not persuaded that he is subject to an inescapable reality claim absolutely above him, he will orient his life according to his whim and fancy. We cannot expect that an inescapable reality claim will be acknowledged by the world at large. But we can expect the Christian community to be aware of this claim. Jesus Christ embodies the ultimate reality claim, and from him we need to learn what it contains. Harding says: "Perhaps, too, the black rebels remember the example of Jesus, the focus of much of Western religion."[16] It is exactly the question of how we must *remember* Jesus as focus of faith that concerns us here.

As long as Christian community among blacks and whites is not forthcoming the black community will more and more function as substitute faith community for the black. Here he will try to find his self-respect and identity. Self-respect or self-esteem is a very necessary condition for man's sanity. Harding feels that the black man must be able to love himself first before he can love the white man. But how can a man really love himself if he does not love God first? "You shall love the Lord your God with all your heart, and with all your soul, and with all your strength, and with all your mind." This is the first and great commandment. Probably with this in mind, Harding asks himself all the right questions:

> If it is assumed — as it surely must be — that black love must begin among black people and find its nurture there, can it be quarantined? What shall be said of a love that is willed towards some men and not towards others? Is this goal in any way related to the deadly disease that has afflicted so much of American life for so many generations?[17]

Harding senses the threat that comes to the black from the white community. There is a disease of the American social organism. Whites have qualified love in myriad ways. Before the white condemns the black for preferences in love he should see the heresy of his own love. But simply seeing the distortion of his love reflected in the black may confirm him in his comfortable acceptance of the misery of the human condition. He must come to see man's true love of God in Jesus Christ judging all human attempts to love and giving them a new motive. It is with this love that we must begin when we consider the proper love of self. Otherwise, our respective self-loves will only make us fall deeper into heresy.

"Black people have imbibed more of American religion than they know."[18] This insight of Harding's has to be taken with utter seriousness. What needs

---

15. Vincent Harding, "The Religion of Black Power," *The Religious Situation* (1968): 15.
16. Ibid., 12.
17. Ibid., 7.
18. Ibid.

to be eliminated from American religion is the whiteness of man's disregard for God. We need to see that American religion puts man in the driver's seat. Man's disregard of God was radically overcome only in Christ. Only in him will black love which seeks to establish community find the power for true community. This is Christ's promise. As regards the problem of creating community, Harding comments: "Perhaps we were urged towards an identification with mankind-at-large (often meaning white mankind) before we had learned to identify with our black neighbors. It is likely that our humanity begins in the black ghetto and cannot be rejected there for an easier, sentimental, white-oriented acceptance elsewhere. So it may be that the question of 'who is my neighbor?' is answered for us."[19] The question "Who is my neighbor?" can be answered adequately only on grounds of response to the question "Who is my God?" And in Jesus Christ identification with God takes *first* place, so that man can adequately identify with the neighbor and create community. It is through him that identification with the wretched of the earth becomes a compelling mandate. "Black Power calls for an identification between black people here and all the wretched nonwhite of the earth. (Some leaders, like Carmichael, now expand this to the poor and oppressed of every color.)"[20] We only dare not forget that it was not Stokely Carmichael, but Jesus Christ, who first made the radical identification with all the wretched of the earth a reality. *It is here that theology must find its focus if it wants to contribute to community building.*

Love, community — man cannot have either one of them unless he grasps who he is. Harding sees that the real nature of man is known in Christ. And from this perspective he can view Black Power critically:

> Most persons who claim to be followers of the Man who introduced zealots to a new way of response have chosen not to follow him at this point. And here is one of the most telling witnesses to the possibility that Black Power may be more fully bound to the traditions of the western Christian world than its proponents would ever dare believe.[21]

The whole point is that Western Christianity does not take Jesus Christ seriously as the normative reality of manhood. The mistake of the Black Power advocates is understandable "because western society now seems unable to offer any normative response to the question, 'What is man?'"[22] If Western *society* is unable to offer any normative response, is it impossible to call the *church* back to its normative ground? The distortions of manhood by Western Christianity have a judge, Jesus Christ, the true man who embodies the true God.

Jesus Christ is, however, not only man's judge, but also his liberator. Man is unable to show forth the perfect reality of manhood embodied in Jesus Christ.

---

19. Ibid., 10.
20. Ibid., 11.
21. Ibid., 22.
22. Ibid. Preston N. Williams, "The Black Experience and Black Religion," has carefully defined the problem insofar as general attempts to define the black man as man are concerned: "In the process the black man becomes invisible and we are left with only our shadows" (137).

"The emphasis on autonomous black action is another of the hallmarks of Black Power ideology, a hallmark that leaves little room for any dependence on what might be called grace."[23] It is difficult to see how men can live without grace. Without acceptance of grace men will always insist on their right, pitted against the wrong of others. But this is not the principle of the Christian community which exists to assist unrighteous men in living together in brotherhood. It is to this kind of community that we must be able to invite one another — ready to see our differences, also our differences in color, acknowledging them and letting the other be in his particularity. The emphasis on Black Power in the Christian community is a preface to our seeing the other as he really is. As long, however, as we do not focus on Jesus Christ, we will not see the other fully. For we will make ourselves the criterion of manhood.

It should be clear by now that the appearance of black theology reopens the whole range of theological questions. Harding sees this quite clearly when he says: "Issues of anthropology, incarnation, the nature of the universe and of God, issues of hope and faith, questions of eschatology and of the nature of the Kingdom, problems concerning love and its functions — all these and more are at stake in the present situation."[24] The whole spectrum of theological issues has to be reconsidered. White theology today tries to make a go of it by identifying with Martin Heidegger, Alfred North Whitehead, and Charles Hartshorne, or secularity in general. "Identification with the wretched of the earth"[25] has not been the focus of recent theology. The question of the seventies for theology will be, What happens to the spectrum of Christian doctrine if the theologian seriously makes this identification?

Man's Liberator

We have reached a point where we can no longer condone the white image of God. Some may still want to talk about perfect wisdom, knowledge, or power as defining God. But it is not that only some peculiar way of talking about God has become incredible; God himself has become incredible because of the way Christians have abused him. In his name Christians have fought crusades and wars of religion. White men have subjugated whole continents for exploitation. Africa for centuries was divided up in colonies of white Christian Europe. It was hardly more than a century ago that large parts of America supported slavery. Christian nations fought two world wars. And behind Auschwitz and Hiroshima lurks the face of the white God — whose infinite power men sought to imitate in acts of infinite violence.

It is with respect to this history that Cone can say, "Whether whites want to

---

23. Harding, "The Religion of Black Power," 26.
24. Ibid., 4.
25. Ibid., 12.

hear it or not, *Christ is black, baby*, with all the features which are so detestable to white society."[26] He goes on to explicate this more fully relative to God:

> Black is holy, that is, it is the symbol of God's presence in history on behalf of the oppressed man. Where there is black, there is oppression; but blacks can be assured that where there is blackness, there is Christ who has taken on blackness so that what is evil in man's eyes might become good.[27]

If one harks back to the average God language one is used to, Cone's ideas will be difficult to appropriate. They compel us to revert to the origins of God language in the Christian community. God's presence, of course, was felt in the early Christian community in a number of ways. But all were centered in the shape of Jesus' public ministry.

It was especially one aspect of the shape of this ministry that made all the difference in the world. For this Messiah was concerned with the wretched of the earth, the lepers, the possessed, and the poor. His concern for the wretched was expressed in his word: "Those who are well have no need of a physician, but those who are sick" (Matt. 9:12). Because of his identification with the wretched of the earth he was rejected by the powerful. He considered part of his task "to set at liberty those who are oppressed" (Luke 4:18). In carrying out his task he himself became oppressed and finally was put to death by the oppressor. Whatever the church experienced of God in him after the resurrection, it was always this aspect of the shape of his public ministry that came through as the cutting edge where people must begin to decide whether they will acknowledge ultimate reality or not. The reality claim his followers experienced in him was most compelling exactly at the point where he had joined the wretched of the earth: "For you know the grace of our Lord Jesus Christ, that though he was rich, yet for your sake he became poor, so that by his poverty you might become rich" (2 Cor. 8:9).

Here the challenge of black theology becomes quite clear. God is not found among the high and the mighty, the glamorous or successful. God is also not embodied in the masochistic or self-debasing. The point is, God is found where human life is most threatened, where it has a hard time breaking through to triumph over the negativities that work against it. While the Christian God is not the God who "out-lowly-services" everyone, he is the one who takes risks for the furtherance of life where no one else is concerned.

The Other. What makes the New Testament witness so strong for us today is that the reality the New Testament calls God confronts us with the unfamiliar, the unexpected, something we are not accustomed to. Jesus risks his life among the wretched in ways that are not the ordinary ways of men, going out of his way to liberate them. Not eliminating their freedom, he invites their response. So in the context of oppression real otherness breaks through.

---

26. Cone, *Black Theology and Black Power,* 68.
27. Ibid., 69.

The New. Real otherness comes across as *kaine ktisis,* a new creation. Until Jesus everything religious had been wrapped up in "law and order." Suddenly Jesus healed a man on the Sabbath. What came through as a reality claim in Jesus was: something *can* be done, change *can* take place. Nothing had been definitively decided upon. There were still new possibilities. God is here no longer seen in terms of the theological establishment, the scribes and the Pharisees, or the theological professor. Occasionally the argument is put forth that man still has some sense of the transcendent even in his secular hang-ups, and that it is here that we must begin to talk about God. The point of the presence of Jesus of Nazareth in the history of mankind is that we must begin with the *new* in him as he identifies with the wretched and try to understand what this entails for our quest of God. Only in identifying with oppression ourselves will we realize where a new grasp of God first broke through.

God appears thus as that ultimate reality that is struggling in man and with man to overcome the negativities of life. This is no omnipotent or omniscient God in the sense of the old theological textbooks. God is the ultimate reality that seeks to increase life. But he can do it only within the world he himself has created. There is no guarantee of a happy end. But there are intimations of God's victory over evil.

The emphasis on the blackness of Christ reminds us of his identification with the wretched of the earth. It points to where God needs to be found, also today. This does not imply, however, that God and the oppressed are identical. God freely comes to man — also to the oppressed. He is not absolutely tied to anyone, except to his son, Jesus Christ. It is in him that we must experience God. There are aspects of black theology that make it a folk theology.[28] That is, it ties the reality of God down to a particular people. Cone, for example, can say: *"The black revolution is the work of Christ."*[29] There is no way of drawing this conclusion on grounds of the biblical word. Cone's kind of folk theology simply mirrors white folk theology. This kind of thing can happen — in the white theological setting. In theology we still speak of German, British, or American theology. Some even feel that we need to develop an even more American theology. Each theology has at one time or other done the same thing black theology is now explicitly seeking to establish. But Jesus Christ is not tied down to any folk, however beautiful it may be. He is the judge of all our folk theologies, and their liberator.

If man were fully free in himself he would not need Jesus Christ. Exactly at the point where man fails in his freedom Jesus Christ liberates him to true manhood.

---

28. There is no pejorative implication in the use of the word "folk" as such. See W. E. Burghardt Du Bois, *The Souls of Black Folk* (Greenwich, Conn.: Fawcett, 1961). The question is to what extent theology and folk can be tied together.

29. Cone, *Black Theology and Black Power,* 89; emphasis in original.

Power and Violence

What I have said thus far can be summed up in a brief thesis: black theology challenges white theology to examine its very foundations. Do we still worship a God who is the judge of all our striving? On the ethical level the issue between white and black theology is most strongly joined when it comes to the use of power in violence. Cone sees the riots in the cities as an expression of the willingness of black people to resort to those means that will help them gain freedom: "This willingness of black people to die is not despair, it is hope, not in white people, but in their own dignity grounded in God himself."[30] We need to look at black theological justification of violence from the perspective of white history. Time and again the church has justified the participation of Christians in violence, especially in war. The black position yields a goodly number of parallels to positions whites have taken. As soon as the white is seen as the enemy of the black,[31] the black Christian may be looking for a "just war theory" for his violent thing with the same justification as a white for his wars.

Black theology today is turning the tables on white theology. In black theology we see our white rationalizations reflected. And it may well be that we do not like to see ourselves exposed. Cone's logic sounds very much like what we have heard all along from whites. Jesus obviously did not act violently and did not condone violence. So Cone also emphasizes that we cannot act in all respects the way Jesus did: "Our choices are not the same as his.... His steps are not ours; and thus we are placed in an existential situation in which we are forced to decide without knowing what Jesus would do."[32]

For blacks, appeals to love and nonviolence, coming from whites, sound hollow. For why should blacks not decide to do in their situation what many whites claim as a right for their particular situation? The task of white theology is not to prescribe for blacks how nonviolent they should be, but to reexamine the white attitude toward violence. Here we must keep in mind the reality of God who judges our easy ways of solving human problems. Our argument about power and violence usually presupposes a God who ultimately sanctions our violence. But actually he identifies with the oppressed in order that we forfeit all forms of oppression. And he creates a new world that defies our familiar understanding of power. He works through his people. Our task is to discover how God's reality can break through to the people of God so that a new community will be built. The church has failed and is still failing in making community real. But this does not mean that Christian theology is entitled to justify violence. Rather, we must discover the power that contributes to helping whites and blacks experience themselves as the people of God.

---

30. Ibid., 30.
31. Harding, "The Religion of Black Power," 7.
32. Cone, *Black Theology and Black Power*, 139.

Eschatology

For Christian theology, in the horizontal dimension of human existence, there can be no other contextual referend than the people of God. If they should have failed to be faithful, this does not mean that anyone has a right to create a substitute. It is exactly the task of theology to recall the people of God to their true identity. Therefore I cannot agree with Cone's principle of the truth of Christian doctrine: " 'If the doctrine is compatible with or enhances the drive for black freedom, then it is the gospel of Jesus Christ. If the doctrine is against or indifferent to the essence of blackness as expressed in Black Power, then it is the work of the Antichrist.' It is as simple as that."[33] It is not as simple as that. Why it is not as simple we can indicate with a brief comment on Cone's eschatology.

Black theology is attacking in white Christianity what needs to be attacked, namely, the perversion of the people of God. Black eschatology is called forth by a white distortion: "The most corrupting influence among the black churches was their adoption of the 'white lie' that Christianity is primarily concerned with an otherworldly reality."[34] One cannot understand black eschatology unless one sees that white Christianity has used eschatology as opium for the black people.

Blacks in America were taught the Christian faith by whites, often with the intention of using the Christian faith to keep blacks docile: "The black man stood on the corner and said, 'take the world and give me Jesus.' So that's just what the white man did."[35] Only if one takes the black experience in America into account can one understand why Cone objects so violently to a certain type of eschatology. Nothing is gained, however, if a white reductionist eschatology is replaced by a black reductionist eschatology.

Individual and Social Eschatology. Cone stresses the immanent significance of eschatology: "With a black perspective, eschatology comes to mean joining the world and making it what it ought to be."[36] In this context he appeals to Jürgen Moltmann, who wrote that eschatology "does not mean merely salvation of the soul, individual rescue from the evil world, comfort for the troubled conscience, but also the realization of the eschatological *hope of justice,* the *humanizing* of man, the *socializing* of humanity, *peace* for all creation."[37] Moltmann's "not merely . . . but also" needs to be taken seriously. Concern for the eschatological anticipation of peace among all men is grounded in concern for the salvation of the individual beyond this life. Only those who acknowledge the transcendent dignity of all men will be able to do effective battle for their temporal dignity. A mere appeal to social justice will hardly change the real root of man's callous attitude toward his neighbor.

The Transcendent Dimension of Life. Cone claims: "The idea of heaven is irrel-

---

33. Ibid., 121.
34. Ibid.
35. Ibid., 123.
36. Ibid., 126.
37. Quoted in ibid.

evant for Black Theology. The Christian cannot waste time contemplating the next world (if there is a next)."[38] The irrelevancy of heaven, however, reflected white thinking long before it mirrored black thinking. White atheism began discarding transcendence by first discarding the symbol of "heaven." This road only led to nihilism. There is little that can convict a man of his human responsibility except his accountability to a judge of his life in the reality that transcends temporal existence.

The Reality of God. What eschatology finally compels us to make a decision about is the very nature of God. Cone stresses that black theology "refuses to embrace any concept of God which makes black suffering the will of God."[39] Everything would be fine if God himself were a heavenly potentate blissfully removed from suffering. There is no indication that black suffering is the will of God. But there is every indication that in all human suffering God himself is agonizingly battling for a new creation. God willed his creation. But he did not will it as the ultimate end (see Rom. 8:20f.). He makes the suffering of his creation his own in order to transform it into the new creation. And he calls us to be his coworkers in its liberation.

In order for liberation to take place a new Christian community has to emerge. The standard images white theology has accepted for centuries no longer do the job. What about the question we started out with, "God: Black or White?" The full answer will have to remain in suspense for a while. The implications of the question are too vast and complex. Thus far we have learned that autonomous man is a self-contradiction. Man is not man without acknowledging a reality that judges his right and wrong. Tentatively, "God is black" means that ultimate reality denies white theological supremacy, which, however subtly, evades identification with the wretched of the earth.

The seventies will probably compel American theology to a complete reconstruction of its material. And it will have been black theology that has called the shots. It will have been especially Cone's merit to have sharply focused the issue. For the first step in reconstruction will have to be the radical identification with the wretched of the earth — as principle of theological orientation. My critique of black theology is not meant as "great refusal," but implies the hope that it can become more radically oriented in the truth of the biblical Word.

The emergence of a new community of faith will probably not be possible without a new church conflict. We might already be in the midst of it. Why has theology not as yet caught on?

---

38. Ibid., 129.
39. Ibid., 124.

– 8 –

The Political Gospel

Before and shortly after coming up with the term "liberation theology," Herzog wrote a number of essays dealing with political theology. Yet in contrast to some of its more famous counterparts in Europe, political theology as Herzog uses the term does not immediately imply a new theological program. As the encounter with acute forms of oppression along the lines of race and class teaches us, theology and the church do not need to be politicized but need to realize how much everything is politicized already. Whether it is aware of it or not, all theology is political.

In light of this situation, theology needs to raise once more a set of questions that appeared to have long been settled: Who governs our life? And, what is the human being? Abstract theological answers that do not take into account actual constellations of power will no longer do, but neither will a kind of social or political activism that lacks theological reflection on its limitations by sin and established structures of privilege.

The die is cast. The publication of James H. Cone's *Black Theology and Black Power* (Seabury Press, 1969) serves notice that Protestant theology in America has come to a decisive turning. Some will ignore it. But the large majority of Christians will take note — sooner or later. For the rise of the black theological consciousness has revealed the dilemma of the white theological consciousness and clarified the direction theological thought must now take.

By citing the dilemma of the white theological consciousness I do not wish to imply that there is no dilemma of the black theological consciousness today. In fact, black theology is a singular outcry over the dilemma in which the black theological consciousness finds itself. But that outcry is also a strong complaint that white theology is offering nothing to help black theologians get their bearings. So it becomes imperative to ask what may have gone wrong in white theology.

First published in the *Christian Century* (November 1, 1970): 1380–83.

A Specific Political Context

Part of the dilemma of white theology is its assumption that it can still operate with a fairly definite image of man, while in fact this image is either eroding or being used as a pretext for exploiting man. Black theology is pained to have to point out that man is still being enslaved and held captive — a fact only too quickly circumvented by many of us. And man's captivity is most evident in the political dimension of his existence.

Black theology reminds the theological enterprise of the specific political context to which it must address itself. Said the "Black Theology" statement issued by the National Committee of Black Churchmen in June 1969: "We cannot ignore the powerlessness of the black community. Despite the *repeated requests* for significant programs of social change, the American people have refused to appropriate adequate sums of money for social reconstruction. White church bodies have often made promises only to follow with default." It is a simple fact that ultimate power in this country is still in the hands of the white majority. In concrete experience, this fact usually comes across to the individual in the minority group as oppression. The gospel speaks to this situation: "The kingdom of God is at hand: repent, and believe in the gospel." This is a political word. The nearness of God's kingdom in Christ demands that we decide who shall *govern* our lives. And the question of government is a political question. For our day it probably comes down to an either-or: God or mammon. But "no man can serve two masters.... You cannot serve God and mammon."

I am a white man in the South. I cannot really grasp what it means to be a black man in the South. But when I encounter my black fellowmen — a goodly number of whom can still say, "My father [mother] was born a slave" — I am driven to ask myself: What does it mean to be a human being conditioned by a slave culture? What is it like to have been brainwashed into servility? All the janitors I know in the South, all the maids, all the yardmen, all the garbage collectors are black. Blacks clean up behind me in my office and in my classrooms. I myself have never had to clean up behind blacks. I do not know how they feel, but I know how I feel: as if I have been disemboweled of what I thought was my inmost being. Recently I talked to a black woman who has to take jobs as they are offered from day to day in the city of Durham. What does it say about my humanity that just recently she had to work eleven hours for six dollars — in the year 1969?

All this may seem rather chatty and out of place in a theological article. But the outcry over continuing oppression brings home to me the fact that some men and women are tied to the lowest rung of the economic ladder just because of their color — and that Christians are accomplices in this oppression. These facts, of course, are not new. They were stated and restated for years before the recent civil rights struggle. What is new is the realization that theology has a definite stake in this whole situation. What frets us today is no longer a problem of sheer decision-making mechanics, but a struggle over a new image of man.

We have been compelled to realize that behind the concrete shaping of man in his historical existence there usually lies an explicitly or tacitly accepted view of man, and that we must come to grips with it theologically.

Economic Man and Political Power

Naive though it may seem, I have been led by my observations of what is happening between the races in the South to believe that Adam Smith's image of man as economic man still dominates our political and economic relationships, in fact, our entire existence. Smith maintained (in *The Wealth of Nations*) that society is best served if the individual "intends only his own gain"; that the true interests of society are most efficiently taken care of when its members are bent each on "pursuing his own interest." This was written at a time when black Americans were still property, nonpersons. In the years since, the attitude in respect to them has, alas, changed very little. Ann Colarusso, writing in the *Durham Morning Herald* (October 19, 1969) about North Carolina industrialists in an encounter with the governor's Committee on Industrial Development, observes:

> Time and again the committee heard the "plantation" philosophy expressed. It goes something like this: "We were the first ones here; we invested time and money turning these farmers into factory workers and we have a right to protect our investment." Implicit in this philosophy is the idea that people are property, and any investment in them is to be considered as an improvement of property and to be guarded as jealously as any other improvement in property.

In other words, the "plantation" philosophy declares that economic man pursuing his own interest is fulfilling his calling as man, is indeed expressing his essential being.

Since economic power has been secured by political power over the years, man is viewed as having the right to exploit his neighbor. It is quite clear that seeing man as property penalizes whites as well as blacks. And it is also quite clear that whites are prejudiced against blacks for more reasons than economic advantage. But the economic factor plays a significant role, and it hits the black hardest because he is still considered the lowest form of humanity, i.e., humanity as property. Politics is often used as the arm to enforce economic advantage over him.

In this context, the Christian view of man, if stressed at all, remains in a Pollyanna world. It hardly ever effects anything beyond the soothing stimulation of innocuous rhetoric. Whether man is understood as alienated from his essence (Paul Tillich) or as imaging the Trinity by way of an *analogia relationis* (Karl Barth) or as a phenomenon of historicity (Gordon Kaufman), none of these definitions relates to political oppression. Oppressed man sees his oppressor operating on grounds of the image of economic man as exploiter with sufficient political power to enforce his exploitation.

As the clash between black and white smolders, it is more and more obvious that the white is operating with a false image of himself, of man. Here a theological caveat must be sounded. Adam Smith wrote as though man had not sinned, were not depraved. But, every day we live through the agony of black-white tensions shows us that man *is* depraved, not merely alienated from his neighbor. The industrial age with its burgeoning technological wonders gave man a new opportunity to demonstrate his depravity in callous disregard of the neighbor as a person. When Malcolm X concluded that the white man was the devil he merely stated the doctrine of total depravity. This doctrine is significant not so much in its insistence that sin began with primal man as in its acknowledgment that sin is inevitable. Man's depravity is total, through and through. And one proof is that today the black man cannot perceive real goodness in generic white man. He continues to be confronted with exploitation, condescension, or callousness. Brotherhood does not come through because man is radically evil (Immanuel Kant).

The second caveat is a *sociological* one of sorts. In America, economic man as ideal man is largely Anglo-Saxon man. Will Herberg put the case succinctly:

> The "national type" as ideal has always been, and remains, pretty well fixed. It is the *Mayflower*, John Smith, Davy Crockett, George Washington and Abraham Lincoln that define the American's self-image, and this is true whether the American in question is a descendant of the Pilgrims or the grandson of an immigrant from southeastern Europe.... The "Anglo-Saxon" type remains the American ideal to which all other elements are transmuted in order to become American [*Protestant-Catholic-Jew*].

It is exactly this image that is radically attacked by the black community today. Blacks counter claims on the *Mayflower* with claims on *before the Mayflower*. Davy Crockett must give way to Nat Turner, George Washington to W. E. B. Du Bois, Abraham Lincoln to Malcolm X. Here the black man's revolt against the lily-white image of man that the WASP paints comes to a head.

But more. The black man senses that the WASP has lost nerve and thus self-confidence, that he no longer believes in his self-image. No longer is the white a strong counterpart for the black's self-identification. American man no longer really knows who he is. This ignorance of his is glaringly evidenced by the widespread interest in psychoanalysis in America of the '50s and '60s. Of course, that interest also showed that American man shares in the general malaise of the Western world. As Philip Rieff says: "Western culture is changing already into a symbol system unprecedented in its plasticity and absorptive capacity. Nothing much can oppose it really, and it welcomes all criticism, for, in a sense, it stands for nothing." It is especially the black American who senses nihilism. That is why he feels the time has come to overthrow what is already crumbling in its foundations.

But the black realizes also that although the white has become unsure of himself he is still hanging on tightly to the reins of political power. In our southern society it is by a political decision that garbage collectors are recruited primarily among blacks; to my knowledge, whites are not first in line for the job. This is not written law. It is a tacit affirmation that to be a white man is to have enough political power that no one can expect you to find your manhood in garbage collecting. The poor black has no political leverage to keep the employment office from channeling him to the lowest menial job, whether in the city, in a university, or in a tobacco factory.

The Political Gospel

Black theology is right in saying that the gospel today must be relevant exactly at the point where some men are powerless to show forth their manhood; else it cannot be relevant at all. If God is not the God of the oppressed he is not the God of the New Testament. He is struggling for new life among the oppressed and not among the affluent (especially the affluent churches). He sent his Son to liberate the captives. In Jesus' day, liberation took on various forms: from demonic possession, from blindness, leprosy, etc. Let us have no naive literalism here: today liberation is needed in other areas. We are invited to be open for experiences of the new, somewhat along the lines of John 14:12: "He who believes in me will also do the works I do and greater works than these will he do, because I go to the Father."

To the extent that we address the gospel to this captivity it proves itself a *political gospel*. This differs from the social gospel in that it does not try to cure all the ills of society. Indeed it rejects Walter Rauschenbusch's "idea of the redemption of the social organism." It focuses on the severest social strain — namely, on political oppression — and seeks to create new structures for self-determination. Once man has been freed, it is up to him to seek his own political boon or bane. The social gospel was a program for the renewal of society, for Christianizing the social order. The political gospel has a much more modest goal. It focuses on the hang-ups of the city power structure, of state and federal government — first of all to the extent that the church is involved in it. Thus it is primarily concerned with the liberation of the church. Many theologians today are beginning to act and write as though the battle on this front had already been won. In fact, that battle is only beginning. The political involvement of the church has never been radically thought through, and church members have never radically faced the implications of their church membership as a political datum. Political criticism of the church is a task still to be learned.

A New Image of Man?

If we are to get at the roots of the dilemmas we face, we shall probably have to dig deep into the recesses of consciousness. It may be that political oppression is grounded in fundamentally wrong conceptualizations of the nature of man. It may be that the primary political act for the church in our day is to rid itself of a false image of man.

Black theology is making it clear that oppression is no superficial symptom of societal relationships that can be easily dealt with. We need to reconsider basic theological concepts. This does not at all mean that black theology should now become the be-all of theological reflection. I have a number of reservations as regards black theology in some of its expressions (for instance, I do not think we can identify Christ with the black community). But my reservations shrink considerably in view of the realization that the white theological consciousness will not change except through radical questioning by black theology.

Thus far we whites had thought we could operate with the premise that we all acknowledge a common humanity. White theologians figure out this "common humanity" on grounds of the *imago Dei*. But the white man has used the *imago Dei* to play God to the fellowman. Regardless of how little William Styron in *The Confessions of Nat Turner* was able to identify with the black slave, he at least realized that the evil done by the white man disproves humanity as something already attained. When Nat's master becomes maudlin about having sold several slaves in order to make money, Styron has him exclaim: "Surely mankind has yet to be born. Surely this is true! For only something blind and uncomprehending could exist in such a mean conjunction with its own flesh, its own kind." This is an insight we still need to apply. So long as mankind "has yet to be born," we had better not try to make our eroding white self the measure of who a black man is. We need to acknowledge our blindness and uncomprehendingness as we try to read the mind of a man of a different color. For the enslavement of others begins with the assumption that we know what is going on in the mind of the man who feels oppressed.

To transcend the wrong relationship to our neighbor and ourselves we should put a moratorium on the concept of man as *imago Dei*. It has contributed to the apotheosis of man. We are learning more and more that man's radical evil so completely conceals the *imago Dei* as to make it unidentifiable. Man is still hidden to himself (*homo absconditus*). The picture is complicated by the fact that the *Deus* of whom man is supposed to be an image has become man-writ-large on the screen of the transcendent — has become the *imago hominis* (as Ludwig Feuerbach and Sigmund Freud repeatedly pointed out).

Man is on the way to becoming what he is destined to be. Could we think of him as *imago futuri*, an image of the future? I am thinking here of St. Paul's idea that Adam was a type of the coming one (Rom. 5:14) and of 1 John's saying: "It does not yet appear what we shall be" (3:2).

Giving up the straitjacket image of man is probably the first step in the repentance required today by the political gospel. Only men who are willing to begin all over again with the task of defining themselves are able to become part of God's present liberation of man. The cutting edge of the gospel differs from age to age. In our specific political context, it is "to proclaim release to the captives...to set at liberty those who are oppressed" (Luke 4:18). Only those who realize that they can no longer approach the neighbor on the ground of the old definition of man can deliver this message. Only men who can give up defining the neighbor on their own terms can bring the gospel to him. Liberated from ourselves, we realize that the neighbor, and we also, are "defined" from beyond ourselves. The mighty act of God's liberation in Christ becomes the basis of our freedom. "If the Son makes you free, you will be free indeed" (John 8:36).

To be governed by God's liberation in Christ means to give up the exploitation of the neighbor. Amassing wealth for wealth's sake, we are not yet what we are meant to be. Only in renouncing mammon can man become the *imago futuri*, which must be understood in terms of an *analogia liberationis*. What this entails can be worked out only in the new community of a *liberation church* as it develops a *liberation theology*.

Salvation as Liberation

Here American Protestant theology must make a radical decision. Much of its disorientation is due to the fact that it still draws its wisdom from two sources: God's revelation and human reason. The appearance of black theology is a radical challenge to reconsider its sources. Radically evil as he is, man cannot produce any sound solution for the present dilemma. Human ingenuity has run its course and failed. Natural theology has come to naught. The mandate upon theology is to propound the divine claim of the Word of God — not a fundamentalist or biblicist claim, but the Word of a living authority that compels man to bend the knee and to act in new ways. We have entered a new church conflict about the authority of the Word of God that in many ways resembles the Reformation conflict. Only now the issue is not the reformation of the church but the liberation of man in the church. Salvation today is liberation. The gospel invites us to live by God's liberation. It is exactly at this point that we experience the gospel as political gospel. And that means not only *thinking* of the neighbor but also witnessing to his *liberation* in creating new community structures (of foremost importance is deghettoizing the oppressed).

Obviously the issues of liberation are not confined to the black struggle. Vietnam, too, makes us experience political captivity and oppression. Resistance against the American war effort in Vietnam is also resistance against a wrong image of man. White American men today believe they know what Asian men are (or should be) thinking. To save them we must first destroy them — white men playing God again! Resisting white man's self-delusions is liberation from sin and error. Resisting man's inhumanity to man is — God's liberation.

– 9 –

THEOLOGY OF LIBERATION

This essay marks a turning point in Herzog's work. It is the first North American essay that uses the term "theology of liberation." While many of the themes of the essay grow out of Herzog's earlier work, the martyrdom of Martin Luther King, Jr., has made a difference. Herzog compares the moment when King was shot to the situation of the disciples after the crucifixion. "Up to that point we were all pretty optimistic. Then it dawned on me that something was going on."[1] In the process of establishing new forms of solidarity with the black community which no longer co-opt blackness,[2] the drama of Martin Luther King, Jr.'s, shooting leads to the final realization that the racial problem is not something society will be able to cure easily.

The racial tensions underscore the truth about the white establishment. The point for white theology is, thus, not first of all to fight for black freedom but to become aware of the oppressive mechanisms of the white system of which it is a part: "Much of reality as it is needs to be negated" (see p. 89 below). We can no longer afford to cover up the painful reality of conflict, most strongly experienced by those at the margins. Realizing that we cannot liberate ourselves, Herzog calls for new reflections on God's liberating power that put us back into closer relations with the oppressed.

The main essays of the Duke Consultation to which Herzog refers are published in The Future of Hope: Theology as Eschatology, *ed. Frederick Herzog (New York: Herder and Herder, 1970).*

April 4, 1968, 6:01 p.m. A shot rings out from a flophouse in Memphis, Tennessee. Across the street on the balcony of a motel a man drops to the ground: Martin Luther King, Jr. In Durham, North Carolina, I had just presented my opening paper at the Duke Consultation, "The Task of Theology Today." In the evening, an hour and a half after the shot, Jürgen Moltmann would give

First published in *Continuum* 7, no. 4 (Winter 1970): 515–24.

1. Author's interview of April 12, 1992; see also Frederick Herzog, "Liberation and Process Theologies in the Church," included in this volume as chapter 29.
2. This is acknowledged by the AME Bishop Philip R. Cousin, "Black Identity and White Identity," *Dialog* 15, no. 2 (Spring 1976).

a summary of his position paper for the consultation. Shortly after his lecture we would learn of King's death.

There are axial moments in one's life around which everything else begins to turn. 6:01 p.m., April 4, 1968, has become such a moment for me. It made me think about the task of theology more radically than ever before.

Toward the end of my paper, I remarked: "Political theology, pressed on by God's waiting, perhaps the strangest form of love, will wish, even in the face of the most oppressive circumstances and even while trying to shake them off, to discover the most viable future. The hazardous guess must be eliminated. So we are compelled to plan for the future. Here lies the major task of political theology."

With this in mind I reflected on the consultation. King's death became its crucible.

How do the issues raised by the consultation appear today in view of King's death? Just what does such a convulsing event indicate for the task of theology?

What we had wanted to learn at the consultation — in terms of the preparatory material we had sent out — was how a few young theologians in America size up the present task of theology in the light of the eschatological question, which simply put is, Where is man going? What is his future?

The question is pressed upon us more and more because of the terrifying events of our time. But it reaches us especially in the form of the political arrangements in which we live. It may well be that ultimately economic security is still the strongest driving force of a man's life. It is nonetheless in political arrangements that economic power controls our mores, hopes, and aspirations, and wields influence.[3] Contemporary history makes theology twin to the political, so much so that a political theology is beginning to emerge. By political theology we do not mean a new type of theology but a new theological focus.[4] The Duke Consultation taught us that this dimension needs further exploration.[5]

At the consultation, there were many references to contemporaneity *in general*. But the task of theology was still largely understood as interpretation, not as engagement with questions of political power. This is not to say that there was no concern along these lines. The tendencies in this direction, however, need to become much more explicit and more strongly focused on the cutting edge of the contemporary sensibility.

We take seriously the modern secularized mentality only to the extent that we

---

3. In order to see how far the political reaches into every nook and cranny of our society we need to take a good look at our institutions. Within the past decade, for example, the United States Supreme Court has been very much the center of public attention. William S. White recently observed: "The court is in human truth a political institution, though ideally it might not be." "High Bench, Challenge and Opportunity," *Durham Morning Herald* (May 21, 1969), 4. Similar comments can be found on almost any other institution of our society. All one has to do is to read the newspaper.

4. See my article "Political Theology," *Christian Century* (July 23, 1969): 975–78.

5. Something similar is noted for the European discussion in Wolf-Dieter Marsch, ed., *Diskussion über die "Theologie der Hoffnung" von Jürgen Moltmann* (Munich: Chr. Kaiser, 1967), 17.

also take into account its political captivity. At the consultation, Van A. Harvey stressed the pluralism of present-day religious thought and suggested that a new task of theology "might profitably be the appropriation of rather than the mere toleration of pluralism and relativism and the adoption of a style that reflects what Karl Rahner calls the radical simplicity and the radical mystery of faith." Only in a subordinate clause did he speak of God, "who calls men to a life of freedom and responsibility for the creation." If we theologians do not join in assuming this responsibility we will continue to be the parasites of society. Other men will risk their lives while we retire to God-talk and contemplations of the mysteries of life.

In the future, a *general* orientation in the dilemmas of the secular mind can only be a secondary concern of the Christian faith. The coming orientation point of theology will be the liberation of man, in world revolution and in the revolution of consciousness. James Baldwin puts it briefly: "The struggle . . . that now begins in the world is extremely complex, involving the historical role of Christianity in the realm of power — that is, politics — and in the realm of morals."[6] Thus far in the West the dominant theological definitions of power are white men's definitions and by intent or default have become part of the system of exploitation in which the white man conceals the man of the other color from the public domain.

It is a hard lesson to learn that white Christianity as organized religion supports the exploiter. It is sometimes a blunt, but more often an ever so subtle instrument of keeping others oppressed.[7] While much ado has been made in the sixties over how Christianity ought to adjust to the modern secular mind, little has been done so far to make theology cope with the new perception of the power dilemmas in which all of us are caught.[8] Theological language is not as yet cued in to the agony of garbage collectors.

Protestant theology at the consultation by and large proved still to be oriented in the problem of faith as it was delivered to us by the Reformation. One can have all the faith in the world, but if one does not understand power, one cannot move mountains. Realizing the inadequacies of the theologies of faith, the recent theology of hope seeks to focus on the future and to find ways for man to overcome his paralysis in facing power. But one can also have all the hope in the world, and if man does not grasp the specific dilemmas that keep him captive in society, he will remain paralyzed. The credibility gap from which theology is suffering today relates not to the unwillingness of man to hope but to the inability of theology to show that God makes a difference in specific situations of power where men organize their public and private life.

One need not look far for situations to which theology must address itself. As a real estate owner, the church itself has now been challenged to share its wealth.

---

6. James Baldwin, *The Fire Next Time* (New York: Dell, 1964), 65.

7. Frantz Fanon, *The Wretched of the Earth* (New York: Grove Press, 1968), 42.

8. One of the first steps in this direction has been taken in Carl Oglesby and Richard Shaull, *Containment and Change* (New York: Macmillan, 1967).

Regardless of how little "civil" such a demand may seem to some, it manifests the plight in which Christianity is caught today.[9] In America, "integration" is no longer a realistic possibility for the blacks.[10] It amounts to little more than token acceptance. In integration, blacks seldom participate in the control of the resources of power. And the wealth of the church is largely still in the control of whites.

So the question of Black Power is not merely an issue for blacks. What is involved is the redistribution of power in America, in our hemisphere, and ultimately in the world as a whole.[11] For Christian theology the focus is thus no longer the question of immortality, or of forgiveness or justification. At stake now is how a human being relates to power in a world dominated by political arrangements. What matters is liberation, being able in society to control one's humanity: "We shall have our manhood. We shall have it or the earth will be leveled by our attempts to gain it."[12]

On what grounds can theology speak to this aspiration? In neoorthodoxy the burden of the argument centered on how the transcendent could be brought into the ken of the limited earthling. Here the theologian was constantly laboring, as it were, at transferring cargo across an abyss. It was not that he was supposed to transfer God across the abyss. God had already crossed it. But the theologian was expected to describe the nature of this transition to church and world. The act of God in stepping out from his transcendent realm was understood as *revelation*.

Meanwhile a bouleversement has happened, witnessed to also by the Duke Consultation. No longer is man concerned about the transcendence-immanence syndrome. This is not a matter of superciliousness or nonchalance. The concept "revelation" has simply turned out to be less of a biblically important concept than it had been made out to be.[13] What is more, we no longer think of a strange world of the beyond behind this world that must reveal itself to man from behind the veil of hiddenness. For us, the world has become a unitary process, with no need for a mysteriously *hidden* realm of transcendence.

Theologians have reacted to this development in several ways. The most widely publicized approach has been the death-of-God theology. In Europe one is trying to come to grips with the new situation by developing a new model of man's relationship to the world. Turning away from the ancient physics-metaphysics polarity and the more recent existence-transcendence polarity, a few younger theologians have begun to stress the history-future syndrome as a context in which to discover a new concept of transcendence. Here the emphasis is obviously entirely on changing worldviews. But besides the importance of

---

9. Stephen Rose, "The Manifesto and Renewal," *Christianity and Crisis* 29, no. 9 (May 26, 1969): 142.

10. Stokely Carmichael and Charles V. Hamilton, *Black Power: The Politics of Liberation in America* (New York: Vintage Books, 1967), 50.

11. Eldridge Cleaver, *Soul on Ice* (New York: Dell, 1968), 123.

12. Ibid., 61.

13. See F. Gerald Downing, *Has Christianity a Revelation?* (London: SCM Press, 1964).

changing worldviews that evoke different conceptual models of man's relationship to the world we must also realize the crucial significance of different models
of value. At least this is where things have become pressing in America.

Central to the understanding of God in America today is the tension between
black and white. It may still come as a surprise to some, but the question today
is not whether God is dead or alive, but whether he is black or white. Involved
in the question is whether there is any Valuer of human action, any ultimate
Judge independent of the white man's value structure of prestige and success.
The theodicy question of the Old Testament comes alive again: is there any
ultimate righteousness that measures man's deeds? James Baldwin was forced
to begin his life with the idea that God is white. But why, he soon wondered,
did God not take care of blacks as much as of whites? "God...is white. And
if His love was so great, and if He loved all His children, why were we, the
blacks, cast down so far?"[14] Somewhere along the line the Black Muslims entered
the scene and claimed that there was also a black Ultimate: "God had come a
long way from the desert — but then so had Allah, though in a very different
direction. God, going north, and rising on the wings of power, had become — for
all practical purposes, anyway — black."[15] White men have used God to sanction
their concealment of the neighbor. What does this say about God?

The issue is simply whether or not man stands under a claim, that is, whether
or not he must obey a reality that is not of his own making, a reality greater
than himself that does not sanction his every whim. It can no longer be settled
simply in terms of the debate about *transcendent* revelation. What is at stake
is a reality different from man, a Valuer who judges man's values or lack of
values. Theorizing about transcendent revelation does not help man to discover
a Valuer.

Those who take their stand in the Christian tradition can only point to the
originating events of the Christian faith and wait for others also to experience
their import. These events are mediated through the biblical Word. What we
are confronted with initially in this Word is not a theory of revelation, but an
account of the history of the people of Israel and of the life of one of their
sons, Jesus of Nazareth. As the biblical Word lets Jesus of Nazareth sum up the
history of his people, it confronts us with an otherness that judges and liberates
us. Strictly speaking, there is no revelation of hiddenness taking place in him,
but an acknowledgment of that Valuer who is always unconcealed to man as
judge and liberator and who does not play hide-and-seek with him. The hiding
is done by man.

In focusing on the Word that relates the history of Jesus we discover that it
turns into the heuristic principle of theological thought. The reality of human
life and history as a whole must be examined in its light. The story of Jesus' life
speaks of a paradigmatic "waiting on," a reality different from man that liberates

---

14. *The Fire Next Time*, 46.
15. Ibid., 66.

him to new possibilities of humanity. It opens man for freedom, but it does not overrun man's own choice. It waits on man, in coming to his aid. But it also waits on him to respond freely.[16] But we can discover this only in letting the Word itself probe human experience.

Theology today has widely lost the nerve for action. It had been characteristic of Jesus of Nazareth, however, to act. And he acted through a Word that was "other" as compared with man's words. Through his Word he negated human self-deception and liberated men to an open life. His Word contains the promise that it can still be effective today as it confronts men with a liberating otherness.

In the present situation one is struck by the inability of theology to come to grips with the social turmoil in terms of the Word.[17] For example, demands of black Christian militants are often understood by whites as blackmail. Conversely, good will gestures of white Christian liberals are frequently interpreted by some blacks as brainwashing. We must learn to approach one another in new ways.[18] Obviously this is more easily said than done. And it is also easily said that the biblical Word liberates us to an understanding of man that reflects a dialectic of human existence which we hardly discover on our own. But we have to start somewhere to introduce a new theological determination to be truthful about what is real.

What man never discovers on his own is how all of human life stands under judgment, his loves as well as his hates, his accomplishments as well as his failures. He learns this only in confrontation with the Word that speaks of Jesus. The judgment is that man does not live in terms of the quality of Jesus' life. What makes Jesus' life important is the costliness of his love.

What a man who responds affirmatively to the Word that speaks of Jesus learns is that human life is already liberated and that he will have to change those conditions that keep him from living according to costly love. The costliness is ultimately the discipline to let the other be himself. A price must be paid for letting the other find his freedom.

We should not think that man in the biblical Word becomes subject to a regimentation that confines his freedom. Rather, it offers new possibilities for being human. The biblical Word proves its authority, its power of bringing into being, in that it liberates. The Bible, as an essay on liberation,[19] differs from other essays on liberation in that it ties liberation to a reality other than man. Man can be free because reality has already been liberated in Jesus of Nazareth. And he is invited to prove his liberation against all forms of captivity and exploitation that still exist.

---

16. See Frederick Herzog, *Understanding God: The Key Issue in Present-Day Protestant Thought* (New York: Scribner, 1966), 107.

17. A notable exception is James H. Cone, *Black Theology and Black Power* (New York: Seabury Press, 1969).

18. How change is possible also beyond the pale of the church was, for example, borne out by Malcolm X. See *The Autobiography of Malcolm X* (New York: Scribner, 1966), 413.

19. See Herbert Marcuse, *An Essay on Liberation* (Boston: Beacon Press, 1969).

With the emphasis on the Word as *liberating* Word we have perhaps struck at the heart of the debate about the relationship between American theology as reflected in the American papers at the Duke Consultation — and European theology — as represented by Jürgen Moltmann. At the consultation, Langdon Gilkey commented with respect to how biblical reports are used in European theology: "Perhaps the authority of *das Wort* in the German theological tradition is sufficient to explain psychologically the authority, for theologians, of these reports." It is, however, exactly this type of relating to the Word that Jürgen Moltmann has tried to overcome, at least in intention. The real issue in theology, whether European or American, today is whether it is *authorized* — brought into being — by a reality "other" than itself. It is the living power of the "otherness" of the Word that theology needs in order to make sense at all.[20] And it is exactly at this point that the attempt must be made to mesh the concerns of American and European theology.

Herbert W. Richardson, in *Toward an American Theology*, gives an analysis of the difference between European and American theology that can serve as a clue to understand why both need to be related more adequately: "The Puritan and spiritualist program to create a righteous society in history (i.e., establish the kingdom of God) is usually called 'theocracy.' Theocracy seeks to attain God's kingdom in this world, not the next. This is the fundamental theme of religion in America. Because of its concentration on God and His kingdom, American Christianity has tended to reduce the Reformation concentration on human sin and Jesus Christ the Redeemer to a secondary emphasis. When, as in Reformation theology, human sin and the need for redemption are made primary emphases, the kingdom of God must be a secondary emphasis — for the very possibility of attaining that kingdom in this world must be denied."[21] Assuming that Richardson's view of the European situation is accurate, a significant aspect of such a theological project as that of Jürgen Moltmann lies in its attempt to move beyond the sin-redemption syndrome to which Richardson objects. Moltmann as much as Richardson is interested in moving from the *cur Deus homo?* to the *cur creatio?* We are no longer as far apart as the old clichés have it.

And yet the emphasis on the Word — as much as it may stand in need of some American corrective — challenges the one-dimensional understanding of attaining God's kingdom on earth through human effort. The Word does not deny that God's kingdom comes to this world. But it does deny that it comes through human effort alone. It liberates man from the illusion that everything

---

20. Just how important the emphasis on the liberating Word might be will have to be examined from denomination to denomination, perhaps in the way J. Robert Nelson has already tried to do this for the Methodists in "As Others See Us," *Christian Advocate* 13, no. 14 (July 10, 1969): 7: "The Bible is revered but not often used...Specific texts are adduced in support of preconceived ideas, which may or may not have been derived from the Bible. In the leap to escape uncritical literalism, the denomination has by and large failed to land on a place where there can be discerned, with all critical reading, the decisive acts and purposes of God."

21. Herbert W. Richardson, *Toward an American Theology* (New York: Harper and Row, 1967), 109.

depends on him. It calls attention to two dimensions: God's initiative as well as man's response.

The European emphasis may not be altogether as obsolete for contemporary American Christianity as Richardson would have it. It is simply a fact that with all the emphasis on building God's kingdom in America our society has become oppressive[22] and totalitarian.[23] American theologians must ask themselves once more why it is that human activity has not as yet brought in the kingdom. It is of the Christian world that supposedly has been bringing in God's kingdom that James Baldwin writes: "The Christian world has revealed itself as morally bankrupt and politically unstable."[24] Unless man is liberated from political captivity, there will be no new society. Remember the Great Society? Where have all its programs gone?

It is tragic for theology that the need for a new understanding of the power of the biblical Word is not even seen by those who have realized how bankrupt Christian civilization is. Take Michael Novak's assessment of contemporary German theology: "Modern science has entered a new cycle, the printing press has been replaced by electronic media, and now it is time to turn from Germanic eschatology to Mediterranean nature. Camus refused to surrender the present moment to the future. Visions of the future must share time with the world of total present experience."[25] One can easily agree with Novak on the importance of the present. The question remains *which reality* determines the content of the present moment. Mediterranean nature did not escape the oppressive politization of society and the captivity to the powers that be.[26] So the issue we face is whether there is a power that can liberate us from the powers of nature as well as of history. Nature is still groaning in travail and cannot liberate. Its pain and evil negate God. There have been other modern religions of nature, for example, Nazism's worship of *Blut und Boden*.[27] *Principiis obsta!* From the very outset, we must resist this sort of thing.

A theology of liberation is the first step toward challenging present-day theology to think of changing itself radically. Does it wish to take the liberating power of the Word, a reality other than man, seriously, or does it wish to continue to gaze at its navel? The task of theology is not determined by human ingenuity, but by the Word that bears witness to the liberator of human ingenuity.

Much of American theology today is absentminded. There is no other primal task for theology today than to make the liberating Word of the Bible effective. To say this does not mean to invite a new biblicism, a naive rehash of the biblical

22. See Herbert Marcuse, *One-Dimensional Man* (Boston: Beacon Press, 1964).

23. See Erich Fromm, *The Revolution of Hope* (New York: Harper and Row, 1968).

24. *The Fire Next Time*, 73.

25. Michael Novak, *A Theology for Radical Politics* (New York: Herder and Herder, 1969), 110ff.

26. See Jacques Ellul, *The Political Illusion* (New York: Vintage Books, 1967), 14ff. See Mercer Cook and Stephen E. Henderson, *The Militant Black Writer in Africa and the United States* (Madison: University of Wisconsin Press, 1969), 82.

27. See Arthur C. Cochrane, *The Church's Confession under Hitler* (Philadelphia: Westminster Press, 1962).

Word. What it says is that we need a new high regard for the *liberating power* of the Word of God.[28]

The need for a theology of liberation appears at a time when liberal theology in America is becoming more and more irrelevant. In Europe, it is generally understood, it was Karl Barth's theology that initiated the decline of liberal theology. For the American scene, however, it was by no means the case thus far that liberal theology had come to the end of the rope. Until recently it was still holding full sway in university theology.[29] Now with the emergence of black theology the theological scene is being changed.

What is suddenly appearing as the downfall of American liberal theology is its glorying in pluralism and relativism, something that seemed a virtue thus far. In the present crisis into which American civilization has been catapulted, truth, however, proves a much more precious thing than heretofore supposed. As a black, James H. Cone is able to size up the present dilemma of liberal theology with a sharp eye: "The liberal, then, is one who sees 'both sides' of the issue and shies away from 'extremism' in any form. He wants to change the heart of the racist without ceasing to be his friend; he wants progress without conflict.... He wants change without risk, victory without blood."[30] What still needs to be done is to inquire into the real basis of the liberal dilemma. What is it really that makes for the ambivalence of a liberal theologian? Karl Barth spoke of a conflict of faith with itself.[31] Ultimately it is unfaith that wants to satisfy everyone; in the process it contradicts the truth of faith. We are learning again that faith at its core is an utterly difficult thing and that it is by no means immediately clear what faith is. We must struggle anew to find out what faith is and must liberate it from the dross of unfaith.

There is no other way to do this than to measure our words by the biblical word that speaks of Jesus of Nazareth. In doing so we find out that he demands not right thinking but radical action, a commitment to the neighbor that goes beyond the commitment a man himself can generate. The time has long past that the Christian faith was understood as a communicable body of truth whose effectiveness could be demonstrated on grounds of a logical argument. Even so, liberal theology by and large still thought it could somehow make the Christian faith palatable to the modern mind, if one only knew the right argument. Secular theology today is merely a modified version of liberal theology in this respect. But today no one is really convinced by a mere argument as far as the relevance of the Christian faith goes.

This does *not* mean that we are calling for *inarticulate* action. If there ever was

---

28. It is from this perspective that one needs to evaluate any theology of liberation. An initial proposal for such a theology is John Pairman Brown, *The Liberated Zone: A Guide to Christian Resistance* (Richmond, Va.: John Knox Press, 1969).

29. See Schubert M. Ogden, ed., *Existence and Faith: Shorter Writings of Rudolf Bultmann* (New York: Meridian Books, 1969), 9ff.

30. Cone, *Black Theology and Black Power*, 27.

31. Karl Barth, *Church Dogmatics*, I/1 (New York: Scribner, 1936), 33.

a time when action needed to be undergirded with a clear rationale it was ours. But in theology we can no longer argue a separate point, say, man's knowledge of God, without relegating it immediately to a particular lifestyle. The new shape of life has to be based on the Word that speaks of Jesus Christ. Only in yielding to this Word does the radical discipleship originate that introduces the new life-style, or the new society.

We still live far removed from this radical discipleship. What we usually live for is an intact institutional theology for a civil religion,[32] sanctioning the status quo. Black theology and Forman's recent issuing of the Black Manifesto have introduced a new sensibility. The Third World is right in our midst. The haves have been served notice that they must give an account to the have-nots. The old model of Euro-American theology has become obsolete. There are new referends for the human sensibility.[33] We can no longer be reconciled to reality as it is. Much of reality as it is needs to be negated. No one can serve two masters. Either he will take the side of the one who conceals the neighbor or the side of the concealed. In order to be neither the concealer nor the concealed, man needs to be liberated. He cannot liberate himself. While liberal theology may see this it does not fully realize how much the working out of these issues calls for identification with the concealed and oppressed. Only in complete identification can we fully appreciate the act of liberation: "If the Son shall make you free, you shall be free indeed" (John 8:36).

Liberal theology needs to make way for liberated theology, a theology in which the initiative and power of God's liberation unite the theologian more fully with the lot of the disadvantaged. Liberated theology will probably find that its first reward in engaging society is conflict and not applause.

According to a well-known legend Jesus appeared to Peter leaving Rome during the persecution of the Christians. Peter asked the Lord, *Quo vadis, Domine? Where are you going, Lord?* To which Jesus responded, *Venio Romam, iterum crucifigi.* To Rome, to be crucified again. Thereupon Peter, the legend claims, went back to Rome where he too suffered the death of crucifixion.

In view of our present concern for the future we ask one another, Where are you going? No one wishes to be sentimental in our day of hard sell. But no one who feels some commitment to Jesus of Nazareth can even today avoid also asking the question, *Quo vadis, Domine?*

At the center of Christian theology lies a commitment to realizing one's discipleship where one is, witnessing to the liberation of life exactly where one has been placed at the moment.[34] Without willingness to risk everything at this place there will be no theological progress. The concomitant of risk is conflict. Christ's

---

32. See Robert N. Bellah, "Civil Religion in America," *The Religious Situation* (1968): 331–56.

33. On the change of sensibility see George S. Hendry, "Reconciliation, Revolution, and Repentance," *Princeton Seminary Bulletin* 61, no. 3 (Summer 1969): 15–24.

34. These reflections need to be specified in terms of what the life of the church demands as renewal. See Douglas W. Johnson, *A Study of New Forms of Ministry* (New York: Dept. of Research, Office of Planning and Program, National Council of the Churches of Christ in the U.S.A., 1969).

sacrifice on the cross was the climax of open conflict.[35] A liberated theology will de-honkify Christ. He was a warrior who brought the sword (Matt. 10:34) and battled for our liberation. It was the sword of the spirit, but nonetheless a sword. Radical discipleship must do battle in society on grounds of this liberation. This is what Martin Luther King's death reminds theology of. Providence made it co-incide with the Duke Consultation. For a brief unforgettable moment it showed us the direction in which theology must go.

---

35. On this level there may be a few answers to some of the problems Vincent Harding is wrestling with in "The Religion of Black Power," *The Religious Situation* (1968): 27ff.

– 10 –

THE EATING AND THE GLORY

In Herzog's later work the Eucharist plays an important role as the place where we encounter Christ's presence in ways which take on the tensions and struggles of the present. This sermon illustrates an early stage in the process. Bringing the strange power of the eucharistic event together with the "harsh reality" of the Vietnam War, Herzog explores the new reality of God's work in Christ's death and resurrection.

Three decades later Herzog would still quote from time to time fragments of the third stanza of the hymn "Once to Every Man and Nation" referred to in this sermon: "Truth forever on the scaffold, wrong forever on the throne! Yet that scaffold sways the future...." No wonder theologians and church people have so much trouble when looking for God's glory: we often look in all the wrong places.

The text for the communion meditation is found in 1 Corinthians 10:31: "Whether you eat or drink, or whatever you do, do all to the glory of God."

A few weeks ago there was some discussion in the letter section of *Time* about a picture that appeared in the May 28 issue showing a beheaded victim of the Viet Cong in Vietnam. Some readers approved of the picture being printed. They felt it gave a realistic picture of what America is up against in Vietnam. Others canceled their subscriptions, claiming that their sensitivities had been slighted.

The picture of a beheaded man, his body torn apart: the image of the broken body of mankind! Regardless of whether we object to such a photo in print or not, we cannot escape the harsh reality of mankind's war against itself. The body of mankind is torn asunder time and again: in cold and hot wars, in the battle of ideologies and the battle of guns. As the escalation of the war in Vietnam continues, the best in us rebels against mankind's ceaseless failure to be one.

The Lord's Supper for which we are gathered this morning speaks mainly of two things: the broken body of our Lord and the broken body of mankind. In our eating and drinking they become related. But this is by no means obvious. We can only understand it in faith.

Unpublished communion meditation in Duke University Chapel, August 1, 1965.

Eating and drinking are basic life-preserving functions. In our culture today they are very much commonplace, although we should not generalize on that too much. For example, Harry Golden in *Only in America* can still speak of food as the *symbol of tomorrow*, that is, the symbol of survival among the Jews on the Lower East side in New York where he grew up. Even so, for ancient man who was captive to mythology, eating and drinking were more mysterious yet. To be strong like a lion a man would eat a lion. For he believed that a man was what he eats. To be one with his god he would eat him. The idea might appear naive today. But for ancient man it made a lot of concrete sense. St. Paul had this depth dimension in mind when he spoke of eating and drinking. But as he spoke of it he filled it with new meaning, a meaning still relevant today, the meaning of faith.

Whether you eat or drink, do it to the *glory of God!* Glory is here not the popular type of glory, the glory of fame or success. Glory for St. Paul was true being, the ultimately real, that which truly is. God's glory, this was the inside of all things, as it were, their source and center. It had become fully known to St. Paul only in the death of Christ on the cross. Thus he could say, "As often as you eat this bread and drink this cup, you proclaim the Lord's death..." (1 Cor. 11:26). A man had sacrificed his life for all men, Jew and Gentile. And God had shared in the sacrifice. A price had been paid. Costly love had been shown. This had been God's glory, not the glory of a kingly throne, but of a cross, not the glory of a crown of gold, but of a crown of thorns, not the glory of easy success, but of suffering. To eat to God's glory thus means *to eat in awareness of God's costly love on the cross.*

St. Paul pondering the cross had a new vision of reality. In part one can better understand it as one compares it with poetry — as a creative interpretation of reality. Wallace Stevens wrote a poem called "The Man with the Blue Guitar." It begins: "The man bent over his guitar. A shearsman of sorts. The day was green. They said, 'You have a blue guitar. You do not play things as they are.' The man replied, 'Things as they are are changed upon the blue guitar.'" When we encounter St. Paul's concept of glory for the first time it is as though we also would want to say to him: "You do not play things as they are." And he might answer: "Things as they are are changed upon my blue guitar." Things are as they are, the way we see glory: our status, our fame, our bank account, our guns and bombs. Things as they are! Here a dollar is a dollar and a gun a gun. But this is not ultimate reality, true being.

There is much ado in some theological quarters today to the effect that God is dead. If God is dead, God's glory is also dead. But God is not dead — or absent or silent. God is *unnoticed*. We fail to notice him. That is our *real* problem. For God in his glory appears where *we* do not expect him: on a scaffold. Truth forever on a scaffold, we sing. That is God — forever on a scaffold. "He had no form or comeliness that we should look at him," says the prophet. Little wonder that we fail to notice him! He is inglorious — if measured by our standards of glory. Dietrich Bonhoeffer, the modern Christian martyr, did not speak of the dead God, but of the suffering God, the God who suffers in costly love, bearing our foibles and frailties. It is this God who is near us, who is present in the eating of the bread and the drinking of the cup. The late secretary-general of the United Nations, Dag Hammarskjöld, wrote in his *Markings,* published last fall in English, about the death of God: "God does not die on the day we cease to believe in a personal deity, but we die on the day when our lives cease to be illumined by the steady radiance, renewed daily, of a wonder, the source of which is beyond reason." But how can we notice God? How can we find the wonder beyond reason?

In the broken bread of the Lord's Supper we have the most concrete symbol of the *unnoticed God,* the God we ignore as long as we are captive to standards of worldly glory. The breaking of the bread reminds us of Jesus' broken body as the sacrifice of God's love. The drinking of the cup points us to his shed blood as part of the sacrifice of love. Jesus' suffering was not dumb suffering. Although he was "like a lamb that is led to the slaughter" (Isa. 53:7), he transformed suffering from within so that it became costly love. The resurrection witnesses to the victory of this love.

In view of the escalation of the war in Vietnam faith in the ultimate victory of costly love seems unrealistic. What appears to count is the glory of crude power. But in the eating of the broken bread and the drinking of the cup we view reality in a new way. We affirm our faith that costly love is quietly disarming crude power. Now we understand St. Paul as he invites us in all our eating and drinking, that is, in all our preserving of life, to remember the true source of life for ourselves as well as our neighbor. The sharing of bread among the nations is part of God's goal for mankind.

If we, participating in the Lord's Supper, do not dedicate ourselves anew to the sharing of costly love among all men, we deny its innermost meaning. For the Lord's Supper is the meal of the unity of mankind in the suffering God. As we grasp the glory of God in the Lord's Supper, the picture of the beheaded victim of the Viet Cong becomes transparent to the broken body of our Lord uniting us in the work of healing the broken body of mankind. Thus we begin to share in the resurrection. Concretely this will also mean that each one of us in his place of responsibility, whether large or small, commits himself to wise political decisions, supporting the forces of peace in this country and in the United Nations, never fearing to negotiate.

Jesus Christ has created, as the letter to the Ephesians put it, "in himself one new man in place of the two, so making peace . . . [reconciling] us both to God in one body through the cross, thereby bringing the hostility to an end" (Eph. 2:15–16). In the Lord's Supper, in our eating and drinking, we are made participants of his reconciling work among men and thus share in the glory of God.

PART TWO

RESHAPING THEOLOGY FROM THE MARGINS

Encountering the reality of oppression and suffering at the margins, Herzog develops proposals for a new way of doing theology which still bear the potential to revolutionize the field. One reviewer compares the challenge of Herzog's book *Liberation Theology* to the challenge of Karl Barth's famous commentary on Romans: "Like Barth, Herzog is not content to play according to the going rules of the theological and ecclesiastical game."[1]

Where theology begins to pay attention to the tensions and conflicts of the present, the smooth correlations between God and world, or gospel and culture, that provide safe havens, especially for liberal contextual theologies, break down. God is not necessarily on the side of the powers that be. Yet the sort of rupture introduced by neoorthodox and other critics of liberalism will no longer do either. Even the notion of God's otherness, the rupture between God and humanity, can be domesticated or remains abstract if it is not connected to the rupture among human beings.

In other words, the dominant modes of theology fail precisely in light of the conflicts and tensions of everyday life whose most destructive and deadly manifestations are usually noticed only by the victims. Liberal theology, built on visions of identity and harmony, is unable to cut through the layers of false peace that protect those in power. Various orthodox and neoorthodox theologies, focusing almost exclusively on the vertical struggle between humanity and God and thus neglecting the struggle between the powerless and those in power, also tend to work in favor of the powers that be.

In the attempt to see our relation to people at the margins together with

---

1. James C. Logan, review of *Liberation Theology: Liberation in the Light of the Fourth Gospel*, in *Review of Books and Religion* (Mid-May 1973): 1.

our relation to God, Christology becomes a focal point. In Christ Godself joined humanity precisely at the level of nonpersons, and this divine act of solidarity opens the door for new encounters with God and neighbors. Christ, according to Herzog, redefines the relationship between self and other and prepares the way to overcoming the contemporary tug-of-war along the lines of race, class, and gender, where those who consider themselves persons establish themselves on the back of those who are considered nonpersons. These insights set new standards in Christology.

In Christ personhood becomes communal, bringing together persons and nonpersons, from the bottom up. Herzog interprets the biblical commandment "Love your neighbor as yourself" as "Love your neighbor as [being] your self."[2] While liberal theology often emphasizes the love of self ("you cannot love your neighbor unless you love yourself"), and a certain conservative stance promotes the depreciation of self in ways that do not lead to a reconstruction of the selves in charge ("we are all sinners"), the point is the formation of a new self in the encounter with the other. Only when dominant images of personhood are restructured in the encounter with nonpersons can real transformation happen.

The trouble is that even today in much of the social involvement of the church, reaching all the way back to the Social Gospel movement, this aspect is still missing. The selves of those in power, acting in terms of charity or social service, are often not reconstructed. Herzog formulates the challenge of nonpersons in this way: "I have often heard it said in debates about liberation theology that first of all we must define oppression and who the oppressed are. I believe it's the other way around: the oppressed define us."[3] This remains one of the major lessons for theology in the twenty-first century.

In the encounter with nonpersons and with Christ a new theological project develops. In ever closer encounters with the oppressed, theology finally begins to understand the seriousness of the situation. While in the 1950s and 1960s, both in the civil rights movement and in the relationship to countries of the "Two-Thirds World," high hopes were placed in gradual development, in the seventies it becomes clearer that progress may not happen without a break.[4] Rather than smoothing over the tensions, theology needs to face the existing asymmetries between those in power and those without power, which, even three decades later, continue to reinforce themselves.

Theological reflection, often confined to the realm of universals, needs to learn how to deal with particular issues. Responding to the assumption of mainline theology that universality of religious experience is a better guide than historical particularity, Herzog puts it quite drastically: "We are not employed as

---

2. See Frederick Herzog, "Befreiung zu einem neuen Menschenbild?" *Evangelische Kommentare* 5, no. 9 (September 1972): 518.

3. Frederick Herzog, "From Good Friday to Labor Day," *Journal of Religious Thought* 34, no. 2 (Fall–Winter 1977–78): 22.

4. Frederick Herzog, "Which Liberation Theology?" *Religion in Life* 44, no. 4 (Winter 1975): 451–52.

children of God but as black garbage collectors or red field hands or white-collar workers, as male bosses or female secretaries, and so on."[5] In the encounter with a variety of different people, the closed systems of theology break open. Theology needs to be kept open for encounters both with the human other and the divine Other. Widening the horizon of theology in this way, people on the underside become part of the theological enterprise.[6]

---

5. Frederick Herzog, "Liberals versus Liberationists," *Christian Century* (July 21–28, 1976): 666.

6. While white theologians cannot write theology for black sharecroppers, they can structure their theologies in such a way that "the sharecropper belongs to the context of its hermeneutical premises." Frederick Herzog, "Responsible Theology?" in *Philosophy of Religion and Theology: 1974 Proceedings*, American Academy of Religion Section Papers, ed. James Wm. McClendon, Jr. (Missoula, Mont.: Scholars Press, 1974), 165.

– 11 –

PRAYER

One of the central insights of Herzog's work is that theology needs to be reshaped "on the road." Theological reflections can easily become smoke screens if they do not grow out of tangible practical commitments and a deep spirituality. This prayer models what is at stake: in light of the dynamic of the struggle for peace, theological questioning and Christian praxis are closely interwoven and inspire each other.

Why pray to you, O Lord
when bombs are falling?
Why pray to you when Mars
is calling
young men to war?
Are you like Mars,
a God of blood
and blown-out guts
and early death?

We do not fully
know your ways.
We keep on guessing.
But every man who prays
will find you stressing
that peace
is in our hands
if we but grasp your peace
with our faltering hands
that fashion guns
and bombs
and heavy mortar.

Unpublished prayer at midnight peace rally and vigil, Duke University, May 4, 1971.

O make us see
that it is us
who make your wars
and call them holy,
but that *you* bear the scars
of our treason of your truth.

So cry we out in this thick darkness
of our hate and fear —
may your light lead us
to fashion plowshares from
our swords
and pruninghooks
from spears of death.

Steel you in us the will to peace —
that peace which you have brought
to us in suffering servants —
in Daniel Berrigan and Martin Luther King.
And free us through your liberating word:
there is no way to peace —
peace is the way,
your peace.

Amen.

– 12 –

SELECTIONS FROM
LIBERATION THEOLOGY

Encounters with African Americans at the grassroots such as William Edwards
(see part one, chapter 6) have taught Herzog what he calls the "Bible-in-hand
approach," a rereading of the biblical texts in the midst of life, out in the cotton
fields and in the factories of North Carolina. His second book, Liberation Theology, *is just that: a theological rereading of the Fourth Gospel in the light of*
oppression and God's liberating power which at times displaces even the struggle
with the theological state of the art. In this book Herzog leaves out much of his
extensive previous research on the theological reception of the Gospel of John,
including in-depth discussions of the work of Rudolf Bultmann.

Promoting an exercise in new listening, both to the oppressed other and to the
text of the gospel, Herzog talks about "becoming black," a notion that dropped
into the theological scene like a bombshell. Modeled after the well-known pas-
sages on the new birth in the Gospel of John, "becoming black" talks about a
radical transformation which can only come as a gift, guided and made possible
by Christ's own presence with the oppressed.

Fully aware that he is not in a position to write a black theology, Herzog
thinks through this phenomenon from the perspective of white theology. From this
angle, "becoming black" calls for repentance and a new awareness of how the
encounter with the oppressed selves of blacks reshapes the self-centeredness of
white America, transforming the private selves of the middle class into a cor-
porate self which includes the other. Entering into solidarity with the oppressed,
"becoming black" or "becoming red," has to do with participation in God's own
power which makes the impossible happen: people are being "born again." The
core issues for a liberation theology, such as eschatology, revelation, and a new
interpretive focus, are rooted here.

The translations of the biblical texts are Herzog's own.

First published in *Liberation Theology: Liberation in the Light of the Fourth Gospel* (New York: Seabury Press, 1972), 10–22, 61–67, 136–43, 254–65.

Liberation Theology versus Liberal Theology

Today we are compelled to choose between the bourgeois self and the longing of the wretched of the earth to be free. In first turning to the modern self the theologian does not even ask why there are countless multitudes who do not have the time and the freedom to reflect on their precious, private white selves. The usual starting point of liberal theology is a truncated view of human existence. The liberal focuses first of all on his private self. But are we even free enough to reflect adequately on our self? Anselm of Canterbury said, "You have not as yet considered the weight of your sin!" *Nondum considerasti, quanti ponderis sit peccatum!* As long as the modern middle-class self, the self of secular man, contributes directly and indirectly to the misery of untold millions throughout this country and the world, it may not be worthy of much concern. Is not the secular self part of the ideological glamorization of capitalist society? Who else but the leisure class can today afford the luxury of focusing on the private self?

Suggested in the analysis of the self as starting point of theology is an adjustment to things as they are. They may happen to be *in process* in the self. Even so, what is expected of us is that we adjust to this process.

I am not implying that the raising of a different type of question will result in a widely accepted demonstration of the reality of God. But the reality of God as introduced into the world by Christianity probably cannot be appreciated at all if it is immediately related to the quest of the modern subject for self-certainty. This modern quest begins with the stance of René Descartes: "Today, then, having freed my mind of all care and assured myself of untroubled leisure in peaceful solitude, I shall apply myself earnestly and freely to the general overthrow of all my former opinions."[1] Descartes's intention is understandable within the cultural and philosophical milieu of his day. The question is only whether we are not still aspiring theologically to "untroubled leisure in peaceful solitude" for the analysis of our precious little self. How could we ever think that Christianity and Descartes's primary intention had something in common? "Noting that this truth: *I think, therefore I am,* was so firm and assured that all of the most extravagant suppositions of the skeptics were incapable of shaking it, I judged that I could accept it without misgivings as the first principle of philosophy which I had been seeking."[2]

In the modern age, in America as well as in Europe, Descartes became more and more determinative of the basic theological approach. Friedrich Schleiermacher's entire methodology, for example, is an adjustment to his stance: self-certainty comes first, and God-certainty is based on self-certainty. The problem of modern atheism, within the bounds of Protestantism at least, emerged exactly at this point: the more self-certainty could be had, the less God-certainty was necessary. And of course one had to have leisure and privacy to find self-certainty. So the loss of God had much to do with the gain of leisure and wealth.

---

1. *Essential Works of Descartes* (New York: Bantam Books, 1961), 59.
2. Ibid., 20.

All the anthropological proofs for the existence of God had this difficulty built right into them from the beginning. God-certainty based on self-certainty was thus a very tenuous enterprise, subject to the whim of the thinker. To try to study the vicissitudes of this whole development as it catapulted into the death-of-God syndrome in Europe and the United States and to argue its pros and cons becomes a waste of time as soon as we see through the flaw of its first principle. Why should theology be based on the flimsy grounds of bourgeois self-analysis?

Karl Barth raised this question in his own way, but seeing the issue as an expression of the self-contradiction of the Christian faith in German culture-Protestantism and its political consequences in the Hitler Reich, he gave an answer more pertinent to the European situation. Today we must view the matter in our American context in terms of the quest for radical freedom: How is the self-contradiction of the Christian faith in our culture an expression of a radical denial of humanity? In what way is man's manhood contradicted? The basic objection to the Cartesian presupposition of God-certainty remains the same. We must remember that the argument for God in Descartes grows out of the analysis of the self: "Reflecting on the fact that I doubted, and that my being was therefore not entirely perfect, for I saw clearly that it was a greater perfection to know than to doubt, I decided to try to determine how I had learned to think of something more perfect than myself, and it became obvious to me that I must have learned it from some nature which was in fact more perfect."[3] New natural theology, of whatever provenance, makes the mind move toward the divine on the same grounds — as basic premise. The self here operative is the mind *freed of all care and assured of untroubled leisure in peaceful solitude* (Descartes).

The wretched of the earth turn our attention toward another factor. They are no *proof* of God. But they press us to ponder the character of the Christian view of the self which never relates primarily to untroubled leisure in peaceful solitude, but to the identification of a man with the *marginales*, the marginal figures of life. What theology at present needs to learn on the primal level is to acknowledge this unique dimension of the originating event of Christianity and to tie it to the question of radical freedom the *marginales* are raising today.

There is of course nothing intrinsically wrong with the self-in-leisure. What I wish to point out is that, theologically viewed, the self-in-leisure can as easily slip into answering the question of God with the atheist catchwords as with the orthodox catchwords. It is not at all a matter of *not* thinking, or of right (orthodox) thinking, but of thinking about what is worthwhile.

Does the self encounter God in encountering process (Cobb-Ogden), presence (Dewart), or future (Cox), *or* in a man's identifying with the wretched of the earth? The latter is not something we can decide at leisure. It imposes itself upon us, and only in being grasped by it do we know it as truth.

Obviously the self is involved in all that theology is about. The question is *what kind* of self we focus on, and whether the self-certainty of a particular kind

---

3. Ibid., 21.

of self, the Cartesian self, is capable of carrying the whole weight of theology, as it were, on its shoulders. If I turn from the private self to the oppressed as part of the self, I am subjecting myself to a more primary hermeneutical or interpretive presupposition operative in my theological thought, more primary because it has placed itself there *before* I begin to reflect on it in terms of my bourgeois self. *The oppressed as part of the self*, this is a compelling factor because of the power of the originating event of Christianity over us. And this happens within a corporate self — the community of the church. Here I learn that there are injustices I cannot forget. That the self is in fact isolable and that it makes for some interesting leisure thinking — the Cartesian self proves this without a doubt.

As soon as one rejects the Cartesian self as starting point of theology and turns to the originating event of Christianity within the context of Christian community, the next interpretive step is a fuller appropriation of the import of this event for a new corporate life.

That in a pluralistic society there are countless ways of being pluralistic in the church, and thus also as regards the starting point of theology, should be clear. The issue today is whether in a secularized church we are still talking about Christian faith at all when we do theology. Naturally one can imagine countless ways of continuing to linger with the self as private self. The problem is whether this is really the task of theology in the light of what Christianity stands for in its crucial originating event.

So I am trying to say two things. (1) We have to learn to "think black" theologically. To "think white" is to turn in upon the Cartesian self, to engage in "navel gazing." The black self over against the white self is the compassionate self (*compatior, ergo sum*). It is the corporate self in which the "I" shares. I believe this is a more adequate corrective (from the Christian perspective) of the *cogito, ergo sum* than the "I rebel, therefore we exist" (Albert Camus). To "think black" means to be able to think from the perspective of the underdog. We could also suggest "thinking Indian" — the underdog has many colors in this country and the world over. (2) To think from the perspective of the oppressed, however, is not as yet to think theologically. "Thinking black" ("thinking Indian") has to be radically tied to the originating event of the Christian faith in order to be theological. In fact, ultimately we can "think black" only if we are bound to the originating event. This does not mean leaving reason out of the picture. While the theologian cannot be the man "who is led by reason alone" (*qui sola ratione ducitur*), he is a man who is *also* led by reason, a "black reason" that has been tied to the incarnation. But reason as an agent here is not primary. It does not control the theological endeavor.

To speak of this theology as liberation theology is to imply that the identification of Jesus Christ with the wretched of the earth not merely brought freedom of the individual but also gave him public space for freedom to become operative. Naturally, many objections to this position are imaginable and will be raised. For some it will seem merely another dogmatic assertion or a camouflage of orthodox ideas. The revulsion against a put-on is strong in us all. Why should we orient ourselves in a Jew of nearly two thousand years ago? A billboard sign read: "Christ is the answer." Someone wrote underneath: "But what is the question?" It should be quite clear that in the following the theme is: Christ is *the* question. But we cannot always talk in hypothetical language. We need to make certain affirmations as we become certain of certain things. Even the question needs a formulation, a very articulate formulation. It cannot remain just a vague feeling. An articulate faith affirmation is involved in asking a question. At least some confidence is presupposed that it might make sense to ask a question. And one had better be clear about the content or nature of this confidence lest talking in questioning language turns out to be no more than mumbo jumbo, or mere shooting off of the mouth.

Liberation theology, then, in terms of asking questions, begins with the supposition that through the Christ-event liberation has taken place for being free to see reality in terms of a new question. That the nature of asking the question is qualified by the Christ-event is of course true. So whoever wants to stay with self-analysis, with the pain of self-torture, or the threat of impending suicide must stay there. But whoever wants to ask what *Christ* has got to do with self-torture or suicide, must first ask, What has Christ got to offer *anyway*? It seems that too many who are, for example, asking what Christ has to do with suicide, are unwittingly injecting the expectation that Christ is *the* answer, or at least a partial answer. Thus, many close their minds immediately to the possibility that Christ might have something *new* to say to them, something they have not known before.

Liberation theology as distinct from liberal theology begins not with *any* question, but with Christ as *the* question. It presupposes a community that has experienced the liberating effect of the question. Liberation theology is a function of the liberation church. An event has taken place in the history of mankind that has not been forgotten. A unique configuration of history is remembered in a community that asks *the* question over and over again.

The Fourth Gospel as Catalyst of Liberation Theology

It is useless to try to introduce one or the other biblical term as a stopgap, as it were, when our lofty theological reasoning runs into snags. We must get our field of vision focused on the basic originating history of the Christian faith. There is little promise, for example, in reasoning about the "God of hope" unless we recall immediately "Christ Jesus, our hope" (1 Tim. 1:1). Nothing is gained today by speaking of the God of the future unless we experience how Jesus Christ liberates man from the misery of the present. It is *his life* that we must understand in order to discover our theological task for the present. Our choice of the Fourth Gospel as the basis of our reflection is mainly due to the fact that it is the most reasoned out of all the Gospels, carefully articulating a theology of Jesus' identification with men who had no identity in the eyes of the established church and society of his day.

The primitive Christian writings do not expect us to understand their thought forms on their grounds alone. They invite us to find new forms for our time. The ancient words press us on to find our own words and to discover the Word that liberates us today. In terms of Johann Albrecht Bengel's exegetical rule, "apply yourself completely to the text, apply the subject completely to yourself," the "to yourself" becomes more and more pressing today. The past presses us toward the present. We are compelled to think our own thoughts.

In working with the text of the Fourth Gospel I gradually learned that I was searching for a focus of present-day theology. It did not burst upon me suddenly. It grew out of the taxing process of reading and rereading, translating and retranslating, interpreting and reinterpreting passage after passage.

The focus that gradually showed itself is God's liberation of man. God liberates in a twofold way: in serving and in waiting. He serves in giving life and renewing life. And he waits on us to respond to him by realizing freedom in personal relationships and public structures.

God's waiting creates liberation. Man is freed from bondage to his oppressed self not by the mighty sound of a trumpet or revolutionary rhetoric, but by the lowly ministry of a man called Jesus. His life is accessible to us only in the words of the Gospels. His presence for us is a presence in words, a Wordpresence. Beyond these words there is nothing we can ascertain about him. And whatever is said about God in Christian terms is mediated through words about Jesus of Nazareth. In one respect the Fourth Gospel is merely a piece of literature. In another respect, however, it is God's Word, as it liberates us to a new life. It has the power of creativity that is "other" than human creativity.

God's Wordpresence in the words about Jesus proves to be a claim upon us to find its reality in our own experience. Again and again we must search for its truth in our own lives. The issue is not that we must immediately find an adequate philosophy which would help us to interpret a reality called "God." We must discover this reality where it first was found: in a human being battling against human misery. Biblical stories are not props for pious schemes already thought out beforehand. God's Word is a power that pries open reality and questions the philosophies that seek to interpret it. Reality is asked a new question by God's Word. In fact, it is waiting to be questioned in the light of the liberation of oppressed men. Interpretation of reality is merely a corollary of the change in reality that God's liberation effects.

My *readings* in the Fourth Gospel do not present the central thought in a comprehensive analysis of theological concepts. They try to break down the text into separate units of thought. Every unit demands an exposition of a major theological point. Reflection on the various units led me to an articulation of their central theological thrust.

It should therefore be understood that the present volume is not intended as another commentary on the Fourth Gospel. It contains — besides the introduction and conclusion — readings that reflect the gradually emerging grasp of God as liberator. There are excellent commentaries on the Fourth Gospel today — Barrett, Brown, Bultmann, Dodd, Hoskyns, to mention only a few. It would be naive to think that I could improve on them. What I set out to do was to discover the witness of one New Testament writing to the reality of God in human life.

The language of the Fourth Gospel seems liturgical, as though it were meant to be read aloud in a great cathedral, which accounts for its repetitiousness and, in turn, reflects itself in my readings. This style is not altogether undesirable. It should be possible to ponder a chapter or several chapters and to get at the basic theological intention of the Fourth Gospel without reading all the other chapters. I should point out that I am not introducing my own translation in order to improve on existing translations, but only to form a unity between text and contemporary understanding.

Critical issues, such as the question of the historical sequence of events recorded in the Fourth Gospel, or the problem of which words of Jesus might be original concerned me greatly in the historico-critical research with the text. But it seemed unnecessary to introduce such reflections in a book that tries to grasp the major theological point of the Fourth Gospel: God's liberation of man.

According to John 20:31, the purpose of the Fourth Gospel is to show that "Jesus is the Christ, the Son of God." The problem runs through the entire gospel: what is the unique relationship of the history of this man to a reality called God? The problem is already present in chapters 1–4. But it becomes inescapable in chapter 5 when Jesus is accused of blasphemy: "Now the Jews tried to kill him because he was not only breaking the Sabbath, but called God his own Father, making himself equal to God." This is at the heart of the witness to the reality of God as the Fourth Gospel saw it for its day. From chapter 5 on it is the explicit issue until the end of the gospel: God becomes concrete in the public dimensions and structures of life and makes freedom real.

Before turning to the readings I must emphasize that the Fourth Gospel is deeply rooted in the Old Covenant community. It is not written *against* Israel. The author seems to be a Jew who wants to discover in what sense Jesus in his identification with the wretched of the earth is the Christ of Israel, the Son of God. His anger is directed toward the ecclesiastical establishment of Judaism that rejected Jesus, not against Israel, the people of the Covenant. Today his words judge the *Christian* religious establishment. They attack the organization church, which in its yen for success again denies the reality of God.

So the Fourth Gospel is a nonecclesiastical interpretation of the Christian faith, a "nonchurch" interpretation, but "nonchurch" for the sake of the liberation of the church. It offers a relevant response to the problem of a political theology as it is shaping up in present-day theological discussion.

Contrary to the myth that the Fourth Gospel is mystical and withdrawn, it is a theology of protest, of *protestari*, of affirming truth as counterattack upon the forces of oppression that have established themselves in church and society, robbing man of personhood and dignity. It invites men to join in God's work of liberation in forming the countercommunity of discipleship that as liberation church mirrors the corporate reality of God.

What is thus required is to struggle with the words of the gospel and to discover whether or not they are able to release in us a new self-understanding and worldview. The test of their truth lies in the liberation they bring.

What follows is an attempt to develop an outline of Christian theology and to identify priorities in its present task. Just what are the pressing issues? How can we tackle them? Why is it that probably one first has to go to prison today in order to appreciate *the Word as liberation* (Daniel Berrigan)? I hope the reader will remember that the Fourth Gospel text merely stakes out the area in which I am attempting to identify present theological priorities. It occasionally turns out not exegesis of the text but even antithesis to the text. And yet it is reflection on the text. The strange silence of the Bible in the church (James Smart) must be broken. American theology, by hook or by crook, must be compelled again to read the Bible. This has nothing to do with bibliolatry. The point is that liberation history has been at work for a long time. The Bible is its Wordpresence inviting us to share in it and to increase it in history as a whole.

Becoming Black (John 3:1–21)

[1]*Nicodemus, one of the Pharisees, a leader of the Jews,* [2]*came to Jesus by night. He said, "Rabbi, we know that you are a teacher sent from God. No one can do the signs you do unless God is with him."* [3]*Jesus answered, "Believe me, no man can see the kingdom of God unless he becomes black."* [4]*Nicodemus wondered, "How can a man become black when he is white? Can he again enter his mother's body and be born different?"* [5]*Jesus said, "Believe me, if a person is not born of water and Spirit he cannot enter the kingdom of God.* [6]*Flesh creates flesh, and spirit creates spirit.* [7]*Do not be surprised that I told you, you must become black.* [8]*The wind blows where it wills. You hear the sound of it, but you do not know where it comes from and where it goes. So it is with everyone born of the Spirit."* [9]*Nicodemus asked, "How can this be?"* [10]*"You are the teacher of Israel," replied Jesus, "and you do not understand it?* [11]*I assure you, we speak of what we know and witness to what we have seen. But you do not accept our testimony.* [12]*If I have told you about things on earth and you do not trust me, how can you trust if I tell you about things of heaven?* [13]*No one entered heaven except the one whose origin is in heaven, the Son of Man who is in heaven.* [14]*The Son of Man must be lifted up as Moses lifted up the serpent in the wilderness,* [15]*so that everyone who trusts him may have prevailing life.* [16]*For God so loved the world that he gave his true Son, so that everyone who trusts him should not perish but have prevailing life.* [17]*God did not send his Son into the world to doom the world, but to liberate it through him.* [18]*He who trusts him is not doomed, but he who does not is already doomed, because he has not trusted in the selfhood of God's true Son.* [19]*This is doom: Light has entered the world, but men preferred darkness to light because their deeds were evil.* [20]*Everyone who does wrong hates the light and shuns it lest his deeds be exposed.* [21]*But he who does the truth comes to the light, so that it becomes clear that his deeds are done in God."*

Now we are told how man can attain freedom. He needs to go through the shock of recognition: he does not want to change. It takes liberation of consciousness for man to become free. But this is a gift. Without it there can be no real freedom.

The Fourth Gospel does not say what made Nicodemus come to Jesus. It is not very graphic in portraying the persons who participate in the story. Types are sketched without great concern for their background, motives, or personal characteristics. It is concerned with the shape of Jesus' public activity and how men relate to it. All the Fourth Gospel points out in this instance is that Nicodemus apparently had been impressed by Jesus' signs. While somehow close to sensing the point of the mission of this man, he does not really understand it. He addresses him as God-sent teacher: God is with him. God seems somehow involved in the life of this man; otherwise he would not be such a great teacher (v. 2).

In response, Jesus revamps Nicodemus's worldview. He offers a new idea. What it involves in our day is plain: "Believe me, no man can see the kingdom of God unless he becomes black" (v. 3). Doesn't the idea seem absurd? "How can a man become black when he is white? Can he again enter his mother's body and be born different?" (v. 4). Jesus' reasoning is based on another logic: "Believe me, if a person is not born of water and Spirit he cannot enter the kingdom of God. Flesh creates flesh, and spirit creates spirit" (vv. 5–6). Nicodemus is still reasoning on grounds of wanting to retain white superiority, private selfhood. Jesus is concerned about a different self, corporate selfhood, which man controls as little as the wind (v. 8). Here the brutal logic of retaining one's identity as the superior white self or the "private I" no longer prevails.

It is significant that the challenge to man's renewal (3:1–21) is prefaced by events that show how much man distorts his selfhood (2:1–25). Culture and religion contribute to man's enslavement, compelling him to view himself other than he is.

The Fourth Gospel presupposes that man has been enslaved in a false relationship toward himself, a false self, a private self. Jesus' open way of acting confronts man with corporate selfhood. It challenges man to begin anew with being human. But beginning over again is not a matter of course. It calls for a radical change, liberation of consciousness. Man is asked to grasp his selfhood anew. Many ask like Nicodemus: "How can this be?" (v. 9). Nicodemus at least ought to have had a hunch: "You are the teacher of Israel...and you do not understand it?" (v. 10). He ought to have had an inkling because of the partial acknowledgment of the light in Israel. As a teacher of the church he had to be aware of it. As a human being, the *sensus communis* should have taught him the truth. But being a theology professor does not mean much when it comes to knowing corporate selfhood.

"No man can see the kingdom of God unless be becomes black" (v. 3). Man needs to go through the shock of recognition that he does not want to change. He needs to know how radical the change required is. "Rebirth," of which Jesus is usually made to speak in this chapter, has become something trite. One goes through it in a revival, enjoys it, and comes out of it quite unscathed. The change demanded in confrontation with Jesus is something eviscerating, something that touches the core of our being. It destroys the self-made self, that is, man as self-made man. Today it is usually the successful exploiter who preys upon others and uses their labor to build up his beautiful white front. It is all that "whiteness" stands for in the eyes of the poor, despised, and oppressed. To become black means to give up one's glamorous white self-image. "Blackness is an ontological symbol and a visible reality which best describes what oppression means in America" (James H. Cone). We could also speak of redness as an ontological symbol of oppression. The Indian, too, is debased. To be freed is always a question of being enabled to identify with the *marginales*, the people on the borders of society, through the power of the one who started doing it. Through Jesus we are able to enter the kingdom of God (v. 3), the realm in which all men are free as the truly free man rules over all. To worship one's beautiful private self is enslavement. To be related to corporate selfhood through Jesus is freedom.

There are a few additional dimensions in chapter 3 that need to be lifted out. The kingdom of God, the realm of freedom, was embodied in a bruised body lifted up on a cross (v. 14). God rules (as king of his realm of unconcealment) as Jesus freely chooses to take death upon himself in order to identify fully with all the wretched of the earth. Here we meet man reborn. Here is opened up a new direction of human destiny, affirming that man is not "real" in the mask of the "white" pseudoself. Here Jesus, the Son of Man, is "in heaven" (see 1:51), which is standing in the openness of all things by embodying man's corporate self (v. 13).

In fact, God's very character is embodied in Jesus' freedom on the cross. For faith, God himself waits on man in death, breaking the ironclad law of death. For faith, this freedom prevails in resurrection and offers unoppressed life, free from negation, to all who trust it (vv. 15–16).

Becoming black through Jesus does not mean now to have a handle to identify him with any contemporary figure, group, or power. "Then if anyone says to you, 'Lo, here is the Christ!' or 'There he is!' do not believe it. For false Christs and false prophets will arise and show great signs and wonders, so as to lead astray, if possible, even the elect. Lo, I have told you beforehand. So if they say to you, 'Lo, he is in the wilderness,' do not go out; if they say, 'Lo, he is in the inner rooms,' do not believe it" (Matt. 24:23–26). The blackness or redness of the man reborn is always related to *Jesus'* blackness or redness. It is always *his* kind of blackness or redness that counts. It is not *our* identification, but *his* identification with the wretched of the earth that counts and brings the great change among men. Therefore it is always called a rebirth *through the Spirit*. It is a gift mediated through the Jesus event (v. 5). Man needs to be reminded time and again that of his own accord he does not want to find liberation of consciousness through this event.

Human life is still lived by the law of the jungle. We doom ourselves time and again, taking one another's lives in war and in peace, exploiting one another, rejecting history's true possibilities and producing a state of fear and doom. The design of unconcealment — a new direction of our destiny — is not doom, but liberation, freeing man in the structures of life. If a man trusts freedom as the Son embodies it he is not doomed. God liberates *in Jesus.* Doom is lack of trust in what this man embodies: the new corporate selfhood (v. 18).

Jesus' corporate selfhood is the judgment on man's life. Mankind's doom is that his presence illumines man with the potential of true freedom and we keep rejecting it, dooming ourselves. Doom is not choosing death freely and thus not rising to life. Loving concealment, camouflage, private success, we do not wish to be openly what we are becoming to be. This is darkness — pitch darkness. The lily-white deeds are dark because of the cover-up (v. 19). Since we sense that the deeds of our pseudoself are not in accord with our true selfhood, we go into hiding before the new direction of our destiny, continuing to construct a pseudoworld (v. 20).

We go into hiding in myriads of ways. But today it is especially obvious what the hiding is as white men still conceal themselves from black men and red men — imprisoned in ghettos and reservations. It is only as we openly face one another as we really are and destroy ghetto and reservation that truth becomes manifest. Truth is ultimately not known, but done as men begin to see one another in terms of new corporate selfhood. This is not an easy thing, since it means facing one another as sinners (v. 21).

Lest anyone think we are talking here about an utopistic scheme, let him remember the water. The new life is tied to rebirth by *water* (undoubtedly a reference to baptism as practiced by the church) and Spirit (v. 5). The water says that the new life finds external expression. There is a space for freedom. There is liberation. It is in new corporateness that the new life is experienced: in the church as liberation church (see chapters 13–17). Since the Spirit is God himself (4:24), it is *God's* action that creates the new corporate life. Rebirth by *water* and Spirit is therefore the new corporate life wrought by God himself, outwardly as well as inwardly: identification with the wretched of the earth. Flesh — desire for make-believe, false fronts, status, deception, illusion — creates only more of man's hiding from one another. "Flesh creates flesh" (v. 6). By nature man is born into the realm of flesh. But the Spirit draws men into new corporateness.

To be reborn, to become black (or Indian or Vietnamese peasant or Soviet Jew), is thus to find a new selfhood. Jesus offers it: "Light has entered the world" (v. 19). In him man already is the new man. He who trusts him enters into new community — which is ultimately the realm of liberation, "the kingdom of God" (vv. 3–5). In the community of the church man receives in liberation a foretaste of the kingdom.

At the Intersection of Anthropology and Christology

With the emphasis on *unblinding reason* a massive continental shift is taking place right now in theology, a moving away from the hang-ups of modern man to an identification with oppressed man. The movement is away from thinking white to thinking black. White theologians have never taken a good look at themselves in the mirror since Puritan days.

For generations, theology in the United States has assumed that its basic landmarks remain fixed. No longer so. Whirl is king. What becomes clearer and clearer is that the sure image man had of himself has been eroding. And whatever of the old image is still around must go: *our image of man must go.*

In this regard theology is compelled to dig down to bedrock, to begin over again at the beginnings and to consider what the foundations were and what they still might be for us. Here theology needs to be involved in *storytelling*, trying to retell one story of the gospel after the other in order to discover something of the bedrock of faith. The one who retells the story must view himself as a "poet"; that is, he must be creative as well as faithful to the original. It is like translating a poem from another language. The original must still be there, and yet it must be there in another form!

In the retelling Jesus appears as the counterself, the true self, the open man. One has to understand this primally, for example, in terms of John 9:39–41. The remark refers, of course, to the hearing of the boy born blind who represents mankind. Man does not as yet see what he is supposed to become. But we white churchmen have claimed that we see. And we have promulgated an image of man that is supposed to give us direction. It is exactly this hubris that has led us astray. And so Jesus must first of all be appreciated by us as the verdict on history: that the blind are unblinded and those who see are blinded.

We modern theologians have said that we see. We know who modern man is. He is the steersman of the cosmos, "the point where the cosmos begins to think and to steer itself" (Cox). Man has begun to understand life and to control it in technology. Along comes David Rockefeller at Senate hearings concerned with poverty in the ghetto and claims: "As a banker, I invest money in order to make money; and if you want private enterprise to go into the slums, you have got to make it profitable." So what is left when the cosmos begins to steer itself? Rockefeller's kind of reasoning. We theologians, of course, still have some pragmatic inhibitions. But truly secular men have long drawn out the consequences of Cox's steersman principle. The exploiter image of man is the real referend of theological concern, even if only for making the writing of theological books profitable. If the theologian got into the slums he was writing about — again it was to make his work profitable. There is a remarkable passage in William Styron's book on Nat Turner, clarifying our white problem. After Nat's master has sold some slaves in order to salvage his farm with the money received in return, he cries out: "Surely mankind has yet to be born. *Surely* this is true! For only something blind and uncomprehending could exist in such a mean conjunction with its own flesh, its own kind. How else account for such faltering, clumsy, hateful cruelty? Even the possums and the skunks know better!...In the name of money! *Money!*" Underlying the profiteering is an image of man that today is still being promoted also by the church. This image of man must go.

There has been a hardening of man's self-image as exploiter. Probably many influences have shaped the present image. At the core today is perhaps a fusion of the Puritan and the Cartesian. But the principle of the fusion seems nothing new. In the context of theological thought in the New Testament, we are also confronted with such a hardened self-image of man. The man called Jesus appears on the scene to confront this self-image. Jesus is the Christ (and thus Christology begins) because he meets man with the offer of a new self.

Christian anthropology and Christology *intersect* at this point. In fact, Christian anthropology is merely the other side of the coin of Christology. As we talk about man's self we also need to take into account the counterself. This must be understood in terms of John 9:39–41. This self is the verdict on history, the judgment on corrupted human selfhood. Jesus did not bring all the conditions the Christ was expected to bring in terms of the fantasizing about the future of Israel. But as the counterself he gave a nonecclesiastical interpretation of the Messiah. His self-offering in confrontation with the white churchmen of his day became the primal christological stumbling block. Man as a prideful white self is not concerned about a new self. And as a *religious* white self he is mainly concerned about building up a glorified self that he can use as escape mechanism from his social responsibility — which happened in part in the development of christological dogma. Christ against culture as liberator of culture stands at the beginning of Christology, not the "acculturated" Christ. If we forget John 3, the motif of the liberation of consciousness, then as we get to John 6 and John 9, we cannot develop an adequate contemporary Christology or anthropology. What is at stake in the new selfhood Jesus confronts us with is radical freedom that can liberate us from the ironclad necessity in which we are caught. At its core lies transcendent freedom, not just abstract otherness. The real christological and anthropological issue is how transcendent freedom and human freedom can be fused.

The difficulty arising in many contemporary Christologies lies at the point where it is assumed that what is necessary is merely a rearranging of the metaphysical or doctrinal "toys." But that is a cop-out. What is here assumed is what can be assumed the least: that man in his present state can be the *measure* of who God and Christ are. The Christ-event in the New Testament is first of all a radical questioning of all of man's self-images. God liberates: this is the sum of the Fourth Gospel. Of course, we must ask: liberates from what? The answer is: first of all from a false image of man.

It is exactly this insight which is not a matter of course. We must protest that too many theologians today assume that their presuppositions — ontological, epistemological, hermeneutical, etc. — are just fine, unquestionable, drawn from some modern worldview or some critique of the modern worldview — without ever looking at themselves as political and economic beings. The ease with which the liberal and neoliberal theologians assume to know who we are — secular men! — is difficult to take. All we need to do, it seems, is to adjust God and Christ to secular manhood!

A case in point is the Christology of John A. T. Robinson, which is widely accepted among liberals and neoliberals in America as standard truth. From the perspective of our present black-white confrontation in theology, we can see how on Robinson's grounds the theological enterprise is grinding more and more to a halt. On several levels one can be quite sympathetic with the dilemmas Robinson sees. But without taking a good hard look at man's self-image the melancholy over these dilemmas is to no avail.

If we look at contemporary man's view of himself in the light of the biblical story we need to take one particular difficulty into account, one that has not as yet been mentioned. Besides liberalism and neoliberalism there is still a strong current of fundamentalism around in this country. The general reaction of the young college-trained religionist is to reject it as irrelevant. So he turns to religious-language analysis, all the while still assuming, however — unconsciously, that is — the basic fundamentalist posture toward the biblical categories. All that needs to be done, he thinks, is to interpret these categories in terms of the more epistemological framework of religious language. But the real problem is that fundamentalism misunderstood the biblical categories in the first place. They are not at all significant in themselves. The story to which they point must be recaptured. Here lies the theological difficulty. Part of the task of liberation theology is to smash the misconstrued biblical categories of fundamentalism relative to a new image of man, so that God's story can break through.

In principle, the struggle against liberalism/neoliberalism and fundamentalism is the same. What we are up against we can briefly specify in regard to John A. T. Robinson. In a November 1970 *Christian Century* article he claims that Christ is the one who says that men's attitude to him will determine God's attitude to them. He is "God's representative, called to stand in God's place. He does not assume identity with God, but he desires to represent God: he claims to be sent by God as his representative." This is interpreted to mean: "A representative is one who keeps your place *open*. What Christ the representative does is to hold God's place open, to enable man to believe and hope in the unrealized transcendent possibilities. And the church in turn exists to hold the world open for God." In summing up the new Christology, Robinson is quite plain as to what results on these premises: "The realization is fitfully dawning that 'God' now means, for us, not an invisible Being with whom we can have direct communication on the end of the telephone, but *that by which he is represented,* his surrogate — the power of a love that lives and suffers for others." Robinson's Christology does not want to eliminate God. It wants to say that Christ is the one who holds the world open for God. But man, too, can hold the world open for God. Again, God becomes quite manageable. What does it mean to keep the world open for

God? Is God not able to keep the world open for himself and for us? Is not man here again producing God as the *imago hominis*, the image of man? Here is no otherness, no judgment under which he stands. "God is made dependent on man and man's response." According to Robinson, it seems any man would agree to this Christology, consent to its truth, if only properly explicated. This is a primal mistake. All the enterprise amounts to is some rearranging of the metaphysical "toys" with no horror over man's corruption.

The basic flaw in the neoliberal presupposition is that man's inability to grasp Christ lies in poor Christ's inadequate adjustment to the modern worldview. But Jesus did not at all introduce himself in terms of a mythological event that would have to be rearranged. One of the first things Matthew says about him is that "he went about all Galilee, teaching in their synagogues and preaching the gospel of the kingdom and healing every disease and every infirmity among the people" (Matt. 4:23). The issue of grasping Jesus as the Christ on the primal level is not at all a problem of the modern worldview, but of man's persistent corruption of his self. Jesus is the Christ because he brings a new self: he is the liberator of man's every disease and infirmity. This presents the *difficulty* of appreciating the man called Jesus.

John 3:3 must be taken with utter seriousness: "No man can see the kingdom of God unless be becomes black." No naive conversionism is involved, but a radically different perspective of thought: a grasp of the corporate self, *seeing* the wretched of the earth, experiencing the *unblinding of reason.* Robinson bases his Christology on an utterly unexamined self. He takes for granted that so-called modern man is the proper self that can appreciate the Christ.

The turning from the private modern self to the corporate self will not come easy. It will take, for instance, an examination of the history of selfhood in the past three hundred years of Western civilization. R. H. Tawney points out that individualism "became the rule of English public life a century before the philosophy of it was propounded by Adam Smith." In the older medieval view man had been related to the church "in a mystical corporation, knit together by mutual obligations," so that no man could press his private advantage to the full. This is also the perspective of the Old Testament. Hebrew faith was a corporate faith in every respect. In Puritan economy things gradually came to be viewed differently. It was understood as an undeniable maxim that "everyone by the light of nature and reason will do that which makes for his greatest advantage. . . . The advancement of private persons will be the advantage of the public." No longer was the social character of wealth understood. In fact, according to Tawney the whole theology of the poor had to be changed: "A society which reverences the attainment of riches as the supreme felicity will naturally be disposed to regard the poor as damned in the next world, if only to justify itself for making their life a hell in this." In the words of Karl Marx, the dissolution of the medieval bonds between man and man "left remaining no other bond between man and man than naked self-interest and callous cash payment." The person determined by naked self-interest and callous cash payment is a peculiar kind of self: the private self that cannot understand the gospel. Not a wrong worldview is the obstacle, but a wrongheaded view of the self.

This of course can be said only from within the context of a particular community. The self is not self without being self-in-community. The real difficulty for the Protestant theologian today — whether he be black or white — is that the Christian church has become disincarnate or Gnostic. For this reason we need to covenant anew so that talk about the corporate self does not remain private. Here the inevitability of the liberation church becomes evident. The "anthropological" premise for the realization of the liberation church is the unblinding of reason.

Liberation in the Light of the Fourth Gospel

The readings in the Fourth Gospel are an experiment in a new form of Christian theology. Paul Klee liked to quote a fellow artist: "Drawing is the art of omitting." Today theology too must understand itself as an art of omitting. We tried to lift out the most salient features of contemporary theology as the ideas of the Fourth Gospel impinged on our contemporary experience. We will briefly sketch in conclusion the core issues as they shape up for the development of a liberation theology. Crucial for our understanding of liberation became the tension between the present and the future as it pervades the Fourth Gospel.

Eschatology and History

The relationship between the present and the future in the Fourth Gospel is often viewed as the difference between realized and final eschatology. Raymond E. Brown finds a useful example of final eschatology in the apocalyptic view of Albert Schweitzer, who claimed that "in speaking of the coming of the *basileia* Jesus was speaking of that dramatic intervention of God which would bring history to a conclusion."[4] He sees the opposite pole represented by C. H. Dodd, who holds "that Jesus proclaimed the presence of the *basileia* within his own ministry, but without the apocalyptic trimmings usually associated with the event."

According to Brown, the Fourth Gospel seems to present the most advanced form of realized eschatology in the New Testament. Here the disciples see God's glory. The judgment is now. Eternal life is a present possibility. But does this mean that there is no apocalyptic element in the Fourth Gospel? Brown discovers also indications of a future coming, a resurrection of the dead, and a final judgment (5:28f.; 6:39f., 44, 54; 12:48). If these indications exist, how are they related to the so-called realized eschatology of the Fourth Gospel?

---

4. For this and the following see Raymond E. Brown, *The Gospel according to John* (Garden City, N.Y.: Doubleday, 1966), cxii ff.

Brown believes that in "Jesus' own message there was a tension between real-ized and final eschatology. In his ministry the reign of God was making itself manifest among men; and yet, as heir of an apocalyptic tradition, Jesus also spoke of a final manifestation of divine power yet to come.... The passages in John that treat of apocalyptic eschatology are a remembrance that this theme is found in Jesus' own preaching." For systematic theology, the juxtaposition of these two strands is felicitous. While some biblical scholars give the future prior-ity and others emphasize the present, it is important for systematic theology that neither present nor future appears to the exclusion of the other. If the "future" of the future appears less stressed in the Fourth Gospel, this is because it is less concrete. The "presence" of the future is more central insofar as the Fourth Gos-pel is crucially concerned about the concrete. In terms of principle, eschatology is never absolutely realized, but embodied, as we said. The point is well articu-lated in the words: "The hour is coming, and now is" (5:25). What now is, is still coming. And what is coming, already reaches into the present.

Systematic theology must learn to work with the dialectic between the two. Jürgen Moltmann has wondered as regards the relationship between the present and the future: "Does the present determine the future in extrapolations or does the future determine the present in anticipations? Is there a third factor in which present salvation-in-faith and not-yet-present salvation in hope can be meaning-fully united?"[5] The Fourth Gospel may provide us with a clue for answering the question. Here the present and the future appear for some to contradict each other. In one instance the present takes priority over the future. In another in-stance the future determines the present.[6] We are probably confronted here with perspectives that complement each other in their difference. There can be no meaningful final eschatology without its anticipations in Jesus Christ, and there can be no meaningful embodied eschatology without the prospect of the final consummation.

What actually creates the forward movement of history, however, is the power of liberation that in Jesus Christ encompasses present and future as a "third factor." The movement of history is not set in motion primarily by human ex-trapolations, but by God's constant unlocking of the present through liberation. It is also not merely determined by the past. Says Jürgen Moltmann: "Only when the world itself is 'full of all kinds of possibilities' can hope become effective in love."[7] From the perspective of the Fourth Gospel, it is God's liberation that fills the world with all kinds of possibilities and enables man to hope.

---

5. Jürgen Moltmann, "Antwort auf die Kritik der Theologie der Hoffnung," in *Diskussion über die "Theologie der Hoffnung,"* ed. Wolf-Dieter Marsch (Munich: Kaiser, 1967), 209.

6. This has led to rather contradictory interpretations of Fourth Gospel eschatology. Lodewijk van Hartingsveld, *Die Eschatologie des Johannesevangeliums* (Assen: Van Gorcum, 1962), 154, claims that affirmations of realized eschatology are possible only on grounds of affirmations of final eschatol-ogy. Joseph Blank, *Krisis* (Freiburg: Lambertus Verlag, 1964), 353, asserts just the opposite: without an eschatological presence there is no eschatological future. There seems no point in trying to merge these two views. Rather, we must see that in the Fourth Gospel they complement each other.

7. Jürgen Moltmann, *Theology of Hope* (London: SCM Press, 1967), 92.

As soon as the issue of eschatology has been put on this level, the nature of history itself becomes clearer. History is not primarily a matter of recollection in turning to the past in faith, or of turning to the future in hope, but of God's liberation breaking into the present through the coming of Jesus Christ. History is thus always created by what opens man up in giving him freedom.

The problem of eschatology, while not solved in the Fourth Gospel, is focused on the anthropological issue of man's inability to appreciate either God's presence or God's future. Already early in our readings we were compelled to stress man's self-deception, his blindness to the reality of God. It is not that man cannot grasp God because full liberation has not as yet occurred; rather he does not care for God's liberation in the first place. So the lack of appreciation for both present and future liberation brings man under judgment. He does not acknowledge God from whatever angle he is approached by him — be it the present or the future. The rejection of eschatological truth makes man all the more inexcusable in terms of the Fourth Gospel.

God's Unconcealment

The debate on revelation in twentieth-century Protestant theology has been confounded by the fact that revelation was understood as disclosure of something that is hidden not only in fact but also in principle. As we have seen, however, God is not hidden in principle. And in fact he is hidden only because man blinds himself to him. It is man's sin that hides God. The presence and future of God always reach man. The real trouble is that man does not acknowledge it.

"Seeing God" is nonetheless a possibility of liberation. From God's side nothing stands in the way of seeing him. But only the one who with his entire being responds to God's unconcealment really sees him. This total response took place in the man called Jesus. And through him also the disciple can see God. But it is a mediated "seeing": "Anyone who has seen me has seen the Father" (John 14:9). The disciple shares in Jesus' seeing of God. It remains for the disciple a seeing "in part," focused in the liberation Christ brings.

So it should be clear why we cannot accept the way in which the problem of revelation has been formulated in twentieth-century Protestant theology. Jesus Christ is not God's act of self-revelation, but the acknowledgment of his unconcealment. God working together with the man who acknowledges his openness to his creation labors toward a fuller opening up of the world to its destiny. Man is now able to see himself in a new way. He can understand life more fully. He can walk toward the openness of God. But this is merely the effect of the acknowledgment of God's openness in Jesus Christ and need not be called an act of revelation.[8]

---

8. Long after the idea of God's unconcealment was formed in my thought I encountered an observation of Daniel Callahan in "The Relational Nature of Theology," *Frontline Theology*, ed. Dean Peerman (Richmond: John Knox Press, 1967), 169: "I am increasingly skeptical of any talk of a 'hidden God.' To put it more precisely I am doubtful that Christians can continue to have their God a hidden God and yet at the same time continue to talk about him as if he were quite visible....I am

In terms of the Fourth Gospel, God is the light that illumines man's darkness. He always reaches into man's experience and struggles with him in judgment and grace. Nevertheless, although man may be *aware* of the presence of the light, he may not understand it at all.

So we must try to grasp the reality of God where it is first of all acknowledged: in the life, death, and resurrection of Jesus Christ. Here we learn that God is not found where we might expect him, in the temple, in the sanctuary, or in the pious conventicle, but where the pain is: in audacious suffering in the battle for survival.

Even where man only raises the question of survival is God at work. It is in view of this *awareness* that the theological enterprise begins to make sense. It is merely an awareness, however, not a preunderstanding.

God's unconcealment is most "obvious" where it is not obvious at all in terms of the criteria of greatness and power. The discovery of the presence of God where the pain is, is impressed on us by the biblical story. And yet it is not at all easy to acknowledge that this is the case. It is even more difficult to find its truth in concrete contemporary situations. The scales covering our eyes as regards the biblical witness persist also as regards God's unconcealment in our historical experience.

Political Theology as New Interpretive Focus

We said in the Introduction that our interpretation of the Fourth Gospel would offer a response to the emerging political theology of our day. We now need to address this point more fully. It is a complex task to describe how theology originates in a particular historical experience. It is never a matter of sheer repetition of biblical ideas. The work of theology is always at least bifocal. Besides the biblical matrix as a focus there is also the focus of the contemporary situation. While the past cannot be changed the present still is changing, and changing swiftly. The unchanging gospel must always be translated into the changing present. Here a major aspect of the interpretive or hermeneutical problem emerges.

The contemporary situation is so multifaceted, vast, and complex that it is impossible for theology to address itself to it as a whole. A choice has to be made as to where the focus of the theological work actually is found. In a sense, the choice is being made for us by the situation itself. Of course, an individual theologian may decide that he wants to concern himself with a particular facet of the contemporary situation that personally interests him. But he can do so only at his own peril. The result may turn out to be very privatistic. What the

---

actively exploring the plausible hypothesis that the whole concept represents the Christian's special way of coping with the threat which the patent absence of a personal revelation from God normally poses. How much better, as a psychological device, to posit a hidden God (which is compatible with any facts at all) than to do away with belief altogether." On account of a similar argument, on the basis of the Fourth Gospel, I arrived at the idea of God's *unconcealment*. We must give up the idea of a *principally* hidden God.

theologian needs to do if he wants to be responsible is to discover where the church is already being touched by the cutting edge of life.

It appears that in the American church today the focus is more and more on the political dilemmas in which we find ourselves, the hurt inflicted in the power struggle over public issues and in the exploitation bolstered by political power. Why are people still in bondage? What is the church still contributing to man's unfreedom? Where is the church itself in bondage? These are questions impressed upon theology by the church, whether theology likes it or not.[9]

In response to these queries, political theology is emerging as a new interpretive focus, a center around which a new theological understanding is gradually being developed. By interpretive focus we do not mean an interpretive or hermeneutical principle which would inform much of theological construction as a consciously accepted hypothesis determining the shape of theological enterprise as a whole, so that issues of a political nature would become dominant *in principle*. And we certainly do not mean by interpretive focus *the* hermeneutical norm that would determine the actual *content* of the developing theology. There is a measure of disagreement on these points in theological circles today. Some regard political theology as having already attained the status of an interpretive principle and some would even wish to use it as the interpretive or hermeneutical norm. We want to indicate that while in our perspective the whole enterprise of political theology in America is still in a somewhat amorphous stage, it has at least attained the status of a prelude as regards the total theological enterprise. It is unmistakable that the questions of political power, group loyalty, or national prestige are strongly influencing the basic quality of church life today. So we wish to speak of an interpretive focus.

The worst thing that could now happen would be that political theology were understood as invitation to developing a Christian ideology for this or that political task. What political theology can help us to understand is why religious people still exploit their neighbor. We must see ourselves time and again in the mirror of the Christ-event, so that we realize how much we continue to conceal ourselves. The shaping of an ideology would probably afford us a new opportunity for hiding behind a front. Much of our exploitation of the neighbor is due to our placing between ourselves and him an ideology according to which we want to mold him. Ideology continues exploitation because it does not let us see the neighbor as he is. It approaches him in terms of what he is expected to be in our utopistic schemes. It is especially the idea of revolution today that dare not again become the beginning of a new Christian ideology. What it can do is to provide a master image for the change that is the fabric of modern life. We must be open for this change. But the liberation to openness does not basically originate in revolution. It springs from the encounter with the open man. Only in

---

9. I have tried to give a fuller account of these questions in "Political Theology," *Christian Century* (July 23, 1969): 975–78, and in "The Political Gospel," *Christian Century* (November 1, 1970): 1380–83 (included in this volume as chapter 8). See also my essay "Political Theology in the American Context," *Theological Markings* 1, no. 1 (Spring 1971): 28–42.

openness to oneself and the other as first acknowledged by Jesus Christ can we hope to participate creatively in the so-called revolutionary processes shaping modern man.

Liberation Theology

The discoveries we made in the biblical matrix of thought have influenced our concern for political theology as new interpretive focus. And the concern for political theology triggered new questions addressed to the biblical matrix of thought. It was in this context of reflection on theological principles that we developed our readings as an outline of Christian theology. Political theology as new interpretive focus was constantly present in our deliberations. We concentrated especially on the freedom-bondage syndrome in contemporary American experience.

Within the structures of our society we not only become interdependent as human beings, but also interfere with one another immediately curtailing one another's freedom. Throughout the past decade many have tried to alleviate the interference. The civil rights struggle was by and large one great effort by many well-meaning people to make room for freedom so that everyone would have enough space to be human. But in the process events occurred that pulled us only deeper into the mire of hate or mutual interference. The more we tried to improve, the more difficult relationships became. The gargantuan idealism of Christians who understood themselves as servant church ended up in the stark realism of the militant church, the *ecclesia militans:* the church in conflict with itself.

So, running through the present conflict in society and church there is an increased yearning for liberation, for being freed from interfering with one another, from being master and slave. The yearning is expressed in many ways, by young and old, by people in all walks of life. It has been beautifully expressed by Felix Cavaliere in a lyric, widely known through a recording by the Fifth Dimension, where he observes how men everywhere just want to be free. This yearning is not at all a merely selfish thing. It is not just freedom *from*, it is also freedom *for.* It is often quite clearly understood in terms of the coinherence of all men, a hope for a time when in the whole land no man is living in pain. But when will there be such a time? So concomitant with the increased yearning for liberation comes the realization, at least for some, that liberation is not our thing. We can do various things to overcome certain aspects of the captivity in which all of us are caught. We can put new laws on the books. We can put up new buildings for the poor. But the spiral of dissatisfaction seems to grow with every new law and every new building. Why? We never rest satisfied with our best accomplishments because we want perfection. "Man's reach is always beyond his grasp" (Reinhold Niebuhr).

The importance of liberation theology on the very primal level lies in its new stress on the difference between the perfect and the sinful, the absolute and the finite. The major impression one often gets from recent American theology is that we humans are expected to play God. It is supposed to be *our* task to revolutionize society, to reform the church, and to renew the mind. As a consequence, we are more and more bereft of the basic Christian experience: that man can only live by grace. From the perspective of the Fourth Gospel, the basic human disease is for man to think that he must carry the world on his shoulders and must heal himself.

Once we grasp the basic Christian experience we will also see that it does not leave us paralyzed, but enables us to become agents of liberation in the world. It will always issue, however, in contingent balances of power, relative improvement, finite progress. A grasp of our limitations will make us all the more willing to risk everything in making life more human — after receiving the power of liberation. We do not wish to downgrade the concrete possibilities of liberation, but would like to make its dynamics unmistakably clear so that true liberation can occur.

Lerone Bennett, Jr., states the concrete issues of liberation quite succinctly: "A philosophy of liberation requires a frank appraisal of the institutions and policies of the white communities. A philosophy of liberation also requires an advance program of economic democracy. Racial integration requires economic integration. And this, in turn, requires a recognition that the race problem cannot be solved without profound structural modifications in 'America,' without real changes in the tax structure and the relations between the public and private sectors, without redefinition of all values and a redistribution of income and power." All these things also become the concern of a new liberation theology. In fact, they are already the concern of the churches, as a recent report of the United Church of Christ indicates: "The theme of 'liberation' is appropriate for the United Church of Christ in its attack on white racism in the 1970s. As a predominantly white denomination in the United States, we need to be aware that as white Christians we are a double minority in terms of the world's population. The vast economic and military power in the hands of this 'white minority' constitutes a serious 'minority' problem for the world's peoples. 'Liberation' from the burdens of excessive power is also a demand upon white church members to disassemble those racist institutions they cannot change and to redirect their resources to support the oppressed peoples of the Third World." Theology's task is to articulate what the dynamics of liberation are. It is not that we are discovering a theme for the church. But we are trying to state in what way it can function effectively. The next step will be to show how liberation theology offers specific suggestions for the solution of our political dilemmas.

Initially, however, liberation theology is interested in radically witnessing to the power of liberation, the grounds on which the goals of liberation can be tackled sanely, with a measure of effectiveness. This calls for stressing the core point of the Fourth Gospel once more: *we* cannot generate the power of liberation — God liberates.

– 13 –

THEOLOGY AT THE CROSSROADS

This essay grows out of a set of dialogues with black theology that began in the early seventies. Herzog was a key figure in bringing together white and black theologians, encounters which later included Europeans as well. This issue of the Union Seminary Quarterly Review *is dedicated to such a dialogue. The participants are James H. Cone, C. Eric Lincoln, Herbert O. Edwards, Paul L. Lehmann, Helmut Gollwitzer, and Frederick Herzog. The fact that all essays appeared also in German in the journal* Evangelische Theologie *shows the international significance of these conversations.*[1] *Herzog functioned as "mediator," and most of the translations into German and English were done by him. Later Cone would talk about this symposium as "the most significant conversation between White and Black theologians to appear in print."*[2]

What brings theology to the crossroads is an insight into the difference of God and the powers that be, and a glimpse of God's own "poverty in Christ." Mainline theology must rethink its position in light of the challenge of the oppressed. This challenge cannot be settled by merely entering into a theological dialogue with various theologies of liberation. Mainline theology needs to learn how to think through its own relationship with the oppressed in past and present. Cone's work is addressed as an example of how theology is already taking the oppressed seriously. The specific references are to James H. Cone, "Black Theology on Revolution, Violence, and Reconciliation," included in the same volume of the Union Seminary Quarterly Review. *Herzog's own observations add another aspect to the challenge, reminding us that, since oppression is a complex phenomenon, liberation along the lines of race is incomplete without liberation along the lines of class.*

Why should whites listen to black theology? The primary issue is not dialogue but the underdog. We whites need to get away from the idea that by all means

First published in *Union Seminary Quarterly Review* 31, no. 1 (Fall 1975): 59–68.

1. *Evangelische Theologie* 34, no. 1 (January–February 1974).

2. James Cone, *Black Theology: A Documentary History, 1966–1979* (Maryknoll, N.Y.: Orbis Books, 1979), 139.

we must talk to black theology. In awareness of the underdog we need to address white theology first. Black theology makes us aware of the underdog as the relevant orientation point of theology.

This does not mean that we should not stay in contact with one another, not critique each other's position, or not "check in" with one another as to our several purposes and goals. But for the time being at least the primary task for white theologians is the examination of the white theological past — in regard to the underdog. Whose servant has theology been in the United States? The servant of the Lord of the Church? Or the servant of the almighty dollar? Some forty years ago John Dewey scanned the American scene and observed: "Nowhere in the world at any time has religion been so thoroughly respectable as with us, and so nearly totally disconnected from life.... The glorification of religion as setting the final approval on pecuniary success, and supplying the active motive to more energetic struggle for such success, and the adoption by the churches of the latest devices of the movies and the advertisers, approach too close to the obscene."[3] Only a few clear-sighted Americans discerned the signs of the times. When theologians were among them, did they think of changing the theological hermeneutic on account of it? Is it not fair to say that until the appearance of black theology there was no American theology related to the underdog? Some will protest that the Social Gospel was an exception. But it was not really a theology. It did not bring its insights effectively to bear on a change of theological outlook.[4] By the time Paul Tillich began to publish his theological system the mood again was such that the underdog had no chance for an input into the ground rules of the system. Friedrich Schelling had much more to say in Tillich's system than any poverty-stricken black or Indian.

Paul Tillich is representative of what continued to happen in the United States during the past two decades in Protestant theology. In fact, in many ways he became its twentieth-century lawgiver. It was he who laid the ground rules of the basic approach. His continuing influence is a matter of record.[5] Protestant theology in America today stands at the crossroads of the decision whether or not to continue the approach represented by Tillich.

The Gospel and Counterfeit Christianity

Will theology persist in turning to the creative self-interpretation of man in culture or will the social self-contradiction of the church be its major concern? It is black theology that reveals the crossroads at which theology now stands.

---

3. John Dewey, *Individualism Old and New* (New York: Capricorn Books, 1962), 14.

4. The most known effort in Social Gospel theology is Walter Rauschenbusch, *A Theology for the Social Gospel* (New York: Macmillan, 1918). The "fathers" to whom Rauschenbusch appeals are the great liberal theologians Friedrich Schleiermacher, Albrecht Ritschl, and Richard Rothe. Not one move was made by Rauschenbusch to show that these men had not at all taken the radically social problems into account.

5. For example, in a work such as that of John Macquarrie, *Principles of Christian Theology* (New York: Scribner, 1966). The basic philosophical theology approach is here retained.

Protestant theology in the United States has let its starting point be too much
determined by the needs of the modern mind, neglecting the needs of the underdog. The dilemma is brought forcefully to the fore in James H. Cone's article.
There is first of all the historical fact of counterfeit Christianity which we have
failed to relate to the premises of theology.

> It is unfortunate that Christianity did not offer a serious challenge to modern
> slavery in Europe and America. Calvinism seemed especially suited for America
> with its easy affinity for capitalism and slavery. While John Wesley, the founder of
> Methodism, did not endorse slavery, he appeared to be more concerned about a
> warm heart than an enslaved body. And his evangelist friend, George Whitefield,
> publicly defended the slave institution in Georgia. It is a sad fact that Protestants
> not only bolstered slavery but many actually encouraged it. (6)[6]

Since it is difficult to pinpoint the basic callousness to slavery in all Protestants, it is revealing to focus on the *leading exponents* of the Christian tradition
who acted representatively. "For the most part, the chief exponents of the Christian tradition have been identified primarily with the structures of power and
only secondarily with the victims of power" (7). While there have been exceptions to the rule (for example, the Quakers), white Christians usually did not
come to understand the *basic dynamics of the Christian life* in regard to the underdog. "White Christians in America tend to think of 'love' as an absence of
power and 'reconciliation' as being indifferent to justice" (7). Thus a counterfeit
Christianity has resulted in which the holistic grip of Christ on man is rejected.
This happens as a matter of course as Christ is being acculturated. One way
of stating the acculturation is saying that Christ is white. There is the untruth
of "the unverbalized white assumption that Christ is white" (9). Anyone who
thinks that this is not a problem, let him take note, for example, of a Christmas
hymn still found in a hymnal:

> Softly to the little stable
> Softly for a moment come;
> Look and see how charming is Jesus,
> How he is white, his cheeks are rosy....[7]

Counterfeit Christianity in the church is not a far-fetched matter, but white
theologians in regard to the organization of the theological materials are hardly
bothered by it. The Tillichian question-answer scheme would have to be given
up, and the immediate significance of the modern mind would have to be rejected. Apologetic theology as a program would have to be scuttled. "Theology
formulates the questions implied in human existence, and theology formulates
the answers implied in divine self-manifestation under the guidance of the questions implied in human existence."[8] The pressure black theology puts on the

6. Page references to Professor Cone's essay will appear in parentheses throughout this response.
7. In a hymnal of the United Church of Christ, *Pilgrim Hymnal* (Boston: Pilgrim Press, 1966), 124.
8. Paul Tillich, *Systematic Theology* (Chicago: University of Chicago Press, 1951), 1:61.

church and theology as a whole proves of primary importance in regard to *the question the theological subject matter puts to us.* It may as well be that the questions we formulate in our existence are so limited that we immediately screen out radical questions that might turn our existence around. Why should theology always be a matter of middle-class anxiety answered by revelation? It is one thing to predicate theology on the statement: "I am anxious. What's the answer?" It is another thing to base theology on God's question: "Your neighbor is oppressed. What is your responsibility?" It is crucial to discover God's poverty in Christ: "Foxes have holes, and birds of the air have nests; but the Son of man has nowhere to lay his head" (Matt. 8:20). What does it mean that this Son of man asks us to repent and to believe in the gospel? He calls us to consider life from a perspective completely different from our everyday view. It immediately implies identification with him who did not determine his answers by the existential questions of man, but by God's claim, therein showing complete solidarity with the poor.

Slavery, exploitation of black labor, the creation of a labor pool from underprivileged minorities — all these things have been and are still being justified by appeal to a God of love who apparently does not care for justice.[9] No claims can be made that an appeal to the God of justice will make the world perfect in a jiffy. The basic issue is whether we still acknowledge God as God and his claim upon our lives. Whatever Cone's theology does for blacks, it makes it inescapable for white theology again to ask the question of its starting point. Theology again is compelled to think from the subject matter toward the contemporary situation and let the subject matter determine the basic theme of its inquiry. Thus the gospel confronts counterfeit Christianity, which is not so much the rejection of pure doctrine as the negation of the life that embodies Christ in the world in liberating the oppressed.

Theology and Ideology

The issue of doctrine today in regard to the Christian life is not that of pure teaching but that of ideological "malpractice." In what way does the teaching undergird societal values? Cone explains: "Because black liberation is the point of departure of black theology's analysis of the gospel of Jesus, it cannot accept a view of reconciliation based on white values" (13). American Protestant theology has not made the question of the influence of white values on the content of theology a significant query. This is partly due to its immediate flights into the ultimate. Tillich again can be viewed as representative: "Theology should never leave the situation of ultimate concern and try to play a role within the arena of preliminary concerns."[10] Obviously theology should not try to become kingmaker in politics or write Ann Landers columns. But the demand that theology

---

9. Cf. Herbert O. Edwards's article, p. 25 of this issue (*Union Seminary Quarterly Review* 31, no. 1 [Fall 1975]).

10. Tillich, *Systematic Theology*, 12.

should not play a role in the arena of preliminary concerns does not mean that it should not be challenged by preliminary concerns. The basic model of theology is still the academy with its rarefied air of debate for its own sake so that theology becomes semiphilosophy. The basic rhythm of thought in operation here is "theology *and philosophy.*" If one now turns to "theology and black theology" as a more basic model, preliminary concerns of the oppressed begin to question the abstract elevation of ultimate concern to the position of priority.

It may well be that ideological distortions hide themselves under the umbrella of ultimate concern, making the theological enterprise a tool of white values from the outset. It is exactly this kind of reflection, however, that does not enter into the definition of the theological premises. Karl Marx and Friedrich Engels wrote in *The German Ideology:*

> In every epoch the ideas of the ruling classes are the ruling ideas, that is, the class that is the ruling *material* power of society is at the same time its ruling *intellectual* power. The class having the means of material production has also control over the means of intellectual production, so that it also controls, generally speaking, the ideas of those who lack the means of intellectual production.[11]

Tillich was quite aware of the Marxist critique,[12] but he did not apply it to the premises of theology. One need not, as Tillich intimates, attempt to preserve evils on grounds of a theoretical justification. One need only to *close one's eyes* to existing evils and keep one's theological constructs aloof from the victims of evil. The present problem of United States Protestant theology is its unwitting participation in the ideas of the ruling class.

The way out is taking concrete human beings more seriously. The needs of the oppressed appear as the propelling challenge of theological thought as truly as the Lord of the church identified with them. It is not necessary to move into the black community in order to make all this real. Rosemary Ruether writes:

> The white liberal comes of age in the black community when he learns how he can be of genuine service ... when he overcomes paternalistic and sycophantic relations to black people.... The white person comes to the point where he can realistically and sympathetically recognize the faults of black people without this either reinforcing his superiority complex or "shattering his idealism." Rather, he dedicates himself all the more to the welfare of the black community, in understanding of — and solidarity with — its great wounds. Therefore he begins to become human in the black community and to be of service to human life there.[13]

It is a moving statement. And yet one gets the impression that reconciliation is again defined in white terms: after the lesson of Black Power has been learned, communication between blacks and whites might be established again. Then once more we might be able to talk to each other.

---

11. Lloyd D. Easton and Kurt H. Guddat, eds., *Writings of the Young Marx on Philosophy and Society* (Garden City, N.Y.: Doubleday, 1967), 438.

12. Tillich, *Systematic Theology*, 92.

13. Rosemary Ruether, *Liberation Theology* (New York: Paulist Press, 1972), 141f.

The matter is not that easily tackled because we whites have a scale of values which is very much unchanged in its core, for example, in regard to John Dewey's point of pecuniary success. Along with it goes the whole scheme of competition and individualism that is still the hallmark of capitalist society. Status and prestige are still the aspirations of competing individuals. It may well be that through whites working in black communities these patterns will change among these whites and the blacks they come in contact with. But the white society still remains intact. The white working in the black community cannot help ultimately reaching for the integration of the black community into the white system, especially if once more coming to speaking terms is stressed. And the white system is not changed or challenged at all.

The task is not so much working *in* the black community as changing the values of the white community. For example, changing the value of power. Solidarity with the oppressed in the battle for survival means changing the white value scale, countering "the glorification of religion as setting the final approval on pecuniary success" (John Dewey). But this is a complex task that pertains to changing the whole value system of white society.

Theology cannot begin with ultimate concern in the abstract. From the very beginning it needs to take the ideological distortion of the Christian faith into account in which the needs of suffering persons have been disregarded. The pain of the oppressed belongs to the starting point of theology. Ultimate concern without concern for this pain is always an escape mechanism. The concern syndrome has to be changed from ultimate concerns to bodily concern as the starting point of theology. Marx and Engels need to be mentioned once more:

> In direct contrast to German philosophy, which descends from heaven to earth, here one ascends from earth to heaven. In other words, to arrive at man in the flesh, one does not set out from what men say, imagine or conceive, nor from man as he is described, thought about, imagined, or conceived. Rather one sets out from real, active men and their actual life-process and demonstrates the development of ideological reflexes and echoes of that process.[14]

Authority and Norm

A yet larger issue looms on the horizon. It may seem a good idea to eliminate the oppressor ideology from theology. But why should this be so? Why should we not let the oppressed fend for themselves? What gives us the sense of obligation to get involved *here* rather than somewhere else? So the issue of *authority* injects itself inescapably. This is also the case in the issues Cone poses in this regard: "To understand the Christian view of reconciliation and its relation to black liberation, it is necessary to focus on the Bible. Here reconciliation is connected

---

14. Easton and Guddat, *Writings of the Young Marx on Philosophy and Society,* 414.

with divine liberation. According to the Bible, reconciliation is what God does for enslaved man who was unable to break the chains of slavery" (13). The whole force of the question of Christian authority hits us once more. It is obviously not a matter of calling attention again to verbal inspiration or some obsolete view of authority. The issue is more primal: what is the character of the originative events that bring the Christian worddeed and deedword into being? As we all know, these events appear to us only in the form of the biblical words. So we are drawn to their convicting power. It so happens that these words reach us in the church — in its several traditions. And in the church we are compelled to give reasons for the convincements of the biblical words.

The situation created by black theology in regard to the Bible is "abnormal" in at least two respects. (1) In recent memory the biblical word has not been appealed to in the mainstream of American Protestant churches as a significant orientation point in the adjudication of disputes over the shape of the Christian life. (2) There is a principal openness in black theology to acknowledge a court of appeal that transcends personal religious preferences.

On these premises one can well imagine readers finding James Cone's essay wanting on a number of points — wanting from the white perspective that has used the Bible to its advantage time and again.[15] One does not have to be a coward, however, if one forgoes pointing out inadequacies in the black use of the Bible. All one has to do is to wonder about one's own theological decency: in what way is white theology at all willing to acknowledge the same authority as black theology? This is what we need to focus on in the white camp. It is in confrontation with the originative events of the Christian faith through the biblical word that one senses the obligation to the oppressed. I know, others find other reasons for their sense of obligation. But we are not these persons of other faiths. We are white churchfolk. The biblical word convicts us of one thing: there by the grace of God go I. The other is part of my self. I am still concealed to myself because I do not see the other.

Appeal to the biblical word is constructive in Rosemary Ruether's recent reflection on black theology. It is from this center of her argument that her contribution receives its strength:

> An authentic black theology of liberation...would be a demand for order over against systematized disorder and an affirmation of the humanity of all men as the context for affirming black humanity. Such a black universality would not be abstract. It would take black humanity as the particular which it celebrates as the concrete place where the universal is being realized. This particularity would not contradict its universality, but could draw on the other side of Biblical theology; namely, its contextualism. Biblical theology is universal, but never abstract.[16]

---

15. H. Shelton Smith, *In His Image, But...* (Durham: Duke University Press, 1972), brings one example after the other of the white misuse of the Bible in regard to the black, beginning with slavery up to the twentieth century.

16. Ruether, *Liberation Theology*, 130f.

However, is not the move to the universal barred by the biblical story? Is it not rather that concrete blackness and concrete whiteness are called before the judgment bar of God's incarnation without universalizing human beings? "Participation of the individual in the universal"[17] is the Enlightenment stance (on which we still depend), but not the biblical view. We need not repeat Marx's critique of Feuerbach in our generation.[18] We should have learned from the civil rights struggle of the sixties not to repeat Feuerbach's mistake. The Bible demands that the particular be taken seriously. Nothing is gained if once more we make the particular subject to the universal — "the concrete place where the universal is being realized" (Ruether). For Cone the problem is that blackness is the place where whites usually see no concrete humanity whatsoever, only janitorhood, maidhood, shoeshineboyhood, garbagemanhood. Ralph Ellison's *Invisible Man* is pertinent here.[19] The biblical word invites us to take seriously the concrete encounter, the boy born blind, the man thirty-eight years sick, Lazarus. Universality antecedently conceived seems always to result in covering up the individual person with his or her particular needs. Unless we "see" the concrete black we shall not see any manhood or womanhood at all.

This brings us to a radically new appreciation of the norm of theology. Norm is not the same as authority. It is the biblical word that brings our Christian thought into being and thus proves itself authoritative. What is normative for us, however, depends not only on the biblical text. The context in which we live is also important. As long as we see the context in relation to universal man our norm will tend to bank on universals. Paul Tillich, for example, banked on the German philosophical universal of Being, so that his norm became the new being in Jesus as the Christ. But seeing an individual person, one black person, in a new way would mean that we have already begun to see Jesus Christ in a new way, as liberator of this particular person, and because of our encounter with him in regard to this individual, also as our own liberator, so that freedom would be gifted to us. *New freedom in Jesus as liberator* functions as norm where the other is really seen as one particular person. And talk about universals ceases. We become concerned about changing our inner eyes, so that we can finally see a human being as a person. Said an invisible man: "That invisibility to which I refer occurs because of a peculiar disposition of the eyes of those with whom I come in contact. A matter of the construction of their *inner* eyes, those eyes with which they look through their physical eyes upon reality" (Ralph Ellison).[20] What is called for in white theology is the change of the inner eyes, in other words, an altering of consciousness.

---

17. Claude Welch, *Protestant Thought in the Nineteenth Century* (New Haven: Yale University Press, 1972), 53.

18. Easton and Guddat, *Writings of the Young Marx on Philosophy and Society*, 400ff.

19. Ralph Ellison, *Invisible Man* (New York: Random House, 1953).

20. Ibid., 7.

Black Theology and the Black Bourgeoisie

The neat separation between black and white theological responsibilities breaks down at the point where the black liberation struggle issues once more in the bourgeois captivity whites have been caught in all along in this country. Cone writes: "To be reconciled with white people means destroying their oppressive power, reducing them to the human level and thereby putting them on equal footing with other humans" (14). Theoretically, this is fine. But what does it practically look like? It has proved possible in the United States for the black to chip off a piece of the white power rock. Some blacks *have* put their oppressors on an equal footing. *But what does equal footing mean in this society?* Can we afford to overlook or not mention its *concrete socioeconomic dimensions?* Does the black become less a capitalist than the one he puts down?

Black theology makes us aware of the underdog, we said. But what does it do when the underdog becomes merely a moneymaker in the well-established business society?

Take, for example, the recent resignation of Ralph Abernathy as head of the Southern Christian Leadership Conference (now superseded by his reappointment). His complaint was that many black people who now hold positions of black power made possible through the struggles of the Southern Christian Leadership Conference "will not support it financially and make it possible for this organization to meet its obligations and commitments." He pointed to the black middle class who have meanwhile "turned a deaf ear to our call."[21] I am not attempting to imply that Abernathy's problem is *also* a white problem. Blacks will have to come to grips with these recent developments themselves. What hits blacks and whites alike, however, is the reality of the business society values in the United States which can make one feel like having arrived after having put down the fellowman. Can Cone understand that his argument breaks down for me at the point of reconciliation because he has no image of the human being to offer other than the bourgeois? Is not the black who gains power *in the capitalist system* bound to be a bourgeois and not just an equal citizen? Now that the influence of Black Power has peaked, the anguish of some young blacks in this regard is understandable: "It raises all the issues that many thought were long put to rest with the manifestation of the Black Power movement, i.e., the problem of individualism and indifference toward the plight of the black masses."[22] In what sense can Cone's theology today still identify with the plight of the black masses? In what way does the sharecropper or the garbage collector appear for him as a concrete identification point in the actual theological *practice* of liberation?

Over a decade ago E. Franklin Frazier wrote his book *Black Bourgeoisie: The Rise of a New Middle Class.* One of his conclusions was that "the black bourgeoisie has failed to play the role of a responsible elite in the Negro commu-

---

21. *Durham Morning Herald*, July 10, 1973.
22. George Napper, *Blacker than Thou: The Struggle for Campus Unity* (Grand Rapids, Mich.: Eerdmans, 1973), 116f.

nity."[23] Does Cone provide us with an alternative to Frazier's black bourgeoisie? The American tragedy is more horrifying than what usually meets the eye. Freed from slavery, the black in a business society seemed to know only one possibility of being a human being: the bourgeois.[24] Without a new image of man, what else can there be but the further display of the black bourgeois competing with the white bourgeois — possibly now under the aegis of Black Power with a smattering of violence, which is indeed as American as cherry pie? Does violence need justification in a capitalist society? The big fish always eat the little fish. Christian rhetoric is superfluous as the halo of any carnage. Let us just admit what we are made to be: cutthroat capitalists.

Without a new image of man, can there be reconciliation? Can there ever be reconciliation between bourgeois and bourgeois? And in order for a new image of being human to arise, do we not need a new order of society? I know, Jesus Christ *is* the new man. But in our cutthroat system there is no place for him. Do we therefore not need to consider an alternative system? What about socialism in America?[25] I do not expect a black theologian to quote Karl Marx on every page, but should what he represents not be considered as equal in importance as the cherry pie of American violence? Without economic and political change, what hope is there for Cone's reconciliation?

The problem is in part that revolutions always resulted in something different from what one initially hoped for. "Hidden in the *citoyen* of the French Revolution was the *bourgeois*. God have mercy on us as to what hides in the comrade!"[26] Who is hidden in the Black Power advocate? Again the black bourgeois.

Protestant theology in the United States stands at the crossroads. It is compelled to decide between continuing to sanction the old image of a human being as bourgeois and finding a new image grounded in the originative events of the Christian faith, an image that includes the oppressed.

In closing, four brief questions:

---

23. E. Franklin Frazier, *Black Bourgeoisie* (New York: Macmillan, 1957), 235.

24. Joachim Schwelien, "Schwarz und Reich," *Zeitmagazin* (June 8, 1973): 6–10.

25. As an American alternative, see Michael Harrington, *Socialism* (New York: Bantam Books, 1972).

26. Ernst Bloch, *Spuren* (Frankfurt: Suhrkamp Verlag, 1959), 30. Since the initial drafting of my article goes back several years, it seems indicated that *Union Seminary Quarterly Review* readers hear part of the story that goes along with it. German interest in getting a better handle on black theology through publications goes back to a course I taught at the University of Tübingen in 1970. During that time I also contributed the introduction and epilogue to the German translation of James H. Cone's *Black Theology and Black Power*. There were publications on the general issues of Black Power available in the German, for example, Volkhard Brandes and Joyce Burke, *USA — Vom Rassenkampf zum Klassenkampf* (Munich: Deutscher Taschenbuch Verlag, 1970). But there was nothing dealing with the theology of the blacks. One caveat needs to be added. Obviously publication of these essays does not mean that we have solved the horror of *racism in theology*. What we wanted to do was to face it finally. For our 1971 meeting in New York I wrote a paper, unpublished thus far. The final sentences read as follows: "It is impossible to redress the sins of the past. But we can work for not committing new sins in the present. One important step in this regard is the attempt to come clean in theology *as to the terms which compel us today as blacks and whites to go our separate ways*, in the hope that someday they will converge." That's still the stark realism of the situation for me also in 1975. And yet just because of facing the separateness — things look different.

1. What keeps black theology from being ultimately only one more notch up the totem pole of the black bourgeoisie?

2. What keeps black theology from producing merely more black capitalists?

3. What is black theology's new image of man that liberates blacks from money-making (Frazier) as the supreme human value?

4. Could black theology consider socialism as alternative to the present American system?

– 14 –

LIBERATION THEOLOGY
OR CULTURE-RELIGION?

In the North American context liberation theology provides a first step beyond the bifurcation of mainline theology into two camps, one liberal and the other conservative. This bifurcation is also reflected in the ongoing opposition of two civil or "culture" religions that clash at present in the religious manifestations of what we now call the "culture wars." While some of the positions of those camps as described by Herzog may have shifted in the past twenty-five years (conservative religion has become more politically active and liberals see themselves as being more on the defensive), our need for alternatives is greater than ever.[1] The self-serving character of those tensions is largely due to the fact that both camps operate in the context of the powers that be.

A theological alternative needs to work through the limitations of the contemporary scene. Herzog finds that in the context of new encounters with the invisible human other and the divine Other in Christ as portrayed in the Bible, the "vertical" and "horizontal" elements of theology can be pieced together in new ways. In Herzog's own words, "Liberation theology in the South requests: let us see what happens if on grounds of the biblical Word we radically bring theology in confrontation with the concrete sufferer, the concrete oppressed."

We shall begin with the fact that the same word, or the same concept in most cases, means very different things when used by differently situated persons.

—KARL MANNHEIM[2]

The mood of the community generally was one of piety.... In my case, and in the case of thousands of other Southerners, it was an experience which went well beyond my life upon the immediate plantation where I grew up and the church I attended. It was, in addition, an experience with a system of society, a plantation

First published in *Union Seminary Quarterly Review* 29, nos. 3–4 (Spring–Summer 1974): 233–44.

1. In later years Herzog and John B. Cobb, Jr., one of the theologians addressed in this essay, began to interact more constructively in the search for alternatives. For Cobb's account see John B. Cobb, Jr., "Liberation Theology and the Global Economy," in *Liberating the Future: God, Mammon, and Theology*, ed. Joerg Rieger (Minneapolis: Fortress Press, 1998), 127–42.

2. Karl Mannheim, *Ideology and Utopia*, trans. Louis Wirth and Edward Shils (London: Kegan Paul, Trench, Trubner, 1960), 245.

system, including all the institutions in that system. In it I was located and knew who I was supposed to be and what I was expected to do and to think.

—Edgar T. Thompson[3]

For good or for ill, the term "liberation theology" has entered the forum of theological debate in the United States.[4] One of the first things of which we need to be aware in order to employ it adequately is the recent turning from "universalizing" theologies.[5] For centuries theologians lived in the realm of abstract ideation. In the formulation of the hermeneutical premises of theology, the concrete pain and hurt of suffering humankind went begging. Liberation theology means "the times, they are a-changin'." It also means that in the church no one is going to do your theology for you. There is no way that what happens, for example, in Latin America could somehow suffice for doing significant theology in North Carolina or Georgia.

> The success enjoyed by Latin American theology in the West worries some of its representatives, men like Hugo Assmann and Paulo Freire. They believe we are witnessing a "mythification" of the Latin American situation. Thus in Europe the word liberation covers anything you like to think of, whereas in reality throughout history it has been the instrument of a struggle.[6]

"Liberation theology" does not necessarily mean the same thing in Latin America as it does in the South of the United States. Everything goes wrong if one thinks of it as a "movement" and fails to see the locally grown theologies dealing with locally different idiosyncrasies of liberation.[7]

Liberation theology in the South began with the frightful awakening that man's religious story seemed much more important than the Christian story.[8] Taking one's own religious pulse seemed more exciting than listening to the

---

3. Edgar T. Thompson, "God and the Southern Plantation System," in *Religion and the Solid South*, ed. Samuel S. Hill, Jr. (Nashville: Abingdon Press, 1972), 59.

4. Martin E. Marty, *Context* (January 15, 1974): 5. Richard J. Neuhaus, "Liberation Theology and the Captives of Jesus," *Worldview* 16, no. 6 (June 1973): 41, claims that Gustavo Gutiérrez is widely credited with coining the term "liberation theology." The fact is that several liberation theologies have existed for a good while, not side by side, but in several contexts. If one wants to talk about liberation theology in Latin America one would do well to specify in terms of Latin America. See the excellent essay by Phillip E. Berryman, "Latin American Liberation Theology," *Theological Studies* 34, no. 3 (September 1973): 357–95. See also Thomas G. Sanders, "The Theology of Liberation: Christian Utopianism"; Rubem A. Alves, "Christian Realism: Ideology of the Establishment"; and Archie LeMone, "When Traditional Theology Meets Black and Liberation Theology," all published in *Christianity and Crisis* 33, no. 15 (September 17, 1973). The continuation of the discussion appeared as "Liberation Theology and Christian Realism," *Christianity and Crisis* 33, no. 17 (October 15, 1973): 196–206. For recent observations on liberation theology in the U.S., see my "Liberation Theology Begins at Home," *Christianity and Crisis*, and "The Liberation of White Theology," *Christian Century*, both to be published sometime this spring, 1974.

5. David Jenkins, "Man's Inhumanity to Man," *Ecumenical Review* 25, no. 1 (January 1973): 5–28.

6. Marnie Mellblom, "Media Roundup," *Risk* 9, 2 (1973): 9.

7. For a discussion of liberation theology in the South, see *Duke Divinity School Review* 38, no. 3 (Fall 1973): 126–70. For liberation theology of the women's movement, see Rosemary Ruether, *Liberation Theology* (New York: Paulist Press, 1972).

8. Recent emphases on the "theology of story" are nothing new for southern sensibility.

pulse-beat of society. There can be no doubt that in the Bible Belt the Bible is read more than in any other part of the country. But for what reason? To acknowledge the Holy? Or to increase mystification? It stands to reason that where so much "Bible" and "back to the Bible" are emphasized, some get fed up with the Scriptures. As a southern UCC minister declared recently, "For my money, the Bible should be shelved and not be used in the pulpit. Period." He did not want to "preach from the Bible" anymore.

This situation seemed to be an issue of the standing and falling of the church, *stantis et cadentis ecclesiae*. It demanded taking a fresh look at the biblical word. Was the Bible really nothing more than a fundamentalist textbook? Was it little more than religious literature, as the liberal theologian seemed to think? What was especially dumbfounding was that the person of Jesus of Nazareth had become so silent in the church. Often it seemed the preacher was producing himself, sharing his private opinions, telling the people how he had felt during the week, rather than sharing God's Word. A sea of subjectivism was engulfing us.

What was more, society seemed a frightening maze of misplaced aspirations, misguided efforts, mislocated ideals. On campuses, everyone was trying to explain it in terms of alienation. But it actually seemed more like concealment. Ralph Ellison's *Invisible Man* had a true word to say. There were garbage collectors. But who knew their faces? There were janitors and maids. But who knew their names? That's the way Ralph Ellison had seen it:

> I am an invisible man... I am invisible, understand, simply because people refuse to see me.... Nor is my invisibility exactly a matter of a biochemical accident to my epidermis. That invisibility to which I refer occurs because of a peculiar disposition of the eyes of those with whom I come in contact. A matter of the construction in their *inner* eyes, those eyes with which they look through their physical eyes upon reality.[9]

As I began to discover how deeply we all are involved in this concealment, I began to take stock. It was not just a southern phenomenon. Charles A. Reich had observed it all over America: "We do not look at faces very often in America, even less than we look at ruined rivers and devastated hills."[10] I noticed, however, that this wide-reaching American experience could be gotten hold of *theologically* only in one's own setting. There were sharecroppers left unseen in the South. Blackness turned out to be the place where whites usually saw no concrete humanity, only sharecropperhood, janitorhood, maidhood, shoeshineboyhood, garbagemanhood. Not that whites acted *very* differently toward whites. That was part of the enigmatic dilemma. But in regard to the "inferior race," one could discover the real roots of the deception. That we all live concealed from one another in realms of mystification — the greatest of which is religion — is

---

9. Ralph Ellison, *Invisible Man* (New York: Random House, 1960), 7.
10. Charles A. Reich, *The Greening of America* (New York: Random House, 1971), 165.

due to our unwillingness to see *one* oppressed person as person. We are so callous toward one another even among peers because we are so callous toward the lowliest of people and their pain.

Can anyone be faulted if he concludes that a radical rupture with all this is necessary?[11] In sheer subjectivism there can be no genuine communion with the transcendent. In atomistic privacy there can be no genuine communion with the neighbor. This is not just an anthropological dilemma. For theology, it is a christological one. The bearing of the incarnation is forgotten. So it seems that complete restructuring of theology is called for, orienting it radically in the concrete — where theology functions as praxiology.

Southern Culture-Religion

At the center of the essay lies the hypothesis that *without careful analysis of our regional dilemmas in church and theology we will not make headway with the renewal of the church hoped for and prayed for on all sides.* At this time, it is the small negative concrete that hinders theology's progress in the South. It is "the little foxes that spoil the vineyards" (Song of Solomon 2:15). Samuel S. Hill, Jr., in *Religion and the Solid South,* has done a pioneer job of helping us to understand where we are in this regard. He contends that the South when it comes to religion is still in "a self-conscious and publicly identifiable culture."[12] It is essentially a qualitative reality, not just a matter of geography. Southern theology departs from the overall American theology pattern "in that it does not feature worship and incarnation in preference to sin and crucifixion. On the contrary, southern preaching and teaching are centered in the themes of man's depravity, Christ's atoning death, and the assurance of salvation." Disengagement from secular matters in the interest of minding one's own business is important. And yet there is concern for such public issues as the control of liquor or the use of drugs. But

---

11. See the stress in literature on the radical rupture with the Western tradition; for example, W. M. Frohock, "The Revolt of Ezra Pound," in *Ezra Pound,* ed. Walter Sutton (Englewood Cliffs, N.J.: Prentice-Hall, 1963), 93.

12. Hill, *Religion and the Solid South,* 17. In the following we will mainly use Hill's essay, "The South's Two Cultures," 24–56. At the point where we deviate from Hill's terminology, substituting culture-religion for culture-ethic, some might wonder why the term "civil religion" was not used. The reason is simply that this term has been abused so much in complete disregard of its author's intention that one should not add more insult to injury. See Robert N. Bellah, *Beyond Belief* (New York: Harper and Row, 1970), 168: "While some have argued that Christianity is the national faith and others that church and synagogue celebrate only the generalized religion of 'the American Way of Life,' few have realized that there actually exists alongside of and rather clearly differentiated from the churches an elaborate and well institutionalized civil religion in America. This article argues not only that there is such a thing, but also that this religion — or perhaps, this religious dimension — has its own seriousness and integrity and requires the same care in understanding that any other religion does.... It should be clear from the text that I conceive of the central tradition of the American civil religion not as a form of national self-worship but as the subordination of the nation to ethical principles that transcend it and in terms of which it should be judged." It should be clear from the foregoing that Bellah's civil religion is different from culture-religion as we will use the term.

the core effort focuses on the need for a culture-ethic, "a framework of meaning and order for fruitful life in society." Thus, southern religious leadership is hard at work "to establish orthodox religion as the basis for a culture-ethic."

The one modification of Hill's terminology I should like to introduce is the substitution of the term "culture-religion" for "culture-ethic." If the Christian religion as a whole is used to legitimate society the way Hill describes it, it does not merely give birth to a culture-ethic; it has itself been metamorphosed into a culture-religion. Wherever men try to "legitimate, consolidate, and perpetuate the secular culture" on grounds of religion, whether by means of conservative Protestantism or liberal Christianity, it is the Christian religion itself that becomes subservient to culture as a culture-religion. Hill himself says of southern orthodox Christianity that it is "the cultural system needed to tighten and sanctify culture" so that culture can be cast "in the mold of ultimate truth."

Significantly, Hill does not evade the "racial attitudes of the white South." Usually today the reaction to the racial issue is one of déjà vu, a big yawn: we've been through all this before, we've heard enough of it. One year of Watergate is enough! Ten years of civil rights struggle is enough! And yet the inescapable truth is that it has not been thought through enough. The *promise* of the dilemma has been slighted, that is, the real achievement that can still grow out of the pain, the tears, and the blood. This essay wishes to be understood as a contribution to the possibility implied in the promise, that is, that a new shape of theology might emerge from the pain and the stress.

The real difficulty is that the ethical and the religious have been so neatly separated that one often functions without the other. The root of this compartmentalization is the christological vacuum.

Hill makes the point that southern culture-religion has contributed to tightening the hold of racially biased convictions. "What seems to have happened is that religious assumptions deflected moral earnestness." This can be readily explicated:

> Southern churchmen have been taught that the high God of heaven, who is life's ineluctable reference point, issues a single directive to each person: find forgiveness for your personal sins. This being the divinely imposed, overriding obligation of mankind, consideration of the unloving character of relations between persons of distinct races, is bound to be depreciated, though not intentionally abrogated.[13]

Religion is here defined as status before a morally righteous God. Somehow Christ does not function very clearly in this relationship. Few questions are asked as to who Christ really is. Everything seems focused on the vertical. Christ is God's outstretched hand to the sinner, or the divine vessel through which God's love is poured out to man. *That Christ could also be the fundamentally new structure of human selfhood is not envisioned.*

This "accident" became possible since there was no clear christological reflection. So also any turn to moral earnestness, whenever it occurred, did not have

---

13. Hill, *Religion and the Solid South,* 33.

the *power* to prevail. Hill refers to the significant number of southern ministers who sought to affirm the unity of black and white under God, often at their own peril.

> Despite their courageous proclamation and example, when the evangelical concern shapes perceptions, this message is viewed as "tacked on," perhaps very important, but neither the central concern nor an organic by-product of the religious life. This is to say, the main practical impact of the churches' message does not penetrate the racial situation of the South.[14]

The term "tacked-on" is all-important. Christian activity in the racial situation that is not grounded in a new grasp of the selfhood of God in Christ can only appear as "tacked-on" activism. *What we need first of all is not a new socially oriented Christianity, a new Social Gospel for the South, but a new Christology that adequately expresses the corporate selfhood embodied in Jesus' life, death, and resurrection.* The point is that Jesus is not the Christ without the poor, the needy, the outcast, the oppressed. In facing him, we also face them, not just a lonely God. Where they are excluded we have a packaged Christ, made snugly to fit our ideology of the good life. The Forgiver-Christ is a kind of heavenly station conductor who lets the train of forgiveness run in and out, but who in no sense is determinative of the kind of cars that run on the tracks. Christ has been neutralized in much of southern theology. So there is a christological explication for the social concern being "tacked-on."

As active as the southern churchman may seem, his basic categories are associated with *being* rather than *doing*. Hill believes:

> The rhetoric of doing, so common to southern church life, is actually self-contradictory, since doing, according to this view, consists of *interior* states, resolutions, and convictions. Rhetoric notwithstanding, the principal mode of southern religious sensibilities is not operationally the moral — and no one supposes that it is the aesthetic. In the classical philosophical division, it must then be the ontological.[15]

This is a brilliant insight. It is exactly on this level that the christological foundation of theology operates. It is not that we must immediately try to get away from ontology. What is called for is a different ontology — what I have called the corporate selfhood of Christ.

Hill describes the ontological dilemma as delineated by a sense of interiority. The religious goes on inside a person. Hill thinks that interiority as such is bad. But what if the real problem were *false* interiority, a false consciousness? "The habit of mind which generates this form of consciousness emanates from a fundamental conviction that the locus of religious reality is 'heaven' or 'between heaven and earth' or 'the interior self.' "[16] Obviously it makes no sense for the Christian faith ultimately to separate the outer from the inner. But the point

---

14. Ibid., 33–34.
15. Ibid., 35.
16. Ibid.

that needs to be made here is that a sheer move from the interior self to some new perspective of "outer" activity will also seem "tacked-on" and be doomed to failure. At the core of a human being lies an "interior self" (Christ), different from the isolated atomistic religious self presupposed in much of southern religion. At this point the issue is joined. For *on a change in the "interior self" hinges the whole present-day debate of Protestant theology in the United States.*[17] Once there is a "private Christ" in the interior self all the distortions of the Christian faith become possible that change it into a culture-religion.

The rest of Hill's essay amplifies these distortions. The problem becomes, how can one belong to both the South and the church? "Potential conflict is aroused by the fact that the Christian Church demands a total loyalty, while the South as a cultural system presents itself as a nurturing and teaching agency lacking in self-critical powers. In very different ways both Christianity and Southernness lay exclusive claim upon white people of the region."[18] What, then, is the power that can wrench a person free from this conflict of loyalties? It is not an utterly inescapable conflict. For the loyalty demanded by culture is supported by a form of Christianity that need not exist. Without a measure of counterfeit Christianity, southern culture in its present form could not continue

Does Liberal Theology Provide an Alternative?

What I have tried to do thus far has been to offer a kind of phenomenology of the christological problem involved in southern culture-religion. It centers on *a struggle between faith and bad faith.* The irony of the situation is that the language used by southern culture-religion is not — on the surface at least — altogether "wrong." But it is crippled language. Important aspects of the Christian language are *repressed.* What we have here is a collective repression of highly important aspects of Christian truth. So even what is right in the use of Christian language in the South may often be doing the right thing, but for the wrong reasons. And that is often the greatest treason — doing the right thing for the wrong reason. The term "treason" here means betrayal of trust, breach of faith.

Is there a theology abroad in the land that can help us in this situation? What is still most alive in the Unites States is new natural theology. God is still taken seriously here, also in the South. Sometimes it seems that the new natural theologians are the only ones around still doing serious theology. Fortunately, we have a recent book where this theology is presented in summary fashion in

---

17. The idea of a need for such a change is nothing new. Even the Reformed tradition — my own — can speak of this change in quite explicit terms. See the *Heidelberg Catechism* (Philadelphia: United Church Press, 1962), 46. The catechism declares that by Christ's power "our old self is crucified."

18. Hill, *Religion and the Solid South,* 48. Hill speaks of the Social Gospel as not having made an impact on the South without indicating that the Social Gospel itself had no clear-cut Christology that might have changed the core of the theological difficulties shaping up in the South.

terms of liberal Christianity. It reaches in many ways also into the South. I am referring to John B. Cobb, Jr., *Liberal Christianity at the Crossroads.*[19]

We need to acknowledge that Cobb also sees the problem we are wrestling with in regard to the structure of selfhood:

> Christians today must face honestly this problem of the mutually isolating character of selfhood. We cannot solve it simply by reemphasizing our traditional teaching. We must incorporate that teaching but we must also go beyond it. Love can show us the way. Empathy and *agapē* both challenge the final separateness of my self from other selves. If my feelings are shaped by empathy for others, then I receive their feelings into my experience on the same basis that I relate to my own past.... I live from others and for others. But not only so. In a community of empathy and *agapē* others live from me and for me as well. We become Christs to one another. Obviously I am describing a state of affairs that is very distant from what we know. But we need such a vision in order to appraise what is now happening and to guide ourselves as Christians through the multiple possibilities now appearing for self-transformation and new types of relationship.[20]

This passage is key to understanding liberal Christianity as it seeks to launch out in new directions. Cobb does not intend to turn away from liberalism. He wants to improve it. In a sense, one could say that what Cobb presents is unreconstructed liberalism. But then, Cobb himself injects a caveat of his own: "I am personally troubled by the extent to which we [liberal Christians] have lost our centeredness in the gospel, but I remain quite sure that the gospel requires of us to be liberal."[21] What does "centeredness in the gospel" really mean, however? Is it not centeredness *in Jesus Christ*? One would expect so. But can a liberal understand what a radical concentration *on* Jesus Christ that requires? It is remarkable what a role grace plays in Cobb's book. One can only be grateful for the emphasis. Nevertheless, in the final analysis Cobb always turns to the thoughts of Alfred North Whitehead for his authority. To be sure, there is nothing wrong with Alfred North Whitehead. He is a great philosopher; one of the greatest. But when one wants to know how *grace* is really to be understood one learns: "The understanding of grace, which is the single most pervasive theme of these chapters, is derived from him."[22] From Whitehead! Cannot one at least begin by acknowledging the primary role *Jesus Christ* plays in the understanding of grace?

All the fine things Cobb says about the isolation of selfhood, etc., are ultimately non-christologically oriented. Cobb is "describing a state of affairs very distant from what we know."[23] But if we were to concentrate on the selfhood of Christ, would we not be describing something *very near* to us? In fact, the nearest the believer knows, his very existence *in Christ*? What is more, is *agapē* really something I *have* for others as for myself? Is not exactly the mystery of

---

19. John B. Cobb, Jr., *Liberal Christianity at the Crossroads* (Philadelphia: Westminster Press, 1973).
20. Ibid., 114f.
21. Ibid., 10.
22. Ibid.
23. Ibid., 115.

Christian existence that *I do not have agapē*, but that Christ has it *for me* and gives it *to me* as to others? This question lies at the center of the christological controversy today. The order of priorities is reversed in Cobb. The value scale appears upside down. It does not become clear in Cobb that acting in terms of *agapē* is basically impossible for man, unless he is reborn by the Spirit of God, i.e., unless a transplant takes place — which is that the selfhood of Christ is transplanted into him.

The whole problem really opens up as soon as we turn our attention to the oppressed. Empathy? That is what Cobb wants. And at one point, he even presses toward solidarity. But it is *general* human solidarity, "our solidarity with one another in both good and evil."[24] If one asks about the oppressed they seem to appear on one level with the "white supremacists" — as a special interest group.[25] So Cobb might be moved by the story of the oppressed as he might be moved by the story of the KKK? I wonder. The conclusion is not surprising: "As liberal Christians we distance ourselves critically from all of them."[26] Which side is Cobb on? Only his own? So it seems. But the issue is to be *where Christ* is. As God in the flesh, was he not moved by the people mangled on the wheel of history so as to make their lot his own? For those into whom his self had been transplanted, is it possible to be anywhere else than where he is?

Before we "uncover and articulate our own inchoate story,"[27] we need to un-cover and articulate *his* story. If we but knew the difference! The whole point is that we need to start with the reasons for his story. Albert Schweitzer, in *The Quest of the Historical Jesus*, speaks of the immeasurably great man whose man-gled body still hangs on the wheel of history which is rolling on. His mangled body hangs there because of the mangled bodies of countless others with whom he came to show solidarity. He was mangled, not because of a freak of history, but because of his free choice to be in solidarity with the mangled. It is this mangled body, and the reasons for it, which need to be the starting point of Christology.

There is a very good insight early in Cobb's book: "The past two decades have forced us to re-view our history. We must see it through the eyes of Indians and blacks and Orientals and Mexicans, and it is transformed into a story of greed and exploitation, racism and nationalism, all papered-over with a transparently hypocritical rhetoric."[28] But this good insight remains christologically unrelated. It does not function as a center. What I miss is a clear grasp of grace in the corporate selfhood of Jesus most concretely embodied in the mangled body on the wheel of history on which he shares the lot of countless lost. The white heat of this grace I miss in Cobb.

---

24. Ibid.
25. Ibid., 30.
26. Ibid.
27. Ibid., 31.
28. Ibid., 18.

Is liberal theology not one and the same as culture-religion? The major point of Cobb's book is that liberal Christians should articulate their own story. The insight is there that we live in a "time of spiritual poverty."[29] So the question is understandable whether or not we could "also develop life-styles that would give more satisfaction to people while reducing consumption."[30] And Cobb keeps insisting that we act "zestfully for justice."[31] What remains to be seen is how this is to be done. There is the comment at one point: "We should indeed be mindful of those who are less fortunate, but that has its own dangers."[32] Then there is also the injunction: "Christianity cannot share in belittling the value of wealth, sex, and success. Christians think of the world as creation.... The Christian cannot be indifferent to worldly goods. He is instead grateful for them."[33] Somehow one thinks that through Jesus Christ one would be able to see "the less fortunate" related to the issue of "worldly goods." But Jesus appears mainly as a "disturbing figure"[34] with an "unsatiable demand," on the one hand, and a forgiving power, on the other.[35] At no point does he function in terms of corporate selfhood. The comment of Albert Schweitzer finally comes to mind: "There was a danger that modern theology for the sake of peace, would deny the world-negation in the sayings of Jesus, with which Protestantism was out of sympathy, and thus unstring the bow and make Protestantism a mere sociological instead of a religious force."[36]

On this level we need to look carefully at what Cobb offers in regard to worship. In a strange way, he is caught up mainly in the horizontal dimension:

> Our worship has tended to desexualize us. We can rejoice to see the return of the dance and the physical embrace to our services, but that alone does not suffice.... Traditional worship focuses on our relation to God and to our neighbor in such a way as to obscure our kinship with animal and plant life.... We must learn this as a new lesson in our own context of beliefs and understanding of man.[37]

But if anything is missing in many of our present worship services it is a grasp not of the horizontal but of the vertical dimension. What is so disturbingly absent is the experience of Sacredness — and thus, of Reverence for life. For Christian experience this can best be learned in contemplation of the "Sacred Head, now wounded, with grief and shame weighed down." It becomes a question of who has the power to force us down on our knees as far as worship is concerned. The involvement of God in history on the cross, in the life, death, and resurrection of Jesus Christ creates the intellectual drama for us that compels us to fall down

---

29. Ibid., 93.
30. Ibid., 103.
31. Ibid., 99.
32. Ibid., 60.
33. Ibid., 61.
34. Ibid., 37.
35. Ibid., 40.
36. Albert Schweitzer, *The Quest of the Historical Jesus* (New York: Macmillan, 1948), 402.
37. Cobb, *Liberal Christianity at the Crossroads,* 36.

on our knees because it is more than mind-boggling. It is awesome. It sweeps us off our feet into the posture of true prayer: "Who has known the mind of the Lord, or who has been his counselor?" (Rom. 11:34).

Theology between the Potomac and the Rio Grande

In the fifties, we spoke of piety at the Potomac. What is worse, though, is that theology often ends at the Potomac — for the Yankees in the theology centers of the North and Midwest. And we in the South often act as though we would have to accept the Yankee judgment. Liberal theology, dominant in other parts of the country, does not offer any alternative for what we are up against between the Potomac and the Rio Grande. One need not be a southern chauvinist in theology to observe that liberal theology is as crippled in the vertical dimension of the faith as southern culture-religion is crippled in the horizontal dimension. Obviously the handicap in the one dimension also reflects itself in the other. Southern culture-religion will also not grasp the dimension of true Sacredness in the "Sacred Head, now wounded." The last thing I would like to have understood would be that we in the South already have an answer on all the issues raised earlier. In one context Cobb remarks: "On this point I dare say that Christianity has the answer."[38] In this regard today we in the South have to say that we do not know of any answers. But we have some questions.

The major question is that of the role which Jesus Christ plays in the shaping of theology. The point is to realize how imprecise is the use of some of the language that is being heard in the church and how easily it can become deceptive. "We become Christs to one another," says Cobb at one point.[39] This sounds like Martin Luther. But what did Luther say?

> First, let us contemplate the inner man, to see how a righteous, free, and pious Christian, that is, a spiritual, new, and inner man, becomes what he is....One thing and only one thing is necessary for Christian life, righteousness, and freedom. That one thing is the most holy Word of God, the Gospel of Christ....Let us then consider it certain and firmly established that the soul can do without anything except the Word of God, and that where the Word of God is missing there is no help at all for the soul....You may ask, 'What then is the Word of God, and how shall it be used, since there are so many words of God?' I answer: The Apostle explains this in Romans 1. The Word is the gospel of God concerning his Son, who was made flesh, suffered, rose from the dead, and was glorified through the Spirit who sanctifies...so that if you believe in him, you may through this faith become a new man.[40]

It needs to be made clear that nothing of these dynamics of Luther in principle appears in Cobb. The whole issue of the priority of the ministry of the

---

38. Ibid., 80.
39. Ibid., 115.
40. Martin Luther, *Treatise on Christian Liberty* in *Luther's Works* 31, ed. Harold J. Grimm (Philadelphia: Muhlenberg Press, 1957), 344–47.

Word is brushed aside in liberal theology. Luther says: "Nor was Christ sent into the world for any other ministry except that of the Word. Moreover, the entire spiritual estate — all the apostles, bishops, and priests — has been called and instituted only for the ministry of the Word."[41] The concentration on the priority of Christ as embodiment of God and the new man is central in Reformation thought.

Missing in Luther is an arguing-through of the new selfhood in Christ, so that in principle becoming a Christ to the other, on Luther's terms, at least seems to imply a charitable condescension of the one who "has" to the one who "has not." Without taking into account that the one who "has not" is actually — through Christ — already constituted as the one "who has" and is part of our very selfhood, we misconstrue the reality of Jesus' own selfhood. But this shall not deter us from making use of Luther's principal insight. He at least showed the way wherein the dynamics of the new selfhood are to be found. This is what is crucially absent in liberal theology, even with all the new emphasis on grace in Cobb.

What is missing in southern culture-religion is a clear grasp of the sovereign power of the Word. God's Word seems in the control of mankind, so that it says what the religious person wants it to say. So southern culture-religion and liberal theology both become a barrier to truth in the church. They keep the people from entering God's kingdom: "Woe to you lawyers! For you have taken away the key of knowledge; you did not enter yourselves, and you hindered those who were entering" (Luke 11:52). My explanation of it all is that there never has been a radical break in the South between "old Massa's"[42] theology, plantation theology,[43] and what we have today. But without a radical rupture we will not understand ourselves theologically in the new days into which we have entered in the culture as a whole. Theology in the South, in some of its most visceral orientations, is still very much nineteenth-century, pre–Civil War theology.[44] It is only now with men like Sam Hill that a radical break between pre–Civil War days and the post–Civil War era is looming on the horizon.

The basic issue is that we have to begin all over again with the Bible. Question: If others identify their theological problems within the framework of the new Bible of Whitehead or Martin Heidegger, why should we be scolded for turning to the Bible in order to identify the crucial theological dilemmas of our region? Why should it be wrong to be working toward modeling theology on the gospel history rather than on the method of correlation (liberal theology) or the orthodox creeds (southern culture-religion)?[45] And why should we

---

41. Ibid., 346.

42. The expression "old Massa" is well-known from the song "Carry Me Back to Old Virginny."

43. Thompson, "God and the Southern Plantation System," *Religion and the Solid South*, makes a clear point about plantation theology.

44. For the account of the lack of a break in southern theology see H. Shelton Smith, *In His Image, But...* (Durham: Duke University Press, 1972).

45. My book *Liberation Theology: Liberation in the Light of the Fourth Gospel* (New York: Seabury

not begin in the Bible with Jesus' identification with the "invisible man" (Ralph Ellison)?

Liberation theology in the South requests that we see what happens if on grounds of the biblical Word we radically begin theology in confrontation with the concrete sufferer, the concrete oppressed. This stress on the concrete accounts also for the differences in the particular orientation of the several liberation theologies. We have to talk in each case about the concrete setting. This then leads to new christological struggles. The basic issue for the South turns out to be one of Christology. In an earlier reflection on theology in the South I observed: "The peculiar burden of Southern theology is its struggle over the shape of the human self in racial confrontation."[46] This needs to be amplified now in christological reorientation. Basically we are involved in a christological struggle, perhaps in some respects as crucial as the struggle over Christology in the third, fourth, and fifth centuries.

The fundamental question that we are facing now is whether in the matrix of what we call the Christ-event, the personhood of Jesus of Nazareth, his life, death, and resurrection, there took place a radical *mutation* of human selfhood and thus of the human race, a change in human quality — and not just an incarnation of God. Was the human self constituted anew in this history as corporate self, so that also we are enabled to become a new self?

Why should one not mind one's own business? Why should Jesus of Nazareth get involved with lepers, lame, blind, poor, outcast? Why not stick to his business in the carpenter's shop? Why must he be about his Father's business? In 1850, Iveson L. Brookes of South Carolina declared: "Next to the gift of his Son to redeem the human race...God never displayed in more lofty sublimity his attributes, than in the institution of slavery."[47] This southern God has no place for a Christ in solidarity with the oppressed. As a consequence, the human self becomes a private self. It is always one atomistic little self pitted against another atomistic little self.[48] Today we are invited to learn again what it means for the constitution of human selfhood that St. Paul declares: "If any man is in Christ, he is a new creation" (2 Cor. 5:17).

Press, 1972) has triggered "wondrous" responses in this regard. One reaction is complete unbelief over the use of Scripture as "home" of theology — in the freedom of the Spirit. Apparently the only use for Scripture among some people is either slavishly to repeat the text or not to use it at all. But to use the gospel history as "home" of theological thought? Impossible. The ossification of American Protestant theology in these matters seems almost perfect. Any new venture is precluded by the agreed upon options.

46. "The Burden of Southern Theology: A Response," *Duke Divinity School Review* 38, no. 3 (Fall 1973): 152.

47. H. Shelton Smith, *In His Image, But...*, 145.

48. The social Darwinism that later gripped wide parts of the U.S. was well prepared in the South. There was no theological fuse that could have interrupted the currents of thought unleashed, for example, by William Graham Sumner (1840–1910). It is instructive to read H. Shelton Smith's *In His Image, But...* side by side with Sumner's *What Social Classes Owe to Each Other* (New York: Harper and Brothers, 1883).

15

LIBERATION THEOLOGY IN THE SOUTH

*A crucial step in the development of liberation theology is the genesis of libera-
tion communities which identify with the oppressed. Initially, liberation theology
develops in oral rather than written discourse. (For a reproduction of such a dialogue see, for instance, Perkins Journal, Summer 1976.) The following paper
also grows out of such a discourse. Written in collaboration with a group of
women and men, black and white, it briefly tells the story of the development of
liberation theology in the southern United States, and its different implications
for African Americans, white males, and — now explicitly included — women.*

*Liberation theology in North America is not the invention of great theological
minds or an import from south of the border. It is born among those who are
oppressed. One of the basic premises of the paper is the theme of Herzog's entire
work: liberation theology is not social ethics but theology, a new reflection about
God which includes life as a whole. In the confrontation with the oppressed,
theology encounters God's transcendence in new ways, not in "right angles to
history" but as a challenge of unjust structures.*[1]

It began with the black struggle — on the shores of Africa some four hundred
years ago.

Throughout centuries of slavery on U.S. shores blacks believed that through
Jesus Christ "their freedom would come in this world and their salvation in the
world to come" (William J. Walls).

To the extent that whites share in the liberation struggle in the South they
derive their vision from the black struggle finding its most recent expression in
the civil rights battles of the '50s and '60s. Some had participated in earlier dia-

---

Unpublished statement by Joseph B. Bethea, Helen Crotwell, Herbert O. Edwards, Nancy Ferree,
Lea Harper, Ruth Harper, Frederick Herzog, Archie Logan, C. G. Newsome, and Robert T. Osborn,
March 1976.

1. The reference to "right angles" appears to be a response to the critique of Herzog's contribution to the Theology in the Americas Conference where some participants felt that he was stressing
divine transcendence too much; see the report in Gregory Baum, "The Christian Left at Detroit,"
in *Theology in the Americas*, ed. Sergio Torres and John Eagleson (Maryknoll, N.Y.: Orbis Books,
1976), 418.

konia efforts of the church among the poor and oppressed. Many soon discerned, however, that the civil rights focus more radically engaged the root causes of poverty and oppression.

With the '70s a new era of the struggle began. Our groping toward clearer understanding found a new center. We had our first North Carolina conference on liberation theology in the fall of 1970, followed by a more intensive one in the spring of 1971, with blacks, women, and white males. We did not as yet fully know where we were going. But we were on our way.

At times we have been working separately, at times very much corporately. Apartness and community at the same time have put us in creative tensions with one another as well as in constructive unity.

For us, *liberation theology is born among the oppressed.* The premise of all our action, it grew out of radical reflection on the Bible with Jesus as *the* oppressed at the center identifying with other oppressed folk.

We do not romanticize the oppressed. All of us are finite and frail. But if the cries of the oppressed are silenced in theology, the stones will cry out.

Part of our growth process was the insight that liberation theology and social ethics are not one and the same. Much of what passes as "liberation theology" in this country thus far has been little more than Christian social ethics with a Marxist vocabulary. It is not theology. Writes Alice Hageman: "Liberation theology relies on Marxist methodology and concepts."[2] We object to totalitarian definitions. There is no one form of liberation theology. For us, liberation theology born of the suffering of the oppressed in the South is struggle with *theology*, Christology, and Christian anthropology — in concrete situations of oppression. In our situation theology instantly self-destructs when reduced to ethics. We do not deny the usefulness of Marxist analysis. But it cannot take the place of *theology*. Of the Detroit conference Alice Hageman claims: "The conference's prevailing terminology was Marxist."[3] Karl Marx, in our opinion, would have walked out of the conference, had he come at all. Too much mystification among some U.S. participants.

In the name of Karl Marx we protest whatever U.S. mixing of religion and Marxist analysis in the Detroit aftermath is being turned into dogma. At the same time we declare our solidarity with our Latin American sisters and brothers in their struggle for liberation. But because of the all-pervasive mixing of culture and religion in the South it would be courting disaster to counter it with a comparable mixture of culture-religion and Marxist analysis. It would bolster the socioeconomic oppression we are battling.

The liberation theology that has developed in the South, however tender the shoot, is now trying to forge ahead toward a hermeneutic of our North American reality. Unless we think historically, we will pontificate categorically. We need to

---

2. *Christian Century* (October 1, 1975): 851.
3. Ibid., 852.

reflect in terms of our southern story lest we force reality into straitjackets. In groping ways we are involved in separate struggles toward this hermeneutic. Yet we covenant to be accountable to God and one another.

As *blacks* we have a vital and abiding faith in the sovereign God. We recognize God as a source of our life and meaning. Our struggle for survival in America has often found us seeking and making allies. But we were often left behind when minute progress toward liberation in certain areas had been made.

We have devised methods of analysis and protest which have subsequently been adopted or co-opted by other oppressed groups. That experience gives us pause as we ponder alliances in the task of doing theology. We affirm our person-hood and therein our preordained oneness with humanity in corporate existence, though not in corporate experience.

We do acknowledge the universal commonality of our existential experience with those whose personhood, like ours, is denied by the forces of racism, sexism, classism, and economic exploitation. However, those who have not had limits placed on their humanity cannot share the experience of those whose humanity has been denied.

In a condition of oppression, we proclaim the activity of God in the liberation and salvation of ourselves and all oppressed persons to whom Jesus Christ has come as liberator.

As *white women* we are both the oppressed and the oppressor, while our black sisters are doubly oppressed.

Through the church, which continues the work of Jesus as liberator, we were made aware that God does not support any institution or system which places more value on one group of people than another. In fact, not only does God not support, but God seeks to break down these oppressions.

As southern women we were molded by our church which teaches the value of humility and self-giving and by our southern culture which idealizes the non-assertive woman who needs to be "taken care of."

Our role in history has been that "behind every great man there is a woman." We have told our story in relation to men. Until recently we were not aware of our foremothers and the battles they fought, for example, Elizabeth Cady Stan-ton's feminist critique of the Bible or Sojourner Truth from whom we hear the unity of the oppression of blacks and women.

In our work in the civil rights movement and the peace movement we became aware of being given menial tasks and being excluded from leadership positions in the movement. While we kept as top priority black liberation, we learned that we also had to work for our own liberation. While some of us have moved — or felt pushed — out of the church in this work, others of us are convinced that God's action is the liberating action. So we stay in the church where we trust that God will continue to use us as a liberating force.

The church has nurtured us. It is our faith in God's action on the side of the oppressed that sustains us.

We know the dangers we face: that we who are oppressed, in fighting for our liberation can become oppressors. Therefore, we work in close community with our brothers and sisters.

We also know, given our "molding," that we have to gain clarity and confidence in our ability to do theology and in our understanding of the critical issues we face. This means we still have to do some work separately, so that we can come to the larger context of dialogue as people who are able to share, to give, to listen, to correct, and be corrected. But even as we do this, we remain in dialogue with our brothers.

As *white males* we believe that God in Jesus Christ is the liberator, working for the liberation of the oppressed, and that apart from God's work our work is in vain. We learned this in the situation of the oppressed, who taught us anew who Jesus is. We are called in the Christian community to set the captives free. God's work is witnessed to by the Bible and only through its witness do we come to share responsibility in that work, destroying also the oppression we ourselves engender. What is more, there is enough oppression built into the theological systems we inherited that their restructuring alone will keep us occupied for a lifetime.

Our theological conflicts as *blacks, women,* and *white males* are grounded in social and political conflicts and are insoluble as theological conflicts until the underlying causes have been changed. We no longer make each other theologically responsible for our divisions in abstraction from our socioeconomic and sociopolitical divisions. We may not be able to write theologies together, but we can do theology together in creatively struggling with the causes of our conflicts.

However harsh these conflicts, we identify God's battle on the side of the oppressed through the biblical Word and not according to human whim or fancy. In the South we have learned that as Christians we cannot know liberation apart from God's struggle in the liberating Word for the recovery of which we also struggle.

It is exactly the recovery of the Bible as the empowerment of the just church that compels us to go through history as race, sex, and class conflict and thus to discover the unity of liberations. Here theology does not appear as an adjunct of liberation struggles in general, but as the praxis of God's liberation in global history.

The first result of the biblical recovery in the South is a new view of God's transcendence. This was also understood in Detroit. Writes Beverly Harrison: "Those Latin Americans who responded made it very clear that they would accept no paradigm of God's transcendence that did not emerge from the world-historical struggle for human freedom, nor any account of divine transcendence that dichotomized God's action and human historical agency."[4] We will not accept any paradigm of God's transcendence that does not acknowledge the transformation of transcendence in Jesus as the fusion of God's action and historical agency. We do not hold a vertical view of transcendence at right angles

---

4. *Christianity and Crisis* (October 27, 1975): 254.

to history. The controversy pertains to *two different views of historical transcendence*. We know, there are possibilities of ideological distortion in the biblical story. But the possibilities of ideological distortion are no less in any paradigm of God's transcendence growing out of the "world-historical struggle for freedom." In our struggle in the South we found the corporate discipline of the church in history an inescapable reality mediating to us God's historical transcendence. We are not accountable to every little god of culture-religion or civil religion. It is God in Jesus who inescapably confronts us among the oppressed. It is the God of Israel who confronts us with sacred justice.

The recovery of the just God of the Bible impels us to disciplined analysis of the socioeconomic and political causes of our conflicts. This comes down to hard-nosed study in economics and political science, in particular capitalism and socialism, but study in action/reflection appropriate to our North American reality. We are working for the realization of justice in a pluralism of races and creeds. We dare not fall prey to sibling rivalries in the church. There is a much wider picture. There will be no liberation without a new relationship also between Christian and Jew, and a reconciliation between the political owners of the land and the spiritual owner of the land, the Native American. Responsible for the overall oppression are the destructive dimensions of capitalism that themselves need to be destroyed. The poor of the global village point to us as co-responsible for their plight. While the struggle began on the shores of Africa some four hundred years ago, it all the same continues on the shores of America even some four hundred years to this day.

We are committed to God's liberation. The agenda of the '70s is the unfinished business of the '60s. Here we need staying power for years to come. Standing by each other in the freedom struggle of each, we battle together for the freedom of all.

16

ON LIBERATING LIBERATION THEOLOGY

Written as an introduction to the English translation of an important book by a Latin American liberation theologian, this essay begins with a comparison of theology in North and South. At a time when many of the ideas of Latin American liberation theology were being imported into North America with little consideration for the different challenges in each setting, Herzog is ahead of the game. The problem is that using the concerns of liberation theology in Latin America to dress up the position of liberal theology in the North will only end up reinforcing the powers that be.

This essay serves as a reminder, still highly relevant at the beginning of the new millennium, that theology can no longer be done in terms of the import and export of ideas, the way we often deal, for instance, with artifacts and styles from other parts of the world. Theology of the future needs to grow first of all out of encounters with God's own resistance to the pain and suffering of particular settings at home. Only on these grounds can we start to learn from each other, make use of differences in constructive ways, and thus develop new kinds of relationships across national and denominational barriers which allow for mutuality and self-critique. At this point the reality of double or even triple forms of oppression along the lines of race, gender, and class comes into focus. For Herzog's interest in socialism, see chapter 18 in this volume and my introduction to it.

Two recent books bring the continuing ferment in Latin American theology to the North American reader: José Míguez Bonino, *Doing Theology in a Revolutionary Situation*,[1] and now Hugo Assmann, *Theology for a Nomad Church*, one Protestant, the other Roman Catholic. After the appearance of the pioneer works in translation, we are here confronted with refinements and ramifications of the new approach.[2] This does not mean that the Assmann volume does not

First published as the introduction to Hugo Assmann, *Theology for a Nomad Church* (Maryknoll, N.Y.: Orbis Books, 1976), 1–23.

1. José Míguez Bonino, *Doing Theology in a Revolutionary Situation* (Philadelphia: Fortress Press, 1975).

2. Both Assmann and Míguez Bonino in one way or another appeal for foundational thought patterns to such works as Gustavo Gutiérrez, *A Theology of Liberation* (Maryknoll, N.Y.: Orbis Books,

present a theologian in his own right. It makes for rewarding reading because it confronts us forthrightly with the increasing complexity of the issues. The book is written in a direct either/or style, and the style is the man: Behind every sentence stands the person of whom Míguez Bonino writes: "Hugo Assmann is a Brazilian priest.... His participation in the struggle for liberation has successively forced him out of Brazil, Uruguay, Bolivia, and lately Chile. He now teaches at the Department of Ecumenical Studies of the University of San Jose (Costa Rica, C.A.)."[3] In several ways, the fortunes of some of the Latin American theologians remind one of the Reformation, when theologians existentially had to express a *theologia viatorum*, a pilgrim theology. Circumstances of politics force upon them a nomad existence.

In reflecting on a theological text from Latin America we need to keep in mind at least two things: (1) Middle America and South America are teeming not only with hungry peoples but also with torture chambers, concentration camps, and firing squads. In Chile alone, according to some figures, since September 11, 1973, 150,000 have been imprisoned and 20,000 have been killed. In Paraguayan villages where peasants have resorted to self-help in the face of hunger and starvation martial law has been declared in order to quell resistance. (2) Thus Christians in Latin America are living in an emergency situation. "Normalcy" as a way of life in U.S. cities, towns, and countryside is practically unknown to them. Whereas North American Protestant theology largely reflects middle-class normalcy, Latin American theology is confronted mainly with social abnormalcy.

Due to the increasing interdependence of peoples, the questions we face in theology are these: In what sense can we in the United States learn from sisters and brothers struggling in dire circumstances? Can we take over their theology? Or are they challenging us to develop a theology of our very own, yet true to their plight for which we, too, are accountable?

One major focus of this introduction — in trying to answer these questions — will be on the liberal approach in Protestant theology within the past hundred and fifty years in the United States. "Those who fail to comprehend their histories are doomed to reenact them" (George Santayana). What is more, the cancer in our liberal traditions sits deep. It is more than skin cancer. Unless we are willing to cut deep into our history, we will hardly bring about needed change. It is to be hoped that Roman Catholic readers will not be put off by the analysis of a Protestant struggle. What follows is largely an attempt to discover where we are in U.S. Protestant thought in regard to the issue of liberation as raised by *Theology for a Nomad Church*. I often think that Roman Catholicism in North America is only now arriving at a truly liberal stage. Protestantism might offer a

---

1973), and the five-volume *A Theology for Artisans of a New Humanity* by Juan Luis Segundo (Maryknoll, N.Y.: Orbis Books, 1974).

3. Míguez Bonino, *Doing Theology*, 83.

model of the dilemmas theological liberalism has produced. Learning from this model, none of us might want to reenact the mistakes of the past.

Theology South of the Border

Anyone who has spent some time delving into liberation theology materials from Latin America knows that something new is in the making. In one respect, the new is best understood as the determination of a few theologians to take their geographical limitations utterly seriously. What these few are about is a *theological hermeneutic for Latin America.* This is partly due to the realization that the European theology which for so long had informed Latin American theology no longer offers solutions to the new challenges emerging with the revolutions of rising expectations. A number of Latin American theologians have been trained in Europe. As a consequence, even those who have not been across the Atlantic have been influenced by their European-trained colleagues. That is to say, we should not be surprised that Assmann's book begins as a debate with European political theology.[4] But the Europe orientation often creates for us the first obstacle for getting "in" on Latin American theology. For a goodly while some of us in the United States have given up measuring our dilemmas by the criteria of European debates.

As soon, however, as one grasps the need for the Latins to cut the umbilical cord to Europe one finds an easy "in" on Assmann's theological argument. We are on the same channel, as it were. Going back at least as far as the Reformation, Assmann objects to a dualistic view of the relationship of church and world:

> Although the reformers talk much of the world and of service to the world, they are still working within a dualist framework.... This is a basic theological issue: the true unitary view of the world cannot see the Church as having a mission to build a separate history, but as the conscious emergence and most explicit living example of the one meaning of the one history. The Church...does not possess in itself (in sociological terms, in its intra-ecclesiastical structures) the point of reference needed to establish the criteria for redirecting its service to the world.[5]

It is especially the unitary view of history that distinguishes much of the theology of liberation as it emerged in Latin America beginning with the 1968 Medellín conference. Analysis of present reality and basic sources of faith now become intimately linked:

> This insistence on the links between analysis of underlying realities and the basic sources of faith is one of the main differences between the approach to theology in Latin America and in Europe. And that means a different approach to the nature of political theology.[6]

---

4. Ibid. Míguez Bonino states that Assmann served as assistant professor in Germany.
5. See Assmann, *Theology for a Nomad Church,* 36.
6. Ibid., 38.

What Assmann proposes as liberation theology, however, is not just a different approach to *political* theology as practiced by some Europeans, but to theology *itself*:

> It is...false to state that the whole biblical framework, with its infinite variety of paradigms and situations, is an adequate basis for establishing a satisfactory complex dialectics of hermeneutical principles. The theology of liberation sees itself as critical reflection on present historical practice in all its intensity and complexity. Its "text" is our situation, and our situation is our primary and basic reference point. The others — the Bible, tradition, the magisterium or teaching authority of the Church, history of dogma, and so on — even though they need to be worked out in contemporary practice, do not constitute a primary source of "truth-in-itself."[7]

So it is not surprising that in summary fashion Assmann can define liberation theology almost entirely in reference to the liberation struggle:

> The theology of liberation can become a permanent and indispensable critical adjunct to the struggle for liberation.[8]

Before one rushes into criticism one needs to keep the Latin American situation in mind: people in abject poverty, pressed against the wall, in prison, dying of hunger, shot to death. As we said, it is quite unlike what prevails on the North American continent. Who are we to tell Latin Americans how to run their theology? Problems arise at the point where the expectation is that the new hermeneutic developed in Latin America *can* be transcribed to North America, with no questions asked. The book itself does not present us with that inference, which is felicitous. One might say that Assmann going about his struggle in Latin America invites us to go about our struggle in North America. Obviously the few quotes do not adequately cover his position. And certainly not the perspectives of all Latin American liberation theologians. But they do give us an indication of what is new in the recent theological developments south of the border.

Theology North of the Border

What, then, can we derive from the new Latin American approach to theology as we go about our struggle north of the Rio Grande? Despite the many preconference disclaimers, the prevailing impression on most journalists of the August 1975 Detroit conference "Theology in the Americas: 1975" seems to have been that it was an attempt to import Latin American liberation theology into the United States: "Can liberation theology, primarily a Latin American phenomenon, be imported into the United States? This was to be the central question addressed by nearly two hundred persons who attended a six-day conference...which brought together for the first time the fathers of liberation

---

7. Ibid., 104
8. Ibid., 86.

theology and their North American disciples."[9] To put the question that bluntly shows with equal bluntness the profound ignorance surrounding the present U.S. discussion of liberation theology. A theology so radically seeking to tie herme-neutically into its own geography, how dare it be co-opted for a U.S. import? If for no other reason — and there are a goodly number of others — Latin Amer-ican liberation theology itself already stands in need of liberation: some North Americans packaging it as a consumer good are talking about it as an "import." The word itself reflects the prevailing consumer mentality north of the border.[10]

For any Protestant liberation theology in the U.S. it would be suicidal to ap-propriate the most distinctive feature of Latin American liberation theology, the unitary view of history. The thrust of Assmann's struggle for "one history" south of the border can only be applauded. But what may be good for theology south of the border may not be equally good north of the border. What may be liberating in Latin America may create further bondage in North America. U.S. Protes-tantism in crucial respects has long abandoned the dualist view of the reformers. The unitary view of history is initially a merely formal idea which can be given content any number of ways. In the United States it has unfortunately been filled with the covenant idea of the Puritans, America as God's chosen people, leading a straight line of self-interest logic to the notion of Manifest Destiny.

The "beastliness" of the American empire is partly due to blind Christian legitimation of American history, the *one* history of Manifest Destiny. This is something Latin Americans will want to take into account. We can agree with them on a unitary view of history defined *on God's terms*. Some of us, however, vehemently disagree with the unitary view of history defined on Uncle Sam's terms. That is, we cannot agree with an acculturated view of the one history of God. The U.S. Protestant has to undergo an altering of consciousness before he or she can grasp that the one history of God is not identical with the history of "God's own country." God in history is always the antagonist of the vainglorious one history we concoct as God's chosen people.

Recently Richard John Neuhaus has again confronted us with the dilemma. I refer to him because he is so keenly aware of the tension between history and transcendence. His premise is not that the United States is a religious culture ab ovo. It is rather that it ought to be such a culture today: "Some new legitimation must be found, if indeed there is legitimacy to American power."[11] Neuhaus finds much of the new legitimation in the old idea of God making a covenant with the creation: "The covenant relevant to America is but a specific instance of that covenant with the creation."[12] That point then is tied into the argument of the one history:

---

9. Thomas C. Fox, "Liberation Theology Tests U.S. Conscience," *National Catholic Reporter* (September 5, 1975): 1.

10. See Míguez Bonino, *Doing Theology*, xix.

11. Richard John Neuhaus, *Time toward Home* (New York: Seabury Press, 1975), 45.

12. Ibid., 47.

It is simply to say that I look for the vindication of myself in my historical particularity, and of the American experience of which I am a part.... All of history is
Heilsgeschichte, salvation history. All history is the history of redemption. There is
not a sacred history and then a secular history. There is one, universal history to
which God has irrevocably committed himself.[13]

Nazi Germany and Communist Russia present problems for Neuhaus, but not
insurmountable ones, he thinks. Both *deified* historical realities and thus seem
to fall outside the limitations Neuhaus thinks he has put on his scheme. But
Nazi Germany most surely pursued its self-deification on grounds of the history-
as-*Heilsgeschichte* thesis. As I see it, the real dilemma emerges when we do not
distinguish between the history we humans make and the reality of God as mover
of all history. While Neuhaus uses all the correct words, a language expansion
takes place that takes language to the breaking point and beyond it. An accident
happens; the language breaks to pieces. God is not committed to *all* history as
Heilsgeschichte.

Here we have a good Lutheran, Richard John Neuhaus. On Luther's terms,
however, the divine vindication has already happened — in cross and resurrection. We do not have to be worried about history having to be vindicated time
and again. There is a New Testament *ephapax,* the once-and-for-all act of God:
"The death he died to sin, once for all..." (Rom. 6:10; see Heb. 7:27 and 9:12).
Not all history is the history of redemption. Cross and resurrection see to that.
One might want to say that all our little histories are tied into the history of
redemption. But history is not *Heilsgeschichte.* We in the United States need a
radically critical distance from any view of history *as redemptive* so as not to fall
prey to "a doctrine of America's providential destiny to provide an example of
equality and democracy to redeem the entire world."[14]

We need to make a distinction between Christ and history and as a consequence honor an order of priorities which precludes labeling history in general
as redemptive. Neuhaus made a sterling record in the struggle of the sixties. For
many of us he was a bright beacon in the dark night of those turbulent days. It
is hard to grasp why he now considers it right to claim the American experience
as revelation. Is it not exactly in an arbitrary decision, such as that of Neuhaus,
identifying American experience and revelation, that God in Christ finally cannot help legitimating almost anything that might seem precious in our self-made
history? In any case, we need to remember that the identification of God with
history has time and again in the United States legitimated the doctrine of Manifest Destiny. But God in Christ came to exorcise the demonic claims that all
history is redemptive, in order to be able to redeem history in God's way. If we
do not begin with God's way, we probably will continue to redeem history our
way. A purely secular approach to history would simplify things considerably. But

---

13. Ibid., 64. It is quite clear to me that Neuhaus has some outstanding critical things to say about
American civil religion (188ff.). My argument here relates to the leverage we need in order to make
the critique stick irrevocably.

14. Robert Jewett, *The Captain America Complex* (Philadelphia: Westminster Press, 1973), 33.

here we are, confronted with the injection of the religion dimension. It always tempts us to absolutize our own involvement in history and thus to create the ideology that legitimates our way of life. God in Christ redeeming history is the counterpoint of all self-legitimation in history or outside of history.

Thus we arrive at a first principle for the Protestant hermeneutic of our North American reality:

> *Protestant theology needs to recover not the one history, but the one just God as the radical counterforce of all unjust history.*

The Bane of Theological Liberalism

The "religiosification" of the American Empire in one redemptive history is possible because of a theological cover-up. Partly responsible for the persistent cover-up is a theological liberalism that celebrates the unity of culture and religion. The United States has long been viewed as a predominantly Protestant country. The Protestant theologies that have become influential in the past two hundred years have not been able to develop a clear leverage for American self-critique. And in the twentieth century a theological liberalism has begun to reign supreme that by definition excludes the supremacy of any reality other than cultural experience.

This Protestant liberal approach goes back to the German theologian Friedrich Schleiermacher. North American theology never really understood what it was doing as it imported the Schleiermacher scheme to this continent. On the surface Schleiermacher seemed solidaristic,[15] and yet pervasive of the whole argument was his view of the theologian as virtuoso of religion, playing the score he himself has written. Bible, tradition, and the teaching authority of the church as well as the history of dogma no longer sufficed as primary sources of truth itself. They all had to be connected with the historical "now" of truth-in-religion.

What becomes determinative here of who God is in Jesus Christ is the immediate self-consciousness of cultural experience defined as feeling of absolute dependence. That is a cultural phenomenon yielding to culture and taking it at face value.[16] The ticket to the Christianity still acceptable among the "cultured despisers of religion" is the demonstration of personal religiosity. The cultural system itself is not questioned. How could it be questioned? The theology here projected is based on the very foundational premises of this culture. There is no vantage point external to culture that could offer critical leverage. So the major

---

15. Even Walter Rauschenbusch in the United States banked on that Schleiermacher concept without asking a principal critical question. See Walter Rauschenbusch, *A Theology for the Social Gospel* (New York: Macmillan, 1918), 27.

16. See Yorick Spiegel, *Theologie der bürgerlichen Gesellschaft: Sozialphilosophie und Glaubenslehre bei Friedrich Schleiermacher* (Munich: Chr. Kaiser, 1968). It is surprising that in the United States we have not paid more attention to the European reappraisal of Schleiermacher on grounds of sociology. This probably is partly due to the fact that Protestant theology in the United States is far behind the social sciences in its radical critique of liberalism.

work of Schleiermacher climaxes in a legitimation of bourgeois society. Reflecting on the ministry in relationship to the prophetic office of Christ of which the working of miracles was a part, Schleiermacher bluntly rejects the need of miracles today on grounds of the "miraculous" superiority of Western civilization:

> Even if it cannot be strictly proved that the Church's power of working miracles has died out (and this the Roman Catholic Church denies), yet in general it is undeniable that, in view of the great advantage in power and civilization which the Christian peoples possess over the non-Christian, almost without exception, the preachers of today do not need such signs.[17]

There could be no more devastating affirmation of the bourgeois system. Paul Tillich working a century later, with Karl Marx having interfered, knew well that things could not really continue unabashed.[18] And yet when he came to this country he made a strong point about continuing the work of Schleiermacher. While he had become critical of much of bourgeois theology, he had not changed its fundamental premises and outlook. All former authorities, Bible and tradition, were still to be connected with the historical "now" of truth-in-religion within this culture. Tillich's system thus was ultimately predicated on the viability of the present socioeconomic system. It does not begin with the need for revolution, i.e., the replacing of the present system with a different one. Over years of hard struggle it gradually dawned on me why it was impossible to use Tillich's theology (or any other theology falling into the pattern of his method) in the clash between black and white in the South. I could not forget the courage of his resistance in Hitler's Germany. He himself had become a victim of oppression. But with the publication of Hannah Tillich's *From Time to Time* (1973) I realized why Tillich's system was not really a radical attack on our dehumanizing social system: Tillich apparently often was able to compartmentalize his various interests. He apparently could "turn off" the economic, political, or social concern at will in certain contexts. It was not part of his lifeblood. Or so it seems. Therefore it is not surprising to read in him the expectation that "one of the great powers will develop into a world center, ruling the other nations through liberal methods and in democratic forms"![19] The best Tillich knows how to offer us here is development. One of the great world powers will *develop* into a center

---

17. Friedrich Schleiermacher, *The Christian Faith* (Edinburgh: T. & T. Clark, 1928), 450.

18. Especially Tillich's early work needs to be taken into account in this regard. See, for example, Paul Tillich, *Die sozialistische Entscheidung* (Offenbach a.M.: Bollwerk-Verlag, 1933). For the later Tillich, see his *Systematic Theology* (Chicago: University of Chicago Press, 1963), 3:343f., 388f. My problem is that Tillich's concern for revolution does not enter into his basic hermeneutical premises of the first volume of his *Systematic Theology*. Radical critiques of U.S. culture have occasionally arisen in Protestant theology. The early work of H. Richard Niebuhr is one such example. During the 1920s and early 1930s, he produced a series of articles sharply critical of the socioeconomic structure in the United States. Since Niebuhr's analysis of capitalism also included consideration of the Marxist communist alternative, his early articles merit reexamination in light of Marxist contributions to contemporary discussions of liberation theology (see especially "The Irreligion of Communist and Capitalist," *Christian Century* [October 29, 1930]).

19. Paul Tillich, *Love, Power, and Justice* (New York: Oxford University Press, 1954), 105.

of justice. A lot more would have to be said in order to offer an adequate picture of the assets as well as the liabilities of Tillich's work. One thing can be said with surety: Tillich did not offer us a revolutionary principle that would have radically questioned the bourgeois system in a theological way.

The strange circumstance now arises that Assmann's approach transcribed directly as applicable to our culture will be absorbed by liberal Protestantism as just one more *situational* theology. Assmann understands the situation in quite different terms. But the situation *as such* in liberal Protestant thought is also the reference point: "Its 'text' is our situation, and our situation is our primary and basic reference point."[20] It is exactly the situation (as understood by us) that has blinded us more and more to the dilemmas our nation as empire inflicts on other peoples. Situationally oriented bourgeois minds love new situational talk. So one can get involved in newfangled analysis. Twenty years ago we got enamored with analysis on the couch. Now it is analysis of poverty, but situational analysis all the same. The Latin American situation, for all I know, may well tolerate situation analysis. Our North American situation does not without first radically shifting the ground of the whole theological endeavor.

One has to be keenly sensitive to how things religious get co-opted in U.S. capitalism. Among us situation analysis can assimilate almost anything that comes along on the successive waves of U.S. fads. "Religion," Martin E. Marty has said, "in America seems to be a game played by innings."[21] To wit, the *New Theology* series begun in 1964 — by now how many volumes? One forgets to count. Social change theology was absorbed by the capitalist situation, the death-of-God theology was absorbed, so was the theology of revolution, the theology of the dance, and similar efforts. Now some of us are on to liberation theology. Will capitalism change in its assimilative capacity just because of a new label for a more radical theology?

We have to remain utterly critical and see that North America presents a temptation all by itself with the infinite absorptive capacity of capitalism. The Bible, tradition, the teaching authority of the church, history of dogma, and so on (Assmann) among mainline U.S. Protestants have been subject to extreme ridicule and rejection for years. Several years ago a minister of my denomination told me: "The Bible? We should take the book off the pulpit and shelve it." Capitalism can be so strong in this country because nearly every critical vantage point has either been co-opted or otherwise made innocuous. "Religion," someone from the South said recently, "that's God and the free enterprise system." In the United States we do not need to discover that Bible and tradition are not a primary source of truth itself unconnected with truth-in-action. Bible and tradition have already been dissolved into truth-in-capitalist-action. And everyone has become his or her own judge.

The whole biblical framework, as Assmann puts it, with its infinite variety

---

20. See Assmann, *Theology for a Nomad Church*, 104.
21. Martin E. Marty, *The Fire We Can Light* (Garden City, N.Y.: Doubleday, 1973), 87.

of paradigms and situations is of course *inadequate* for establishing a satisfactory complex dialectics of hermeneutical principles. But a few of us in North America have begun to read the Bible again as adequate for establishing one crucial vantage point outside the capitalist experience: the revolution of God in battling for justice. So the Bible is not a textbook of doctrine, as in neoorthodoxy, but a handbook of liberation (Ernst Bloch has also been talking along these lines). We need not fear for the unity of the biblical witness. "There is one body and one Spirit" (Eph. 4:4). The task of Protestant theology in the United States today is very much centered on the reorientation in the one Spirit who provides critical leverage from the outside in order to enable us to shift grounds radically in regard to capitalism.

Here we discover the second principle for the Protestant hermeneutic of our North American society:

> *For recovery of the one just God Protestant theology needs to rediscover the Bible as empowerment of the one body of the church with the one Spirit of freedom.*

The New Hermeneutic of our North American Reality

We would be presenting a false picture of the North American reality if we were to give the impression that all the work for a hermeneutic of this reality were still ahead of us. Much has already been done to make us aware of a new perspective. It is becoming more unfortunate every day that the "public myth" ignores the body of work already available. The August 1975 Detroit conference was no exception: "The conference revealed that North Americans do not yet agree on a single approach to an understanding of the social realities of the United States. Blacks spoke for a racist analysis, women spoke about sexism and others of economic imperialism."[22]

In some respects, of course, there can never be a uniform argument on the approach to the social realities of the United States. There will be no plebiscite with a 100 percent yes vote on this matter. But there are dominant configurations in our social life that are indicative of where we might be going in concert, at least in certain quarters. One can only hope that theologically the area of this country called the South will be taken more seriously in the future. For in the South a new hermeneutic of the North American reality had years ago already begun evincing a fairly coherent pattern to work with and to develop more broadly for the North American reality as a whole.

Nearly a decade ago Martin Luther King, Jr., wrote:

> The struggles of the past were not national in scope; they were Southern; they were specifically designed to change life in the South, and the principal role of the North was supportive. It would be a serious error to misconstrue the movement's

---

22. Fox, "Liberation Theology Tests U.S. Conscience," 4.

strategy by measuring Northern accomplishments when virtually all programs were applied in the South and sought remedies applicable solely to it.[23]

By the time of his death, King was trying to move "the movement" out of the South. The fact that he was assassinated before he could make good on his new goals does not undo his particular accomplishments with regard to a new hermeneutic of our North American reality in one area of our country. As to the further development of such a hermeneutic it becomes increasingly important that we do not wipe out the Martin Luther King decade from our memory. It is equally important to see that whatever we reflect on as liberation in this country has a direct relationship to the civil rights struggle in the South. Our hermeneutic cannot emerge without a historical memory.

Martin Luther King, Jr., was not able to tie it all together. But he realized very well that the Southern struggle was linked to the struggle going on in the country as a whole. In fact, he was able to develop a vision that encompassed the world: "All over the world like a fever, freedom is spreading in the widest liberation movement in history."[24] It is at our own peril that we blind ourselves to King's pioneer work and act as though he had never existed, implying that the theological hermeneutic of the North American reality has to begin from scratch.[25]

Where are we today? The race conflict has not abated. But new dimensions of our utterly conflictual North American reality have been revealed since King's day, especially those of sex and class. One need not at all speak for others as one ponders these conflicts. One needs only to draw together the various voices on the scene to realize that a unitary view of the conflicts is emerging as a matter of course. It would be pointless not to dare a description of what is such an obvious phenomenon.

1. *The Race Conflict.* King saw the economic cause of racism in terms of its historical origins. But at the same time he realized that economics was unable to explain the peculiar quality of racism as it had developed in this country. As to the economic factor, the explanation is simple:

> It is important to understand that the basis for the birth, growth and development of slavery in America was primarily economic.... Since the institution of slavery was so important to the economic development of America, it had a profound impact in shaping the socio-political-legal structure of the nation. Land and slaves

---

23. Martin Luther King, Jr., *Where Do We Go from Here: Chaos or Community?* (Boston: Beacon Press, 1968), 13.

24. Ibid., 169.

25. I tried to make this point in two preparatory papers for the Detroit conference "Theology in the Americas: 1975," August 17–23, 1975. The first one was titled "Pre-Bicentennial U.S.A. in the Liberation Process" (later published in *Theology in the Americas*, ed. Sergio Torres and John Eagleson [Maryknoll, N.Y.: Orbis Books, 1976], 139–74). The other was called "Race, Sex, and Class in a Technological Civilization." Unless we are willing to tap the specific history of our North American hermeneutic as it was shaped during the past two decades in regard to liberation, we probably will continue to flounder in matters of liberation theology.

were the chief norms of private property, property was wealth and the voice of wealth made the law and determined politics.[26]

But slaves as private property is not racism as yet. Racism is a legitimation of white supremacy that sanctions the status quo of property and a praxis that embodies it in every nook and cranny of our nation. Its theoretical rationale was found in the Teutonic Origins Theory, which declares that only the Teutonic race is capable of building stable governments. In due course, religion was co-opted to support the theory: "The greatest blasphemy of the whole ugly process was that the white man ended up making God his partner in the exploitation of the Negro."[27] As much as I try to stretch my imagination I find it difficult to see how U.S. Protestant theology can get rid of the doctrine of white supremacy by simply ignoring it. Every dimension of our systematic theologies has been drawn into its circle of influence. It is the fundamental teaching that the human being acts together with God in history, determining human fate by sovereign decision, for example, entitling the WASP at a particular time in our national history to regard the black as merely three-fifths of a person. Obviously when there is a religious legitimation for human beings as property individuals pass for nonpersons.

2. *The Sex Conflict.* The struggle of feminist theology hardly even loomed on the horizon at the time of King's death on April 4, 1968. In a sense, it is more far-reaching than the race struggle in this country, since in sheer numbers it encompasses a larger portion of the population and crosses racial lines as well. It also has to delve much further back into history (5000 B.C., or when did the problem arise?). It is impossible in this brief introduction to touch on more than the most salient dimension of the feminist struggle. To know its history in this instance is utterly important. But not all the monstrosities inflicted upon women throughout history reach into our present North American condition. Much of what we are up against today is continuing authorities that insist on "women's subordination."[28] In my view, it would be helpful for a development of a hermeneutic of North American reality if female oppression would not immediately be merged with racial oppression. In our country both did not originate together. Whether or not the notion of a qualitative leap between racial oppression and women's oppression might be helpful for women is not for a male to decide. The point is that there is no Teutonic Origins Theory for female oppression in this country. The white supremacy rationale is not simply the same as the male supremacy factor. Women in this country are not nonpersons the same way all blacks are nonpersons because of color. Obviously black women stand in "double trouble." What is more, minorities usually claim that they are victims of white male *and* female oppressors alike. The female claim of being oppressed — un-

---

26. King, *Where Do We Go from Here: Chaos or Community?* 71f.
27. Ibid., 75.
28. Sheila D. Collins, *A Different Heaven and Earth: A Feminist Perspective on Religion* (Valley Forge, Pa.: Judson Press, 1974), 40.

less you are a black woman — on its own terms, falls more into the category of being treated as a minor rather than as a nonperson.[29] On these grounds it might make some sense to speak of qualitative leaps between various forms of oppression in our conflict-ridden society, so that suddenly the white woman who sees herself as oppressed is not too surprised when on another level she in turn is being attacked as oppressor.

3. *The Class Conflict.* Neither race nor sex conflict touches directly the brutal struggle of economic classes. And again there is a kind of musical chairs happening. To put it bluntly, whoever may think of himself or herself as oppressed racially or sexually may, in the perspective of a lower class, clearly appear to be an oppressor. The recognition breaks through today in the protest of those who live as a lower class on the fringes of the American empire, manifest now so strongly in Latin American theology. This in turn again shows that what is in need of being critiqued and overturned ultimately is not only the supremacy of a race or a sex, but the entire system of oppression that pits races and sexes against each other as much as classes. In fact, we need a global analysis of oppression in terms of class.

Martin Luther King, Jr., still believed that the problem of race was solvable in the present socioeconomic system. "Black Power" was the step that led beyond that first pioneering move on the North American scene. The work of James H. Cone raised the whole matter for the theological perspective to a level on which an alternate system could be contemplated — in terms of revolution — and struggled for.[30] With Cone it also becomes clear that for the U.S. capitalist system revolution cannot be conceived of in the abstract, but needs to be seen through the hurts and expectations of particular oppressed peoples and groups. Obviously the feminist position underscores the dilemma. The road to revolution in the United States is narrow and arduous, and few are they who dare travel on it.

This leads to a third principle for the Protestant hermeneutic of our North American reality:

> *The recovery of the Bible as the empowerment of the just church compels us to go through history also as race, sex, and class conflict and thus to discover the unity of liberations. Here theology does not appear as adjunct of liberation struggles in general, but as the praxis of God's liberation in global history.*

The Greatest Conflict

It would be circumventive of the great stakes between theology North and South in this hemisphere if the introduction would not at least attempt a brief discussion of the Detroit conference "Theology in the Americas: 1975." There was a

---

29. Ibid., 160.
30. See especially James H. Cone, *Black Theology and Black Power* (New York: Seabury Press, 1969).

clash of views between a Latin American and a North American perspective —
what in *Christian Century* has been called the "greatest conflict."[31] In Detroit for
the first time Latin American liberation theologians as a group expounded their
position as a seemingly monolithic perspective to a North American audience.
It was a unique occasion to compare notes and to see which way the winds of
change are blowing in theology today. One hard point of difference came down
to a disagreement between Hugo Assmann and the writer of this introduction.
Alfred T. Hennelly summarizes the core issue: "Hugo Assmann, with his usual
passion, leaped to the microphone to assert that 'your North American theology is God's action in history without going through history,' the latter phrase
referring to social analysis and commitment."[32]

The hard point of difference! One needs to plead for a fair understanding of
the North American struggle for liberation. From the perspective of Karl Marx,
it is not just the economic gap between classes, but also the ideological ob-
fuscations which keep people from seeing that a gap exists in the first place.
Whites who think they are superior may have a hard time shedding their white
supremacy even after turning Marxist.[33] *Going through history in the United States*
means taking our own reality seriously[34] — with racism as the "chronological"
point of entry for our initial grasp of the liberation process. The race conflict
involves as hard an analysis as any other conflict of this type.[35]

From within the capitalist "beast" things look different than they seem from
without. Especially tactics and strategy of the struggle may be different *inside*.
It would be unfortunate if all liberation theology would regard the U.S. liberal
as its principal or only ally.[36] It is a simple fact that much theological liberalism has become a henchman of capitalism, humoring it along over its more
precarious dilemmas as a "kept" critic — no more dangerous than a mosquito
for an elephant. We, too, in the United States are in a tremendously conflictual situation.[37] Those of us committed to liberation stand over against "liberal"
interpretations in theology that concentrate on cultural assimilation or on a

---

31. Alice Hageman, "Liberating Theology through Action," *Christian Century* (October 1, 1975):
852.

32. Alfred T. Hennelly, "Who Does Theology in the Americas?" *America* (September 20,
1975): 139.

33. Documentation in this regard is not confined to material available in the United States. It is
internationally available. For example, see Volkhard Brandes and Joyce Burke, *Vom Rassenkampf zum
Klassenkampf* (Munich: Deutscher Taschenbuch Verlag, 1970), 247.

34. I stressed the need to be faithful to our own reality in a paper presented at the AAR meeting
in Washington, D.C., October 24–27, 1974, published as "Which Liberation Theology?" *Religion in
Life* (Winter 1975): 448–53.

35. See the article "Warum schwarze Theologie?" *Evangelische Theologie* (January–February 1974),
now also published in *Union Seminary Quarterly Review* (Fall 1975).

36. One also needs to take into account how from a revolutionary perspective the political liberal
is viewed in the United States. See Michael P. Lerner, *The New Socialist Revolution* (New York: Dell,
1973), 115–38.

37. It is one of the strengths of Latin American liberation theology that the conflictual situation
there is squarely acknowledged. See Gustavo Gutiérrez, *A Theology of Liberation*, 136ff.

"universal" gospel (with an a priori universal) which denies the very *going through history* Assmann is asking for.

We take seriously "historical mediation" in the United States as we pay careful attention to the concrete dimensions of our conflicts. If we can be given the benefit of the doubt that we in the United States also are premising our thinking on solidarity with the oppressed and that our emphasis on God's action in history and its biblical witness does not keep us from hard-nosed social analysis, we will be able to look forward to one of the most fruitful developments in theology on this continent. We should not be afraid of more confrontation. If we do not battle through the issues with one another as we disagree, we can only look forward to cheap togetherness and finally cheap liberation.

1. We need to battle through the *premises* on which we operate in the liberation struggle, the prejudgments, the doctrines felt as facts. It is more than surprising that so many U.S. theologians are still in love with the liberal premises when our comrades in the social sciences have long abandoned them in their life-and-death struggle with secular liberalism.[38]

2. We have to learn to be able *to live creatively with conflict*. The church is not a monolithic structure of one mind and heart, but a confederation of *peoples*. The denominational differences and family quarrels have become next to obsolete. The goal is now a confederation of the various liberation covenants in the hope that in a "network" of peoples a new structural unity will emerge which creatively undergirds the needful unity of a culture.

3. We ought to admit the almost insurmountable difficulty for traditional theology to begin anew in *identification with the struggle of the oppressed*. Unless one oppressed person benefits from liberation theology in the United States the new effort in this country is a sham. It is only in dying, however, that we live. So the seeming failure of liberation theology in the United States thus far reveals that, in the end, it is always God who liberates, not theology. As our theology together with Christ is crucified, God resurrects our freedom spirit, our determination never to give in — never.

Wrong People?

Put a cat before a mouse, Ernst Fuchs once said, and you will know what a cat is — one of the best hermeneutical "rules of thumb" I know. Put Servetus in front of a good Calvinist, and what do you get? "Wrong people" (Alice Hageman).[39] Latin American theology on its largely Roman Catholic premises may in Latin America well be able to trigger a creative image as it uses the term "orthopraxis." But that is a Latin American phenomenon. In our North American situation we will have all kinds of difficulties if we take the "ortho-"tack. Some might claim that the times of *orthodoxy* have long past and that therefore no false

---

38. See Victor Ferkiss, *The Future of Technological Civilization* (New York: G. Braziller, 1974), 1–60.
39. Hageman, "Liberating Theology through Action," 852.

expectations will be created when we carry the connotation of *orthodoxy* into orthopraxis. But are not the times of neoorthodoxy in U.S. Protestantism just of yesterday? And did not neoorthodoxy have a lot to do with *right thinking?* Was not — as little as one might wish to admit it — the right thinking seen as done by the *right people?*

It has been part of the bane of my theological generation in Protestantism that we had to stand against our "fathers" on this issue — an always painful and often destructive struggle. With those who want to import liberation theology from Latin America the same "ortho-" appears. So today there is an in-crowd of the right *posture.* The in-crowd idea remains strangely ingrained in American religious thought. The destructive "supremacy" game manifests itself not only in white supremacy or male supremacy. With the hankering for supremacy we touch on the issue of power that has hardly been dealt with as yet in U.S. Protestant thought.

Vestigia terrent. The tracks of the past horrors of right thinking loom forbidding in our Protestant memories. People are people. In God's liberation there are no right and wrong people. The struggles of all are drawn together by God as the sacrament of history where Christ concelebrates cross and resurrection. What counts for U.S. Protestantism is not orthopraxis but *Christopraxis.* This is exactly what the struggle of liberation, in the end, is all about: that God in Christ is right, and that there are no wrong people anymore. Not even our enemies are left as wrong people. God in Christ died for them, too. Since the self-righteous religionist, however, cannot live without enemies, one thing is left: "We have met the enemy, and they is us" (Pogo). Blacks struggle with whites, women with men, Native Americans with foreign Americans, and Latin Americans with North Americans in order that one people may arise: *God's* people.

Liberating Liberation Theology

"At Detroit there was much projection on the Latin Americans of things which they did *not* say."[40] Beverly Wildung Harrison (in her eminently fair attempt to tell what happened at Detroit), with an almost uncanny sense of our dilemmas, minces no words as to our liberation bondage. When a new phenomenon of national or international import bursts on the North American scene, myth-makers usually have a heyday. It would be a waste of time to list in detail what is being projected on theology south of the border. The important thing is to realize *that* it is being done. Often it is a strange compensation for copping out of the work at hand. Some seem to find a measure of satisfaction in celebrating revolution — stillborn in this country in the '60s — by Latin American proxy in the '70s. Meanwhile the development of a North American hermeneutic goes begging. The more the fixation on Latin American theology as problem solver

---

40. Beverly Wildung Harrison, "The 'Theology in the Americas' Conference," *Christianity and Crisis* (October 27, 1975): 253.

of our North American dilemmas grows, the more shackled to capitalism we will become. Thus the effort of this essay to free the creative potency of Latin American thought from being muffled in "God's own country."[41] Unless in U.S. Protestant thought we learn critically to deal with our immediate past of the last one hundred and fifty years of liberalism, no liberation label will keep us from further losing our identity.

The great strength of Assmann's book lies in its uncompromising struggle for the reality of the Christian faith under abject Latin American conditions. Great strides ahead would be in the making among us were we only half as clear about our goals.

As first steps in clarifying our goals the Assmann book compels Protestant theology in the United States to do three things: (1) We will see how the attempt to develop a hermeneutic of our North American reality cuts deep into theology itself. Judgment begins at the household of God. What first of all needs questioning is racism *in theology*, sexism *in theology*, and class conflict *in theology*. It is the ideological orientation of theology itself that requires criticism. (2) We will learn to distinguish between theology and social ethics in the liberation movement. There is much people can come up with in terms of rational social choices. U.S. Protestant theology cannot afford further to give the impression that social ethics understandings are identical with christological, anthropological, and ecclesiological understandings. *The confusion of theology and social ethics is one hermeneutical error that keeps U.S. liberation theology from getting off the ground.* (3) In regard to the change in the social system necessary in the United States we need to take a familiar southern tack: why we can't wait. There is no question in my mind that socialism has to be examined as alternative to the attrition of the capitalist system. But this also can be done on purely secular grounds. The Christian need not develop the coherent rationale for the socialist alternative. It exists already. Christian theology needs to articulate why Christians ought not to abstain from working on it with all their might. And this involves global analysis.

My North Carolina sisters and brothers in the liberation theology struggle all along were looking over my shoulder in the genesis of this introduction: Joseph B. Bethea, Helen Crotwell, Herbert O. Edwards, Nancy Ferree (meanwhile our "missionary" to Portland, Oregon), Lea Harper, Ruth Harper, Archie Logan, C. G. Newsome, and Robert T. Osborn. They do not want me to be their

---

41. The notion reappears in various ways time and again, most recently in the title of the October 20, 1975, *Time* review of Richard John Neuhaus's *Time toward Home:* "Again, God's Country" (60). In order to counteract the "religiosification" of the U.S. we need to do more than polish old terminology. There is a radical (going to the *radix*, the root) effort necessary to rediscover the view of God in the originative witness of the Christian faith, the original liberation Christology of the Bible, and its implicit Christian anthropology. There is so much romanticism of liberation around that the backlash is already on the horizon. See Elliot Wright, "The Good Ship *Oikumene*," *Worldview* (November 1975): 17–20. For an attempt to develop a radically theological view of liberation grounded in the originative witness of Christianity, see my *Liberation Theology: Liberation in the Light of the Fourth Gospel* (New York: Seabury Press, 1972).

mouthpiece or their scribe. But they do expect me to sing — the song of the South: sisterhood is powerful; brotherhood is powerful.

Furthermore, between California and North Carolina, the Pacific and the Atlantic, our continent was spanned these months by brotherly caveats of Robert McAfee Brown. Also here: brotherhood is powerful.

This piece could not have been written, however, had it not been for the life of William Edwards, bilateral amputee and paraplegic, who died in 1969. He was not able to mount any barricades, walk any picket line, or go to jail. But he was there, too, all the same. For me he embodied the liberation struggle of the marginals we shut out of sight who are yet the real bearers of the struggle. In his memory I conclude: unless one struggling person creates for us liberation theology, our efforts are in vain. God in the marginal person also liberates liberation theology — the mystery of God's Christopraxis.

17

LETTER TO GAYRAUD S. WILMORE

Convinced that the challenge of black theology must not be ignored by white theologians, Herzog organized a number of consultations between black and white theologians starting already before the publication of James Cone's A Black Theology of Liberation *and his own* Liberation Theology. *His essay "Theology at the Crossroads" (chapter 13 in this volume) is also related to these conversations.*

This letter, which chronicles an exchange between Herzog and Gayraud Wilmore, one of the fathers of the black theology movement, grows out of one such conversation which also included Shelby Rooks and Edward Huenemann. (James Cone and George Peters were part of earlier conversations.) It shows once more how liberation theology is done "on the road," raising tough questions for mainline theology and promoting a self-critical perspective. It does not immediately lead to the finished product but rather invites further dialogue.

Dear Gay,

Since we did not touch upon question number 1 of my prepared question sheet, let me stick to the two questions we dealt with. Number 3 received the least attention. So let me begin there.

I would like to stress once more what I said to you in parting: unless the sharecropper benefits from our conversations they will not be worthwhile.

Herzog: How does, for example, Paul Tillich function in all this? . . . a thorough reading of Paul Tillich . . . (292).[1] Paul Tillich would give us an example of how determinative norms of white theology function.

Wilmore: It isn't clear to me why you refer to Tillich (this is the way I remember your response in New York).

Herzog: Let me explain more fully. In order to make my point I probably should quote the full passage in which Tillich appears in your book: "Calling upon Protestant theologians, from Karl Barth to Jürgen Moltmann, Cone showed how a radical, but historically accurate, interpretation of the Biblical story and a

---

Unpublished, May 3, 1973.

1. The page references in the text are to Gayraud S. Wilmore, *Black Religion and Black Radicalism,* C. Eric Lincoln Series on Black Religion (Garden City, N.Y.: Doubleday, 1972).

thorough reading of Paul Tillich, Albert Camus, and Frantz Fanon leads to the indisputable conclusion that Black Power is the affirmation of Black being and humanity against the nonbeing and dehumanization of white racism" (291f.). The question for me is *in what way Protestant theologians, if they have not specifically dealt with black suffering, can at all be useful in coming to grips with the issues of black theology.*

In a term paper this 1973 spring semester Bill Turner, one of our black students, indicated (rather revealingly, in my opinion) how he felt about the syndrome of white Protestant theology functioning in black theology: "Black theologians have appealed to the established white theological authorities for their authority. They have used the same categories and inherited some of the same bugaboos. When they draw on some white theologian they may not be intending to invoke the entire theological system; but how is the reader to know how much of a given system a theologian is buying in on if he is not radical enough to forge new categories of his own? It must be assumed that he is accepting the epistemological matrix out of which the system grows, unless he explicitly states otherwise. So far no black theologian — with the exception of Cleage — has stated otherwise. Cone brings great insights on the issues of blackness, oppression and liberation; but he is still boxed in by Barth and Tillich. Cleage's assessment of his work appears to be correct: 'My very good friend Dr. James H. Cone is undoubtedly a most interesting and meaningful Black theologian. His task is certainly not an easy one. He is our apostle to the Gentiles. He drags white Christians as far as they are able to go (and then some) in interpreting Black theology within the established framework which they can accept and understand.' (Cleage, *Black Christian Nationalism,* xvii). Major Jones in his theology of hope is so tied to Moltmann that he has almost lost his middle name. Roberts is so bound up with the classical approach that he feels the urge to defend it against any perceived threat. Cleage does not want to go the traditional route; but he still does not give us a way out. While he is not bound up in the traditional epistemology his matrix does not go far beyond a socio-cultural analysis. And when he does attend to some theological matter he picks up the woes of nineteenth century liberalism by taking the historico-critical approach to establish his authority."

I quoted from Bill Turner's paper at length in order that you might get a feel for what I see as penetrative insight among the younger generation of black theology students. The white theologians Bill alludes to have not specifically dealt with black experience. Barth addressed the Teutonic syndrome that grew out of Schleiermacher and some Roman Catholic heresies. Paul Tillich tried to develop, in his own words, "a systematic theology which tries to speak understandably to a large group of educated people" (III, 4). By no stretch of the imagination is the sharecropper anywhere in sight as significant for theology discourse.

Today the ground rules of theology have to be changed, so that we radically move away from the needs of the anxious middle-class person to the needs of the wretched of the earth as starting point of theology. The first issue of theology for me is not the bourgeois question, "I am anxious, what's the answer?" but God's question, "Your neighbor is oppressed, what's your responsibility?"

To use Cleage's term of the "established framework" — must not the white theological framework go before we can make headway with the task of theology facing us in this country?

What are the really *determinative* norms of white theology from the black perspective? Wilmore says: "Black theology breaks with the determinative norms of white theology and unveils the deepest meaning of human freedom for all men" (297).

Wilmore: Let me quote from an article by William H. Becker for "openers" in regard to defining such norms of white theology: "Jews and blacks are 'post-secular' in that they see themselves as having gone beyond, and therefore as having to question and even reject as inappropriate for themselves, certain basic assumptions about man and democratic society which have characterized secular Western, and especially American, culture. Some of these secular assumptions are a confidence in continuing 'progress' and the basic good will of the educated, 'progressive' man; a high evaluation of 'autonomy' or individual freedom, and confidence in the 'Democratic Way' as the proper road to freedom; trust in reason, particularly 'scientific' reason, and the technological-material gains it makes possible" (*Soundings* [Winter 1970]: 415).

It is especially individualism which needs to be singled out among the secular assumptions. It gave us emphasis on individual salvation, individualistic justification by grace alone, and the priesthood of all believers as "denominational individualism." Turning to systematic theology specifically one can trace this in terms of metaphysical abstractions or in epistemology where faith is stressed as knowledge and not as dependence. The concept of God here appears more transcendent than necessary. The individualistic tendency also prevails in Christian anthropology and in Christian ethics. While there is much stress on love, the yield is powerlessness of love. And power itself is viewed as evil. All in all, autonomy becomes all-encompassing. Which finally leaves us with the question: has there ever been such a thing as authentic Christianity?

Herzog: For further discussion I plead for concentration on the premise or starting point of theology. How is the individualism you refer to spelled out in the very premise of theology (white theology) — which is theological epistemology or hermeneutic? My contention is that white theology *may* have arrived at the notion of a social self, but thought of sociality in terms of the suburban Joneses primarily, and did not incorporate the wretched of the earth in the notion of selfhood. *Liberation Theology* thus tries to speak of a corporate self at the very beginning of theological reflection in which God's identification with the oppressed becomes the criterion of every Christian teaching or doctrine. God in Christ — identifying with the oppressed — is authentic Christianity for me. Or?

Gay, I've run our conversation through my mind as best I could remember the logic of the discussion from my notes. Obviously this is simply a "primer" for further discourse. Since copies of this letter also go to Shelby and Ed, let

me thank both of them as well as you for the significant exchange on April 14.
Ed, I believe, will continue to act as monitor and moderator of further plans,
especially now as regards the meeting in Atlanta.

As ever,
Fred

P.S. Obviously I have "filled in" at points. The quote from Bill Turner I did not
mention in New York, for example.

– 18 –

OPEN LETTER TO JÜRGEN MOLTMANN

In this open letter that was never published, Herzog responds to his longtime friend Jürgen Moltmann on the occasion of Moltmann's "An Open Letter to José Míguez Bonino," published in Christianity and Crisis *(March 29, 1976): 57–63. Since this debate between European and Latin American theology has been picked up in the North American context without regard for underlying differences, Herzog addresses the need for alternative solutions in the United States.*

In a situation where economic interests have taken over both politics and religion, Herzog searches for possible antidotes. Theology needs to understand that simple denouncements and condemnations will not solve the problem. The central question is how we can begin to develop alternatives to a system that favors a few and neglects the majority of the people. In this context socialism, understood as an effective way of connecting people at the grassroots and not as another absolute system, might have something to say to us.

Nevertheless (like his teacher Karl Barth and unlike the religious socialism of Paul Tillich and others), Herzog is not interested in dressing up the social-ist alternative as a religious ideal. Socialism is not the kingdom of God. It is merely one mode of bringing together people at the grassroots in more mutually accountable ways in order to analyze and transform their situation, as some of the established European models have shown (many of which continue even after the fall of communism in the East). At the verge of the twenty-first century and the much celebrated "victory of capitalism," we might do well to ask ourselves once again what alternatives still exist to the dominant system.

Dear Jürgen,

You are obviously entitled to tell your Latin American colleagues where they've been misjudging your position. Your self-explanations are sterling. But I have also had reason to wonder: how is some of this being read in the United States?

I certainly do not wish to get ahead of Míguez and his Latin American friends as they ponder responses. But meanwhile we had better clarify a point or two in

Unpublished, June 22, 1976.

regard to North America lest our exchange seem like an afterthought to their responses. Your letter offers us an unexpected chance to state precisely what pertains to theology in West Germany and what to the United States in matters of socialism.

You know as well as I that some North American theology is still little more than a shunting yard, a *Verschiebebahnhof,* where ideas from Europe (yours not among the least) and Latin America (Míguez's not among the least) are constantly switched back and forth from one track to another — world without end. We both agreed a good while ago, it is difficult to find a truly indigenous North American theology.

I referred to one sentence in your March 29, 1976, open letter: "In the European countries — and here we include also the United States — one cannot develop socialism at the cost of democracy" (61). In our exchange about this sentence I have had the difficulty thus far of making clear to you its "non-indigenizing" character for the United States. I understand full well that the United States are not the center of the universe. What concerns me is that we're seen and that we see ourselves in real terms, not in mythical terms. Haven't you misunderstood our U.S. situation and in part also the Latin Americans?

You rightly claim Marx and Engels for Germany, the one for Trier, the other for Barmen (58). What have we got to offer on this side of the Atlantic of similar importance instead? The social Darwinist William Graham Sumner? Or Henry Ford? So we face some one hundred years of a development with much different sensibilities in most respects. Of course, Marxism also reached these shores. Karl Marx himself for several years was a European correspondent of a New York newspaper. Early in his life he had claimed that socialism and communism "did not originate in Germany, but in England, France, and North America." Also in North America! But the actual social function of Karl Marx for the average United States citizen got lost in the shuffle. In some respects it's like Rudolf Steiner and his anthroposophy with you in Europe, a kind of esoteric sideshow a goodly number of intellectuals know about, but the populace pays no attention to. Socialism is not as yet a realistic option.

We still have to learn *how* beholden we are to capitalism in this country. Recently there has been much discussion of TV personality Barbara Walters getting $1 million a year in her switch from NBC to ABC as coanchorperson for the evening news. Soon Erik Sevareid and others were in on the fray: newscasting becoming show business? Horror of horrors! Obviously this is merely one recent instance of the malaise of our socioeconomic system. But one has to mention cases or one does not notice the dilemmas we're up against every day. The worth of a person in "God's country" seems to lie somewhere else than in Europe. One does not need to get nasty on the subject. Angela Rippon, the British counterpart of Barbara Walters, gets $14,000 a year. Says she: "I'm delighted for Barbara Walters. But things are on a different scale here. We're not in the personality industry. We are journalists, not performers."

I do understand that you did not write your letter to a United States citizen. But for those who read your letter in this country, the difference between the German and the United States social systems needs to become utterly clear. For countless people in the United States, democracy and capitalism are still indistinguishable. I cherish the civil liberties of democracy and will defend them tooth and nail. But on the level of ideas the first thing that needs to be done is to disengage democracy from capitalism. A complicating factor is civil religion as ideological undergirding of the fusion between capitalism and democracy. "Religion," someone said to me not long ago, "that's God and the free enterprise system." The disengagement of capitalism from democracy on the level of ideas, however, will not go very far unless we get deep into the nitty-gritty of party politics. In West Germany you can write about socialism as a theologian with the Social Democratic Party in power. Millions of West Germans are imbued with at least rudimentary principles of socialism. There are only a few minuscule socialist parties in the United States. And which average North American citizen knows even their names? Thus I need to say that *one cannot develop democracy in the United States at the cost of socialism.*

I hope you could understand that we cannot develop socialism in the United States without the concrete political party base you already can depend on in West Germany as a people's party. I believe I also know the problems of genuine socialism that party presents to you. But apart from such a concrete political base, appeals to democratic socialism in the United States remain altogether wishful thinking. I know, I'm focusing on one reference to the United States in your letter. But the letter *is* also being read in this country. Recently our good friends at *Christian Century* (May 19, 1976) picked it up and stressed your message to the Latins that it may be "more important to maintain a connection with the people than to travel alone into the paradise of the future." On the face of it, who would want to disagree? But in terms of socialism, you as a theologian in West Germany are able via the Social Democrats to identify with the people the way we on this side of the Atlantic cannot. And what really is bothersome, ultimately none of us can produce on paper these connections with the people for all to behold. But we can state a principle: when two do the same thing it need not be the same thing by a long shot — *duo quum faciunt idem, non est idem.* We both hope to identify with the people. In the United States, however, the political base for the identification is practically nonexistent, at best in humble beginnings.

So what about the road to socialism in the United States? I read the New Testament — and compared with our socioeconomic system the clash is absolute. The first thing we *still* need to work on is opening our eyes to the difference between the gospel of Jesus and the gospel of profit. Jesus' gospel dare no longer be used to legitimate our socioeconomic and sociopolitical system. It involves a radical change in theological education and the use of money by the churches. Rejection of capitalism implies for theology commitment to a new socioeconomic and sociopolitical rationality. We dare not simply flip-flop and now use Christianity to legitimate a different social system. Being liberated to a new rationality we had better first of all develop alternative futures. But within the perimeter of this rationality I need to commit myself to a political base which includes scientific socialism.

It would be important for us that you explain the difference between socialism in West Germany and what in the United States is still a lacuna of an alternative to capitalism. There are two subpoints where we might learn from Europe's experience: (1) How does one at least in principle define the connection of theology with the people? (2) How do we avoid abusing the gospel for legitimating socialism rather than capitalism, and instead make the choice for socialism as the more humane economic and political system on rational grounds?

Sincerely,
Fred

Death, Be Not Proud

In this sermon Herzog touches on the foundation of his theology. While theology needs to learn first of all how death manifests itself in our society and even in the church, there is hope in Christ's resurrection which establishes a new reality. Since the power of God's justice rests here, Herzog does not shy away from a clash with the dominant views of the resurrection, both liberal and conservative.

Scripture Lessons:
   Old Testament: Isaiah 53:1–12
   Epistle: 1 Corinthians 15:51–58

"When the perishable puts on the imperishable, and the mortal puts on immortality, then shall come to pass the saying that is written: 'Death is swallowed up in victory.' O death, where is thy victory? O death, where is thy sting? The sting of death is sin, and the power of sin is the law. But thanks be to God, who gives us the victory through our Lord Jesus Christ. Therefore, my beloved, be steadfast, immovable, always abounding in the work of the Lord, knowing that in the Lord your labor is not in vain" (1 Cor. 15:54–58).

> *Death is always looking over our shoulder.*
> *God is always giving death the cold shoulder.*

These are the two emphases of our text we will ponder briefly this morning. Lent begins this week. And death plays a significant role in Lent. But we cannot understand Lent without Easter.

I

Death is always looking over our shoulder, even in places where we do not expect it. On a September Sunday last year I was in Burg (East Germany) in the morning service offering a brief meditation *at* the steps of the altar of one of the churches. There was a unique altarpiece with the crucifixion among other scenes from the life of Christ looking over my shoulder. I referred briefly to the scene of death behind me, trying to say what it means in contemporary terms.

Unpublished sermon delivered in Duke University Chapel, February 25, 1979.

About the same time somewhat farther South (in another East German church) a young minister burned himself to death in front of a large congregation — *on* the steps of the altar.

I was not aware of the incident at the time, of course. I learned of it shortly afterward. The self-immolation, as best one could tell, was not a protest against the communist government, as an earlier self-immolation of another East German minister had been. Rather, it was supposed to offer a signal in the strife of the local church the young minister seemed unable to bear any longer.

Things of this nature impress themselves on one especially within a sealed-off country where everything the church does takes on a sharp profile against the backdrop of an atheistic culture. And yet the self-immolation of a minister in church would have left an indelible mark on me under any circumstances. It makes us reflect on things we otherwise do not like to admit. While the good news is being shared in our churches, at the same time rather threatening things may be happening in our assemblies. In any case, death is present with us, most of the time not in that traumatic a way as in the East German church, but with a threatening sting nonetheless.

Death is present as death of our ambitions or as death of our loves. But also in our personal death. The cold scythe of death is already being put to our lifecord, even though death may still take a little while, or quite a while, until it cuts us down.

Who *wants* to think much about death this very moment in a beautiful church? With the season of Lent soon upon us we cannot avoid taking another hard look. According to church tradition, Lent is nothing but learning to share in the remarkable death of Jesus on the cross. Here death appears as the last enemy, a real threat to life. Can we still understand this tradition? Why was such a tragic death necessary, such a great sacrifice of a young person, perhaps not even thirty years old?

Death is not viewed as threat *by all*. Some poets have long borne testimony to a friendly death. "We love to sleep all, and death is but the sounder sleep" (Beaumont). Or, "Death is a commingling of eternity with time" (Goethe).

In Christian terms, death is not a lying down to pleasant dreams. It is rather an attack on human identity, the threat of annihilation. So St. Paul speaks of death as our "last enemy" a little earlier in the chapter (v. 26). He contemplates the possibility that death, given a chance, might win out in the end over all people and all things — as a victory of death eternally.

In facing that possibility St. Paul, as it were, shouts out an Easter song: "Death is swallowed up in victory. O death, where is thy victory? O death, where is thy sting?" (v. 55) Then he goes on to explain why death is such a threat: "The sting of death is sin, and the power of sin is the law" (v. 56).

The argument of St. Paul seems somewhat complex. The language is not twentieth century, for sure. But when we break it down to its component parts it can make sense in Christian experience. For what makes death such an awesome killer? St. Paul answers, sin. *Sin as an accomplice of death.* We ourselves alive this morning do not know the experience of death itself. But we know the *anticipation* of it. The anticipation is painful in Christian terms, since it seems to finalize all the injustices we do, or we feel inflicted upon us.

God has a right to be God. As humans we have a right to be human. But we turn that right into a farce, not understanding it as a gift, arrogating it unto ourselves, trying to play God. We become unjust. Suddenly we lose control.

We do not have to search around a lot to understand St. Paul's point even today. The *Durham Morning Herald* three weeks ago discussed at length the question, "Why Is Suicide Appealing?" with 732 suicides in North Carolina in 1977, as compared with 514 in 1968. Professor Bressler of this university suggested that those who kill themselves seem to have an increased sense of lack of control over their own lives.

We begin to play God ourselves, St. Paul implies, and seek to determine right on our own terms. But when we become aware that we overreach ourselves, i.e., when we become aware of sin, we see death, emptiness, no real foundation to our life or of our achievements. We lose control. Only relatively few commit suicide. But the phenomenon of suicide reflects how many of us notice death. The *sting of sin* in us rips away the mask that often hides death.

St. Paul digs into the issue from one more angle: "The power of sin is the law" (v. 56). It seems again first of all somewhat obscure what is intended. But he wants to say that through the law sin comes alive. Without law we probably would not notice it. Law for St. Paul is what is laid down as just and right between God and human beings and between human beings themselves.

For a long time a person may be blind to law. But then may come a moment of revelation when one discovers how one defies the bond of common obligation. The discussion between UNC and HEW of recent weeks on the black campuses of the North Carolina University system is a helpful case in point. For the longest time the dismal situation of black colleges seemed to go unnoticed. Now the law comes in and we discover, as it were, our common obligation to justice. Even the governor of North Carolina, Jim Hunt, is quoted as saying Thursday, "I go into some of these campuses and my heart aches for some of these buildings these children have to go to school in." St. Paul is right. The law makes us suddenly notice wrong, human sin, and admit it.

We might not want to make St. Paul's argument our own for any number of reasons. The question is whether it is true. And if it is true, what language do we want to substitute for it if we don't like the ancient terms?

Right now a goodly number of people on this campus are experiencing the dark night of the soul. The particular sting may differ from St. Paul's. The specific law we notice may also differ. But many of us feel the deadening pall of death once we see ourselves in the mirror Holy Scripture holds up to us in the words of St. Paul — there is a destroyer of our identity, whether we are the perpetrators of injustice or the victims of the injustice of others — or both.

II

The whole chapter, 1 Corinthians 15, is mainly a proclamation of the resurrection. God is always giving death the cold shoulder. There is no Lent without Easter. There is no dark night of the soul without the light of the Easter morning.

Plato thought that philosophy was training in dying. And well it may be. There is no one-upmanship involved when we say that Christianity is *training in living.* It is a different focus on the meaning of life because God has done a marvelous thing. God in Christ has taken death upon Godhead and has conquered death.

The whole modern debate about the resurrection stares us in the face at this point. Theological modernism time and again has stressed that the resurrection of Jesus dare not be understood at face value: a bodily resurrection is impossible. We cannot avoid the clash with the modern perspective. The modernist theology approach leaves us ultimately only with a mere historical relationship to Jesus of Nazareth. It knows nothing of Jesus as very God of very God.

The biblical witness, however, also does not want to confront us with a mystifying magical event feeding only sheer credulity. A merely literalist understanding of the resurrection is also excluded by St. Paul. He speaks of a new creation body transcending this creation. "Death is swallowed up in victory." Something has happened to death itself. Recently the Swiss theologian Hans Küng defined resurrection as dying into God. But that still leaves death holding its sway over us. Resurrection in St. Paul's way of thinking is rather the dying of death itself, of that death which disintegrates human personhood eternally. On those grounds John Donne could say, "Death, be not proud...Death, thou shalt die."

In Jesus' resurrection, God appears in the new creation body — a spiritual body, death in this firstfruits of the resurrection having died. The dogma of the church sought to safeguard this resurrection as the liberating and redemptive current of history that moves all of us to God's goal.

God sheds new creation light into the dark weeks of Lent, into the dark night of the soul, into all the dark recesses of history to re-create us as new beings. If a person is in Christ, this woman or this man is a new creation. Death, be not proud.

This is the center of the Christian faith which is not grounded in itself, but upon the God who reigns eternally in the resurrection Christ over the death that attacks our human identity. This is how God rights the human condition, fulfilling the law. Righting the human condition is God's justice — making love possible.

In a stroke of genius, as it were, St. Paul winds up his strange message about Easter in Lent with a clarification of the fundamental terms of Christian living: "Therefore be steadfast, immovable, always abounding in the work of the Lord, knowing that in the Lord your labor is not in vain" (v. 58). The key words here are "in the Lord." Because in the resurrection Lord eternal life is implanted into us in faith, we can be steadfast and immovable. It is the bedrock of our life, the core of our being. We cannot force Christian living on anyone. It's simply there or it isn't — as result of the resurrection life, an expression of thankfulness: "thanks be to God" (v. 57).

Resurrection life at the core of our being: this is justice in Jesus, God's justice prevailing eternally over death, making us just. It is not as yet the new heaven and the new earth. But it is God's inroad into sinful humankind through us, making justice counter injustice. This pertains as much to the struggle for equal treatment of black colleges as it pertained to equal treatment at lunch counters. It pertains to justice in the classroom between teacher and students as much as in the home between husband and wife or parents and children. It pertains to the relationship of a student to the fellow student. Be immovable in justice. It makes love possible. Abounding in this work of the Lord we can sing: we shall not be moved.

It would be misleading if we were not to stress that God relates justice first of all to the struggles of the individual. Resurrection life at the core of our life makes a person just. It is to be made free, to be forgiven, to be saved, to be enabled to love, even in the face of the worst maltreatment others inflict upon us or we inflict upon ourselves. Becoming just through God's justice we know that our labor is not in vain, however long the struggle, however distant the goal. Becoming just through God's justice — this is Christian living. Death, be not proud. Amen.

PART THREE

TRANSFORMING THEOLOGY AND THE CHURCH: CONSTRUCTIVE PROPOSALS

How can theology, in the midst of competing attempts to control its subject matter, keep the view open for what God is doing? This is the common thread of the essays that follow, branching out into specific proposals for the future of theology and the church. A first step, according to Herzog, is to shift from theologizing about ideal concepts to analyzing what is actually going on (see the selection from *Justice Church* included in this volume as chapter 21). This leads to two related questions: What is actually happening in theology and the church today? And, what is God doing?

In order to address these questions, theology needs to develop a broad perspective. At a time when socioeconomic and political factors more and more shape both living and thinking, theological reflection can no longer afford to neglect them. Herzog puts it quite drastically: "All doctrine today which is not explicitly also a critique of the present economic system eo ipso also becomes a justification of the system, and opium for the people."[1] Without turning into a subfield of sociology or cultural studies, theology needs to do a better job of analyzing those factors that go into theological reflection.

All theological analyses lead back to God. God, at work in both church and world, cannot be relegated to the ideal realm. Herzog's work is at its most constructive in rethinking the work of God. In a North American middle-class setting where people are used to thinking about God as being on their side, the surprising news is that God is at work in places where we least expect it.

---

1. Frederick Herzog, "United Methodism in Agony," *Perkins Journal* 28, no. 1 (Fall 1974): 6.

Both the tradition of the Reformation and the developing tradition of liberation remind us in their own ways that God is at work in suffering and in the cracks and fissures of this world, working toward salvation and liberation in ways that we cannot control. God's work, which includes Christ's life, death, and resurrection, challenges the activism of those in positions of power and control, those who can rest assured that the popular slogan "Just do it" (recently picked up by the Nike Company) works for them. God reconfigures existing structures of power and empowerment.

Rediscovering the roots of theology in praxis, an insight shared by liberation theologies all over the globe, Herzog introduces a distinction between Christian praxis and God's own praxis (in his last book *God-Walk* he brings together the notions of Theopraxis, Christopraxis,[2] and Spiritpraxis in trinitarian fashion). Christian praxis needs to be remodeled according to God's own praxis. Here, the tug-of-war between two major camps in contemporary mainline churches, rallying around the notions of either doctrinal correctness (orthodoxy) or social action (orthopraxis), breaks down. Theology does not start with doctrine or action but with God's own praxis, which in turn reshapes both the doctrines and the actions of the church.

If God's praxis deals with the pain of those who are pushed to the margins, theology and the church can no longer afford to avoid these contexts. Entering new worlds, theology becomes a matter of life and death.

---

2. The term "Christopraxis" appears in Herzog's work for the first time in 1976, in "Doing Liberation Theology in the South," *National Institute for Campus Ministries: Southern Regional Newsletter* 1, no. 2 (January 1976): 7, and in "Introduction: On Liberating Liberation Theology," in Hugo Assmann, *Theology for a Nomad Church* (Maryknoll, N.Y.: Orbis Books, 1976), 18, included in this volume as chapter 16. It is picked up in Frederick Herzog, *Justice Church: The New Function of the Church in North American Christianity* (Maryknoll, N.Y.: Orbis Books, 1980), 50. Herzog is the first to use this term and not Ray S. Anderson, who in his book *Ministry on the Fireline: A Practical Theology for an Empowered Church* (Downers Grove, Ill.: InterVarsity Press, 1993), 212–13, n. 2, assumes that he invented the term in 1984. Already in 1974 Herzog had raised the question whether "Christology offers some cogent reasons for a praxiology not oriented in middle-class values." Herzog, "United Methodism in Agony," 8. See also Frederick Herzog, "Liberation Theology or Culture-Religion?" Included in this volume as chapter 14.

– 20 –

Quo Vadis?

In the mid-seventies an earlier activism appeared to be settling down in the United States, making room for what many saw as a turn to inner values and religiosity. Many theologians and church people were relieved, feeling more at home again in this new cultural climate.

In this poem (printed in a publication of Duke Divinity students), which he identifies as "a somewhat odd pre-Lenten 'meditation,'" Herzog attempts to let the extremes touch and reshape each other. More important, however, with the reference to Christ's cross and resurrection a new focus is introduced which remodels the dialectic of activism and quietism.

Students — they say —
    have quieted down.
Clenched fists don't even draw a frown.
    Still is the town
    And the Academy to boot....

    Who gives a hoot?

Injustices in prison and in slum?
The face of justice has turned glum.

It's Tolkien now, and Kierkegaard,
And C. S. Lewis for a start,
And Zen and Yoga, Tao, and Nu
With meditation as the glue.

    So quick the fiery activist
    Has turned into the quietist.

But why so must we always fly —
Extremes exchanging as we try —

First published in *Response* 6, no. 4 (February 1975): 18–19. The text refers to the legend according to which Jesus on the Via Appia met Peter, leaving Rome in despondency over Nero's persecution. Peter asked the Lord, *Quo vadis, Domine?* (Where are you going, Lord?) Jesus answered, *Venio Roman, iterum crucifigi.* (To Rome, to be crucified again.) On hearing that, Peter returned to Rome.

From one pole to another one?
Is that the way life needs be done?

Are we not barking up some tree
Dissembling schizophrenically?
And as we bark we do not see
    The unimpeded unity

      Of thought and deed
      And do not heed
      The wholeness lodged in
      History?

Have we not heard — have we not read
That God in Christ in our own stead
Has offered faithfulness as faith,
So that we ne'er need end as wraith?
But substantive with character
Be actor, not sheer re-actor?

"Where are you going?" Christ was asked
Near Rome — and fearsomely unmasked
St. Peter stood, as Truth outcried:
"To Rome t'again be crucified."

Thus perseverance, suffering, death,
True staying power's awesome breath,
Is at the core of all we be
At Calvary for trust to see.

      In Rome 'twas also to be seen
      And other rugged crosses' scene.

An -ism does not match *that* Tree.
All activism makes us flee
Away from "I" and also "We" —
And quietists invert the spree.

Can we ne'er learn just plain to be
Wayfarers of eternity?
Grasping the simple task to live —
In wholeness, soul to take and give,
To ponder, act, breathe in, breathe out,
And all therewhile to find the clout
For joy in singleness of mind
And thus be one as humankind?

No action — that is human loss.
Without the deed there is no Cross,
Without the Cross there is no Life,
But merely mumbo jumbo strife.
Or rubber cells of various sorts
In which we humans play our sports
In isolation without names —
Nuts playing silly inmates' games.

"The center cannot hold," cried Yeats.
Pack into one your loves, your hates,
And stretch the breaking point of act,
And heap together dream and fact:
The horror and the splendor's hue.
The blood, the smile, the false, the true,
The cry, the song, the bird, the Tree,
And grasp at last who makes you — free.

You *can* hold opposites in one —
Extremes will touch. It has been done
Before. The Wonder of it all
Makes thought walk tall
And deed resound — the Freedom Call.

Epilogue

The media can't really set
The rules for what you love or dread,
Or do or don't, or think or not,
Assigning you a beehive slot

In Orwell's 1984.

Still, you yourself can write the score:
What life through death is really for.
On that no one has closed the door.

21

POWER DILEMMAS IN THE CHURCH

Justice Church, the book written after Liberation Theology, addresses a "second stage" in liberation theology. It grows out of the expanding horizon of new experiences of Christian accountability which by now go far beyond those of Christians in the southern United States who struggled together against racism (the context of Liberation Theology). *At this point Herzog begins to focus increasingly on the function of the church in the conflicts of the present, developing more detailed proposals for retooling theology in the process.*

The following text was published as the first chapter of Justice Church. *The problem with the church is not primarily of a moral or sociological, but of a theological nature. While the new function of the church is not fully developed yet, new emphases are emerging where theology begins to analyze the church in light of God's work on the underside of history, rather than idealize about it. The divisions in contemporary theology and the church, not only along denominational lines, but also along the lines of race and class, point to the need to reinvent both theology and church on grounds of new forms of praxis in touch with God's own praxis, from the bottom up. Only in this way can the church be liberated from its (often unconscious) captivity to the powers that be and join God's liberation.*

"The theology of our church stinks." This statement made recently by a layperson in Sunday school may seem unsavory. The honest truth for him was that we were doing a lot of good things in our church, but mostly for the wrong reasons. Our theology was no longer in touch with the real world.

For some time many of us have been telling ourselves that our church is in trouble. But the reasons for the trouble have turned out to be different from what they had seemed.

Many of our churches still create an atmosphere of respectability. But they are living on borrowed capital, the memory of saintly souls, the spiritual aura still reflected in the religion sections of our newspapers, and the awe the label "Reverend" still exudes. So for a while I concluded that what we are up against

First published in *Justice Church: The New Function of the Church in North American Christianity* (Maryknoll, N.Y.: Orbis Books, 1980), 8–29.

is a moral issue: respectability on Sunday, credibility gaps on Monday — in the real world.

At times we were able to close the credibility gap. But then there was also the role society assigned the church in the sociopolitical and socioeconomic power play. Society often expected the church to sanction its ways. This brought in a sociological dimension.

Neither the moral nor the sociological dimension, however, explains the dilemma fully. What is in bad shape is the basic doctrinal view of the church. While not unrelated to the moral and the sociological, the dilemma is concerned principally with how we see the church functioning in the global village. What we have thought of as church thus far is one thing. What it needs to be in the global village is quite another.

We are no longer living in the age of universal Christendom. The Constantinian era is over. The church is no longer the sacred center of society. But what is it? The new function of the church is still developing.

The Old Concept of the Church?

Of the acme of Christendom Juan Luis Segundo claims: "The Church was universal because all men belonged to her. The chief byproduct of this view was that missionary activity ceased to be the task of *each* and *every* Christian. The pagan was no longer someone you lived with or near; in a Christian world there were no pagans, just good or bad Christians. The pagan was someone living beyond the borders of the West, specifically in the Islamic world challenged by holy crusades."[1] That has changed radically. Pagans are again in our midst. But the change has not been fully grasped as yet. The churches are still widely regarded as integrative centers of holiness in terms of an American Christendom. The idea of a civil religion implies no less.

Countless laypersons as well as clergy are trying to break out of the old mold. Almost daily our newspapers carry items to that effect. In the case of foreign policy, for instance, the question has once again been raised, "What do we do in the face of increasing Soviet power?" Speaking from a Christian perspective Father Theodore M. Hesburgh, chairperson of the Overseas Development Council, observed that "the emphasis today tends to be distracted to political problems, like...how strongly we speak to the Russians." He believes we should rather be discussing "the place of America in a world in which we're surrounded by great concentrations of poverty and hopelessness."[2]

The abandonment of the old vision of the church has led to new conflicts in the churches. For years the developing polarity has been summed up in the for-

---

1. The difference in historical situations is very much the framework of Juan Luis Segundo, *Our Idea of God* (Maryknoll, N.Y.: Orbis Books, 1974). See esp. 74–79.

2. Peter L. Berger, *Pyramids of Sacrifice* (Garden City, N.Y.: Basic Books, 1976), is one of the best examples of what is happening in reorientation in the United States in this regard.

mula: the church as challenger versus the church as comforter.[3] Only gradually is it dawning on us that the struggle over the nature of the church is over the church immersed in history versus the church separate from history.

Thus far in the debate we have usually talked about the conflict between a more liberal and a more conservative view of the church. The liberal view often still sees the church as an end in itself, conceptually at least, existing apart from the vicissitudes of history. The theology of Paul Tillich may still function as a test case in regard to liberal U.S. Protestant thought. Here for the last time a liberal theologian in this country has taken it upon himself to restate the Western ontological tradition on a grand scale.

Tillich's doctrine of the church appears within the ontological framework. He speaks of the "ontological character of the Spiritual Community."[4] Since Tillich wants to stress the church as the bearer of the New Being, he first describes what *is*. The sacramental character of the church is implied and a dual dimensionality becomes operative, a visible reality dimension, on the one hand, and a depth dimension, on the other. The latter does not meet the eye and yet accounts for the real nature of the church.

So, for a good stretch of the way, the challenge becomes how to put two churches together, the existential church and the essential church. We are familiar with the basic argument: "The Spiritual Community does not exist as an entity beside the churches, but it is their Spiritual essence, effective in them through its power, its structure, and its fight against their ambiguities." What we are faced with as church is people trying to draw more and more spirituality into reality. But that is not an easy thing to do. And so Tillich ends up with paradox: "The churches are holy, but they are so in terms of an 'in spite of' or as a paradox." A big issue for Tillich, therefore, is how the churches can prove their mettle in terms of expressing Being.

Tillich's doctrine of the church appeared at a time when Gibson Winter and Peter Berger, among others, were already developing sociological critiques of the American churches. Within this new context, Langdon Gilkey published the important study *How the Church Can Minister to the World without Losing Itself* (1964). Gilkey's concern was that the transcendent dimension, the Holy, was being lost in the shallow secularization process rampant in the American denominations. He was searching for a new language that could once more capture "the dimension of transcendence or of the holy in the church's life." In some sense that might have seemed like holding on to the ontology of the church the way Tillich had seen it. And yet, in principle, Gilkey's study was a first step in a new direction. What Gilkey really thought important was an analysis "of the actual social community we label church." The advance was related to his contention that theological language, whether denominational or ecumenical, "has seemed

---

3. Jeffrey K. Hadden, *The Gathering Storm in the Churches* (Garden City, N.Y.: Doubleday, 1969), 6.

4. Paul Tillich, *Systematic Theology*, vol. 3 (Chicago: University of Chicago Press, 1963). The quotes are taken from 162ff.

to refer to some other church than the actual one." Gilkey was also very much aware of his limitations. He expressed the hope "that far better historical and theological analyses will replace this brief one."[5]

Our analysis does not pretend to be better than Gilkey's. Rather it attempts simply to take into account a few developments since the time of Tillich's and Gilkey's contributions. Our effort will be based on a premise already important to Gilkey: *In our day we need to be keenly aware of the shift from theologizing about an ideal church to analyzing the actual church.*

A New Concept of the Church?

It is beginning to dawn on us that the church exists not apart from history but in the rough-and-tumble of history. The result is a turning away from apologetics, in other words, from the primary attempt to convince the elites of the logical consistency of Christianity. We are discovering in the world countless people who do not have the privilege of being part of the modern mind: the nonpersons, that is, the marginals, the voiceless poor. It is not so much that *we* are discovering them as that they are imposing themselves on us as persons no longer to be overlooked. The nature and mission of the church need now to be formulated in regard to our inability thus far to make creative use of this new situation in which nonpersons are making claims on us.

With full awareness of the problem Gilkey was trying to tackle, I tried almost a decade later to tie theology to the claims of the victims of society:

> The church is never an end in itself....Its task is to witness to transcendence.
> ...Insofar as it does point to transcendence, God's involvement in the wretched of the earth, it is the liberation church....To admit that God struggles among the oppressed means to join the battle in opening up public space for freedom for those who have no access to it. Opening up white churches for black members makes little difference for those who suffer. The real point is to open jobs and better housing. On a wider scale it is granting unionization rights to *Chicanos* and self-determination to Vietnamese.[6]

While the church here is understood no longer as a community alongside history, but as a people joining God in the liberation struggle in history, it is not at all clear in detail how a local church might go about embodying this new concept.

The organizational framework in which the churches exist cannot give credence to this new insight. We need a different organizational structure. This is not meant to be another move in "modern" culture accommodation. It is rather an effort to grasp what the Christian movement is all about on *its own grounds*.

The theological point seems fairly clear. In Jesus of Nazareth something happened outside the temple. After death and resurrection the story is carried

---

5. Langdon Gilkey, *How the Church Can Minister to the World without Losing Itself* (New York: Harper and Row, 1964), 140.

6. Frederick Herzog, *Liberation Theology: Liberation in the Light of the Fourth Gospel* (New York: Seabury Press, 1972), 22f.

beyond the temple to the pagans. Worship of God as the Holy can no longer be confined to temples made with hands. God proved to be struggling with all humanity, especially those who had been excluded from being human. People in the Gentile world had been battling for solutions to their historical destiny. Greek mystery religions and Greco-Roman philosophers were no longer providing satisfactory answers. The enterprise of civilization was grinding to a halt. Especially the lower classes felt the purposelessness of life. They were the "expendables." But Jesus included them. The church also included them and thus thrust itself deep into history.

Since that time, much has changed. Other parts of this book will try to give a more detailed account of the dimensions of the changes. Here we need to point out that insight into *the dilemmas of power in the church* does not spring directly from the new concept of the church like Athena from the head of Zeus. For example, H. Richard Niebuhr, as early as 1929, offered a good historical explanation of the dilemmas when he observed: "The same causes which brought on political and economic conflict promoted religious controversy and schism. For the churches of America, no less than those of Europe, have often been more subject to the influence of provincial or class environment than to the persuasions of a common gospel."[7] A European, Friedrich Hufendick, in recent reflection on H. Richard Niebuhr describes the result of this environmental influence: "The churches of the bourgeoisie have separate organizations aiding them in avoiding economic conflict between the classes."[8] But why did H. Richard Niebuhr not make headway with his insights? Why did he end up with a middle-of-the-road Schleiermacherian liberalism almost looking the other way in social conflict?

Who has a satisfactory answer? It seems that as long as churches and theologians do not engage in a praxis that cuts across denominational lines the church is bound to fail. Individual mergers between denominations are usually gargantuan agonies over wedding the class interests of one class of Christian people thus far separate. One result is bigger corporations. In the process Protestant theology continues either to plug into a separate denominational setting or to diffuse its energies in trying to be relevant to the general cultural context.

The denomination is one of the basic hindrances to an embodiment of a new concept of the church. And yet it is precisely here that we have to start anew, principally in terms of analysis. The denomination, once upon a time fulfilling the role of cultural home base for the immigrant, has become a closed society — a prehistorical monstrosity. We know only faintly what is going on in a denomination not our own. As a consequence, theology suffers immeasurably. For example, those of us who are not Presbyterians probably know more

---

7. H. Richard Niebuhr, *The Social Sources of Denominationalism* (New York: Henry Holt, 1957), 140.

8. Friedrich Hufendick, "Von der Individualethik zur Gesellschaftsethik," *Junge Kirche* 6 (1976), Beiheft, 6.

about communist politics in Italy than about the United Presbyterian Church (UPCUSA).

John R. Fry recently published *The Trivialization of the United Presbyterian Church,* a study of the UPCUSA from the Confession of 1967 to the present. The struggle of our sister denomination this past decade did not remain entirely unknown to us on the outside. But how can we adequately judge the agony of this Presbyterian author? Fry is struck by the disproportion between the 1967 confession of reconciliation and the actual historical role of present church dilemmas. Our Presbyterian sisters and brothers went through a radical restructuring of the bureaucracy, supposedly in keeping with the confession of reconciliation. Fry views the process as an exercise in futility: "The reorganizational effort grew a life of its own; once in place as an actual organization, it tried to function in independence of existing denominational dynamics although it insists all along that it is the very incarnation of the Presbyterian spirit."[9] Thus trivialization increased. The intended UPCUSA impact on the world decreased: "The UPCUSA *has* retreated; moreover, it *has* retreated from a once considerable and highly visible ministry to the nation into a ministry to itself."[10]

We have no way of adequately judging the truth of Fry's analysis from the outside. In "God's country" Christians are kept at a distance from each other. Most theology exists only in the awkward gaps between denominational pains and trials. When one member suffers, we do not suffer along by a long shot. Many Protestant Christians in the United States are increasingly retreating into a ministry to themselves. We are kept from battling in concert in the conflict of history by self-serving denominational machinery. This is perhaps the major reason why theology in the United States today is in such dire straits. Theology cannot flourish in closed societies. The common praxis from which alone liberation theology can grow has been hermetically sealed off by the churches themselves. But we cannot hope to develop a new praxis base alongside the churches. Uprooted from the church, theology always turns into something different from Christian theology. So, theologically speaking, we had better take our existence as separate denominations seriously.

The constant complaint that "it's off-season" for the ecumenical movement can best be explained in this context.[11] For a while the cerebral Faith and Order differences between the denominations seemed a good conversation piece. The trade flourished. Meanwhile, the differences have either been ironed out or gone up in smoke. At least they no longer grip the imagination. All the while the plight of the world's poor is growing and the plight of the churches as well.

This does not mean that all problems are confined to the area of Life and Work. There is a wholeness to the present church mandate that can best be

---

9. John R. Fry, *The Trivialization of the United Presbyterian Church* (New York: Harper and Row, 1975), 55f.

10. Ibid., 67.

11. Charles E. Brewster, "Off-Season for Ecumenism?" *New World Outlook* 36, no. 9 (May 1976): 34–36.

grasped as *praxis seeking understanding*. Praxis gives rise to thought. So we cannot understand the ministry of the church apart from the praxis interdependence of the denominations. Obviously one can try to go it alone. But that becomes more and more absurd. Thus we arrive at a first principle in regard to a liberation doctrine of the church: *From now on it will be absurd to try to carry out the ministry of the church in abstraction from interdenominational praxis.*

Divide and Conquer?

While interdenominational praxis cooperation is occasionally taking place in broad terms, we dare not forget that the U.S. churches are also divided by race. After the emancipation of the slave, dealing with the race problem in terms of denominational pluralism was the safest way to keep the U.S. socioeconomic and sociopolitical system intact. The situation today remains very much the same. The debate about black theology that raised so many eyebrows obviously was an event triggered by the racial apartheid involved in denominational pluralism.

One of the first attempts to overcome apartheid in the South centered on the notion of "becoming black." The emphasis was not placed for shock value.[12] There was a shock effect, it cannot be denied, but this was an unexpected by-product. Originally it meant (in Christian humor) white Christians discovering the inclusive structure of human selfhood in Jesus of Nazareth. As the debate developed, we learned that in the church pluralism functions as camouflage for racism. The other side of the coin is that pluralism in the church often also provides the occasion for ethnic nationalism, which, in the end, is part of the power dilemma.

The issue has not as yet fully crossed the threshold of theological conscious-ness in Protestantism. Since I have become part of the debate, I would like to refer to a few comments of Donald G. Shockley which reflect the popular re-sponse to the issue. In a review of Benjamin A. Reist's *Theology in Red, White, and Black,* Shockley wrote:

> Reist begins to make the tired word "liberation" meaningful for all of us. Until now liberation has implied for whites some kind of escape from their whiteness, e.g., Frederick Herzog's *Liberation Theology.* For Reist liberation means that whites at last come to terms with *their* particularity, i.e., become white for the first time. The conversation around the theological triangle requires the presence of white theologians who are willing to sit on *their* side of the triangle and participate as equals, no more nor less.[13]

There is a misunderstanding involved. We cannot escape from whiteness ever. We never intended an escape. The point was to become aware of our separate identities in the corporate selfhood of Christ.

---

12. Herzog, *Liberation Theology,* 61ff.
13. Donald G. Shockley, review of Benjamin A. Reist, *Theology in Red, White, and Black,* in *Religion in Life* 44, no. 4 (Winter 1975): 510.

The real intention was stressed by AME Bishop Philip R. Cousin: "As we see it, exactly in 'becoming black' (identifying with the black in our common history) whites can wish only one thing, namely to be white, that is, to be what they are. This new experience has the strange effect of making whites more conscious of themselves as whites. In the same vein, it should be noted that Herzog also spoke of becoming red, identifying with the Indian. The issue of our common history in North Carolina has at least this 'triadic' dimension."[14] In the South we learned years ago that only because of the confrontation with the black and *the red* could the issue of "becoming white for the first time" be raised. Solutions, however, are not easy to come by. It is a sad commentary on our complacency when we assume we can already sit around tables as equals with blacks and reds. Equals we will not be for a long time. Racism runs too deep. And we whites know it: we have the power.

Has anything been gained by this discussion? In the black/white/red confrontation we have become aware of the subtle "victory" of the social system over the church. We now see the great distance between us, basically a societal one. At times the evil distance due to racism is turned into the virtue of ethnic pluralism. On this level, though, we discover ourselves even more radically out of each other's reach. Pluralism due to racism is totally negative. Pluralism legitimating ethnic nationalism is often viewed as positive. But what does it do to Christianity? Even the seemingly good dimension of ethnic nationalism pits us against each other — just what the social system wants, to keep us in rivalry with one another.

Ethnic nationalism proves a positive good only when measured by the pluralistic ideology of our society. Ethnic pluralism as much as denominationalism is a code word for rugged individualism or even social Darwinism. Illusions are no longer possible in the church on this point. Because of the racial confrontation in the theology of the late sixties and early seventies our eyes have been opened to the great distance still existing between the various nationalisms of the churches. The sociocultural system ultimately determines who we are as human beings, not the church. This is the way sociocultural power functions in the United States.[15] We can be churches in terms of our various nationalisms, but we cannot be the *United* Church of Christ. Obviously several denominations have "alien" ethnic groups within their folds. But that is no solution to the dilemma. The ethnic group in a denomination usually still functions as an ethnic nationalism inside a denomination and intentionally so. Those who have the power can thus more easily rule — as they divide us against each other.

Harold Cruse makes the significant point that America is a group society. So we need to think of this nation primarily in groups. While the overall economic principle remains the same, it uses ethnic groups to inject itself ever deeper into

---

14. Philip R. Cousin, "Black Identity and White Identity," *Dialog* 15, no. 2 (Spring 1976): 148.

15. See Arnold M. Rose, *The Power Structure: Political Process in American Society* (London: Oxford University Press, 1967), 33ff.

the body politic: "Negro workers, just like white workers, adopt the individual-istic ideas of free enterprise and accept its values."[16] In order to understand our peculiar difficulties we have to view society "more cogently in terms of groups than in what the Marxist called class alignments."[17] Thus Cruse concludes: "The Negro question, contrary to Marxist dogma, is more a group problem than a class one, simply because Negro businessmen must depend on the Negro group for their support, regardless of class differentiation."[18]

Cruse offers his comment on the basis of research into "five decades of Marx-ism"[19] in the black community. One of the reasons why socialism is unable to make much of a dent among blacks in the United States is that the oppressed are boxed into ethnic groups and would be sold down the river if they would follow Marxist advice and integrate into a national multicolored class. The U.S. Marx-ist "class" would consist of ethnic groups continuing to seek domination within the overall competitive framework of our society. Says Cruse: "It has come to this! At its roots the American nationality problem is a group power problem, an interethnic group power play; only when the American Negro creates an ethnic group social and cultural philosophy will he be able to deal effectively with this dilemma in real terms."[20] The reasoning is not beside the point. The ethnic nationalisms are a parallel to the nationalisms of the international la-bor movement prior to World War I. The creed of international solidarity in the laboring class broke down as soon as national allegiance became the deci-sive factor at the outbreak of the war. The labor movement as an international movement has not recovered since. The dynamics operative there is also at work among us.

The poor or oppressed in our society are prevented from becoming an effec-tive class by ethnic nationalism. The same is true of the poor and oppressed in the churches. That's how our system works. It has perfected the "divide and con-quer" rule by which the high and the mighty have always controlled dissent.[21] In our context ministry here is up against its greatest limitation. Interethnic praxis is next to impossible in the churches.

Thus we arrive at the second principle of a liberation doctrine of the church: *Since interethnic praxis is next to impossible at this time, and yet ministry is unify-ing activity among humankind, ministry turns into subversive activity in the United States today.*

---

16. Harold Cruse, *The Crisis of the Negro Intellectual* (New York: Morrow, 1967), 157.
17. Ibid., 161.
18. Ibid., 174.
19. Ibid., 257.
20. Ibid., 260.
21. In understanding the dynamics of power in our society I have been much helped by Theodore J. Lowi, *The End of Liberalism: Ideology, Policy, and the Crisis of Public Authority* (New York: Norton, 1969).

What Dare the Church Think Again?

Ministry becomes subversive where it opposes the church as a mirror of the present state of American culture, especially the various pluralisms that sustain the division of the churches. There is no reason to think of a subversive ministry as a sign of megalomania. Methodism, for example, has a good record of subversive ministry. Wrote Bishop Asbury in his journal for December 26, 1806: "The work of God is wonderful in Delaware. But what a *rumpus* is raised. We are subverters of government — disturbers of society — movers of insurrections. Grand juries in Delaware and Virginia have presented the noisy preachers — lawyers and doctors are in arms — the lives, blood, and livers of the poor Methodists are threatened: poor, crazy sinners! see ye not that the Lord is with us."[22] With this kind of tradition, should Methodism be surprised if the same thing happens in its ranks today? The church always seems to get caught in the fangs of culture. Let us take Methodism as an example of what is happening in a U.S. denomination. A good focus is a paper authored by John B. Cobb and published by the United Methodist Board of Higher Education and Ministry.

John B. Cobb, while realizing that the "concrete life of the church largely reflects the society and culture of which it is a part," wonders whether or not the church can "enter into and advance the frontiers of Western thinking."[23] His considerations take place under the aegis of "Can the Church Think Again?" Cobb uses liberation theology as one of the foils of his argument:

> There are others who see little importance in the internal life of the church. They are concerned that the church's energies be mobilized for social reform or the liberation of the oppressed. Among the liberation theologians, some are sharing in the cutting edge of thought insofar as that thought is the ideology of repressed groups seeking freedom. If the basic condition of the church were healthier, their leadership might become significant. But we can hardly expect to mobilize for sacrificial action in the world a community which does not experience its inherited faith as relevant to its own internal activities. And we can hardly expect persons outside the church to be moved by a prophetic word which cannot be heard within it.[24]

There is a shifting of focus going on here. Liberation theology, as I understand it, has indeed directed itself to "the internal life of the church." Perhaps during the past decade when, according to Cobb, the church got accustomed to getting along without thinking, some of us thought along lines *not approved as thinking* by some academic theologians. The impression is given by Cobb that all along we have known the theological subject. What we have failed to do is to tie it "into the current state of cultural and intellectual life of the West." But what about theological amnesia among the theologians as to their real subject matter? Might

---

22. Emory Stevens Bucke, ed., *The History of American Methodism,* I (New York: Abingdon Press, 1964), 324.

23. John B. Cobb, "Can the Church Think Again?" *Occasional Papers: Issued by the United Methodist Board of Higher Education and Ministry* 1, no. 12 (August 9, 1976).

24. Ibid., 6.

there not be a great difference between Cobb's apologetic interest, "sharing in the cutting edge of thought"[25] today, and the specific theological task? Could it not be really unthinking for theology right now not to do specifically *theological* thinking? What about the claims God makes on us through the poor as we are caught in our denominational power dilemmas?

Besides the struggle between the "truth" of the church and the untruths and truths of the Western world, there is also the theological struggle over truth and untruth in the church itself, the issue of apostasy and heresy. The way I read Cobb, he implies that sharing in the ideology of nonchurch groups is what needs to be done. In liberation theology a few of us do not in the least intend to share in the *ideology* of repressed groups as the foundation of theology. It is rather a question of discovering the reality of God in Messiah Jesus. Here *God's* praxis happens to include oppressed groups: "Blessed are you poor" (Luke 6:20).

The crucial task for theology is to make clear why God's praxis is not as yet becoming relevant to the "internal activities" of the church. In a church that mirrors the pluralism of culture, God's praxis in Messiah Jesus is effectively locked out. People in the churches become agents of the countervailing power pluralism of society. The impossibility of interethnic praxis in the churches is partly due to the fact that society keeps Christians apart in hermetically sealed denominations. The church has no power left to determine its own internal activities. It no longer controls its own life. The task of thinking in theology today is to clarify why a prophetic word cannot be obeyed in the church.

What happens to power in a praxis that shares in God's praxis? A theology that takes into account only the educated, the cultured, or the elites as its hermeneutical starting point has a hard time serving him who "has nowhere to lay his head" (Matt. 8:20). The New Testament tried to think through the power dilemmas of the poor as well as the worries of the rich. While not excluding the rich from God's concern, the New Testament church was struggling hard to keep witnessing to God's identification with the poor and the lost. I am not assuming that we already know what all this entails for being a Christian today. But it appears that we first of all have to think through what exercise of power God's praxis in Christ demands before we can hope to tie effectively into any cultural trend of the West today.

Can the church think again? Is not the more adequate question — in the light of God's praxis — *what dare* the church think again? We are constantly misled by the false assumption that we already know what to think. If we think through God's praxis in our church context we learn that sharing in the internal activities of the church means focusing theology on the internal power vacuum in the church. Thus we arrive at a third principle of the liberation doctrine of the church: *Cultural pluralism imported into theology is the Trojan horse that destroys the internal life of the church, keeping us at war with each other in the church, and at*

---

25. Ibid.

a safe distance from real history. It does not let us see history as the place where God struggles for justice.

Theological Education as Crucible?

Unless theological education as a whole can be reoriented, theological interest-group pluralism, reflecting society's countervailing power play, will continue to undermine theology from within. Obviously in trying to rectify a power dilemma of this magnitude we cannot do all things at once. The tendency to think of "two churches," referred to in the beginning of the chapter, still shows in even very progressive approaches to the doctrine of the church today. We need to see how the church cannot be the church in history as long as the power dilemma is disregarded, that is, as long as the internal activities of the denomination are not examined from the viewpoint of God's involvement in history. As long as the church is so structured that it cannot be involved the way God is involved in history there is no point in entering into or advancing the frontiers of Western thinking.

Much theological education is still under the influence of the Niebuhr study of the fifties. Niebuhr speaks of the ministry twenty years ago as the "perplexed profession." Almost immediately he can tie this to the confusion of the church itself: "The contemporary church is confused about the nature of the ministry. Neither ministers nor the schools that nurture them are guided by a clear-cut, generally accepted conception of the office of the ministry, though such an idea may be emerging."[26] A clear-cut, generally acknowledged conception of ministry has in fact not emerged since. From observation of U.S. seminaries and churches, Niebuhr called for what he thought was the newly emerging ministry image, the "pastoral director." He was intrigued by the office from which the minister was directing the activities of the church. Niebuhr makes much of the place that determines how the minister functions: "The place in which the minister functions always signalizes the Church's idea of his task."[27] He was very sensitive to the dual history orientation accompanying the notion of the pastoral director:

> Today there is uncertainty about the ministry in Church and world partly because it is not clear whether the Church is fundamentally inclusive or exclusive, whether therefore the minister's concern is to extend to all in his reach or only to the faithful elite. Is the rural, the suburban, the inner-city, the college minister a parish person or a builder of a separated community? Is the theological teacher a minister of a separate ecclesiastical science or of a university subject?[28]

The internal activities of the church are not looked at in a levelheaded fashion. It is not seen that there is no place for a separate community. The tasks of the church are the tasks of history because of God's involvement. The task of the

---

26. H. Richard Niebuhr, *The Purpose of the Church and Its Ministry* (New York: Harper, 1956), 50. To bring change in this regard has been the intention of "Theological Education and Liberation Theology: An Invitation to Respond," *Theological Education* 16, no. 1 (Autumn 1979): 7–11.

27. Niebuhr, *The Purpose of the Church*, 80.

28. Ibid., 75.

theological teacher is neither a separate ecclesiastical science nor a university subject.

Theological education in the eighties has to cope with several contradictions. Foremost is the contradiction between the actual accommodation of the Christian faith to culture, which makes it impossible for the church to function as a community with an identity of its own, and the taxing demand for the Christian community to join God's own involvement in history. Christians are involved in history but never notice it. We are so much involved in it that what shapes us is what culture and society are doing with history. Yet we ask little what God's involvement in history does to shape us.

The contradiction between our culture accommodation as church and God's involvement in history is partly grounded in the contradiction between a historicist relationship to Jesus and a living relationship to God's work in Christ in present history. In his analysis of theological education, H. Richard Niebuhr regards Jesus of Nazareth mostly as a historical figure to which we have a historical relationship. That reflects an overall attitude of much biblical scholarship. Practically this means that Jesus of Nazareth is safely removed from the present scene of history. Somewhat in the vein of H. Richard Niebuhr and taking the premises of the first fifty years of theology in the twentieth century into account, Van A. Harvey has developed a position that moves back and forth between (a) the historical Jesus and (b) the memory-image of Jesus. While acknowledging the historian's inability to outline a life of Jesus in detail, he lets the basic shape of Jesus' ministry come through as an orientation point for theological work. The basic yield of his reflection is the notion of Jesus as paradigm of awakening faith. Jesus' role was that "of having raised and answered the basic human question of faith. It was this role which made him the paradigm of God's action, for he had taught them to think of God as the one whose distinctive action is to awaken faith."[29] The whole paradigm function seems exhausted in God's faith.

It is not unimportant that Harvey sees Jesus as paradigm of *God*, not just of human existence. But he never draws out the positive strength of this emphasis. There is a specific warrant that accounts for Jesus as paradigm. Before Harvey outlines God's awakening of faith in Jesus he speaks of the distinctive characteristics of religious paradigms. Thus Jesus is part of Christianity as a religion, which functions as a common denominator of many expressions of faith, non-Christian as well as Christian. Once the common denominator has been announced, religion provides the basic matrix of understanding the memory-image of Jesus.

Harvey does not slight the *historical* character of the paradigmatic Christian events. They "do not direct the community away from history but have as their focus the life of responsibility in history."[30] Our peculiar responsibility in history, however, remains largely concealed. Harvey's religious catchall confuses things: "The basic concern was a religious one. Whether we may presuppose that the

---

29. Van A. Harvey, *The Historian and the Believer* (New York: Macmillan, 1966), 270.
30. Ibid., 265.

disciples came to this event with a religious question or whether the event itself raised the question for them we need not decide."[31] In Harvey everything is determined by the religious warrant. For religion it seems not very important to ask whether or not the event itself raised the question for the disciples. But this is the most crucial question: What does the event itself do to us? Does it raise a question different from the religious question?

Harvey is too careful a historian that he would not at least see other dimensions. But with the common denominator of religion they cannot become paradigmatic. He notices that Jesus "represents a radical reinterpretation of the concept of righteousness and of the ideas of God's power held by those who hoped to be justified by the law. Jesus consorts with the outcasts and the sick and the weak, those the 'righteous' call unrighteous."[32] What Harvey does not consider is whether Jesus' consorting with the outcasts is raising a paradigmatic question for us that cannot be subsumed under the general category of religion. The question of religion does not worry about a living relationship to God's work in Messiah Jesus in present history. Religion can leave Messiah Jesus in the past and do its own thing with God in the present. Here the contradictions in the contemporary church lie open before our eyes.

Theological education as crucible? A crucible is something "that tests as if by fire." What is being tested is our endurance in facing the contradictions. The internal activities of the church are being tested by God in Messiah Jesus in regard to a *radical reinterpretation* of righteousness. Since Jesus rose not just into the life of the church, and certainly not just into the kerygma, but into history, the challenge is to discover in what sense theology today can relate to the history into which Jesus rose as Lord.

God is still active in history in terms of Jesus' life. Practically this means that theological education will begin with the premise of praxis, not just with theory, doctrine, tradition, and ideas alone. What has been at stake all along this past decade has been hard thinking, thinking through in what sense each theological doctrine relates to the involvement of the Risen One in history. It does not mean in any sense an immediate call to action. The sociopolitical and socioeconomic problems we are facing are so vast we cannot hope to solve them by just wading into them. As we begin to act in terms of relating to history's sociopolitical and socioeconomic struggles *in which the church itself is caught*, we might be able, however, to become utterly aware of the present powerlessness of the churches and to begin to fight it with all our might.

Our present experience as Christians is dominated by the captivity of the churches in culture accommodation. There are many Christians who by now grasp the contradiction between the captivity and God's involvement in history. Theological education often stays at a distance from the living God in history by concentrating on the historicist Jesus. That is, it stays in a safe realm of ideas.

---

31. Ibid., 270.
32. Ibid., 272.

As soon as one turns from labeling Christianity a religion to a radical interpretation of God's righteousness, the praxis mandate cannot be avoided. We begin to understand God's righteousness as the *justice* that praxis seeking understanding is struggling for. What happens if one begins, not by modeling Christianity merely on a distant faith paradigm of the historical Jesus, but by relating it to historical reality today? We discover the poor. What we are being told by the poor in view of the gospel is that theology grows out of praxis. Praxis gives rise to thought. And the first thought we think here is the powerlessness of the churches. The increasing pressures put on us by vast global structures, politically, economically, and technologically, are not effectively dealt with by the churches. The divided denominations are part of the problem. This is the most concrete form of the contradiction in which Christians live.

The old principle of theological education can only make Christians more religious. It practically means keeping the church apart from history. From now on, theological education has to risk examining each doctrine or teaching in regard to the mandate of justice.

Praxis Seeking Justice?

Theological education will grow responsible in new ways if it sees itself interlocked with the praxis tasks of the local church, especially in regard to liberty and justice for all. The contradictions in which theological education finds itself today are basically the same contradictions experienced in the local church. What the local church does not fully understand as yet is how it is tied into the power struggles of the global village. In many instances the local church does not even have an inkling of being accountable to the power play. Predominantly white mainline churches first need to discard the smoke screen of civil religion that still conceals the radical demands of justice.

Such a turning will be possible if theological education and Christian education can mutually inform each other in terms of forming the local church as an action-reflection group where the principles of our sudden awakening in the global village are thought through. This does not relegate worship or prayer to a secondary place. But the acts of service to God have to be seen much less exclusively as meditation or contemplation. There is not enough corporate social analysis informed by biblical analysis, not enough contemplation and celebration growing out of thoughtful involvement in concrete issues. The primary principle in every American is individual striving: "They would just make that little trip across the ocean! America — that's the country where a poor devil can get ahead."[33] But now there is a new principle: There is a global village where *all* poor devils need to get ahead. This fundamental shift in principle is not grasped as yet. We continue to disregard the exercise of power. We still act as though we were not limited by the global village.

---

33. O. E. Rölvaag, *Giants in the Earth* (New York: Harper & Brothers, 1965), 218.

There is nothing extremely difficult about the basic point. Theology and the church are met by the claims of the poor all over the world. The gospel cannot be understood from the top down, only from the bottom up. Yet millions and millions of Christians are not close to the poor and do not want to get close. Someone might object that we cannot think of the poor all the time. But limits are inevitably imposed on us. We might as well face what is limiting us in the human family: not all people are in a physical condition to grasp the gospel. They are too poor.

Our vision in the churches is not yet focused on our global village existence. The gospel is still interpreted in terms of the *splendid isolation* of that "tiny island of Christianity" called the United States. But can the gospel still be understood at all in terms of such splendid isolation?

This book, then, is in large part an exercise in *new seeing*. It is a question of what we had better see in order to be responsible human beings. Since this is an attempt at seeing in the church, we are fundamentally asking what kind of church helps us in that seeing. No great vision of the future is offered. A few words of Peter L. Berger's come to mind: "Our time is full of visions of the future, loudly and arrogantly proclaimed. Moral self-righteousness is evenly distributed throughout the political spectrum. . . . Yet they know so very little, all these self-confident prophets of doom and salvation. It is necessary to cultivate the quiet art of disbelief. It is necessary to act quietly and disbelievingly, out of compassion which is the only credible motive for any actions to change the world."[34] To this I respond: It is necessary to cultivate the quiet art of seeing. Without seeing the powerlessness and understanding the reasons for it, there can be no change in the church.

The task is a complex one. Pointing the finger does not aid insight. We will try to follow through the issue of power from Christian origins to the present in terms of several turns in outlook and attitude. Basically today in the United States we are up against a Leviathan of organization constantly interfering with clear thinking about what the church is called upon to do in regard to power. Arnold M. Rose has put the matter succinctly in claiming "not simply that power is pluralistic in American society, but that the society itself is pluralistic. The different spheres of life do not interpenetrate each other in the way in India, for example, religious values and institutions permeate the average man's political, economic, family, artistic, educational, and other spheres of life. . . . In the United States . . . practically every person has differentiated roles and values for the various spheres of life, and so power too usually does not significantly cross the boundaries of each sphere in which it is created."[35] The examination of power and powerlessness in the church involves a long thought process. It makes us turn first of all to the head of the church and to analyze Christology in the face of power and powerlessness.

---

34. Berger, *Pyramids of Sacrifice*, 255f.
35. Rose, *The Power Structure: Political Process in American Society*, 33.

22

PRAXIS PASSIONIS DIVINI

This essay commemorates the fiftieth anniversary of the 1934 Barmen Declaration of the German Confessing Church resisting Adolf Hitler's Third Reich. Herzog writes on the boundary between two continents, Europe and North America, and two traditions that have been formative within these settings, the liberation tradition and the Reformation tradition, two traditions that shaped his own theological thinking. As a bridge builder across the Atlantic, Herzog never stopped searching for what each side might learn from the other. The German tradition of resistance against the identification of the church with the dominant powers of culture and the Third Reich, as manifest for instance in the dialectical or Neo-Reformation theology of the 1930s, becomes an important stepping-stone for the critical task of theology today. In the web of relationships already in place between North America and Europe, the liberation tradition, which is rooted in the black church and oppressed groups, adds a new impulse.

In dialogue with the German theologian Gerhard Sauter's interpretation of the common heritage of dialectical theology, Reformation, and Neo-Reformation, Herzog develops the challenge of the liberation tradition which ushers into a dual praxis concept that reshapes the life of the church. In light of both Reformation and liberation traditions, praxis can no longer be the activism of the autonomous modern person in power, used to taking things into his or her own hands. Such praxis, as the Reformation tradition knows, never reaches God; the liberation tradition might teach us that such praxis never really reaches the oppressed either. Theology needs to understand that God's own praxis at work in suffering and liberation, so vividly described for instance by the liberation tradition of the spirituals which take much of their imagery from the Bible, comes first, and that the praxis of the church flows from it.

The March–April issue of *Evangelische Theologie* (1984) occupies a special place in contemporary discussions about the meaning of the legacy of dialectical theology. Once again, sparks generated by focusing a lens on this new beginning could ignite the power of thought. The various issues which were raised revolve around a basic question: What direction do we take from here?

First published in *Evangelische Theologie* 44, no. 6 (November–December 1984): 563–75; translated from the German by Mary Deasey Collins.

The complexity of the discussion can here be acknowledged only by condensing it to a few points. At the same time, we should take into consideration that by reprinting the preface of the first issue of 1934, the "anniversary" volume of 1984 takes on a certain "atmosphere" in which the Neo-Reformation approach of Christian thought plays godfather to a self-critical approach in 1984.

By taking up the principal question, I would like to emphasize points of convergence between two continents (Europe and North America) and places where we can discover common tasks by starting from our Neo-Reformation heritage. I will limit myself to the following points:

1. An as yet unexplored mutual responsibility of Christian theologians toward various traditions — implying a widening of the ecumenical horizon.

2. A new starting point in Christian theology centered on God's action and not just on a particular understanding of the word of God, with emphasis on the Gospels (*viva vox evangelii*) and not only the Pauline tradition — implying an illumination of the ecumenical horizon through God's contemporary "radiance" in the church and in history.

3. The working out of a double praxis concept, according to which the theopraxis always precedes Christian theology — implying a clearer outline of the ecumenical horizon.

Broadening the Horizon of Christian Thought

We will make no headway unless in some respects we break with the thought pattern of the Neo-Reformation approach. I will refer here mainly to Gerhard Sauter's essay "Was heisst 'Evangelische Theologie'?" He proceeds from the conviction that Christian thought derives its themes from those things which concern the church, "especially also the church's activities in the world within the ecumenical realm."[1] Surely there is broad agreement among us that the horizon of Christian thought is the ecumenical horizon. But what do we mean by the term "ecumenical"? Sauter's summary brings us closer to clarity: "By 'ecumenical' at that time was not meant the relationship between the 'big denominations' and their theologians, but rather the conversation of Protestant theologians beyond national boundaries."[2] Today, this conversation has an extremely binding character and initiates a complementary process. Already in 1934 the Neo-Reformation approach would have needed a counterbalance from the ecumenical sphere. Today it could even lead to a mistaken thought process if we would orient ourselves only in the Neo-Reformation direction. By "counterbalance" I do not mean that we should *twist* the Reformation insight, but rather that we should *turn* with it onto a broader horizon.

---

1. Gerhard Sauter, "Was heisst 'Evangelische Theologie'?" *Evangelische Theologie* 44 (1984): 122.
2. Ibid.

It was apparent again last year, during the celebration of the five-hundredth birthday of Martin Luther in the United States, that Dietrich Bonhoeffer's essay titled "Protestantism without Reformation" had exactly hit the nail on the head. Of course there is no tree or bush in the United States which would have been hit by Reformation lightning. No monk ever stood on the prairie crying, "Help me, St. Anne, I want to become a monk!" Naturally there was no Augustinian monastery in the sixteenth century in the Dakotas where a young law student could have knocked at the gate and asked to be admitted. There were only Native Americans with their wigwams and an entirely different understanding of God. The entire historical basis is lacking for an understanding of the Reformation in the New World.

This of course does not mean that for us in the United States the Reformation has no significance. However, the learning process, which seems more pressing now than ever before, is a broadening of the Reformation horizon through traditions which have shaped the Protestant faith through new experiences. Why is this event important also for Europe? (1) Europe gave birth to the New World. In America, Europe sees herself once again in a new form. (2) Middle European life, particularly that of West Germany, has already been partly shaped by North American life for several decades. In this sense we would all do well to consider what kind of a world we are dealing with as church in the ecumenical realm. Certainly it was never the world determined by the Holy Roman Empire of the German nation which turns the problems of the Roman Curia and the Papacy into major themes. Also, it was never exclusively a movement against justification by works, the pretext by which the teaching of the church politically defended the papal moneybags. The answer of Protestantism taking shape at the time continues to be confessionally binding, pointing the way for the churches of the Reformation: *sola scriptura, sola fide, sola gratia,* and so on. But since there was no Reformation in American Protestantism, there was no coalescence of Protestant consciousness on the confessional level.

In the United States, there is no parallel to the alignment (*Gleichschaltung*) of religious consciousness as experienced by European Protestantism. The more than 250 denominations which exist here should be proof enough. The sole exception which even comes close to this is the Great Awakening in the eighteenth century. Even so, there was no formulation of a common creed. The Enlightenment largely preceded or ran parallel to this pietistic movement, and therefore American Protestantism is to a large extent a mixture of Enlightenment notions and Pietism (Puritanism), enlightened piety.[3]

If one puts this together with denominational individuality, the United Church of Christ, which since 1980 has existed in communion with the Evan-

---

3. The relationship between European Enlightenment and North American piety has not yet been sufficiently researched, although there is an extensive body of literature available. For example: Henry Steele Commager, *The Empire of Reason: How Europe Imagined and America Realized the Enlightenment* (New York: Oxford University Press, 1982).

gelical Church of the Union, is a good example.[4] There is in part still alive the legacy of the German Reformation through the Lutheran and Reformed traditions, but equally strong is the Anglo-Saxon tradition. In addition, there are the American influences of pragmatism and pluralism. The ecumenical character of this denomination, however, is attributable to its black, Asian and Native American roots. In addition, there are church members of Latin American origin. Also, Hungarians and Armenians represent significant ethnic groups.

Concealed within this slim enumeration lies a great problem which we cannot avoid in the Protestant theology of Middle Europe (or in the journal bearing the name *Evangelische Theologie*). The decisive question is whether or not we have to do theology out of several Protestant traditions. There are at least two traditions in North American Protestantism which we need to acknowledge, the *Reformation tradition* and the *liberation tradition*.

There is yet a huge assignment also for Middle European theology. So far it has been engaged, at times thoroughly, in North American theology at some points, but not to the extent of confirming its challenges or insights. *Liberation* is particularly related to the black churches, who owe their origins as independent churches to slavery or the emancipation from slavery. Worship, liturgy, hymnody, prayer, and doxology revolve around the emancipation event. Where among the German hymns are we to find anything like, "Go down, Moses, tell ol' Pharaoh, let my people go," or like "before I'll be a slave I'll be buried in my grave and go home to my Lord and be free." This is the counterpart to "A Mighty Fortress Is Our God," i.e., "Were not the right man on our side, the man of God's own choosing."

We in North America have not yet 'processed' this tradition ourselves. However, we can no longer take up the Neo-Reformation beginning from 1934. Concentrating on it exclusively would create a false consciousness. We must examine the Reformation tradition and the liberation tradition side by side, not in order to subsume one to the other, but to process the liberation tradition as a historically different experience of the gospel and to understand it as a second tradition.

There have been times in Germany when preoccupation with anything other than the European world was considered an escape. Should one not do as the gospel tells us: "You should have practiced the latter, without neglecting the former" (Matt. 23:23)? Even by remaining within the European world, we could find ourselves involved in an escape — by undergoing an internal emigration. The end result is the same. It is important now that we take seriously our contemporary ecumenical task, which does not exclude the Third World. Gerhard Sauter's retrospective view of 1934 is exactly up-to-date: "One of the fatal consequences of 'German and only German' theology was that the further it

---

4. I have attempted a commentary on this developing relationship in "Thesen zum Zusammenführen der Ströme der Reformation," *Evangelische Theologie* 43, no. 6 (November–December 1983): 548–56.

withdrew from the Protestant churches of other countries the fainter became their replies."[5] To prevent this from happening again, it is important that voices from the liberation tradition be heard in German theology.

The widening of the ecumenical horizon to North America should not be so difficult when one considers that the American way of thinking is consumed as part of the daily media diet of millions of Middle Europeans — even in the German Democratic Republic, whether it is *The Electric Horseman*, or *Dynasty* or *Dallas*. Emotional intermingling is already widespread, not to mention the intermarriage of the business world.[6] This process is not happening without some quasi-theological experiences.

Naturally, one can no longer say: "When in the box the money sings, the soul at once to heaven springs." However, we all pay into the coffers of television directly and indirectly. In a sense this little Reformation rhyme could be reworded: "When in the box the money sings, the soul at once to dreamland swings." Liberation is long overdue.

Widening of the ecumenical horizon is indispensable if theology wants to remain evangelical theology. Like "Protestantism without Reformation," there is also "Reformation without liberation." Traditions different from our own help us to find healthy self-criticism. The context of the 1934 volume is very different from that of the present day. In those days people hesitated to speak out for fear of losing their jobs. Today there are no grounds for this particular anxiety. We all have good jobs with the church or the government, or want to have them. Young people today, though, certainly fear unemployment. There is also the threat of nuclear war. *Evangelical* theology, theology of the Good News, means that despite all of the difficulties in which we find ourselves, we can continue to do theology as though there were no anxiety.

God's Action as Illumination of the Ecumenical Horizon

The church is God's function as light of the world. Sauter brings his essay to a close with a critical observation on the action of the church: "After fifty years, it has become no easier to talk about this diacritical point without misunderstanding. Perhaps today it is above all the *omnipresence of action*, its presuppositions, opportunities and dangers that make a pause necessary, a pause which must precede theological work and the praxis of faith."[7] From the other side of the Atlantic, we first have to urge a pause for thinking about the *omnipresence of God's*

---

5. Sauter, "Was heisst 'Evangelische Theologie'?" 122.

6. There is a body of literature specifically devoted to the interdependence between the United States and Germany. One of the best new publications is by Marion Gräfin Dönhoff, entitled *Amerikanische Wechselbäder* (Stuttgart: Deutsche Verlags-Anstalt, 1983). This interdependence has been reintroduced into academic circles through the statement made by Dietrich Genscher (December 13, 1983), of the (German) Foreign Ministry, suggesting that German universities should follow the example of American universities. Genscher's proposal to the "Bundesvereinigung der Arbeitgeberverbände" is a telling example of the seriousness of this matter even today.

7. Sauter, "Was heisst 'Evangelische Theologie'?" 136.

action. In the distribution of bread and wine, and with the words of promise (that is to say, by sacrament and word: word-indwelling sacrament and sacramental word) God ever anew calls the church into life and sustains her. Naturally, it is possible that we flee before the words of God's grace into human achievement and thereby transform the theological situation into an ethical situation. It is an equally great temptation to place God in retirement by staying with an "only" theological situation.

The deliberation which has to happen here cannot be a purely North American phenomenon. The basics are located in the worship experience: "Ich selber kann und mag nicht ruh'n, des grossen Gottes grosses Tun erweckt mir alle Sinnen." (Seldom do I care to rest, the works of mighty God awake in me all my senses.) Theology begins when Christian thought is taken up by the great stream of divine action and comes alive in the worship experience. The parishioners have no real image of what the Eucharist and baptism point to. That in them God's action in the church and in history comes to us in a concentrated way is seldom mentioned by theology. Even here God appears as the "sun of righteousness."

The fear that gospel and politics will become indistinguishable, and also the aversion to an apparently recurring demand to go directly from the gospel to party politics, are understandable.[8] But it appears to me that the real problem lies in attempts to trace the route from the Reformation to the *Kirchenkampf* (the struggle between the church and the state in Hitler's time) *without* reflection on conditions as they exist today. The main reference point for the Neo-Reformation principle of *Evangelische Theologie* is always the phrase "proclaiming the gospel." For the Reformation itself, this was an important starting point in contrast to the law of justification by works. The rediscovery of the *viva vox evangelii* was a foundational experience of the Reformation and should be understood as deriving from this *historical* contrast between the grace of the gospel and the Roman Catholic idea of justification by works. Today we must go beyond the *principium verbi divini* to the *praxis passionis divini*.

The peculiarity of our situation with reference to God's action can now be made clear:

1. The Reformation insight concerning the *principium verbi divini* could fully be taken over in 1934. It concerned at the time the proper basis of theology "in confrontation with many additional contents which have to remain alien to its very being."[9] The content of the gospel was still clear and relevant in 1934 as a Reformation voice against National Socialism. The Reformation of 1534 had sufficiently spoken to 1934: one pursues a credible theology only there "where one 'confines' oneself to the subject matter of theology, to the Word of God which reveals the human being as sinner and God as justifying redeemer."[10] Proclamation

---

8. See ibid., 121.
9. Editor's preface in *Evangelische Theologie* 44 (1984): 102–11, 107.
10. Ibid., 106.

of the gospel, the Word of God, the human being as sinner, God as justifying redeemer — this was a sufficient formulation of content for the Reformation's starting point in 1534 and the Neo-Reformation project in 1934. The central question of content for 1984, however, is thereby not yet determined. Simply to repeat the old formulation in 1984, means truncating the content of theology so that it remains foreign to the essential character of Christian theology. The Word of God is not just the preaching of the gospel, not just declaration of the human being as sinner and God as justifying redeemer, rather it is Jesus Christ himself. This has especially been emphasized in the liberation tradition. The first thesis of Barmen does not begin, "The Word of God, as revealed in the Holy Scriptures, is the one Word of God...," but rather, "Jesus Christ... is the one Word of God." The person of Jesus Christ himself must not be suppressed.

2. Alongside the Pauline corpus of justification writings stand the Gospels, which illuminate Jesus Christ as a person. In the celebration of the Eucharist, by bread, wine, and the Word (also in the water of baptism), Jesus comes to us *completely.* This is not just Christ crucified, but the Jesus who, so to speak, already bears the marks of nails on his hands as he offers himself as living water to the Samaritan woman, and who as this *marked one* is not just an advocate for all persons, but also takes them up *into* his being, gathers them and liberates them to new corporate selfhood. Jesus does not say, So if the son justifies you, you will be justified indeed; rather he says, "So if the son sets you free, you will be free indeed" (John 8:36). Liberation doesn't exclude justification, but lets us pause to think about what kind of liberation occurred in Jesus. According to Luke, Jesus' own understanding of his mission began with his public appearance in reading aloud in the synagogue of Nazareth from the scroll of the prophet Isaiah which was handed to him, chapter 61:1–2. This text concerns the preaching of the good news to the poor, the proclamation of freedom to the prisoners and release for the oppressed. Jesus declares: "Today this scripture is fulfilled in your hearing" (Luke 4:16–21). Jesus concretely lived all of this. If we take the witness of his life seriously, then the point of the Eucharist is the presence of this person anointed by God's Spirit, who is still *also* to be found among the poor, the blind, and the destitute. "At the right hand of God," he continues together with God to struggle for all people, especially the poor, the blind, and the destitute.

The incarnation makes clear how God relates to human beings. God creates through Jesus a way of being human in which all people are included in God's passion for justice. God accomplishes both tasks: God *justifies* and God *creates justice.* God is a just God and a God who establishes justice. Concerning the omnipresence of God's action through Christ, also we in the United States do not as yet understand that liberation belongs to the *proprium* of Jesus Christ. However, we cannot bend the confession of this *proprium* into a personal political issue. Misinterpreting the *proprium* as a personal political issue falsifies the gospel. Too easily it becomes a legalistic political issue.[11]

---

11. We must differentiate carefully between the *proprium* as a political issue and our own political

I will resist using here the word "heresy." However, the severity of the issue cannot be avoided. It is just at this point that German/Middle European theology has the huge task of helping to further the decisive action of the Reformation, specifically in furthering the conviction that God is newly illuminated in the person of Jesus, and that God draws "bodily" near to us in the Eucharist and in baptism (including their proclamation of the Word) and becomes "touchable." The peace question and racism — just to name two examples — are in this perspective not to be separated from the *proprium* of Jesus Christ.

We need no new life-of-Jesus research. What we do need is a life-of-God research. That God lives was simply self-evident for the Reformation. We should not unthinkingly take over this self-evidence along with the teachings of the Reformation, because if we do, questions about who and what God is are suppressed or ignored.

3. North American Protestantism at first sight looks very much like its European counterpart. The image of God to a large extent has been shaped by Puritanism and Pietism. Martin Luther was not able to correspond with a theologian in the New World. However, August Hermann Francke (1663–1727), the Pietist, did correspond with Cotton Mather (1663–1728), the Puritan and

---

leanings. I will not go into detail here with regard to the number of political protests or demonstrations I have attended during the past year against nuclear armament, the North American presence in Central America, or the death penalty. What is important is simply not to be silent about it. This is my personal political agenda. But for this very reason I would not dream of expecting all other Christians to get involved in the same political point of view. As my own political stance, this point of view is totally subject to the *pecca fortiter*. Naturally I cherish the desire for as many fellow Christians as possible to stand up in uncompromising opposition to the principalities and powers of our time. But I will not constantly quote Jesus to explain my political position. Alongside me there are Muslims, Jews, Marxists, atheists, and people from all nationalities. My political stance cannot for everybody be directly traced back to the *proprium*. Jesus stood up for the poor, the weak, and the exploited creation. However, even in light of his solidarity with the poor, Jesus does not tell me which political party in the U.S. I should join. Christians in Poland or Guatemala have to make their very own decisions as well. An unmistakable no to nuclear armament, like my belonging to a particular party, depends on an argument, which I, as a North American socialist have to make by way of reasoning. But while setting a particular course, Christian thought may not withhold the political dimension of the *proprium*. What we need to resist is twisting the *proprium* into a legalistic political stance which is forced on everyone. It also does not promote neutrality or a middle-of-the-road policy. "In Gefahr und grosser Not bringt der Mittelweg den Tod" (Friedrich von Logau). (In awful danger and great need, the middle way brings death indeed.) We can make this very clear using the example of the time period after the Dahlem Synod of 1934. In it a word of greeting on November 30, in connection with decisions of the first provisional leadership, stated the following: "The church abstains from every political interference. We seriously decline to become a place of refuge for politically dissatisfied persons. The church has a divine commission. She serves the state and the people with the biblical witness about sin and grace." In looking back on this not very courageous stance, Karl Barth thoroughly clarified the matter in 1963: "Barmen was actually and practically not only an ecclesial affair, but also, with regard to the rise of National Socialism, a political event…a strange incident that a creedal statement is at the same time a political issue." We NATO Christians, however, hardly ever come down on a creed that is a political issue. We waver between an unpolitical confession and a political legalism, into which we twist the *proprium* of Jesus Christ. For more about the post-Dahlem situation and Barth's observations, see Martin Rohkrämer, "Die Synode von Barmen in ihren zeitgeschichtlichen Zusammenhängen," in *Bekennende Kirche wagen,* ed. Jürgen Moltmann (Munich: Chr. Kaiser, 1984), 55–58.

church father in New England. Since American Protestantism was to a large extent shaped by John Wesley (1703–91), one should recall that pietistic influences of the Moravians gave him the distinctive mark of an American church father. The God of Wesley is above all about sanctification — surely not without justification, but God's perfection is emphasized — which helps to understand that *one* word of Scripture is particularly important: "For you should be perfect, like your Father in Heaven is perfect" (Matt. 5:48). The result was an almost romantic notion of God. Certainly one does not get the impression that this popular puritanical/pietistic God is much concerned with history or with justice among human beings. It is a historical question worth asking how Pietism has widely influenced the notion of God in North America (with a basis in Puritanism and additions of Enlightenment thought).[12] To what extent have we constructed a perfect God, not a God who is immersed in the suffering of the world, and thereby constructed a golden calf, so that one could rightly say that God is dead.

If we examine the liberation tradition more closely, there is much that seems unusual to European thought. For example, Theo Lehmann said in his great book on spirituals (1966) in regard to the song "Go Down Moses, Go Down to Egyptland": " 'Egypt' refers to not only the land of Egypt in which the people of Israel experienced captivity, but also a slavery which [black] people must suffer. 'Freedom' is not only freedom from sin, but also freedom from slavery . . . , 'Israel' is not just the biblical people of Israel, but also the [black] people."[13] The point of the spirituals is clear: God behaves today toward those who belong to God the same way God did throughout the ages, particularly through Jesus. One spiritual expresses it this way:

> God raised de waters like a wall
> An' opened up de way,
> An' de God dat lived in Moses time
> Is jus' de same today.
> God locked de lion's jaw we read
> An' robbed him of his prey.
> An' de God dat lived in Daniel's time
> Is jus' de same today.

God acts in the same way, even today. The same point is made concerning other biblical figures or incidents, for example, David:

> He proved a friend to David
> I heed him and I pray.

---

12. Studies of this have not gone far enough for us to form a clear picture. See *Pietists: Selected Writings*, ed. Peter C. Erb (New York: Paulist Press, 1983), 22–26.

13. Theo Lehmann, *Negro Spirituals: Geschichte und Theologie* (Berlin: Evangelische Verlagsanstalt, 1966), 163. The spirituals quoted are also in Lehmann's book, 193f.

> The same God that David had,
> Will save me, come that day.

This is clearly related to the figure of Jesus, so that there is no division between God and Jesus — in the person of Jesus the constancy of God is to be discovered:

> Jesus is de ruler.
> He rule ma soul.
> He rule de hebben.
> He rule de sinner.
> He rule little David.
> He rule old Goliath.

Nothing is left out. Human beings remain sinners — as in the Reformation tradition. However, in the special historical context which is the basis for the spirituals, the sinner was also a slave. We need to remember how God struggles with spiritual captivity *and* with physical captivity. God is not romanticized in the liberation tradition, but God also does not remain in the distance. We cannot simply take over this tradition, but we cannot ignore it either. We must not behave as though it did not exist. Sauter sees in the current situation the danger that theology may be overtaken by an ethical mobilization: " 'Evangelical theology' cannot wish to support a growing tendency of the last few years to allow theology to be absorbed into an ethical movement. In spite of all the pressing concerns for action, it dare not neglect the task of caring for the afflicted conscience."[14] For North America, there remains the task of reawakening the drowsy conscience, to work against a forgetting of God in the Eucharist and in history which leads to unscrupulousness. To me the important point is that there is no evidence of a separation between theology and ethics in the Gospels. Rather, we are invited into the all-pervading presence of God's action, to participate in God's struggle, especially in the Eucharist. One must remember that God's struggle is always a suffering which is concretely realized in the cross of Christ. So naturally God is on the side of the afflicted conscience, but also on the side of the afflicted bodies of human beings. This duality of God's action is irrevocable. We must hold fast to the fact that God is concerned with the afflicted as well as the drowsy or deadened conscience.

---

14. Sauter, "Was heisst 'Evangelische Theologie'?" 130. We must bear in mind that what sometimes looks like the beginning of an ethical mobilization is often the expression of an intensely afflicted conscience. People experience that the no to nuclear weapons does not begin with the atomic bomb and with its mass murder. The conscience is awakened and declares, Every weapon is an instrument of murder. Another step is the discovery that sexual ethics and nuclear ethics are connected. The conscience says, Nuclear power is connected to sexual power. The one who does not care about sexual ethics had better not meddle in nuclear ethics, and vice versa. All of these deliberations appear first of all in the afflicted conscience.

Dual Praxis Concept
on a More Precisely Outlined Horizon

We are today all in the same damnable position, the same difficult global situation, whether we observe the matter from Middle Europe or from North America. Sauter is correct in stating that in 1934, the "theological valorization of a discovered connection — between national-political and religious-cultural matters — was supposed to be rebuffed."[15] One had to take a stance against a historical theology that represented a terrible threat. A distinction between historical signs (Kant) and a perception of the action of God in history would have been helpful at that time. A vote for the life-of-God research is based on the search for recognition of God's action in the Eucharist and in congregational worship. It is therefore not a historical theology but rather an approach to the action of God in history at the place where God makes Godself accessible while acting in history and in the community.

The irony of history, however, causes the "natural theology" that one wishes to avoid to make itself comfortable as our home companion — in our very own theological existence. Sauter stresses: "The phrase 'theological theology' announces a new theological understanding which takes note of the specific *scholarly* task of theology without any strictures."[16] It has turned out, however, that this scholarly aspect is mostly dealt with in a venerable model of theory and praxis which dates back to Aristotle.

It is exactly by retaining the Aristotelian model of theory and praxis that a powerful "natural theology" creeps in which prevents a reform of theology, even though, as Sauter reports, Georg Eichholz already proposed such a reform thirty years ago. Rudolf Bohren's book about Eduard Thurneysen, *Prophetie und Seelsorge* (1982), is especially informative in this respect. As one of the "fathers" of Neo-Reformation theology — the project which the editors of *Evangelische Theologie* were concerned with in volume 2, 1984 — Thurneysen, according to Bohren, simply ignores the *principium verbi divini.*[17]

Bohren finds that despite emphasis on the Scriptures, on the *principium verbi divini*, much thoughtlessness can occur. Thurneysen began with a great prophetic vision of community and freedom. However, in a manuscript of 1932, this discourse turned very bland. "It can't be other than nonbinding. The ritualization of the opening of the book prevents, so to speak, the event of revelation. The concept of community becomes stationary. As early as 1932 [Thurneysen] had overvalued the beginning of the sermon. 'Pay attention . . . to what occurs at the beginning of a sermon. It begins ever and always in the same way. It begins with the pastor ascending the pulpit.' Then comes the book which is opened: 'Preaching is . . . a book talk.'" Thurneysen "did not see what he was doing in an ecclesiological context with this sentence: with such an excessive valuation of

---

15. Ibid., 117.
16. Ibid., 123.
17. Ibid., 126.

ritual it is reinforced. . . . His concept of church was already the result of an old-fashioned attitude." Bohren here takes up a sentence from Thurneysen: "The man who belongs to a church is fundamentally a bound man." He goes on to explain that for Thurneysen, this means that the person wanders incessantly into the cathedral. "Thurneysen was now 'at home' in the cathedral, he was sustained 'by the institution of pulpit preaching,' and more than that, by the loyalty of his listeners. . . . Now theology justifies the theologian, that is to say, the preacher in the cathedral pulpit, and the theologian justifies the institution. The thought process has become hierarchical and moves in the sequence of 'pulpit listener.' The tent of the wanderers has made room for the temple."[18]

Thurneysen's analysis is not as interesting for our context as Bohren's use of it. It becomes evident that the depth of the theory-praxis concept has not yet been plumbed: "We stand before a problem that in practical theology has been inadequately considered. Praxis characterizes our actual image of the church, just as our image of the church determines our action in praxis. Praxis imperceptibly alters theology: therein lies its temptation and cunning. True theology nurtures a change in praxis: therein lies its healing power."[19] As much as I value Bohren's insight, it still operates with the model of "from theory to praxis," without starting out from theopraxis, from the *praxis passionis divini*. This means that *doctrine* takes priority over praxis. He does not then ask which institution *today* determines or occasionally distorts doctrine. So just like the cathedral, there is also the university. It is fortunate that both exist. However, the university may not prevent the access to theopraxis.

The praxis which Bohren has in mind is naturally the ecclesial one, meaning a praxis performed by human beings. However, without the framework of God's praxis, human praxis tends to imprison us. Theory can not remedy this either, because it is theory tied to the university. It is exactly this university-born theory that often produces a massive natural theology when it ignores God's prior action.

As to the search for truth as an academic task of theology (to use Sauter's terminology), is it not to be found in the integration of reflection with theopraxis? Only in this way does it arise again and again from theopraxis, that is to say, from worship, from the Eucharist, in which the stories of judgment and of salvation meet. We cannot continue without a dual praxis concept. Here, it appears to me, we can begin to think beyond the Neo-Reformation approach. Again and again, the point is the distinction between divine and human praxes and their working together.

It seems to me, that the unresolved problem with Bohren lies in his continued

---

18. Rudolf Bohren, *Prophetie und Seelsorge* (Neukirchen-Vluyn: Neukirchener Verlag, 1982), 173f. The rediscovery of the "tents of the wanderers" occurs today frequently in out-of-the-way places. I see such a creative thrust, for example, in B. Klappert, "Die Kirche vor der Namibia-Frage," in "Flugblätter zur Versammlung von Christen, 1.–3. Juni 84 in Wuppertal-Barmen," 9–48.

19. Bohren, *Prophetie und Seelsorge,* 174.

use of a theory-praxis model which connects doctrine *only* to theory — at least in our academic institution.

That will in turn contribute to a narrowing of the horizon which leaves much room to a natural theology in the framework of our universities. Bohren explains:

> It was part of the strength of Eduard Thurneysen that he maintained the priority of teaching before praxis. What he perhaps could not have foreseen adequately was the erosion and corruption of teaching through praxis, its imperceptible change through its situation. Just as the theological method of the new beginning was not acknowledged, so, for instance, the pastor's opening the Bible was not critically confronted with the Word. The corrupting character of ecclesial praxis calls for a questioning of "pure doctrine" as a presupposition of right action. Even more: one must ask whether the theory is defined precisely enough to resist the wear and tear of praxis.[20]

Theory not defined precisely enough? Here we find doctrine indiscriminately equated with theory, and theopraxis is ignored. This is a wide open field for our generation. Church practice can corrupt teaching. However, in the sphere of theory, theory can corrupt itself. How does this happen? In that it doesn't grow out of theopraxis, and does not even permit it to enter the thought process. On this point there is much to think about and to learn. Luther believed that "man solle den Leuten aufs Maul schauen" (one should pay attention to how people really speak). Today perhaps some people think we should pay attention to how the church really functions. However, first of all, we are invited to pay attention to God's life — God's life in the cross of today.

---

20. Ibid., 175.

23

GOD-WALK AND CLASS STRUGGLE

In this short essay, one of the fundamental insights of Herzog's last book, God-Walk: Liberation Shaping Dogmatics, *is developed. Theology in North America can only start over if it does not grow directly out of the tension between right praxis (orthopraxis) and right doctrine (orthodoxy), a tension that is reproduced in the ongoing standoff between liberals and conservatives. Theology will only be able to move beyond this impasse when it begins to focus on God's own praxis on the side of those who need help the most.*

But what does this have to do with class struggle? No doubt, in the United States most calls for orthopraxis and orthodoxy seem to be able to do without an awareness of such tensions. Do the tensions between the rich and the poor, between the races, and between the genders need to be produced artificially, as countless critics of liberation theology have suspected? The point of Herzog's reflections must come as a surprise to mainline theologies, whether liberal or conservative: God's own praxis, which can no longer be conceived without God's preferential option for those at the margins, uncovers those tensions that are already in place and have continued to grow in some ways since Herzog's essay was written.[1]

Encounters with God's presence in the cracks and gaps of this world no longer allow us to worship and to celebrate the Eucharist in splendid isolation. Walking with God, theology and the churches can no longer afford to cover up the wounds of the world. Unwitting participants in the class struggle, we need to wake up and join in a different struggle: God's struggle for justice.

> I saw the world in terms of class-conflict.
> — DOROTHY DAY

Liberation theology is in the news again since the September 1984 publication of a Vatican opposition statement. About the same time, Cardinal Ratzinger and his Vatican Congregation of the Faith interrogated Father Leonardo Boff of Brazil.

First published in *Circuit Rider* 9, no. 6 (June 1985): 4–6.

1. For some numbers illustrating the increasing gap between rich and poor see Joerg Rieger, "Introduction: Watch the Money," in *Liberating the Future: God, Mammon, and Theology*, ed. Joerg Rieger (Minneapolis: Fortress Press, 1998), 5–7.

The Vatican almost willy-nilly seems to become an accessory to a media blitz with even Pope John Paul II getting into the act, telling Roman Catholic leaders they must defend the poor from the "illusory and dangerous proposals" of liberation theology. At least that is the way the media report it.

At this moment opposition is strongest against some Latin American forms of liberation theology. North America has not as yet had major clashes over liberation theology. Our continent is more Protestant, and Protestant churches do not have as controlling a magisterium as Catholic churches, if any. Yet clashes may not be far off here, too.

A Major Issue

Parts of the Vatican document are surprisingly positive in regard to the option for the poor — the central concern of liberation theology. Yet, a crucial theme of the Vatican piece is its objection to the tenet of liberation theologies with Marxist sympathies that "only those who engage in the struggle can work out the analysis correctly." The Vatican says that Christian truth "itself is in question here, and it is totally subverted." This is strong language.

To sum up the subversion, the Vatican statement adds: "There is not truth, [the liberation theologians] pretend, except in and through the partisan praxis." The Vatican bases its critique on the premise that the "ultimate and decisive criterion for truth can only be a criterion which is itself theological."

I would suggest that participation in the struggle is indispensable in establishing the criterion for truth. One might be able to live with a few misunderstandings in the Vatican statement. Yet, the assumption prevalent in much of the document is that the church can state some truth simply in theory without having it grow out of the justice struggle itself. Primitive Christian praxis puts us on a different road.

Only in following Jesus did the disciples find out who he is. Albert Schweitzer has put that in the often quoted words: "And to those who obey him, whether they be wise or simple, he will reveal himself in the toils, the conflicts, the sufferings which they shall pass through in his fellowship."

Only in struggling with the Gentiles over the truth of the gospel did the apostles find out that God also liberates pagans for discipleship. Much of this was connected with bodily abuse by the authorities through persecution and prison.

It seems an easy way out for the authors of the Vatican pronouncement to make Marxist praxis responsible for the notion that only those who engage in the struggle can work out the analysis correctly. It turns into a smoke screen. If one can paint its basic Christian premise as the Marxist thing — good riddance. There is no invitation to reflect on the long liberation theology struggle over a method more truthful to Christian experience. The awesome problems connected with the old methods are swept under the rug. It is a painful moment. How does one argue effectively against a smoke screen?

The God-Walk Hypothesis

The notion that "only those who engage in the struggle can work out the analysis correctly" in Christian thought is rooted in God's own activity in Christ. In suffering on the way to the cross, in the price he paid, Christ worked out the way of salvation and liberation. In his death on the cross, he worked out the analysis of the resurrection: "All authority has been given to me in heaven and on earth" (Matt. 28:18). Correspondingly, it is not those who theorize, "Lord, Lord," who enter the kingdom of God, but those who do the will of God. Christian theory is not primary; the struggle is, life is. This may be the most crucial epistemological contribution of Christianity.

Why so? First of all, it is God in Christ who engages in the justice struggle — standing by human beings precisely in this struggle. Christians find themselves involved because God is involved. Christian liberation thought grows out of theopraxis, God's own God-walk through history. If one claims, as the Vatican statement appears to do, that for liberation theologies orthodoxy usually grows out of "orthopraxy," one might miss the point altogether. Biblically, theopraxy comes first. Is it not first of all God who takes sides with the poor? As soon as God's own praxis becomes primary for our lives, human orthopraxy or human orthodoxy may no longer be the hinge of anything. We need to turn away from our anthropocentric angle on praxis.

Liberation theologians worth their salt primarily wish to join God on the side of the poor. For its part, the Vatican Congregation of Faith tries to show its concern for the poor, for example, by appealing to the clear stand of the Vatican on the arms race:

> The apostolic See, in accord with the Second Vatican Council and together with the episcopal conferences, has not ceased to denounce the scandal involved in the gigantic arms race which, in addition to the threat which it brings to peace, squanders amounts of money so large that even a fraction of it would be sufficient to respond to the needs of those people who want for basic essentials of life.

It is one thing to say this in terms of God-talk, that is, using "a criterion which is itself theological." Is it not quite another to resist the arms race in God-walk by letting pronouncements grow out of actual resistance to nuclear war? As far as our many words are concerned, we are all in the same condemnation. They have accomplished very little in stopping the arms race. Where lies the problem?

Where Marxist and Christian Praxis Coincide

God's justice struggle and class struggle are not two completely separate things. For example, we grasp the real threat involved in the nuclear arms race in its depth dimension only in terms of class struggle. "The needs of those people who want for basic essentials of life" are understood in their stark presence only in the actual struggle against domination.

There are those who own the means of production for making Pershing IIs and other mass murder weapons. There are those who do not own the means of production.

When it comes to ownership, the situation is in principle the same in the Soviet Union as in the United States. Only a radical change in ownership of the means of production would stop the arms buildup. The means of production have to be in the hands of all the people for making peace products and not weapons of war. The time is far off. But the goal is clear.

Whether one talks about the owners as a ruling class or gives them some other label, the owner class and those who do not own the means of production are antagonists in harsh conflict. The conflict does not always flare to the surface. It is not always understood. But it is there. The poor are sometimes blind to it. Their consciousness needs to be altered, too. On the covert and overt violence of the clash, the Marxist point and the Christian point coincide.

Thus, three things are clear: (1) God's struggle for justice antecedes the human struggle; (2) there is no effective insight into justice apart from involvement in God's struggle; (3) the class struggle involves the option for the poor, the refusal of empire, and the refusal of death.

Many other issues connected with the Vatican statement or, for that matter, with the liberation theology method as such we cannot touch on.

Thinking on Our Feet

In this context one is tempted to tell one's story of involvement in the struggle and describe walks for justice one has participated in: the march on Washington against poverty in August 1983 (jobs, peace, and freedom), for example, or another march on Washington against empire in November 1983 ("U.S. out of El Salvador"), or 1984 walks around the North Carolina capitol in Raleigh against the death penalty.

Sure, "We are a gentle, angry people," discovering God in the pain of history, not knights in shining armor. We also remember that in the civil rights struggle and the anti–Vietnam War protests not much happened until bodies in the streets interfered with government machinery.

So, we today may again be involved in the first stages of another such protest. Still, there is no guarantee — history is a messy thing with few regularities. But God's justice struggle does not hinge on our "contemplation in the streets" (Carlo Carretto).

The real issue of the liberation theology method hinges on the Eucharist, the liturgy of the church. It entails an in-depth spirituality we have little thought of before. The "bodily" presence of God for the Christian is felt through the elements of bread and wine as the presence of one who walked the lonesome valley, "despised and rejected" (Isa. 53:3), who battled all manner of injustice — preaching "good news to the poor," proclaiming "release to the captives," and liberating "those who are oppressed" (Luke 4:18).

Present to us in the "elements" of life is the one bearing the cross, the stench of the executioners around him, the soldiers and the vulgar crowd. In the Eucharist we are placed in the midst of brutal history and are not allowed spiritual beauty-culture.

So the Eucharist can never be celebrated apart from history — the history in which God in Christ is still struggling for the liberation and salvation of each person and of the structures of history as a whole. If the word were not so much co-opted today, we ought to call it sanctification. In any case, here the real sanctification takes place.

What about the proclamation of the Word, though? It "walks" in body *language* what the sharing of the bread and wine concretize in *body* language: God's own justice walk through all of history.

"Only those who engage in the struggle can work out the analysis correctly"? The Eucharist puts us in touch with the poor. It makes us aware in our walk that empire still takes its toll among countless poor everywhere. It lets us know in person that too many are still in love with death rather than life.

Suffering the attrition of the struggle concretely is mind-wrenching and soul-wrenching. Yet it is only in this — yet defeated — walk through history that we grasp the struggle as cruel class struggle. It is not a theoretical Marx invention. Class struggle is a fact. Gustavo Gutiérrez has reminded us of that many times.

Acknowledging the fact is all that is at stake in the debate at this time. That some of the poor are also in favor of death in supporting the death penalty makes the struggle all the more fierce. Consciousness-altering is not only for the rich. There is a pedagogy of the oppressed as well as of the oppressor. Taking all these factors of harsh struggle into account, we realize that the primitive Christian experience in praxis repeats itself over and over again.

What liberation theology wants to achieve by rooting itself in primitive Christian engagement in the struggle is the realization that we have to indwell the reality we want to tackle in order to make a difference. We cannot make sense of history or nature by relating to them from a distance. Either you indwell them and you can make a difference, or you keep your hands off. Only direct engagement in the struggle affords a holistic grip on reality, a sense of people and things in their mutual interference and interdependence. The consequences are clear.

The Refusal of Poverty. God-walk bleeds out of history the awareness that the tidbit insights floating around in society about class differences all have their roots in the basic struggle. In 1977, about 25 million people lived below the poverty line in the United States. By 1981, there were close to 7 million more, and by 1983 another 3.5 million. There are now almost as many poor as there were in the early '60s when the war on poverty began.

In reviewing these data, columnist David Gergen, no Marxist he, recently opined: "There is no blinking aside the fact that class differences are sharply growing." The question is, what do we do about it? Engagement in the struggle involves refusal of poverty as "fate."

There is nothing un-American about it. As early as 1775, the Mecklenburg revolutionary convention in North Carolina opposed "everything that leans to...power in the hands of the rich...exercised to the oppression of the poor."

Yet, the churches have seldom taken sides in an explicit option for the poor. In *Sojourners* (January 1985) Jim Wallis points to "new stirrings in the churches" in this regard. Liberation theology tries to embolden the churches in these stirrings, so that in taking sides with the poor they will openly refuse poverty as "fate."

The Refusal of Empire. Since Ronald Reagan speaks of the Soviet Union as "evil empire," we ought to wonder about our own national framework in which our churches do their thing. Are we not an empire, too? Recently, Thomas P. (Tip) O'Neill charged, "This administration has shown that it is ready to starve Africans so that it can kill Latin Americans."

Poverty is also an effect of empire. Nationalism is often used to hide the poverty we inflict in our empire expansion. Are we still continuing what we began in the conquest of our continent? Did we not decimate the Native Americans and hide their remnants in reservations? Leaving them without power, we made them an underclass. We did it through wars, ironically called the "Indian Wars," sealing their fate in a peculiar class struggle.

Teddy Roosevelt explained: "I don't go so far as to think that the only good Indians are the dead Indians, but I believe nine out of ten are, and I should not inquire too closely into the case of the tenth."

We had nearly the same mentality in Vietnam. What we are doing in Central America is too close to Vietnam for comfort. The churches worry little about the fact of empire. Many churches still allow the American flag to legitimate empire in the sanctuary.

Alvin Toffler in *The Third Wave* (1980) makes a sober point: "Nation-states were the necessary political containers for nation-sized economies. Today, the containers have not only sprung leaks; they have been made obsolete by their own success...nationalism is obsolete."

The ecological question is tied into the empire demise. We exploit not only peoples but nature as well. We need to distinguish much more sharply between nationalism as worship of empire, and patriotism, love of country or homeland. A whole worldview is at stake. God-walk involves refusal of empire, an eventual end of global class struggle.

The Refusal of Death. In God-walk we finally move toward the roots of the vast death threat all around us in nuclear death, hunger death, and ecological death. The persistent death penalty debate focuses the dilemma. It reveals how much we are still in love with death. What is more, the poor die earlier, as the statistics tell us. In the United States, with an average per capita income of $10,075, life expectancy is 78.2 years among females, 70.8 years among males. In Peru, with a per capita income of $930, females can expect to live 58 years and males 55 years. The poor are always the first victims.

For millennia the merchants of death have brainwashed us into thinking that institutional violence is right, given the proper conditions. Violence caused by class struggle, however, is supposed to be a devious design of Marx. Class struggle is one expression of the killer instinct that has been trained into us.

If we support the violence of the death penalty and the arms race, we should not be surprised by the violence of the class struggle. If we want to overcome class struggle, we had better commit ourselves to the justice struggle so that the poor need not die early.

This has nothing to do with perfectionism, wanting to make society perfect. It is an issue of trying to keep the world a sane place to live in. Ernest Becker in *Escape from Evil* (1975) pleads for "some kind of life-giving alternative to thoughtless and destructive heroism."

The churches are awakening to the alternative in the face of early nuclear death. But it is still a far cry from the struggle of us all that none will die the early death of poverty. God-walk drives us to refuse all death dealing.

The Truth-Untruth Struggle

The flip side of the class struggle in history is the truth-struggle. Intellectual insight ultimately is not about eternal verities or abstract concepts, but about basic relationships. We are still caught up in Enlightenment priorities with a Kantian orientation: What can I know? What must I do? What may I hope?

Sharing in God's justice struggle, we now ask a few prior questions: With whom do we associate? Whom do we legitimate? What do we indwell? While the Vatican statement claims that the "ultimate and decisive criterion for truth can only be a criterion which is itself theological," in primitive Christian life, the theological is first of all the theo-practical, that which God does through our everyday lives. God makes us associate with the poor because they are part of ourselves. God keeps us from legitimating empire and from participating in state-sanctioned death.

The ultimate criterion for truth hinges on the social location in which we associate with the God of the poor. God in Christ certainly reconciles, forgives, and justifies rich and poor alike. But God also opens our eyes to our complicity in the global class struggle when we are "faking it."

In its 1984 Man of the Year cover story, *Time* celebrates the 1984 Olympics as "Darwinian theater" and by implication the American way of life as Darwinian theater. There could be no more crass acknowledgment of class struggle. The Vatican Congregation pays little attention to Darwinian theater as the source of global poverty. Liberation theologians *will*, we hope.

– 24 –

THE END OF SYSTEMATIC THEOLOGY

While Herzog made few efforts to translate his numerous German essays into English, he commissioned a translation of his reflections on the end of systematic theology. This translation is based on an expanded version of the published article and has still been edited in part by Herzog himself.

What does it mean when a professor of systematic theology talks about the end of his field? Against the suspicions of some of his critics, Herzog does not talk about the end of theology as such. His point is not that, at a time when we are becoming more and more aware of suffering and oppression all around us, theology would have become irrelevant. Just the opposite. Theology plays a more important role than ever where it manages to address self-critically its involvement in the shortcomings of the systems of modernity and even postmodernity. But it is also transformed in the process.

Taking into account God's own praxis and the social location of those on the underside of North American society, specifically African Americans and women, the theoretical and doctrinal mandates of theology pick up new life. Breaking out of the dominant worldview and its unified image of humanity, theology becomes relevant again for all of humanity and all of creation. At the end of the paradigms of modern systematic theology, theology is reshaped where people gather in mutual accountability, seeking to identify the presence of God in specific social locations.

The process of self-critique is the crucial feature of current Christian thought in North America. The ecstasy of North American culture Protestantism under Paul Tillich has been destroyed by the shock of the theology of the death of God. The synthesis between Christianity and culture becomes more and more problematic. At the same time, the question becomes central regarding what it means that the churches are the actual bearers of the Christian stock of ideas.

What is, at this point, the special challenge of the church today to which we should respond? Here the importance of teaching within the church demands a

First published as "Vom Ende der systematischen Theologie," in *Gottes Zukunft, Zukunft der Welt: Festschrift für Jürgen Moltmann,* ed. Hermann Deuser, Gerhard Marcel Martin, Konrad Stock, and Michael Welker (Munich: Chr. Kaiser, 1986), 502–10; translated from the German by Joerg Rieger.

new hearing. There has been a shift from the many options of individual expression to the question of truth. This is demonstrated by the fact that systematic theology itself is called into question. Tillich's major work in North America was his large-scale *Systematic Theology* — his system. This work was the point of orientation for much modern Protestant thought in the United States. This is no longer the case today, although as orientation point Tillich's system is still part of the theological scene.

Similar to North American reflections, Jürgen Moltmann has formulated reservations against systematic theology in Europe: "Systems save some readers (and the admirers most of all) from thinking critically for themselves and from arriving at independent and responsible decisions. For that reason, I have resisted the temptation to develop a theological 'system,' even an 'open' one."[1] At the same time, however, Moltmann rejects the notion of "dogmatics" as well. He argues that dogmatics develops theses which actually distort the meaning of Christian thought. He wants to avoid both "the seductions of the theological system and the coercion of the dogmatic thesis."[2]

North American reservations in this regard have been expressed by George A. Lindbeck in *The Nature of Doctrine*.[3] This book is more or less a representation of the development of North American Christian thought. It is a large-scale effort to come to terms with Christian modernity in dealing with models of systematic theology and in offering an alternate model. The two major models which Lindbeck discusses are (1) symbolic expression of experience (experiential-expressivist) and (2) expression of faith in propositions (propositionalist). His own model is introduced as cultural-linguistic alternative.

A closer look at Lindbeck's analysis reveals that he does not really surrender the formulation of a systematic principle. It is true that he rejects the symbolic expression of experience as developed by Friedrich Schleiermacher. He also rejects a propositionalist formulation of Christian knowledge as a principle, as in dogmatics. His alternative is supposed to be postliberal. But, after all, it is also "principle," as will probably become clear shortly. If one gets to the bottom of Lindbeck's new terminology, he is left with the alternative of systematics or dogmatics. *Tertium non datur.*

I want to show in brief outline why Lindbeck does not offer a fresh postliberal start. Then it will be argued that the end of systematic theology does not immediately produce an alternative; it confronts us, however, with an important question: how does a Christian thought arise at all? Only if we have thought through this basis in North America once more, will we be able to shape a larger framework of thought.

---

1. Jürgen Moltmann, *Trinity and the Kingdom: The Doctrine of God,* trans. Margaret Kohl (San Francisco: Harper and Row, 1981), xi.

2. Ibid., xii.

3. George A. Lindbeck, *The Nature of Doctrine: Religion and Theology in a Postliberal Age* (Philadelphia: Westminster Press, 1984).

Limits of the "Post-Liberal" Position

Like Schleiermacher and the whole liberal tradition Lindbeck wants to root Christian thought in a general concept of religion. Already here Lindbeck's project slows down. How can he assume that he can turn away from the liberal premise, if the general concept of religion is precisely the trademark of liberal hermeneutics? He criticizes the liberal attempt to root Christian thought in personal religious *experience*: It presupposes a religious experience common to all religions. Proceeding this way, Lindbeck argues, no specific aspects of experience can be established. The liberal concept of religion deals with a non-sensuous experience which precedes every concept formation, like for example of religion as unity of meaning and experience.[4]

Lindbeck's cultural-linguistic model, however, does not deal any less with universal concepts, though emphasizing not experiential but linguistic processes. Christianity is a religion for him as well, for which general methodological characteristics have to be found in the first place.

Lindbeck's project presupposes that religion represents a cultural or linguistic framework which forms living and thinking as a whole. He sees the function of religion almost as if it were a Kantian a priori: "Like a culture or language, [religion] is a communal phenomenon that shapes the subjectivities of individuals rather than being primarily a manifestation of those subjectivities."[5]

A number of reasons can be listed which show why it makes sense to argue like this. It goes without saying that Christian life also takes place within the framework of religion. But if we force Christian thought to start with a general notion of religion, we fail to observe more precisely what is the specifically Christian character. When it comes to the question of content, Lindbeck, in his cultural-linguistic framework, is heading straight toward salvation in Christ — saving grace and revelation. At the crucial point, a further reflection of how he actually arrived at those insights does not take place. What is missing is the effort to examine the elementary genesis of a Christian thought. Language conventions in regard to the Christian message are simply taken over.

Where is the social location of such a project? Where is its place historically and in terms of the history of ideas? Andrew Louth has suggested recently that one has to invoke the difference of laboratory and library in order to understand the peculiarity of Christian thought. "Theologians work in libraries"[6] and not in laboratories like scientists. In his description of the cultural-linguistic alternative Lindbeck does not reflect on the significance of the work in libraries as the social location of theology. Certainly, the libraries are by no means to be underestimated. But the real issue of Christian thought cannot be grasped in the library alone. It may sound like a platitude. But we can no longer permit

---

4. Ibid., 32.

5. Ibid., 33.

6. Andrew Louth, *Discerning the Mystery: An Essay on the Nature of Theology* (Oxford: Clarendon Press, 1983), 136.

ourselves today not to expound this further. A systematic as well as a dogmatic principle can be invented anew *in the library,* time and again. But we also have to give ourselves an account of Christian thought in the light of God's activity in the world.

In regard to this crucial issue, however, difficulties in communication arise. Oftentimes it seems as if a direct encounter with the actual subject of the Christian thought in the world would not be necessary. Thus theological reflection moves into a "neutral" social location, an "objective" vantage point. But this approach is not adequate for starters where we need to take God's social location into account. Of course, even on the Eiffel Tower we can do some kind of theology. But does a bird's-eye view result in good theology? Does not God's presence prove itself in Messiah Jesus in the milling crowd of people, where justice and peace, protection and healing are at stake; not an overview from a distance but an inside view from engagement?

In the North American situation as it is now developing, neither religion nor a given framework of religious language can guide our work in the long run. Does not the actual state of affairs render a *preconceived* principle of theological conversation impossible? Do we not have to take the primitive Christian experience of the origins of Christian thought into account?

Of course, this procedure depends on the social location where we develop our thoughts. In this regard we have to resist the temptation to replace the abstract formulation of a systematic or dogmatic principle with a new principle from the outset. Monika K. Hellwig is right: "We cannot begin with the abstract formulation and hope that when people hear that explanation the experience will be generated out of the abstract language."[7] Even this premise must not, however, be used to develop an abstract counterargument.

So we need to think from a new point of departure. Some representatives of systematic theology will of course maintain that experiences can also be deduced from their abstract language.[8] But we have to insist that every experience first has to prove itself in the location of Christian thought. The actual bone of contention among us is how we define this location. North American systematic theology at the end of the twentieth century is only beginning to deal with this question.

North American theologies of liberation attempt to give an account of their social location. They want to avoid abstract principles as starting point of theology. Their social location is the church which struggles to participate in the poverty of God and through God in the poverty of human beings. This location refuses every systematic principle. We are faced with a new claim.

Here, the location of Christian thought is not the library alone, but the Christian community participating in God's protection of the losers and the lost. In

---

7. Monika K. Hellwig, *The Eucharist and the Hunger of the World* (New York: Paulist Press, 1976), 25.

8. George A. Lindbeck, *The Nature of Doctrine*, 36.

order to avoid misunderstanding it has to be underscored that the library is fully part our location in the world, and yet it serves a very special function. Without the library we cannot make do in Christian thought. But the library is not God.

If this kind of Christian thought does not grow out of doctrine as demanding dogmatics, or out of a new religious principle of experience demanding systematics, how shall we grasp it? First of all we have to describe it as mutual accountability for new teaching formation. Accountable teaching in Christian community arises out of the concrete framework of God's activity in the world and constant empowerment of the church through God's presence in word and sacrament in situations of oppression and other human suffering.[9] It is important that we become aware again of the process of teaching formation,[10] the genesis of doctrine. It has to be recalled that from the beginning, in primitive Christianity, teaching is an important mark of the church in the process of constituting itself (Acts 2:42).

The Black Church and Theological Method

The first sign of the end of systematic theology came in the early 1960s from the black church. It became apparent that a unitary view of the human being could no longer be presupposed. The differences between black and white proved to be too strong.

First of all it has to be emphasized that there were the poor black people, who, with the Bible in their hands, tried to make their theology of liberation important to the churches. The black church started with Scripture and thus found the connection to the predicament of black oppression as a task for teaching. Precisely in the way that a new understanding of Scripture arose in the sight of oppression, it became apparent that we are no longer facing a unitary image of the human being.

The problem can be examined from different perspectives. White theologians do not see a problem here up to this day. James H. Cone recently summarized this in saying that "white progressive theologians were saying that blacks cannot think, because they do not exist. That was why some of them could say, and still do, that there is no such thing as black theology."[11] Others claimed that insofar as it might "exist," it would be a passing fad. Cone replies to this: "With over twenty million blacks in the USA, most of whom are extremely poor, how can

---

9. For discussion of this see *New Conversations* 8, no. 1 (Spring 1985), which talks especially about the mutual accountability for new formation of teaching.

10. The formation of teaching is discussed in *Was gilt in der Kirche? Die Verantwortung für Verkündigung und verbindliche Lehre: Ein Votum des Theologischen Ausschusses der Arnoldshainer Konferenz* (Neukirchen-Vluyn: Neukirchener Verlag, 1985).

11. James H. Cone, *For My People: Black Theology and the Black Church* (Maryknoll, N.Y.: Orbis Books, 1984), 69.

you be so insensitive as to ask whether reflection on their religious history is a passing fad?"[12]

Cone implies a critique of the image of the human being among the white thinkers who permit themselves to be human apart from the black situation. In white thought the unreflected presupposition seems to be that the thinker can be a human being without including the other. Whatever doctrinal formulas of the image of the human being the theologian may present, the neighbor who is different in color does not appear in the point of departure of Christian thought in specific terms.

In a situation like the North American one in which there are white and black churches it would make no sense at all to pursue such considerations from either of the two sides in an isolated way. We find ourselves in mutual social and cultural relationships. So the question arises, how can we together bring up differences as well as discuss solutions?[13]

It must not be overlooked that there are many other ethnic Christians in North America as well who have to record similar processes of oppression. The dilemma of women which is reflected in feminist theology is on the same level. The particularity of the situation of the black church was that it could express, as it were, God's struggle for the oppressed for all other oppressed groups in the church. What is at stake is not an advantage of black people in regard to theological insight but the recognition of the reality of God in church and world without white limits. There are limitations of communal activity between blacks and whites, North Atlantic Christians and Third World Christians, women and men. Our most pressing thought challenge in North America is the overcoming of these limitations, in order to find ourselves in God's church.[14]

It is necessary to guard against some misunderstandings. Blacks often think whites assume that being black is not the crucial problem, oppression is. We whites easily overlook the fact that for many blacks, to be black is in fact the decisive issue, since oppression is evoked by difference in color. The one who is not black will hardly see the almost absolute jeopardy of being black in a society in which pigmentation alone stamps a neighbor a nonperson. In the abuse of the neighbor on grounds of color, nonblack Christians are able to grasp God's own struggle with oppression.

---

12. Ibid., 70.

13. Ultimately, such considerations refer to the questions of church formation which confront the United States with specific challenges. We are told for instance by Fritz Schwarz and Christian A. Schwarz, *Theologie des Gemeindeaufbaus: Ein Versuch* (Neukirchen-Vluyn: Neukirchener Verlag, 1985), that there exists a "weak point of systematic theology" which "prevents clear criteria of church formation from being developed" (57). In regard to the situation in the United States one is tempted to say that there exists not only a "weak point" but a zero point in systematic theology, which prevents it from developing criteria for church formation at all. What is at stake is above all mutual accountability in regard to the social location of Christian thought. In the United States we are thrown back to the beginnings.

14. Gustavo Gutiérrez and Frederick Herzog, "Dealing with the True Problems," *Books and Religion* 13, no. 2 (March 1985): 7–8 and 12.

Conclusions cannot be drawn without reference to worship and the life of the churches. The Bible, rooted in the Eucharist, points to Jesus as the oppressed at the cross and makes him appear in the resurrection in persistent identity with the poor. Exactly in this form is he seeking out the outcast and despised. Ostracized Samaritans and scorned women are exemplary witnesses of the eucharistic giving of his life.

To find God among blacks as such, however, does not as yet result in a new image of the human being, only in a new starting point of theological method. We are no longer looking for a new view of the human being from a distance. But it has yet to be shown what our involvement with the world of black people yields. Indeed, from God's involvement with the history of degradation no systematic principle can be deduced from which a systematic theology could be developed.

We are in a new phase of beginnings. Christians are about to develop mutual accountability between the different groups. Among these groups are also Latin American communities.[15] It is the interjection of black people which initiated this new process of teaching in the United States. It confronts us with the task of grasping the relationship of God's justice, on the one hand, and God's justification of the sinner, or God's love, on the other. The new image of the human being will grow out of the dynamics triggered here. What is at stake, in the first place, is learning how to give a mutual account of the changed dynamics in grasping God's activity. In the North American denominations this was not practiced until quite recently.[16]

In a different context in Europe Jürgen Moltmann wonders how, for example, in the light of the ecological crisis, a "capacity for self-control" can be developed by us moderns.[17] Mutual accountability between black and nonblack, male and female, Western and Eastern Christians might be a first step to practicing self-control in regard to the suffering creation, so as to do justice not only to the human creature in all kinds of ways but also to nature as creation. At any rate, this new step of Christian thinking is the beginning of a *eucharistic* method which grows out of common experiences of God's presence in history. Only God makes it possible for us to do justice to creation and God's creatures.[18]

---

15. Harvey Cox, *Religion in the Secular City* (New York: Simon and Schuster, 1984), 167–68.

16. Even now the life in the churches appears to be superficial to the visitor of the United States. See Wolf-Dieter Zimmermann, "Wenn Gott nützt, ist Glaube sinnvoll: Eindrücke einer kirchlichen Amerika-Reise," *Rheinischer Merkur/Christ und Welt* 32 (August 3, 1985): 21.

17. Jürgen Moltmann, *Gott in der Schöpfung: Ökologische Schöpfungslehre*, 2d rev. ed. (Munich: Chr. Kaiser, 1985), 42.

18. Wolf-Dieter Zimmermann, "Wenn Gott nützt," 21, clearly recognized the North American dilemma: "Truth has to be useful — as long as God is useful, faith makes sense.... Thinking starts principally from below, from success. As a result, faith is modified into a personal aid, and God becomes an entity of cooperation. Someone who suffers — according to a common reaction — did not believe firmly enough and did not pray ardently enough." Systematic theology can no longer intervene here at all and is out of place. Something else has to happen first of all — mutual accountability.

Worldview and Social Location

The suspicion arises time and again that to get involved with God's presence in the Eucharist means a relapse into the age of the spiritual obscurantists. Liberal theology often fears that the protest of the theology of liberation against the liberal involvement with the modern worldview could lead to a total rejection of the ethos of our culture. Instead of spurring sociological, psychological, or philosophical analyses, some liberation theologies seem to expect that we first of all do theological homework.[19]

The growing mutual accountability, however, is not about giving each other homework. The point is, above all, to do away with the uncritical entanglement of North American theology with culture.[20] Seeing behind Tillich's influence in the United States the tradition of Schleiermacher, our critique refers not only to Schleiermacher's loyalty to the "official" worldview but especially to his inability to include in his thought project his own social location and to reflect it critically. The theologian is not only the religious but also the modern human being, who wants to control creation and secure and maintain a position of power.

Oftentimes, this problem is not felt to be pressing. If theopraxis, God acting in creation and God's struggling for justice, is left out, and if we move immediately from our doctrines to theological reflection, our social location is easily overlooked.

Yet if we first of all concentrate on theopraxis, that is on God's acting in history, we will not look for teaching formation in the library in the first place, as important as the library is. The Bible, which in a theology of liberation is our starting point, is, after all, not a book which becomes meaningful only in the library. Being the eucharistic book of the church it is near God's justice struggle in the world. We will only understand it in its depth if we read it where God in Messiah Jesus is working in the world. God's standing up for the oppressed and the enslaved creation, which we celebrate in the Eucharist, is the social location of our Christian thinking.

This initiates neither a *sequence* from reflection to action nor a *circle* in which action and reflection are conflated in an ongoing rotation, but a *spiral*.[21] It is still a rotation which takes place in sequences but it does not repeat itself. We are dealing here as little with a dogmatic conclusion as with a hermeneutic circle of dogmatics. From theopraxis does not grow imitation but innovation.

Social analysis is always part of the picture. It grows out of theopraxis, hand in glove with the task of mutual accountability — in the form of a spiral. But it does

---

19. Footnotes 19, 21, and 26 refer to papers which have been presented in a discussion of North American theology of liberation at the annual meeting of the American Academy of Religion, December 20, 1981. This is to say that their thoughts have been "tested" in community.

20. That this is a problem is apparent even to observers who are not theologians. See Herbert von Borch, *Amerika — Dekadenz und Größe* (Frankfurt am Main: Fischer Taschenbuch Verlag, 1983), 140–57, "Die Gesellschaft ist der Gott" (Society is God).

21. See n. 19. For the notion of the spiral I am indebted to Roy I. Sano.

not bring in new preconceptions.[22] Insofar as Marx is part of social analysis he belongs to the spiral, without, however, making him determine preconceptions or prejudices.

It is indispensable for a theology of liberation that social analysis takes place as part of theopraxis. The analysis of political economy is not put off. But it does not become the only determining factor.[23] In social analysis which grows out of theopraxis it becomes clear that the prevailing worldview can no longer offer a homogeneous framework for the starting point of theology. Systematics distinguished itself in its commitment to a particular worldview. As a result the location of the thinker went unnoticed or was concealed.

So far two main conclusions result from our reflections. (1) We can no longer rely on a common view of the image of the human being, as it has prevailed since the Enlightenment. (2) The homogeneous function of the modern worldview in modern Christian thought has become suspicious to us.

In regard to the latter issue, it is obvious that at least since Schleiermacher we are expected to develop some *systematic principle* for the relation of religion and worldview. It is the merit of Albert Schweitzer to have pointed out the advantage which arises if we differentiate the worldview (*Weltanschauung*), which has been elaborated by reason in scientific research, from a view of life (*Lebensanschauung*), which grows out of our will.[24] Armed with a systematic principle the Christian thinker is in danger of turning Christianity into a worldview.

Training in the social location of Christianity means first of all training in the metaphors of the Eucharist. Here is an "image" which requires human participation and which, in "elements," represents our responsibility for creation to our senses and, in a "bodily concrete" way, gives us the power to develop new thoughts. After the Second Vatican Council the temptation was great to develop the starting point of a new worldview out of the liturgical renewal of the Eucharist, giving rational or irrational explanations, while every sensory imagination had been suppressed.[25] Such attempts at an unlimited explanation of the world completely contradict the intention of the Eucharist. What is at stake in theopraxis is not a worldview, after all, but the formation of the heart which does not leave out the feet, *God-walk*. People spontaneously sense that not everything can be explained and done. The heart does not want an explanation but clarification; it does not want to understand the world but to grasp God, because it is grasped by God. Theology of liberation wants to reject not culture but the ethos of culture which restricts us rationalistically and catapults millions of people into

22. Frederick Herzog, "God-Walk and Class Struggle," *Circuit Rider* 9, no. 6 (June 1985): 4–9, included in this volume as chapter 23.

23. What is decisive for theology of liberation is well put in Gustavo Gutiérrez, *We Drink from Our Own Wells*, trans. Matthew J. O'Connell (Maryknoll, N.Y.: Orbis Books, 1984).

24. Albert Schweitzer, *The Philosophy of Civilization* (New York: Macmillan, 1949), 271–77.

25. Alfred Lorenzer, *Das Konzil der Buchhalter* (Frankfurt am Main: Europäische Verlagsanstalt, 1981), 283f.

economic crisis. The modern worldview is finished in its primary function for Christian thought.

Departure from the Janus Face of Systematic Theology

Opposition against parting from systematic theology assumes different forms. Ted Peters, a Lutheran theologian, has criticized liberation theology for presupposing a relationship of theory and praxis that is only represented in our libraries. Now that justice is the great challenge, theologians should not hide behind their desks and play around with terms like theory and praxis: justice is not a question of method but of action.

Peters gives us a telling definition of the prevailing understanding of systematic theology: "A theological system is like Janus, the Roman god who has two faces, one facing inward, the other outward. The two criteria for evaluating the internal system of the doctrinal connections are clarity and coherence. The two criteria for the same process in regard to the outer face of the system are faithfulness to the Bible and being in touch with the present."[26]

Liberation theology, as we present it here, Peters attests has faithfulness to the Bible and proximity to the present. But it lacks clarity and coherence. He further alleges that it would blame theory for the current injustice in state and society. We do not want to denounce theory. G. W. F. Hegel thought that theoretical work would achieve more than its practical counterpart since reality is powerless against the revolutionizing of concepts. But we cannot avoid the question how theory is generated *in the church*. Peters explains that in pointing to the poor we would arrive at a wrong conclusion. We are said to blame injustice on theory while the actual cause is sin, human failure. But the reality is different. We often make use of theory in order to cover up our sin. We develop a theory-praxis paradigm which prevents us from letting God direct us to our social location among the poor. According to the Janus face mentality of systematic theology, we look in two directions at the same time and locate ourselves on seemingly neutral ground.

The second allegation of Peters is the claim that liberation theology makes a category mistake. The relation of theory and praxis belongs to epistemology, the relation of justice and injustice to ethics. In North America, however, we cannot give ourselves permission to neatly separate theoretical and practical reason. The basic question is how Christian theory actually can develop in training the social location of Christianity. We certainly do not want to start with a general notion of praxis. Insight in discipleship grows in concrete theopraxis. Here, theory is already included in praxis. This is not a theory which guides and determines praxis in an abstract and a priori fashion.

---

26. This and the following quotations by Ted Peters are taken from his presentation at the annual meeting of the American Academy of Religion, December 20, 1981. See above, n. 19.

In this way we have renounced the usual arrangement of systematic theology, moving from theory to praxis. It cannot be predicted whether in theopraxis we will settle for justice. It cannot be known in advance whether we can grasp God's justice at all without theopraxis. What is at stake is that we realize our social location in God's struggle for justice and develop a "theory" accordingly — that is, literally, a spiritual "vision" that will enable us to make our decisions. It should be clear from the outset that in Christian reflection our "theory" develops out of the focus of the will of God toward the kingdom of God. We must never forget that it is theopraxis which determines the course. This does not mean that human activity is secondary, but that it is inserted as an essential element in God's cosmic work.

We certainly do not want to argue in favor of a "theology applied after the event" — the opposite of the theory-praxis dynamics — but theory-centered theology is in trouble. The Janus face of systematic theology is going blind. Its place is taken by the open face of discipleship: "And all of us, with unveiled faces, seeing the glory of the Lord as though reflected in a mirror, are being transformed into the same image" (2 Cor. 3:18). What is decisive for Christian reflection is such *clarity*. It is the clarity of the will of God as objective for creation.

Peters raises a basic question: "Can we ever have access to Jesus without christological theory?" Here the big difference between system thought and discipleship thought is evident. Our social location together with the poor is the gift of access to Jesus in the Eucharist — not systematic theory of modern Christianity or dogmatic postulates of past centuries, but the location where theopraxis becomes transparent. Christological vision of discipleship is always rooted in the Eucharist. Here God's justice struggle is at hand in an elementary-bodily manner.

A further question of Peters arises very clearly out of the systematic model: "Should it be possible that, in the twentieth century, we circumvent all thought of the previous two millennia and become the first to proceed from action to thought?" No, we only circumvent a reversal of early Christian basics. Elementary Christian thoughts in all their clarity and coherence grow out of eucharistic discipleship.

It must, of course, be remembered that already in the genesis of the writings of the New Testament "Christian theory" was involved. Theological concepts were responsible for the selection of the material. The naming of Jesus of Nazareth is a theological claim, Peters asserts. But every theological claim is inextricably connected with theopraxis. Therefore we can never say like Peters: "Today we do not have access to a pretheoretical Jesus. Not even the New Testament had such access."

Early Christian thought is different. First of all, churches were formed through acting out theopraxis in discipleship. At stake was time and again an understanding of the genesis of all theory out of discipleship, for instance, the Son-of-God theory, the Son-of-Man theory, or the theory of the Messiah. If we analyze the genesis of thought in early Christianity it becomes clear to us that there never was theory-in-itself but only theory as intellectual expression of discipleship which is already lived out, however poorly.

That is why the Eucharist is so important today. It is the place where even in our time the church continues to encounter a "pretheoretical Jesus" in new ways. Prior to any systematics or dogmatics is the mutual accountability of the members of the body of Christ, where they give an account of the presence of the pretheoretical Jesus in their discipleship. This eliminates the domination of the theological system[27] and reduces distance. It can, of course, be easily shown that theoretical considerations sometimes precede discipleship as well. But they can determine the basic dynamics of Christian existence in which communal teaching grows out of common discipleship.

The Janus face of systematic theology is no longer viable. What is important for us today is the *open face* of Christ, which generates mutual discipleship. Christian reflection today grows out of a eucharistic method — in order to create new mutually accountable teaching.

We have pointed out three aspects of the North American discussion: (1) the lack of a unitary image of the human being; (2) the confusion of theology in regard to the function of the modern worldview; (3) the choice between a theoretical and a pretheoretical Jesus. Under the present circumstances the development of a systematic principle of theology loses more and more ground. This does not mean to stop thinking, but a new challenge for thought presents itself. The question of truth has not been ignored. But we will have to pay more attention to that dimension of our personality where we are holistically drafted into a new relationship to ourselves and to our environment. The metaphors of the Eucharist invite us to adjust the *sense of justice* of human beings to the truth of God's struggle for justice.

---

27. Obviously, it has to be considered which structure of thought grows out of mutual accountability. But it cannot be determined in advance how we will further deal with the new phenomenon of mutual accountability and which form we will give to it.

DOGMATICS IN NORTH AMERICA

In this article, written for the most extensive and prestigious German theological encyclopedia, Herzog provides a unique orientation through the maze of North American theology. Starting in the eighteenth century, it leads to constructive proposals for a new and genuinely North American dogmatics. Here one of the mottoes of Herzog's work shines through: Unless we know our history and deal with it constructively, we are doomed to repeat it.

Taking up the anthropological starting points which connect many of the diverse North American proposals in self-critical fashion, Herzog explores more constructive ways of relating God and humanity theologically. The growing awareness of the specific conflicts and tensions in North American society is one of the factors that leads to a significant shift. Theology's long-standing involvement with the dominant culture needs to be questioned, leading to new ways of living before God.

God and humanity are no longer tied together in networks of control, where God is often used to support the status quo, but in a covenant relationship. Here the church itself becomes a covenant of justice, fashioned after God's own ways of loving and being just, embodied in Christ.

Definition

North America has never experienced the universal claim of dogma in medieval Roman Catholicism. It also never experienced the attempt of Protestant orthodoxy to reclaim the universality of dogma for the Reformation churches. Almost from the beginning the multiplicity of religious experience stood at the center. It is therefore easily understandable that the idea of dogmatics did not have a wide influence. The dynamics of North American theological history is more easily captured in a variety of spiritual movements and geographically conditioned peculiarities than in dogmatic points of view. The material can be organized only by tracing some broad contours of the colorful picture.

Translation of "Dogmatik in Nordamerika," first published in *Theologische Realenzyklopädie*, ed. Gerhard Krause and Gerhard Müller (Berlin and New York: Walter de Gruyter, 1982), 9:104–16; translated from the German by Kristin Herzog.

Within the fast-developing pluralism there were no comprehensive common points of view. Accents that cannot be overlooked are Puritanism, Unitarianism, Neo-Puritanism, liberalism, Social Gospel, and neoorthodoxy. In our time various forms of process theology and liberation theology become visible. Even these key words will help to explain why the word "dogmatics" seldom appears in the titles of theological books. There is a tendency toward the practical and toward experience. In dogmatics research the terms "Christian theology" and "systematic theology" usually were interchangeable. Both of these concepts were considered sufficient to describe the systematically analyzed context of theology. Frequently "dogmatics" was considered the more stringent definition of this scholarly enterprise. For the project as a whole, however, the term usually has been avoided for reasons of a more popular communication.

This self-consciousness in the use of the term is evident in an attempt at definition at the beginning of the twentieth century:

> The name "dogmatics" is here used as a synonym for theology in the technical sense, as distinct from Christian ethics, and the various subsidiary sciences often grouped under that name. In this sense it has been used in Protestantism for over two hundred years (first in 1659; frequently since 1729). In Germany the word *Glaubenslehre* (science of the Christian faith) is often used as a synonym; but we have no single equivalent in English. The popular association with dogmatism renders the word an unfortunate one; yet in itself it is well adapted to the use to which it is put. As distinguished from doctrine (which may include opinion of every kind) the word dogma denotes truth of fundamental and authoritative character, and so appropriately describes the subject matter of our science. It need hardly be said that in retaining the word, we do not use it in the legal sense in which it is understood in Roman Catholicism, but in accordance with the spiritual conception of religious authority which is characteristic of Protestantism.[1]

When William Adams Brown (1865–1943), professor of systematic theology at Union Theological Seminary in New York, formulated this definition, the interweaving of European and North American theology appeared almost as a matter of course. The terminology seems to be outwardly the same. Contentwise, however, a different weighting of interests had developed.

The Beginnings

The Special North American Traits

The beginnings in the seventeenth century in New England throw a long shadow on the total picture which emerges from the colorful multiplicity of fast-growing denominations. Philip Schaff, the Nestor of North American church history, thought that the theologians of New England had mainly been occupied with anthropology. He considered it mainly evident in the disputes over free will. But if one takes a closer look, one discovers that Christology and eschatology

---

1. William Adams Brown, *Christian Theology in Outline* (Edinburgh: T. & T. Clark, 1907), 3.

also play a role, and pneumatology and ecclesiology no less. It is important to realize that soon a colorful picture emerges. At first the New World was an intact world. Besides the psychology of John Locke, Plato too could again gain a footing, religious mysticism beside a pragmatic Christianity. Dry Calvinism had little influence. The relationship to reason was soon no longer determined by guilt feelings. The task of reason merged with the growing interest in a quest for the essential nature of human beings. That, however, necessitated christological considerations. Does Christology limit itself to a transcendental anthropology in which Jesus simply appears as ideal man? Or does reason discover in Jesus an elementary novum which introduces a new way of being human because Godself is active in the process? The rapid development of the continent demanded that special attention be paid to human reason, its possibilities and limitations. The rational penetration of Christology in regard to the problem of what constitutes human nature can be regarded as the characteristic trait of North American dogmatics.

Reason and Method

The primordial theological thoughts in the British colonies which later grew into the United States are well known to be rooted almost exclusively in Puritanism. That does not mean, however, that this type of thought was simply related to a rather trite way of life and to very strict doctrines, like predestination and original sin. There was a new world to cope with! The experience of an untouched and sometimes almost overwhelming nature kindled empirical thought and nature mysticism. The religious inner life became enriched with new experiences of communal life. Great revivals also influenced theology. Christianity had to be comprehended in all its dimensions. Puritanism was, then, not in all respects the bugbear which popular opinion has made of it. Even though intuition and even mysticism played a part, in the end it was reason which structured the new experiences.

That aspect pertained especially to the new concept of God. Jonathan Edwards, the leading theologian of New England, emphasized that reason was very well able to grasp the reality of God, even God's threefold being. Reason, he thought, discovers three differences in God: Godself, the idea of God, and God's self-pleasure. Reason is here understood as a process of finding truth in the logical progression of thought:

> We first ascend, and prove a posteriori, or from effects, that there must be an eternal cause; and then secondly, prove by argumentation, not intuition, that this being must be necessarily existent; and then thirdly, from the proved necessity of his existence, we may descend, and prove many of his perfections a priori.[2]

---

2. Jonathan Edwards, *A Careful and Strict Enquiry into the Modern Prevailing Notions of that Freedom of Will, Which Is Supposed to Be Essential to Moral Agency, Vertue and Vice, Reward and Punishment, Praise and Blame* (Boston, 1754; new ed.: Jonathan Edwards, *Freedom of the Will*, ed. Paul Ramsey [New Haven: Yale University Press, 1957]), 182.

Edwards speaks of his argumentation also as the basic principle of common sense. It is often noticeable how much he was influenced by John Locke (1632–1704), especially by his *Essay concerning Human Understanding* (1690). Self-critique of the use of human reason could hardly be expected in these beginnings of North American thought.

It is not surprising that the theological use of the concept of reason flipped over into a unitarianism in which this very reason simply denies the threefold distinction in God. We do not immediately have to suspect here a glorification of reason. Reason simply continues relentlessly to develop its logic. William Ellery Channing, the leader of Unitarianism in Boston, could declare we would need to come closer to God if we wanted to enjoy God. For this purpose we would have to focus the power of our intellect on God's grace and God's perfections. Here the rational procedure gets the upper hand.

Horace Bushnell, himself already indebted to theological liberalism, has epigramatically summarized this development: "Our theologic method in New England has been essentially rationalistic."[3] Characteristic of this method is also for Bushnell the possibility to understand the Christian religion rationally, in spite of a trust in emotion and intuition. However, Bushnell does not thereby want to have reason placed above revelation:

> Not allowing ourselves to be rationalists over the scriptures, we have yet been as active and confident rationalists under them, as it was possible to be — assuming, always, that they address their contents to the systematic, speculative reason of men, into which they are to be received, and by which they are to be digested into formulas — when they are ready for use.[4]

But what does it mean that reason without self-critique was allowed to interpret Scripture? According to Bushnell's own presentation his project was a parallel to the opinion of Friedrich Schleiermacher and Richard Rothe who held that Christian theology is a speculative or logical expression of Christian consciousness which contains something divine. One attempted to place oneself under the authority of Scripture. But how was this possible by way of systematic-speculative reasoning? Was not Christ increasingly restricted to the limited anthropological field of this reason?

Christian Anthropology in the New World

According to Puritan teaching, human beings were totally corrupt since Adam. In Adam's fall all had by their actions destroyed themselves spiritually. Nathaniel William Taylor (1786–1858), professor of didactic theology at the newly founded Yale University, confronted head-on this difficulty during the heyday of Neo-Puritanism (also known as "New Divinity"). "To believe this, I must renounce

---

3. Horace Bushnell, *God in Christ* (London: Richard D. Dickinson, n.d.), 92.
4. Ibid.

the reason which my Maker has given me."[5] He declared that all human beings are responsible for their own actions. In free decision they would always choose something other than God. Even though human nature was not generally corrupt, it provided the possibility for individual sinning. Human nature as such is not sinful, but it represents the possibility for free decision. It would contradict reason to assume that God were the creator of a sinful human being and therefore the origin of sin. Rather, sin is the deed of the individual, which does not imply that humans are in control of the good deed. Turning away from sin is also for Taylor completely the work of the Holy Spirit. In this regard he is still thinking in line with Puritanism. But human beings can cooperate with the Spirit.

After reason had been discovered as a power able to influence change in human beings, it was only a matter of time until reason would be applicable to a wider frame of reference. Also Christology, the miracles, and finally the biblical worldview were forced to answer to reason. In Bushnell's own testimony the parallel to Schleiermacher is impressive. Taylor was himself a contemporary of Schleiermacher, but was not influenced by him. It is at this time, however, that the direction of thought begins to converge in Central Europe and North America. An anthropological foundation for theology becomes noticeable also in North America, even though the method is not as yet as refined as in Europe.

Covenant Theology and Reasonable Doctrine

The early theological disputes in North American Puritanism were all oriented in the needs of the church.[6] The first theologians were pastors, some of whom advanced to become professors when the first academic positions were created. At about the same time, when North American theological professorships were established, the Enlightenment arrived in the New World. Edwards, Channing, Taylor, Bushnell, whether they were pastors or professors — the Enlightenment put its stamp on their world. In the beginning inconspicuously, but soon very visibly, theology moves away from the interpretation of early Christian doctrine for God's people taking possession of the New World, turning to a self-legitimating of reason within religious ideas. If we take 1758, the year in which Edwards died, and 1943, the year of Brown's death, as orientation points, then the picture has changed within two centuries from a covenant theology to a reasonable doctrine which places the struggle with the modern worldview into the forefront. Brown, one of the main representatives of theological liberalism in the first half of the twentieth century, summarizes the dogmatic task in this way: it has to answer

---

5. Nathaniel William Taylor, *Concio ad Clerum: A Sermon Delivered in the Chapel of Yale College, Sept. 10, 1828* (New Haven, 1828), 6.

6. Williston Walker, *The Creeds and Platforms of Congregationalism* (Boston: Charles Scribner, 1893), 157ff.

responsibly, taking the modern worldview into account, the old question how God works reconciliation with the world (2 Cor. 5:19).

While theology remained fixed on the modern world, it continued to be tied to the church, although a church interpreted by reason. The idea of a covenant is no longer emphasized. Church is now considered a religious society. The foundations of Christian theology are therefore based on the principles of a comparative science of religion: "From the point of view of comparative religion, Christianity is one form among others in which the religious life manifests itself. From the point of view of Christian faith, it is the perfect or final religion, rightfully claiming the allegiance of all men."[7] Now dogmatics is no longer investigating the truth and untruth of the church's proclamation, but changed into systematics it seeks to legitimate reason within the religious framework of society. There is in North America also a reason which separates itself from the religious community and is engaged in "religious studies" in general, especially in the departments of religion at state universities. The dogmatically relevant use of reason in North America, however, can be observed in the continued influence of arguments of reason within the religious community.

The phenomenon of civil religion, of culture-religion, is not thinkable without the influence of reason within the denominations. Civil religion is the attempt of reason to find a sense of societal meaning common to all denominations. If no common understanding of baptism and the Eucharist can be reached, there is still a common loyalty to the nation. The field of religion dare not be kept outside the judgment of reason. It is not easy to find a European parallel to this phenomenon. The necessity of thinking in terms of the Christian religion is widely accepted almost as a matter of course. One is looking for what is religiously acceptable for societal reason and so for what is common also to other religions.

It would be simple in scholarly terms if one could also for the North American context describe this reason as "a reason from within religion itself, not a reason superimposed upon religion from the outside."[8] In North America the type of reason inhabiting religion is from the beginning trimmed and mixed with societal reason. Church and society have been one, so to speak, from the beginning. Christian values are increasingly changed into values of culture, with religion being naturally considered the core of a culture which judges the reasonableness of religion.[9] A possible comparison is Albert Schweitzer's concept of the logical necessity of religious ideas of Christianity,[10] but an unbroken trust in reason, which has not undergone any critique of reason, remains conspicuous in North America.

---

7. Brown, *Christian Theology*, 29.
8. Dietrich Rössler, *Die Vernunft der Religion* (Munich: Piper, 1976), 123.
9. John Murray Cuddihy, *No Offense: Civil Religion and Protestant Taste* (New York: Seabury Press, 1978), 21.
10. Erich Grässer, *Albert Schweitzer als Theologe* (Tübingen: Mohr, 1979), 260.

The Main Problems

Theological liberalism had paved the way for a comprehensive modern system which would confirm North American theology in its most profound expectations. In Paul Tillich was validated for North America what is usually remembered in the hymns of the church as another type of fulfillment: "Was der alten Väter Schar / höchster Wunsch und Sehnen war / und was sie geprophezeit / ist erfüllt in Herrlichkeit."[11] (The highest wish and longing of the fathers of Israel and what they prophesied is now gloriously fulfilled.) In North America Tillich is seen somewhat differently than in Europe. The interest is here his synthesis of religion and culture by way of a complex analysis of reason. Evident contradictions between the teaching of the church and its praxis are not an important object of reflection. The peculiar tie of North American theology to the church remains in place, but to the church as an expression of a religion that favors the merging of Christianity into culture. Therefore systematic theology in North America is primarily focused on an apologetic interest and not on dogmatics. Reason is fitting the Christian religion for the cultural context.

The Function of Reason

Paul Tillich distinguishes between ontological and technical reason. As ontological reason he considers the structure of the mind by which human beings can grasp and change the world. It is the classical tradition of reason from Parmenides to G. W. F. Hegel. Here the cognitive dimension is one access among others. Technical reason, however, is constantly accompanying reason. Here the cognitive dimension is the primary one, especially in view of actions that represent the means toward an end. In the use of the historical-critical method, for example, this rational procedure cannot be avoided. But technical reason should not separate itself from the ontological one. In this way the possibility of merging subject and object in the process of perception is established as is their distance. From the distance, a controlling perception is possible, a mode in which the subject exercises control over the object.[12] There is, however, also the possibility of the object having the freedom to offer itself in its own peculiarity. In this case a receiving perception would result.

The rational process is, then, for Tillich based in the selfhood of the thinker which potentially from the beginning is tied to the object — otherwise it would not be able to grasp the object. A controlling knowledge should principally be excluded, but reason as a whole remains in control because it initiates the receiving of perception. The final identity of subject and object includes a reason which can affirm itself if it so decides. Therefore Tillich has to be asked whether the subject should not also consider *that* object with which in the end it cannot be identical. What about a reason that answers to something really "Other"? Could it be that conscience, in which human selfhood is not constituted by its

---

11. *Evangelisches Gesangbuch* (Gütersloh, 1996), no. 12.
12. Paul Tillich, *Systematic Theology* (Chicago: University of Chicago Press, 1951), 1:71–75.

potential for merging with the object, but by the potential of answering to a truly "Other," would prevent the necessity of regarding the basic tenets of Christianity as logically conclusive?

Christology as Transcendental Anthropology

The unsolved problem of reason in North American theology becomes most visible in the tension between anthropology and Christology. Reason, as long as it is primarily based on itself, keeps Christology from opening the way for essential new dimensions in understanding the human being.

North American theology is widely agreed that the basic historical events of Christianity have to prove themselves as expressions of certain human structures. Thus an existentialist perspective prepares the way for process theology. Schubert Ogden (born 1928), for example, begins his Christology with the presupposition that being a Christian should be understood completely as the original possibility of authentic human existence. The existentialist analysis of reason has previously clarified his theological understanding. Therefore the doctrine of revelation is supposed to be defined in a way different from the dogmatic tradition. Authentic existence is also realizable completely outside of any faith in Jesus or the proclamation of the church. Jesus is only an authentic expression of human existence, an outstanding individual among others, who invites his fellow humans to rely radically on God's grace. He points to a generally accessible situation: the possibility of freedom from the past and openness for the future. Jesus is Adam in his essential being. It takes only a small step of thought from Adam to Jesus. All human beings know the possibilities of their existence. Jesus expresses them in a splendid way.

Reason can here only be understood as a controlling agency. Christology proves itself to be necessarily a transcendental anthropology. Could there also be a reason which does not immediately fit Jesus into the whole frame of human existence? Does not Jesus bring a new human selfhood which, not unrelated to human structures, is new in overcoming the forced rule of reason and is even so fulfilling reason? It is not a completely new reason which is planted into human beings through faith so that they might understand Jesus. But Jesus is not similar to us to the extent that we could find in him only what we already know in our innermost selfhood. If Adam was only a τύπος τοῦ μέλλοντος, a forerunner of the one who was coming, then there would be an analogy discernible between Adam and Jesus, but no absolute identity of Jesus' being and human selfhood. Could not being human be thought from the perspective of the new creation (2 Cor. 5:17)? Is it not also reasonable to think that authentic human selfhood was only brought into being through Jesus?

There is no necessity to understand Jesus from the nature of Adam. That does not mean a denigration of human nature which makes reason possible. But we cannot avoid the question whether under the conditions of sin human existence is subject to a perversion, so that reason is not able to grasp Christology primarily from anthropological presuppositions.

Process Christology

Schubert Ogden has considered whether a solely anthropological foundation of Christology would constitute too narrow a framework. It would be helpful, he thought, if it could be built into a wider context of a process philosophy. Otherwise it might possibly be absorbed by an ontology like Tillich's. Process thought would be able to clarify much more distinctly the necessary logic of the relationship between God and human beings. This has recently happened in the Christology of John B. Cobb, Jr. (born 1925), and his former student David Ray Griffin (born 1939), both of whom make use of the philosophy of Alfred North Whitehead.

Only within the framework of the philosophical thought of God, Jesus appears as understandable, and God is evident as the power working in the world, influencing its individual parts toward developing their highest potentials. Besides the general activity, philosophy also sees a special acting of God which points to God's being and is originally tied to goals that have their origin in God's self. Every person can express such goals.

Jesus does it in an outstanding way. He presupposes Israel's interpretations of reality, but he emphasizes God's love more than God's justice. Based on God's initiative, Jesus' action expresses a strict necessity. Jesus is not important because he realized general human possibilities. He becomes a unique historical figure only by expressing goals which Godself has already put into the world. A Christology merely based on an anthropology would not be very convincing for such a realization of divine goals. Process Christology therefore tries to explain in what way God's action makes Jesus' action unique.[13] But even this position only explains what reason has previously proved as a possible action of God. Reason determines again what God can or cannot do. Only reason determines the process in which Jesus finds a special place.

God in Process

If the identity of human beings and the character of Jesus are derived from the demands of a necessary logic, then the necessary thought of God is also unavoidable. So, for example, in Langdon Gilkey (born 1919) we return to a God who proves Godself as essentially necessary. For him God is necessary being. The flow of time touching all things demands a reality that transcends finitude in order to illuminate the world process in its cohesiveness. There has to be the power of being which makes finite being in the flow of matter possible. God not only needs to sustain what is past, but has to lend being to every present, so that it can indeed be present. Thus God is beyond all time and yet also within time.

For Gilkey all of this is derived from intuitions arising from the depth of reason. If one thinks God, then God has to be thought as self-limiting, time-bound, and changeable. God not only sustains the various individual parts of the process, God also gives it direction and goal. Human freedom, however, is

---

13. John B. Cobb, Jr., and David R. Griffin, *Process Theology* (Philadelphia: Westminster, 1976).

constantly changing this direction, and in the tragedy of evil it destroys God's good purpose. Therefore a reconciling and healing tendency in history, which we experience as God's love, has become necessary.

This kind of reflection limits systematic theology to presenting the personal view of a theologian according to the measure of philosophical ideas. A reasonable view of the world rather easily becomes plausible from the viewpoint of a philosophical theology. Thus one can see also in Gilkey's theological project how systematic theology in North America has largely been built up as a philosophical theology which subjects all doctrines to the concept of necessary thought.

A New Foundation of Reason

Protestant theology in North America has been shaped by its history in such a way that in its use one cannot escape the method of reason. But should this method be continued uncritically? On the one hand, it has kept North American churches from falling into pure sectarianism. On the other hand, however, it has largely legitimated Christianity as culture-religion. Some denominations, inasmuch as they acknowledged confessional writings, have occasionally engaged in heresy trials. But that happened mostly in order to maintain a European tradition of teachings and not as expression of a new doctrinal development which could have produced a new dogmatics.

The Social Gospel, with its main representative Walter Rauschenbusch, gave no impetus for shaping dogmatics in a new way. Rauschenbusch believed in the perfectability of human beings[14] and no less in the possibility of Christianizing society.[15] Here especially the point is once more the self-confirmation of reason in religion, only this time with an emphasis on social concerns. Neoorthodoxy brought little change since it was imported from Europe and hardly took up the specific North American issues of doctrine. Not even through the brothers Niebuhr did it become dogmatically important. H. Richard Niebuhr at the end of his career again returned to the position of Schleiermacher. And Reinhold Niebuhr emphasized that actually he was an ethicist and not a theologian. Thus his work did not really contribute anything to dogmatics and even less to a neoorthodox dogmatics.

In recent times some evangelicals have dared to undertake new dogmatic projects. For the most well-known among them, Donald Bloesch, however, the enterprise is very much oriented in Karl Barth and thereby in Europe. For a new development of dogmatics in North America it is necessary to analyze the North American use of reason and to develop a specific consciousness of the problem. Nothing will move forward without a new foundation of reason.

---

14. Walter Rauschenbusch, *Christianity and the Social Crisis* (New York: Macmillan, 1910), 422.
15. Ibid., 151, 169.

Accountable Teaching

The societal upheaval of the civil rights struggle during the 1950s and 1960s was needed to pull theology, at least in small beginnings, away from its fascination with apologetics, that is, from adapting faith to modernism. The upsurge of black theology, with James H. Cone as its most important representative, pointed out inner self-contradictions of faith. Feminist theology followed suite, at first on the Protestant side with Letty M. Russell and on the Roman Catholic side with Rosemary Ruether. But also the voices of Native Americans, the original inhabitants of the country, became audible. Vine Deloria, Jr., became known as their spokesperson. Soon hardly any of the minorities were without a theological voice. Churches were now forced to reflect critically on themselves and their teachings.

One example was the United Church of Christ, founded in 1957 by merger of the Congregationalist Churches and the Evangelical and Reformed Church. In this case the union had formulated a new statement of faith which is often used in worship services instead of the Apostles' Creed, but it did not change the basic direction of theology. The new denomination was very much engaged in social change, but it often was consumed with "chasing after new tasks," as it is described in a dogmatic interpretation of 1978.[16] Here is discussed how the use of reason in the church has turned into civil religion: that the church increasingly identifies with the values of culture, especially concerning growth and social success. It is constantly tempted to see God on the side of the rich and powerful nation and to find the meaning of life in the national defense of wealth. Even though the church would like to change the nation, it often lets itself be co-opted by the powerful.

There is also a critical emphasis on the state not having the right to rule the church. Therefore terms like "American way of life" or "Manifest Destiny," which are popular images in North American culture, have to be excluded as key words for a Christian understanding of being human. In this culture there are indications of a creeping totalitarianism which by means of technology often prepares for the death of millions. This expansionist culture has no right to determine the frame of values that becomes decisive for Christians. To be truly human, individualism proves itself to be as unfruitful as collectivism. Especially the principle that individuals should first be concerned about, and live only for, themselves — which is still commonly considered one of the cardinal truths of the New World — proves itself to be a false teaching when the church justifies it.

Wherever Christians permit themselves to be shaped primarily by cultural values, the restructuring of the church becomes again an *articulus stantis et cadentis ecclesiae* (a matter by which the church stands or falls). Points of friction, like Manifest Destiny, technological totalitarianism, individualism, or collectivism, as well as racism, cause the development of new teaching, especially concerning the

---

16. Reinhard Groscurth, "Lehren und Bekennen in den USA," *Ökumenische Rundschau* 28 (1979): 277f.

forms of order in the church. Doctrinal declaration does not imply an anathema of false teaching, but points out which teachings today falsify the gospel. Important is not the codifying of binding teaching, but an agreement in accountable teaching. Not mere assent is expected, but accountability concerning the truth in the sense of Colossians 3:16: "Let the word of Christ dwell in you richly; teach and admonish one another in all wisdom." It is not a matter of an authority grafted on and forced from the outside, but of a communal acknowledgment that God is the originator of truth in the church. If the church acknowledges the claim of God, then we need more than a theological systematics which establishes and legitimates the coherence and relevance of Christian teaching in the modern world as a project of reflection. The point is a *new* dogmatics which is not conceivable without a change in the function of the church, even though this is not where it has its foundation.

Given that there are more than two hundred denominations in North America, one cannot proceed with general observations. We can only point out, by way of one or several denominations as examples, which main tendencies are currently prevailing. One has to keep in mind that dogmatics in the European sense of the term seldom existed. Of course, old Christian traditions in many denominations still reach into the present. But without a vivid, commonly acknowledged teaching office that responsibly translates tradition into the life of the church, doctrines will run idle. In some denominations this lack of meaning is already being sensed strongly in view of new developments in society.

It is not a particularity of the North American situation that the function of the church is changing. However, in view of the need to make up for a great lack of dogmatic tradition the change makes a greater difference. Years ago Edmund Schlink described the worldwide change in the situation of theology and church as a shift in "the interest of God's saving action for human beings in the direction of justice and peace and corresponding structures in society." The emphasis was now on the "critique of today's church and its contribution to society as well as the working out of comprehensive social-political programs."[17] This turning point is not strongly sensed in North America because the concern for justice and peace has long been a point of orientation in many denominations, especially since the rise of the Social Gospel. But the lack of teaching for this situation is being sensed increasingly and strongly. Accountable teaching engenders a new dogmatics which certainly has to pay attention to societal dynamics, but which cannot see its task in creating social and cultural compatibility. The new dogmatics develops when its subject matter appears differently in the societal context.

This subject matter is not primarily God-talk, neither is it immediately concerned with the "working out of comprehensive social-political programs." Instead, it appears in an elementary way, only tentatively formulated, as life be-

---

17. Edmund Schlink, "Über die künftige Aufgabe von 'Kerygma und Dogma' in einer veränderten theologischen und kirchlichen Situation," *Kerygma und Dogma* 19 (1979): 3.

fore God. As such, we have to clarify, its content is first of all the one who calls himself the life (John 14:6). In this life, talk about God is included, but it is founded on a new ordering of the relationship between God and the human being. The "God-man" ("human God") of the Council of Chalcedon is not being superseded and certainly not dismissed, but newly comprehended. The old discussion arises again, but forces us newly to state the "content" of the relationship between divinity and humanity. Now Jesus appears not only as Word become flesh, but decidedly as *deed*word, so that from his deed new thought becomes possible and real. God is here not only the triune God of love but also the God who loves on account of the divine triune justice, who in love rules justly. It is the God who does not just take on humanity in general in order to atone for sin and to create eternal life, but who in Jesus inserts into history a certain way of being human, so that every human being is revealed as sharing in a common humanity, not being only an individual.

This understanding of God's self-realization in history does not right away lead to a social-political program that would be valid for all denominations, but to a new struggle concerning Christology which makes a new anthropology unavoidable. Here we are confronted with the characteristic trait of today's North American theology. Accountable teaching tries to call attention to the newly experienced life and to distinguish it from a humanly disgraceful life. It is thereby walking a narrow line between a church isolated from society and a society that would like to influence the function of the church by claiming its teaching in order to direct its various goals. Society, whether consciously or unconsciously, often wants to destroy the identity of the church by initiating an ecclesiastic self-contradiction, so that the church is in tension with itself about its mission. New teaching develops on account of this attack on the identity of the church, especially when counterfeit teaching threatens to suppress accountable teaching.

New dogmatics is the attempt of Christian reflection to think through the teachings demanded for today critically while connecting them to the church's doctrinal tradition. That is not a retreat to orthodoxy, but a progression toward new accountable dogma. It is not primarily a matter of finding a dogmatic phrasing congruent with the tradition in which the inherited concepts of the church can be proved to be still valid today. Rather, the whole church has to be held accountable for a language appropriate to the biblical message, which expresses the communally experienced truth of life before God for human beings today. Thus, accountable teaching consists in what Christians today want to proclaim together about "God's human being" — in view of the dehumanizing of life. New dogmatics is a critical presentation of this accountable teaching.

Answering Reason

Because of the way reason has prevailed in North American theology, it cannot be pushed aside and has to fulfill an important function in the critical presentation of teaching. What is witnessed to in accountable teaching by Christians coming to an agreement cannot develop without the use of reason. But so far reason has usually been understood from a philosophical tradition which essentially tied the cognitive subject in such a way to the object that perceiving reason gained power over the object. However, reason does not have to be based in the cognitive subject. It consists first of all also in the perception of an Other which is not controlled by the subject. Language originally develops when something is communicated to the one who listens. We are spoken to before we speak. Our hearing is a partaking. Our word is primarily answer. In this way reason is based *extra nos*. The *cogito, ergo sum* of René Descartes, which was anticipated by Augustine's *even when I am deceived, I exist*, is superseded on the primary level of reason by an *amor ergo sumus* (I am loved, therefore we are). Before I know, I have been known. The ontological concept of reason is dependent on the historical shaping of reason.

This means for Christian reflection that God can be evident in human perception, but is not a logically necessary concept. If God is perceived in human reason as inevitable, then this happens in the voice of conscience. The insight into good and evil, justice and injustice, is based in an apparently transcendent claim on history. Conscience is rising.[18] In the awakening conscience God is not a necessary but a "memorable" thought. God never proves divine reality directly. In the indirect way of a troubled conscience, however, God is ever anew the unavoidable challenge for human beings. This challenge is not controlled by the perceiving subject. Also Christ and the Holy Spirit cannot be forced into a necessary logic. The contemporary trend of accommodating Christian teachings as logically necessary proves itself increasingly as the wrong track in North America. Especially the influence of civil religion reveals how the Christian values sold to society under the rule of a controlling reason will finally also be divested of their Christian *proprium*, so that in the end it will not appear as grace and gift, but very naturally as that which is humanly thinkable as a matter of course. It loses its character of the Holy and gets lost with other things in what can reasonably be manipulated.

The question is now what, after the trend of accommodation, can again be recognized in conscience as "memorable" Christian truth for a life before God. Accountable teaching will then also call for a philosophical theology which investigates and describes conscience as *praeambula fidei* (a preamble of faith). The doctrine of the trinity, Christology, and ecclesiology will relate to that investigation. But they will understand themselves first of all from the historical self-realization of God. Only the deedword of Jesus makes God as the triune God thinkable as justice-love. Reason *can* think God, but it will always be limping *after* the self-realization of God. It can now rethink the historical event of the self-realization of God and recognize it as reasonable — for conscience it is sufficiently reasonable. Conscience itself, however, does not manage the access to God. It simply answers God's challenge and shows how faith in Jesus can per-

---

18. Herzog is here using the phrase "Das Gewissen steht auf," the title of a well-known German book on the main representatives of the resistance against Hitler.

ceive God's self-realization as sufficiently reasonable. Faith proves itself, so to speak, in light of this reason as reawakened conscience.

The method which is informed by a historically shaped reason does not exclude ontology, but grants it only second place. As historical-ontological method that does not claim a necessary logic, it excludes a Christology as transcendent anthropology. The point is to understand the human being from the viewpoint of Christ as the new creation of common humanity. Here it becomes especially clear how much Christian teaching stands in contrast to logical necessities and restrictions of modern society. Ultimately the situation can only be grasped in conscience. Thus in Christian reflection a very special task remains for reason. It does not address modern society in general and in its various manifestations, but addresses the conscience, which in all its troubles curiously remains the same at all times. As an answering reason, conscience is *conditio communicationis*, the condition enabling communication.

New Dogmatics

If we presuppose that the long North American struggle about reason in the church today turns into a reflection on what is "memorable," then we have to clarify once more what it is that is "worthy of thought," and what a critical discussion of reason in Christian reflection can accomplish. The function of the church as salvation institution usually connotes the image of orthodoxy. Heresy trials, exile, prison, funeral piles — these and similar images we connect with the idea of an orthodox belief. If one stays within the framework of this function of the church, one can change individual themes, but not the principal obedience of individuals toward doctrines of the church. Dogmatics is remaining the same. It interprets talk about God, however critical the procedure may be.

If we, however, no longer see the church as salvation institution, but as justice covenant, then the gift of justice, which makes all church members responsible for accountable teaching, will take the place of an insistence on orthodoxy, because it relates to the deedword of God in Jesus, the origin of all Christian thought and all talk about God. Dogma is here not only a concept, but the agreement of deed and word in Jesus: Jesus' justice-love embodies God's justice-love and thus Godself. The gift of justice becomes accessible by understanding the biblical origin of God's self-realization in history. The character and life of Christ, who calls himself truth and life, become the criterion of a critique of teaching through dogmatics. This point had to be learned especially during the past two decades in the confrontation of black and white Christians in North America. It is only a very small beginning. We have to consider how much the teaching language of the church can ever express.

The church as salvation institution has offered the credo as literal statement of truth. In the last waves of this function in liberalism, the literal faith was supposed to be demythologized by the concept of symbol. But neither literal faith nor symbolic faith can sufficiently grasp God's justice. The very form of the gospel, which is different from the creed, but also differs radically from the correlations of modern symbolic interpretations, offers us a metaphorical reality of the word in which human beings are set in motion toward God and the neighbor: God comes toward human beings with the gift of justice, justifies them, and claims them for divine justice. In this way the image of God and of being human, and therefore the function of the church, are changed. God accomplishes the divine justice in a twofold way. God makes the sinner just and creates justice for the person without legal recourse. Since the one is not without the other, the church proves itself to be a covenant of God by which we become involved in God's struggle for a just life. Jesus is the inner foundation of this covenant, because his way of life makes us desire justice (Matt. 6:33).

The center of the new dogmatics is the witness to a life which embodies God's love. The deedword lived by Jesus precedes his teaching. Thus the old concept of orthodoxy falls by the wayside. The struggle for truth, however, remains. Which injustice destroys life? And which justice furthers life to the extent that simultaneously there is eternal life? The criterion remains the very subject matter of doctrine, Jesus' life before God — which can be scrutinized by the human sense of justice. It is reason as conscience, accepting or rejecting this justice as "worthy of thought." Reason is here asked to see not the unification of humanity as the main function of the church, but the sharing in the establishment of God's justice. It remains to be seen whether this also contributes to the unification of humanity. God and the divine work for justice do not prove themselves as logically necessary, but reason as conscience can be gripped by the common responsibility of being human. That is faith. And the new dogmatics is concerned with a faith based on God's deedword.[19]

---

19. Dogmatic developments in Roman Catholicism and in the Orthodox Churches of North America are here not dealt with, because for a long time they were not in dialogue with North American Protestantism, and they are best understood through self-representations of Catholic and Orthodox theologians of North America.

– 26 –

LIBERATION AFFIRMATION

*This short piece is the product of a collaborative effort of various persons con-
vened by the Office of Church Life and Leadership of the United Church
of Christ in 1976–77. Other than Herzog, the group which formulated the
"Liberation Affirmation" included Walter Brueggemann, Paul Hammer, Ralph
Quellhorst, Henry Rust, and Clyde Steckel. Various other members of the United
Church of Christ were consulted as well. Central themes that can be traced in
Herzog's own work are the emphasis on God as justice, the church as justice
covenant, and the Spirit and conscience.*

*The fact that Herzog included this document as an appendix to his book Jus-
tice Church shows the importance that he attributed to such concrete attempts
to renew the importance of the teaching office of the church, to formulate the
implications of the teaching of the church, and to develop a basis for mutual accountability of the church as a whole. In the contemporary search for doctrinal
foundations which has produced various attempts to develop confessions of faith,
this one stands out: following the structure of other statements of the church in
crisis such as the Barmen Declaration of Christians resisting the Third Reich,
confession is not an end in itself, but is coupled with the resistance to specific
heresies of our time.*

*Statements like this are not comprehensive in the sense that they cover the
whole of the Christian faith, but they arise out of a sense of urgency, addressing
the most burning issues which the church faces at present.*

The United Church of Christ is at a turning. Harsh issues of sound teaching
are emerging that we can no longer dodge. Church and society are caught in
increasing conflict. In this situation, God calls upon us to give a new account
of our hope lest we be "tossed to and fro and carried about with every wind of
doctrine" (Eph. 4:14).

The following emphases appear especially pertinent:

God is Justice. God is struggling with the poor, the outcast, and the lost for a
just life. In Jesus Christ, God takes sides with the poor. God "has put down the
mighty from their thrones, and exalted those of low degree" (Luke 1:52).

First published in *Justice Church: The New Function of the Church in North American Christianity*
(Maryknoll, N.Y.: Orbis Books, 1980).

Faithful teaching excludes the unsound teaching that God is on our side, that of a rich and powerful nation. The meaning of life does not consist of a national defense of wealth, but of struggling with God for justice among all peoples. As a sociopolitical and socioeconomic institution, the church is implicated in the evils of the state. It is called to serve God, not the free enterprise system. Today, racism is the most powerful means of "capitalism" to denigrate human beings into nonpersons. Sexism today is its most powerful means of assigning persons the status of minors. We need to work for alternate sociopolitical and socioeconomic models. New forms of "socialism," including responsible public ownership of the means of production, are live options also for us.

Church is Justice Covenant. The church is people called in covenant to join God's struggle for the new age of justice. Jesus Christ as embodiment of God's justice is our only motivation in the struggle for justice. "Seek first the kingdom of God and God's justice, and all other things shall be added to you" (Matt. 6:33).

Faithful teaching excludes the unsound teaching that the church can transform the nation when it allows itself to be co-opted by the powers that be. Attacked by increasing secularism in our Western nations, the church is called to be in constant conflict in various ways with principalities and powers that legitimate injustice. God is at work in all nations to create a more just life. But God's embodiment in Jesus Christ, and not the American way of life or Manifest Destiny, is the clue to human destiny. It Is Jesus Christ who calls and directs his people in the conflict.

God is Life. God is battling death as the enemy of justice. In Jesus Christ, God provides the power of life over death. "I am the resurrection and the life" (John 11:25).

Faithful teaching excludes the unsound teaching that we ultimately control life in our technological culture. With our vast technological know-how, we can cause death a million times over in our "laboratories" without the majority of the people even being aware of the murder. Totalitarianism is not always discernible by outward emblems or uniforms. It also rules in the cover-up of our "death industry." Christian faith opposes the death dealings of our culture as well as other cultures.

Church is Life Covenant. The church is people drawing upon God's vast creativity in human life. Jesus Christ is Good News as empowerment for sharing the goodness of life — conquering the destructive evils of civilization. "Do not be conformed to the world, but be transformed by the renewal of your mind, that you may prove what is the will of God, what is good and acceptable and perfect" (Rom. 12:2).

Faithful teaching excludes the unsound teaching that the task of the church is to critique culture without showing how to keep together a civilization. The church can be engaged with culture without being co-opted by culture as court chaplain of civil religion. Culture has no right to become the value framework that determines the way of life in Christ. God's rule is to be embodied in culture. Both collectivism and individualism work against God's rule. The church is people working for an obedient culture in keeping with God's will — an unending task.

God is Spirit. God forms in us a conscience accountable to justice and life for true worship. In Jesus Christ, the meaning of life is worship in spirit and truth. "God is Spirit, and they that worship must worship in spirit and truth" (John 4:24).

Faithful teaching excludes the unsound teaching that everyone is an autonomous individual free to do his or her own thing. Worship is first of all God ministering to us, calling us to be daughters and sons. Becoming daughters and sons in turn involves worship of God that overcomes race, sex, and class domination, making us sisters and brothers. Re-creation of people through the Spirit affirms the value of each person. God brings each a vision of life abundant. That life issues in the discipline of piety in each individual Christian. Human beings become persons where the Spirit of justice reigns.

Church is Spirit Covenant. The church is people responding in obedience to God's Holy Spirit as empowering Presence in history. In Jesus Christ, God continues to draw near as Immanuel, God with us, so that the church can be a community of true worship among all people. "By the mercies of God . . . present your bodies a living sacrifice, holy and acceptable to God, which is your proper worship" (Rom. 12:1).

Faithful teaching excludes the unsound teaching that ministry and polity are merely incidental to the life of the church. God in ministry to the poor, outcast, and lost, battles to order human history for the sake of justice and life. Ministry and polity of the church become means of sharing in the struggle in a revolutionary as well as an orderly way. The ministry of Word and Sacrament embodied in just polity seeks to evoke faithfulness to God's action in the lives of all people. The teaching office of the church, responsible for discipline and transformation, invites people to present their bodies as a living sacrifice in the struggles of history.

– 27 –

WHO SPEAKS FOR THE ANIMALS?

No set of proposals for the transformation of theology and the church would be complete without attention to all of God's creation, as this sermon on Luke 2:15–20 shows. The theological concern for people at the margins ultimately encounters other marginalized creatures as well. The silences of church and society in regard to the animals appear to be no accident. They are part of the self-centeredness of the "principalities and powers" that are in charge.

Even environmental issues need to be seen in this broader perspective of power and control. While not mentioned in this sermon, in the context of North Carolina Herzog learns that race, for instance, is an important factor in the location of uncontrolled hazardous waste facilities.

This sermon is directed first of all to pastors — female as well as male. Laypeople will also read it. God keep us all. We are all caught up in the issues of the sermon.

I was pressed into a time bind that made it next to impossible to complete the sermon in time for you to read at Christmas. Unless a print shop miracle happens!

The circumstance could be providential. It might help us remember that there is also Christmas at Epiphany and Christmas at Easter. In fact, at each Eucharist we need to sing inside our hearts: "O holy Child of Bethlehem, Descend to us we pray. Cast out our sin, and enter in, Be born in us today."

We ministers, in our sermons at Christmas, at "Christmas at Epiphany," at "Christmas at Easter," or at "Christmas at the Eucharist" soon need to consider an about-face.

When I read Paul Hammer's keen meditation, about the first thought that occurred to me was, Who speaks for the animals? Hammer says, "The story of the shepherds' response occurs in the context of their daily work after returning from Bethlehem." It has hit me more and more lately how much we in our God-talk focus on the human being. In fact, much of the Christian tradition has been homocentric or anthropocentric. But there have been exceptions; St. Francis of Assisi, for example, whose eight-hundredth birthday we seek to celebrate these

First published in *No Other Foundation* 3, no. 4 (Winter 1982): 14–18.

days. Interestingly the U.S. stamp that calls attention to his birthday has him preaching to the animals.

What about the animals in our Christmas celebrations today, 1982? 1982 is *also* the year of our Lord. But it is at the same time the year of the MX, the year of the Pershing II, the year of the Cruise Missile. What about the sheep?

I recently again pondered Edward Hicks's picture *The Peaceable Kingdom* in the Phillips Collection in Washington, D.C. It's not a very large canvas. But the message comes across loud and clear. Hicks was a Quaker preacher, strongly influenced by the famous treaties William Penn made with the Native Americans (1683–1750), which he honored and which lasted fifty years. The picture shows a harmonious scene near the Delaware. Penn on the other side stands with his associates, peacefully next to a group of Native Americans with some treaty document being held up. On the other side (the right side for the beholder) one sees lion and lamb, leopard and kid, and other animals peacefully lying or standing next to each other in terms of Isaiah 11:6.

> The wolf shall dwell with the lamb, and the leopard shall lie down with the kid; and the calf and young lion and the fatling together; and a little child shall lead them.

There of course are a number of ways one can interpret the picture. The first thing that obviously comes to mind is that here is harmonious nature and history — in the mind of the artist realized in the commonwealth of Pennsylvania. This is the way our forefathers and foremothers dreamed of this New World — a peaceable world free from the ravaging wars of Europe.

My point is that this picture indicates how in our North American history we have not been completely immune to the fate of the animal world. We have not concentrated exclusively on the new "American Adam" or "American Eve." And yet the animal world does not play as conspicuous a role with us today, especially not in our preaching, as it does in this picture.

In our world, even our world of preaching, it often seems already like Rachel Carson's *Silent Spring*. Birds no longer exist. No bluebird, no meadowlark. And so on. Maybe we can get them back at least into our Christmas preaching. The fortunate thing is that in the folklore of Christmas, the animals imposed themselves on the imagination. Drive through the streets of our towns. Look at the crèches people have built on their front lawns. There they are: the sheep, the ox, and the ass, as well as the people. But the text doesn't even talk about the shepherds herding along their sheep to the manger.

My response to the text is *the response of anguish*. How is it that without the animals being mentioned in the *text* as present at the manger, they got into the *texture* of every Christmas scene, in the Christmas tradition, whether in display or in playacting? Why has the Christmas tradition been ready to sentimentalize the manger scene with the help of the animals, but was not ready to thematize the presence of the animals in our midst as part of God's work in creation?

St. Paul comes close to my anguish when he cries out: "The whole creation has been groaning in travail together until now" (Rom. 8:22).

Why is our view of the animals at best *sentimental* in regard to God's scheme of things, and not *sacramental*? In a Christmas hymn we sing, "Ox and ass before him bow, And he is in the manger now." In a more popular Christmas song, we have a whole litany of animal contributions to the birth of the Christ child. It is generally known as *The Friendly Beasts*. All of us, at one time or another, have sung at Christmas: "The friendly beasts around him stood. Jesus, our brother, strong and good." The first animal to speak is the donkey: "'I,' said the donkey, shaggy and brown, 'I carried His mother uphill and down, I carried her safely to Bethlehem town.'" The last animal to speak is the dove: "'I,' said the dove from the rafters high, 'I cooed Him to sleep that He should not cry.'" Beside them appear the cow, the sheep, and the camel.

Yet in our teachings throughout the Christian year — when do the animals ever play a role? What comes to mind is that in these parts there is something like a "Blessing of the Hunt," a "Reverend" appears when the hunters assemble with their hound dogs and blesses them for the foxhunt. Throughout the history of the church, it seems that too often we have turned against the animals, a St. Francis being more the exception than the rule.

Who speaks for the animals? If a nuclear war comes some people think they can save at least a part of the population in shelters. But will there be animal shelters shielding the animals against the effects of radiation? For miles around a nuclear blast the radiation will destroy the pupils of the eyes even of those beings whose bodies have been able to survive the blast somewhat intact. If we have not understood the "groaning of creation" thus far, perhaps we can grasp what kind of groaning among the creatures a nuclear blast will bring.

Who speaks for the animals? They have no choice but to suffer our self-inflicted fate. The Christmas message this year seems grim. "Peace on earth, good will toward humankind." What about: "Peace on earth, good will towards the animals"? Would a change of images be able to shock us into sanity?

In preparing for nuclear war we apparently no longer care whether or not millions of human beings will have to die. That's part of the calculation. Preachments will not change these calculations. But maybe a sudden awakening of moral responsibility for creation, as a whole, will!

The greatest temptation we are facing today is the dulling of our moral sensibility toward creation as a whole.

Sisters and brothers, turn from the sentimental view of the Christmas crèche to the sacramental. All creatures great and small are holy! It is not that there is just — as in India — a holy cow. God has called all these beings into life. They are God's. We have no right to play Armageddon with God's handiwork.

Sisters and brothers, proclaim the sacramental animal Christmas throughout the year 1983 and 1984 and.... The hour is late — Jesus used to say. "Repent, and believe in the gospel." As I was trying to pray through this sermon a letter arrived from a member of the group of seventeen vicars of the Rhineland Church that had recently visited North Carolina. This young fellow minister had been very active in the peace movement in Germany. He rejoiced during his stay here that he found kindred souls. In a meeting on the Duke campus, a Southern Baptists minister had spoken about the power of God to make peace. Referring to that instance, the young German minister wrote: "After the change in our government, I don't believe any longer that the peace movement in Germany can stop the placement of the new Pershing II rockets. Near our town the U.S. Army is already making preparations for installing them. The next phase in stepping up international armament is already under way. Pondering this condition I remember the words of Rev. Robert McClernon: 'If we believe, God will make peace.' I don't believe anymore that God can do it with this mankind."

Desperation is gripping many stalwart souls. All the words of the church for peace these past years seem to have been in vain. We dare not kid ourselves. The times are awesomely tough. "For we are not contending against flesh and blood, but against the principalities, against the powers, against the world rulers of this present darkness, against the spiritual hosts of wickedness in the heavenly places" (Eph. 6:12).

Sisters and brothers, let us resolve to pay attention to what our tradition has not sensitized us to as yet. The animals have fallen between the cracks thus far. The Christian tradition has created or cocreated a vast homocentrism or anthropocentrism. This is where we are because we have concentrated so much on "man" — on *our* salvation, *our* righteousness, *our* sanctification. What will happen if we pay attention to beings we have "tuned out" of our tradition? Who speaks for the animals? If we no longer have compassion for our own kind, perhaps we can learn it again by indirection, by learning compassion for the animals, for all of God's creation. If I can love a bluebird again, and preach to a bluebird, maybe I can also love a Russian again.

I realize this sermon might seem like one great non sequitur. It does not quite follow from the preceding meditation. But in our neatly blocked off theologies we have set up great theological schemes that have not been able to block off disaster in the human race. The gospel is always the good news that we can try a new tack.

The one thing that comes to mind is that "the shepherds returned" (Luke 2:20). It could only have been to their flock, to their "daily work." And the glorifying and praising they did probably also had to focus on tending their flock. That is the story I wanted to tell. We need to become shepherds. We can be shepherds of God's creation — the way it seems intimated in Genesis 2:19–20. It probably will take a conversion the likes of which we have not imagined before. Perhaps humankind still has to be born!

One perhaps can get at the point only in terms of further storytelling. We need a real mutation of sensibility. A fellow feeling for all creation is at the center of the gospel. But it is something that, for most of us so far, is still untapped. How do we grasp it? Reflecting on the slave trade William Styron, in *The Confessions of Nat Turner* (1967), has one of the characters of the novel confess:

Surely mankind has yet to be born. *Surely* this is true! For only something blind and uncomprehending could exist in such a mean conjunction with its own flesh, its own kind. How else account for such faltering, clumsy, hateful cruelty? Even the possums and skunks know better! Even the weasels and the meadow mice have a natural regard for their own blood and kin.... Yes, it could be that mankind has yet to be born. Ah, what bitter tears God must weep at the sight of the things that men do to other men!

The gospel can generate the fellow feeling for all creatures. Perhaps we can get a deeper sense of our mutual dignity as human beings by speaking up for the animals. Alan Troxler created papier-mâché representations of blind animals worn by demonstrators in the June 12 peace march in New York. It was a new beginning of humans, being shepherds of creation.

"And the shepherds returned." Some of their glorifying and praising God can lead us to glorifying and praising God by loving God's creatures. Who speaks for the animals? God yet leaves an opening for us, so that even our children's children will (with a little change in the wording) be able to sing:

> So every beast, by some good spell,
> In the *World so dark is* glad to tell
> Of the gift he gave Immanuel.
> The gift *she* gave Immanuel.

PART FOUR

DEVELOPING ALTERNATIVE VISIONS FOR THE FUTURE

This part contains the latest writings of Herzog, some of them unpublished due to his untimely death. Here he works toward merging the different aspects of his thinking into a more comprehensive structure, extending the horizon of theology beyond the United States and Europe to Latin America in a search for mutual accountability, and developing practical models and plans for reshaping theological education and the church.

Herzog's work in the nineties both broadens and deepens his earlier theological investigations. Already in the late eighties he develops a new string of personal ties to Latin America, especially to Peru. Establishing a close relationship with the Methodist Church in Peru and its theological seminary, with Gustavo Gutiérrez and several Maryknoll priests, and finally with a village for orphaned children on the outskirts of Lima, Herzog expands his theological reflections in light of the common tradition that connects North and South. While much of that tradition has been shaped as a tradition of conquest, Herzog also identifies moments of God's liberation that provide new hope and energy.

At the same time, he continues to work in the context of the ecumenical relationship of the United Church of Christ (UCC) in North America and the German Evangelical Church of the Union (EKU). This ecumenical involvement is characterized by attention to the developments at the grassroots and mutual accountability of two "First World" churches at a time when, especially after capitalism has declared global victory, the power of the market economy takes over more and more dimensions of life.

Yet besides the broadening element, there is also a deepening one in Herzog's work. His analyses of oppression become more specific yet. In different efforts at excavating those structures of oppression which are normally hidden today, the plight of children across racial and national boundaries surfaces time and again. This is where the encounters with Latin America, with the victims of the Persian Gulf War, with the poverty at home and abroad which is intensified by globalizing economic structures that do not pay attention to the underside, and with the self-perpetuating specter of racism, all meet. The oppression of women is also part of this deepening move.

Building blocks for Herzog's vision for the future include an orientation in the work of the triune God, the formation of Christian communities, development of mutual accountability both in small groups and larger settings which maintain diversity, and an understanding of theology as "accountable teaching" where tradition is reshaped and further developed from the bottom up. Everything comes together at the Eucharist as the place where God's alternative economy is rooted. Here a new sense of unity in Christ develops which respects the diversity of the body of Christ.

Herzog's last writings pioneer new vistas for theological studies. Many of them were still waiting for further elaboration before their publication in form of books and articles. But even in their present form they function as guides into charting new terrain of theological reflection at a time when theology as a whole needs to reinvent itself.

– 28 –

PRAYER FOR PEACE

The Gulf War of early 1991 is the setting for this prayer, a war that was met with relatively little resistance in society and in the churches. At a time when most of the churches, the politicians, and even journalists prayed "God bless our troops," Herzog formulated a different prayer.

Hope for peace is nurtured in light of other struggles (Herzog quotes the well-known Black National Anthem), but the cost of this particular struggle needs to be clear: without real acts of repentance and conversion in the face of war, a new way of life cannot be established. No doubt, as we participate in this process, our understanding of repentance, conversion, and new life will never be the same.

As a people we stood before you these days caught in a maze of feelings — some of us angry, some horror-stricken, some crying in our hearts, some crying out openly.

Others were grim, determined to strike a desert enemy with all military might at our disposal. Some have rejoiced, elated that war has begun. We are a divided people in this war.

As a church we have prayed for peace, but there is no peace.

As a church we have hoped for peace, but hope has died.

As a church we have worked for peace, but a night seems coming where we can work no more.

Stony the road we trod, bitter the chastening rod,

Felt in the days when hope unborn had died.

Yet with a steady beat, have not our weary feet

Come to the place for which our mothers (and fathers) sighed?

We confess that we have not labored enough for the Prince of Peace. We have not believed enough that he is our peace and the peace for all humankind.

Give us the strength to become peacemakers in his name.

Give us the will to dream the impossible dream that someday human blood will no longer flow in war.

Unpublished prayer in York Chapel at Duke Divinity School after the Two-Day Fast for Peace, January 24, 1991.

Give us the determination to stretch every nerve and make it become a nerve of peace.

Give us the insight that the transformation of war into peace costs much more than building the war machine.

We have fasted before you for a short two days. Make us grasp that peace will cost the inward fasting of all our days — a strength, a will, a determination, and a grasp that can only come as your gift.

Our God, you are giving us a chance that many of us never have had before: to practice repentance, experience conversion, and rise to a new life with Christ in changing war into nonviolence. Stand by us as we grasp that chance.

We pray for all drawn into the conflict, the parents, the children, the soldiers, the civilians, the leaders of the nations at war, and the leaders of all nations.

Teach us the patience of unanswered prayer.

Teach us the peacemaking of each answered prayer.

Amen.

29

LIBERATION AND PROCESS THEOLOGIES IN THE CHURCH

This essay on the relation of two very different theological efforts illumines the new way of arriving at theological judgments that Herzog develops. Any theology needs to be seen not only in its intellectual commitments but in relation to the tensions and conflicts of the present, its historical genesis, and, most important, in the context of the church as a whole. In this essay Herzog reviews the development of the liberation theology project in the southern United States in detail. Liberation theology grows out of an encounter with God and the oppressed in specific settings.

In this connection process theology will yet have to give an account of its own development in similar ways. Herein lies the challenge for any possible dialogue of various theological approaches in the future of the church: how can theology be developed further in accountability to real-life issues and matters of life and death? Theology can no longer be done in the abstract, on purely academic and conceptual levels, or in response to the movements of the theological market.

Live as free persons, yet not using your freedom as pretext for evil.
— 1 PETER 2:16

What relationship is there between liberation theologies and process theologies? It is impossible for me to begin answering this question, raised by the editors of *Prism*, without trying to view it in our United Church of Christ context.

Three preliminary orientation points: (1) It is impossible to see both theologies apart from the present dilemmas of theology in the North Atlantic community. (2) We need to do justice to the specific histories attending liberation and process theologies. (3) We destroy ourselves as theologians if we bypass the church as teaching body. Christian theology is rooted in the church. If we forget, our theology tends to become a loose cannon. Since *Prism* is the theological mouthpiece of the United Church of Christ, the present essay appears in its true habitat.

First published in *Prism* 5, no. 2 (Fall 1990): 57–68.

1

There still is the perception prevalent that theology in the West is in a bad state. Robert McAfee Brown, for example, states: "Systematic theology is not leading the list of human concerns these days. Few people are grabbed by analyzing the four attributes of God or parsing a complex definition of deontological love. The front lines in the human battles do not seem to be theological libraries and seminar rooms. Perhaps we need a new approach."[1]

The tough theological front lines today are where the church has its front lines. We can be grateful that the United Church of Christ minces no words about its place on the front lines of the human battles. We United Church of Christ theologians have to spell out our direct involvement in these struggles in terms of our personal participation in the life of the church. I underlined this especially in *Justice Church: The New Function of the Church in North American Christianity* (1980). The major thrust of the book is centered in the UCC document that became known as *Sound Teaching.*[2] My book *God-Walk: Liberation Shaping Dogmatics* (1988) retains that angle, especially in reference to our new *Book of Worship* (1986).

One of the major dilemmas facing the theologian in regard to involvement in the life of the church is the popular atmosphere in which religionists are doing theology in the United States today. There is a "conventional wisdom," present also in theological education in the United States, that in the market of ideas we theologians have to sell our intellectual wares. We frequently act as the contemporary Sophists, not too different from the Sophists of the Greek enlightenment.

In the North Atlantic community we are often expected to be the people who sell their private views about the universe, human life, and God, if not the devil. While the Sophists also taught partly out of noble impulse to enlighten their Greek compatriots, "it was nonetheless true that this teaching became their *business.*"[3] They were strong in rhetoric, perfecting the art of eloquence. Ultimately they contributed to a growing sense of relativism in values. Was there anything universally valid? They generally responded with skepticism, "which at first was a genuine scientific theory, but soon became frivolous play."[4]

Are there still universally valid truths in our churches? Obviously we will not be able to offer a quick fix for a rampant relativism. But in many respects the United Church of Christ has made a good beginning in trying to tackle the issue. There is the publication of *Toward Theological Self-Understanding in the United Church of Christ* in *New Conversations* 8, no. 1 (Spring 1985). There

---

1. Robert McAfee Brown, "Liberation as Drama," *Christianity and Crisis* 50, no. 4 (March 19, 1990): 76.
2. Frederick Herzog, *Justice Church: The New Function of the Church in North American Christianity* (Maryknoll, N.Y.: Orbis Books, 1980), 139–54. *Toward the Task of Sound Teaching in the United Church of Christ* was published by the Office for Church Life and Leadership in 1978.
3. Wilhelm Windelband, *A History of Philosophy* (New York: Harper, 1958), 67.
4. Ibid., 69.

is Louis H. Gunnemann's book, *United and Uniting: The Meaning of an Ecclesial Journey* (1987). And we have now the fine book edited by Daniel L. Johnson and Charles Hambrick-Stowe, *Theology and Identity: Tradition, Movement, and Polity in the United Church of Christ* (1990). *Prism* itself, since its founding in 1985, has made a vast contribution to a new era. Yet all this needs to be drawn together in a still deeper common understanding that we are working on a vast mandate of *mutual accountability* for ourselves and for the church in the global village as a whole. We need to discover and articulate very clearly the truths we hold in common. Both liberation theologies and process theologies are crying out for this next move.

2

It was a great and good thing that Latin American liberation theology grew on the soil of the church. So did black theology in this country. Obviously there was also feminist theology, Asian American theology, Native American theology, and so on. It seems difficult at times to count the number of liberation theologies. There are so many. Whatever little some of us were able to develop in the South, besides black theology, also grew out of the church.

It is widely known that Latin American liberation theology was something that grew out of base communities and was conceptualized at the conference of Latin American bishops in Medellín (1968), Vatican II (1962–65) having provided the wind for their sails. The Roman Catholic Church in Latin America at that time very much wanted this theological momentum offering a rationale for the Church's option for the poor.

Wherever we look today in the United Church of Christ, there is no parallel to this type of grassroots church linked to institutional theological mandates agreed upon by the church as a whole. This is the main reason why it is still difficult in our denomination, just as in other mainline Protestant denominations in North America, to make collective sense of liberation theology. Recently our new president, Paul Sherry, has announced nine categories our church ought to work through in "issue concentration teams" until General Synod 1991, where "directional statements" would be shaped for wider church use. The first of the nine categories is *theological reflection*.[5] This is an excellent beginning. The question is: theological reflection from which praxis?

The statement of the "Thirty-Nine" UCC seminary professors already tried something similar when in 1983, more than half a decade ago, it asked that the Executive Council (acting for the General Synod) "constitute a body of theological leadership and reflection responsible for assisting local congregations, associations, conferences, national officers, and instrumentalities in developing teaching consensus."[6] That proposal came to naught. We will have to wait and

---

5. Hans Holznagel, "Sherry: Let's Be Systematic," *United Church News* 6, no. 2 (March 1990): 1.
6. "A Most Difficult and Urgent Time," *New Conversations* 8, no. 1 (Spring 1985): 3.

see how Paul Sherry's initiative is acted upon. One thing is certain: we can keep talking endlessly about liberation theologies, but unless our church finds a moment of decision where we *corporately unite theological reflection and the option for the poor* as mandate for our entire church, our liberation talk will be in vain.

What relationship is there between liberation theologies and process theologies? As I will later try to explain, process theology can provide a philosophical rationale for the liberation *process*, once the question of truth is raised. But process theology needs to be linked to grassroots of liberation lest talk be heaped on top of talk and no one be the wiser for it. Right now as theologians we are generally much closer to nurturing the Sophist line: "With their self-complacent, pettifogging advocacy, the Sophists made themselves the mouth-piece of all the unbridled tendencies which were undermining the order of public life."[7] Unless there is a radical altering of consciousness among us we cannot intelligently debate the assigned topic. We are so blinded by monetary and other rewards for our marketing of religious ideas that we do not see in the least the change called for. The sleazy state of religious affairs in the United States as part of our sleazy culture today often seems perfectly normal to us.

3

It is everybody's guess whether we will be *able* as a United Church of Christ to develop the willpower to take a resolute step in a new direction. I have already lifted out great signs of hope. Some of these are still tied to individuals only.[8] But all of this is not as yet a response to any mandate by the church as a whole. The collective mind of the United Church of Christ at this time gives the impression of being fairly amorphous. But if we as theologians bypass the church, neither liberation theologies nor process theologies will make any difference whatsoever in the actual state of our society. Theology needs to be involved in the most vulnerable dimensions of human life. We have important statements of the United Church of Christ on some of the liberation concerns, for example, the study paper "Christian Faith and Economic Life" (1987). But these are not as yet primal grassroots bases from which a corporate theological commitment to the option for the poor of the United Church of Christ as a whole would grow.

After these preliminary observations, we can now look at liberation theologies and process theologies in brief comparison.

---

7. Windelband, *A History of Philosophy*, 69.

8. It should not be overlooked that much of the work on the local level is as important as "national" publications by our boards and agencies. I especially want to call attention to the many efforts of the Wisconsin Conference of the United Church of Christ under the leadership of Frederick R. Trost. The publications in that context are known far beyond the confines of the conference. In the framework of our present discussion, for example, beginning a new series titled "Koinonia: Issues of Church and Society" with an issue called *Resistance Commitment as Commitment to Justice* (Summer 1988) was a creative step.

Liberation Theology

Instead of describing liberation theologies in the abstract, I will share my own "slice of life" in the matter. Experience of liberation in the South, within the present context, goes back to the civil rights days of the 1960s. It was a time when we encountered history as a process of liberation. I do not remember any significant step in that process that was not related to the black church. The story has been told many times before and is well known. The walls of segregation were crumbling. In North Carolina, Martin Luther King, Jr., came to the Raleigh-Durham area for workshops on nonviolent action. People met in churches for reflection on the dynamics of the liberation process.[9] Before long they found the courage to march out of the churches with liberation songs on their lips and to walk the city streets protesting segregated restaurants, schools, and churches. But to speak of it as "irruption of the poor,"[10] as Gustavo Gutiérrez does in regard to the liberation struggle of the poor in Latin America, would be inaccurate. There were slums in Durham, North Carolina, it is true. But there was not the vast poverty of the *asentamientos humanos,* the shantytowns, of Peru or any other "Two-Thirds World" country. Nevertheless, a change took place. The voiceless found a voice and the nonpersons discovered themselves as persons.

In resisting unjust laws that forced persons to be nonpersons, more and more of us saw the need for radical nonviolent action. I do not recall many United Church of Christ people of the immediate area engaging in resistance activities. But I remember that the national UCC offices sent some monies for our defense in seemingly interminable court actions. The 1960s quickly flew by. Before we knew it, the standard-bearer of the struggle was lying in a pool of blood in Memphis, Tennessee.

It was April 4, 1968, 6:00 p.m. Suddenly it dawned on me: here was not just the liberation process in the death of King, but the theology of liberation. It was martyrdom that made the difference. I sensed then that this was one liberation theology among many other liberation theologies on the horizon. But the liberation process to which all of them would refer was the same everywhere.

Shortly afterward I began writing an article called "Theology of Liberation."[11] As I was responding to the great vulnerability of people in the liberation process, there was no Council of Bishops, as in Medellín 1968, standing behind me.

---

9. In a larger essay a decade and a half ago, I tried to set the whole experience of the liberation process in a wider historical context. See Frederick Herzog, "Pre-Bicentennial U.S.A. in the Liberation Process," in *Theology in the Americas,* ed. Sergio Torres and John Eagleson (Maryknoll, N.Y.: Orbis Books, 1976), 139–74.

10. Gustavo Gutiérrez, *A Theology of Liberation: 15th Anniversary Edition* (Maryknoll, N.Y.: Orbis Books, 1988), xx.

11. Frederick Herzog, "Theology of Liberation," *Continuum* 7, no. 4 (Winter 1970): 515–24, included in this volume as chapter 9. M. Douglas Meeks, "Liberation Theology and the United Church of Christ," in *Theology and Identity,* ed. Daniel L. Johnson and Charles Hambrick-Stowe (New York: Pilgrim Press, 1990), offers a good explanation why it is helpful to use "liberation theology as a single trajectory," although it would be "more accurate to speak of liberation theologies" (152).

I had to reflect intensely on this "loneliness" many times over the past decades, though on one level it was not loneliness at all. What made it possible
to understand the history happening to us as liberation history were the poor
who, with the Bible in their hands, forced us to read the Scriptures in new ways.
These poor have names. They have faces. They are not an abstract mass of
human flesh. They are loving, caring, and real.[12]

In moving beyond that point I have been instructed by Gustavo Gutiérrez in
some sharply profiled observations: "Captivated as we are by the life and death
of the poor in Latin America and by the riches to be found in the Christian
communities that come into existence there and bear witness — even to the
point of martyrdom — to the Lord in their midst, we have perhaps tended to
focus our attention too much on these things."[13] As far as the poor in *our* midst
are concerned, I too, perhaps, may have tended to focus my attention too much
on them. But then most of the white churches in the South were not paying
attention at all to the liberation process. On their foil we *did* appear as "loners
of liberation." But that did not ruffle us a bit. We *had* seen new freedom arise
from the poor as a gift of God. We could only bear witness to that "which our
eyes have seen" (1 John 1:1). It was also like "Mine eyes have seen the glory of
the coming of the Lord" — except that this time the "glory" was not Civil War
violence, but civil rights nonviolence.

There were also two events that kept me from focusing on our southern
poverty dynamics alone. The first was the emergence of black theology. It was
fortunate that I encountered James H. Cone very early in his struggle to shape
a black theology. But some were saying that he too was a loner of liberation. It
was painful to observe that even blacks had difficulties with Cone. In fact, it was
a black minister who told me at the time, "black theology is dangerous."

The second event was a tense racial altercation in the city of Wilmington,
North Carolina. Ten people were arrested in February 1971, nine blacks and
one white. Brought to trial, their sentences ranged from 10 to 34 years (Benjamin Chavis) and totaled 282 years.[14] The court proceedings lasted for almost
a decade. By the time they were over, the Wilmington Ten, as they came to be
called, had accomplished what no one else before had been able to achieve: the
United Church of Christ General Synod had become involved in official advocacy of their cause. The struggle had become a national church struggle, not just
a southern one. My encounter with Benjamin Chavis, the leader of the Wilmington Ten, became as important to me as that with James H. Cone. After an
almost two-decade struggle without firm structural support, I found a link to the

---

12. In some respects, liberation theology is no more than a hermeneutical focus similar to process
theology, neoorthodox theology, existentialist theology, evangelical theology, or kerygmatic theology.
There is one difference: it requires the participation of the theologian in the justice struggle. And
that makes for all the difference in the world.

13. Gutiérrez, *Theology of Liberation*, xxiii.

14. "The Wilmington Ten: A Summary and a Call," A *Statement Prepared by the Wilmington Ten
Task Group of the North Carolina Council of Churches* (October 1977).

national United Church of Christ Commission for Racial Justice whose director Chavis eventually became. His support of some of the continuing struggles in our area has been invaluable.

Other events could be added. I break off my story here in order to make one point only: it took considerable time until I had found the language appropriate to the discovery. Black theology helped. Obviously I was not black. But I learned that it would be possible to acknowledge the same dynamics of the liberation process by all those who cared to open their eyes and engage themselves in the struggle for justice. So I wrote in *Liberation Theology* (1972): "It would be repulsive if we were to try to outblack the black. Anyone looking for repeated invocation of the black God, the black Christ, etc., throughout the book will look in vain. The test of our thesis is that at every step of the way we will be found to be struggling with the same issue as black theology: a new grasp of history as liberation history. The historical space we stand in is the space of liberation."[15]

New freedoms were gained for millions of people. Freedom space thus increased for us all. It was mediated to us by the voiceless who found their voice. The new reality will be etched in our memories forever. It set the following signals:

1. There is a new starting point for theology. We need to listen to the vulnerable, the invisible, and the nonpersons before we can understand the Bible. It is the Bible itself in the hands of the poor that compels us to listen. Theology is a second step. The first step is our own walk into vulnerability.

2. The Bible wants us to be there because God and Jesus are already there. The major christological issue developing for the ecumenical church is the character of God in Jesus. Gustavo Gutiérrez writes: "The ultimate reason for commitment to the poor and oppressed... is grounded in... the God of our faith."[16] Our challenge is, "Opting for the God of Jesus."[17] In our theological textbooks in the past we did not meet a poor God and a poor Christ, a God and Christ who join those struggling for dignity. God does not exclude the rich. But it is "hard for the rich to enter the kingdom of God" (Mark 10:23). There is God's special *protection privilege of the poor.* The Psalms, for example, are full of it (Ps. 9:12, 18; 10:18; 22:24; 35:10; 69:33, etc.). God is not a respecter of persons, be they rich or poor. But God does stand up for those who cannot defend themselves, "the widow and the orphan."

3. There is no diminishing here of God's process of salvation. But for ages the church had proclaimed salvation as pertaining to heaven and the soul only. We had forgotten that salvation is also *Exodus* and not only reconciliation. The liberation dynamics are an equal dimension of God's saving work in history. God

---

15. Frederick Herzog, *Liberation Theology: Liberation in the Light of the Fourth Gospel* (New York: Seabury Press, 1972), ix.

16. Gutiérrez, *Theology of Liberation*, xxvii.

17. Ibid., xxv.

is as concerned about the body as about the soul. God wants human beings to be free in this life and in the life to come.

4. The place where liberation and reconciliation are experienced together is the Eucharist. The fusion of liberation and reconciliation in Re-creation is the Holy Spirit. It is illumined by Jesus' own life as part of liberation history. The proper place for the Eucharist would be the coal mine, the sweatshop, or the cotton mill. It makes sense in our sanctuaries only to the extent that it embodies Jesus' presence in these places. As the Justice Meal, it lets us share in God's own justice struggle.

Obviously I say all this in neat "talk." So we dare not eliminate from our memory that in the civil rights days God's justice struggle took place in the streets and at times near the graves of the dead. It ended in real freedoms, freedom in schooling and business, in access to public services and public buildings, to the mass media and better jobs. But what has become of these freedoms? Some have used freedom wisely, others have abused it. The continuing challenge of liberation is to heed God's Word: "Live as free persons, not however as though your freedom were there to provide a screen for wrongdoing" (1 Pet. 2:16).

Process Theology

What relationship is there between liberation theologies and process theologies? There are several linkages possible. If one thinks, for example, of John B. Cobb, Jr., and Schubert M. Ogden, both have tried to integrate their process project into the liberation thrust. Sooner or later the question of truth arises in regard to any theological claim. As far as the liberation process is concerned, it comes down to the philosophical framework of historical process, so that we do not merely exude a fideistic type of commitment to the poor, but that it makes sense on the foil of the human search for truth.[18]

The temptation is great that we now seek out the wide-flung debate about the relationships between process theologies and liberation theologies.[19] Yet there is no gain in insight for us as church community trying to share in this debate, unless we first of all have sought to subject the challenge to our own church framework. The point is not how many theories we can feed into our denominational pail. The challenge is to ask what kind of *praxis* demands understanding the relationships between process thought and liberation thought. As long as our denomination leaves praxis to individual preference, no genuine answer is possible.

---

18. See John B. Cobb, Jr., *Process Theology as Political Theology* (Philadelphia: Westminster Press, 1982), 138: "For Process theology the quest for the overview within which to understand particular phenomena, including Christian faith, cannot be given up."

19. From the wide range of contributions, significant recent discussion appears in Anselm Kyong-suk Min, "How Not to Do a Theology of Liberation: A Critique of Schubert Ogden," *Journal of the American Academy of Religion* 57, no. 1 (Spring 1989): 83–102, and in Delwin Brown, "Thinking about the God of the Poor: Questions for Liberation Theology from Process Thought," ibid., Summer 1989, 267–81.

The last thing I would want to suggest is that I have found *the* praxis solution for the United Church of Christ. The great thing we are doing right now is that we are examining what Barbara Brown Zikmund calls our "Hidden Histories."[20] In order to make my point about liberation we have to go through a lot of our black history.[21] But in doing so we are already deeply involved in historical process. At the same time we cannot turn away from the contemporary moment of this process. I will mention only three factors. (1) Overpopulation of the globe. Our present world population of 5.3 billion increases by one quarter million a day, 100 million a year. Estimates, fairly conservative at that, are for 10 to 14 billion by the year 2100.[22] (2) Crime increase. In the state of North Carolina alone, the prison population has doubled in less than ten years.[23] (3) The drug war. The ever-increasing meaninglessness of modern life in the burgeoning metropolitan clusters (often close to 20 million people) presses in on us all. So-called controlled substances are "means of survival" for people who have no hope for a meaningful life.[24] War by any name will not solve that problem. Our struggle needs to be for meaningful work, "Jobs with Peace."[25]

It is fortunate that in the collection edited by Daniel L. Johnson and Charles Hambrick-Stowe we now have an essay available by David M. Stowe on process theology in the United Church of Christ that helps us tie together the liberation mandate and the truth question.[26] It makes the contribution I had been hoping for: process theology is brought into the framework of the United Church of Christ. Our learning here needs to be focused on the relationship between Stowe's essay and another essay in the same volume by M. Douglas Meeks titled "Liberation Theology and the United Church of Christ." What relationship is there between liberation theologies and process theologies? The answer for us United Church of Christ people lies initially in our relating these two essays. We need to practice concrete learning in our own household. There are no other solutions today but those embodying *concrete accountability* in church relationships. On the one hand, they may seem insignificant; on the other hand, they are the small miracles of our day.

What the Stowe essay makes clear is that any notion of process has to evidence itself on the foil of the relationship quality of all existence. Any notion of liberation process falls into that framework. It comes down to our trying to understand corporately the primordial point of relating to other beings and structures of creation. Stowe also refers to *Sound Teaching*: "An important document

---

20. Barbara Brown Zikmund has edited two volumes titled *Hidden Histories in the United Church of Christ* (New York: United Church Press, 1984, 1987).

21. For example, A. Knighton Stanley, *The Children Is Crying* (New York: Pilgrim Press, 1979).

22. Hal Crowther, "Clear the Lifeboat," *Independent* (April 12, 1990): 12.

23. Michael Hobbs, "Number of N.C. Crimes Up 9%," *Durham Morning Herald* (April 7, 1990): 1.

24. See "Coca: The Real Green Revolution," *NACLA Report on the Americas* (March 1989).

25. This issue is the same throughout the "Third World," as well as at home. For Latin America see Frederick Ungeheuer, "A Chasm of Misery," *Time* (November 6, 1989): 64–66.

26. David M. Stowe, "Process Theology in the United Church of Christ," in *Theology and Identity*, ed. Johnson and Hambrick-Stowe, 103–16.

reflecting current thinking within the United Church of Christ about the meaning and shape of the church speaks of the denomination as having 'polity in
process.' "[27] As this is spelled out, it becomes clear that liberation has a toehold
in process thought because freedom is crucial to all process: "With its major
emphasis on freedom as well as relationships, process thought naturally leads toward a covenantal understanding of this essential community of faith."[28] The
question is now in what sense liberation is seen as rooted in social location.
Broadly put, Stowe clarifies the verification framework: "Because God is so intimately involved with and deeply concerned about each person, those who would
follow Christ must likewise be involved with and concerned about the needs and
potentials of all human beings."[29] It is clear in which direction process thought
points to a relationship with liberation theologies: the needs and potential of all
human beings and all of creation.

It is important that M. Douglas Meeks also stresses the crucial significance
of *Sound Teaching:* "The most important liberation theology statement to come
out of the UCC is 'Toward the Task of Sound Teaching in the United Church
of Christ....' The statement includes a 'Liberation Affirmation' which has the
character of a declaration/confession."[30] Our mandate is to discover whether we
can corporately affirm "polity in process" and the "Liberation Affirmation" within
the framework of Stowe's process approach.

Until now also in the United Church of Christ theological progress has
been understood as theological "Sophists" talking about each other in ever-new
terms. We need to break the mold. We fool ourselves completely if we keep
playing theological ping-pong with each other as individual theologians. There
will be a rude awakening. Recently Susan Brooks Thistlethwaite and Mary Potter Engel have stated the mandate of liberation theology quite bluntly: "Active
commitment to a specific struggle for liberation, far from being a distorting and
unfortunate occurrence, is the first necessary element in this theology. Critical
reflection upon the communal practice that one is engaged in is the second."[31]

The primal challenge we are therefore facing also in the United Church of
Christ as to relationships between liberation theologies and process theologies
is whether we can agree on the active commitment to a specific struggle for
liberation. If we can get our act together here, a great victory for theological
clarity will have been won. What we thus need to answer right now is the prior
question: do we have a prior commitment to a specific struggle for liberation?

---

27. Ibid., 113. For *Sound Teaching,* see n. 2 above.
28. Stowe, "Process Theology," 103–16.
29. Ibid.
30. Meeks, "Liberation Theology and the United Church of Christ," 159. "Liberation Affirmation"
is included in this volume as chapter 26.
31. Susan Brooks Thistlethwaite and Mary Potter Engel, eds., *Lift Every Voice: Constructing
Christian Theologies from the Underside* (San Francisco: Harper and Row, 1990), 8.

FULL COMMUNION TRAINING

Herzog is fully aware that the grassroots base of liberation theology in the United States is less well developed than elsewhere, for instance, in the base communities in Latin America. At the same time, he has been an active participant and leader in some of those communities that do exist. In the context of the United Methodist Church, so-called covenant discipleship groups have been at work for over a decade, modeled after early Methodist paradigms which emphasize mutual accountability. This is the context addressed in the following essay. Teaching at a United Methodist–related school, Herzog has been a major supporter of, and participant in, these groups as places where different modes of spirituality can be brought together, with the intention of ultimately opening the door to black and Hispanic spiritualities as well.

Theology as a whole needs to be reconstructed in relation to such communities which, reshaping Christian faith from the bottom up, amount to nothing less than a head-on challenge of our whole Western tradition and its individualistic tendencies. The new solidarity with the other that is emerging in these groups also turns on its head much of traditional theological education.

The undercurrent of my remarks will be Charles Wesley's well-known dictum, "Let us unite what so long has been divided — knowledge and vital piety." This challenge, I believe, is what our consultation is all about. Some of you present are far ahead in your seminaries in this matter. So I need to be very modest about what I share with you.

I will divide my remarks into three major parts. The first one will deal with the elementary idea framework that lies behind our spirituality struggle today. The second pertains to Christian spirituality — especially as the praxis of small communities (among us) in *renewal* of our *elementary human relationships*, our relationship to God, to others, to ourselves, and to creation as a whole — in corporate expression as *body* of Christ. The third part will be an analysis of the significance of covenant discipleship for theological education.

Here at Duke, Christian formation in covenant discipleship is not an easy road to walk. We still have a long way to go, I believe, especially also in bringing

First published in *Covenant Discipleship Quarterly* 5, no. 5 (May 1990): 9–16.

together black spirituality with the Anglo spirituality so prevalent among us, not to speak of Hispanic spirituality. So I might as well appeal to the words of Robert Frost:

> But I have promises to keep,
> And miles to go before I sleep.

What's Wrong with America?

In Germany in May (it is sometimes good to look at ourselves from the outside) *Der Spiegel* was loudly proclaiming: There's a downfall of the United States today, and people are depressed about it.[1] No longer is it possible to speak of a new morning in the United States, as Reagan had promised only several years ago. It is late afternoon, and darkness is falling.

The fall or downfall of America has arrived. The time of the U.S. Empire is over. The United States is in the process of joining the already destroyed empires — as Professor Paul Kennedy put it in a large volume on the rise and fall of the great powers. Also philosophy is singing the same tune. Allan Bloom's *The Closing of the American Mind*[2] was mentioned by *Der Spiegel* as philosophical proof of the deterioration.

Already a year ago the German *Zeit* launched a major swan song about the United States: "What's wrong with America?"[3] That question was asked in regard to the Bloom book. "What's wrong with America that such a German-high-school-teacher-like diagnosis of its culture (which we no longer thought possible) becomes the major topic of campus and cocktail party conversations?"

One has to have such a question in mind when one ponders the small community/base community syndrome. We are not dealing with the church only as a theological challenge, but with the doldrums of a possibly dying civilization. It is exactly in such times of crisis that small faith communities try to stem the tide of the downturn of intellectual vigor and spiritual power.

I know, there is a lot being said that is negative about the Bloom book. But the fact is that he does not exactly join in a swan song about the destruction of the United States. Bloom's book is first of all, as I read it, a voice announcing the loss of a definite *landmark* of intellectual and spiritual orientation. In nineteenth-century European terms, it is one of the voices that broadcast the death of God.

Bloom is haunted by the almost incredible and certainly almost incomprehensible relativism of values that has gripped the United States. "Values," the word, is a kind of justification label for the search of comfortable survival. The reality of a truly universal *good* is being denied. Instead, all we have are expediency judgments.

---

1. *Der Spiegel*, May 2, 1988.
2. Allan Bloom, *The Closing of the American Mind: How Higher Education Has Failed Democracy and Impoverished the Souls of Today's Students* (New York: Simon and Schuster, 1987).
3. *Die Zeit*, September 27, 1987.

If we want to understand the loudly proclaimed downfall of the United States among Europeans we probably need to turn to Oswald Spengler's *The Decline of the West,* a tremendously influential book in Europe between the two world wars and subliminally still very significant.[4] For many Europeans today North American culture and civilization is as much subject to the iron laws of decline and decay as Europe. Says Spengler in regard to Europe: "We cannot change the fact that we are human beings born at the beginning winter of our civilization and *not* in the *zenith* of a ripe culture at the time of Phidias or Mozart. Everything depends on making this fate clear to ourselves, realizing that we can deceive ourselves about the fact, but we cannot skip over it."

This is a fatalistic interpretation of history that does not do justice to our situation. Too much has been overlooked, as far as the United States is concerned; too much has been left out. Yet it is helpful to see how others co-opt us into that same sinking boat of fatalism. The empty churches of Europe, the decline in religious interest, and the turning away from Christianity has a lot to do with a yielding to the iron laws of history — in a word, to fate.

Church membership decline among us may also have something to do with yielding to the inevitable. But that is not a decisive factor. In the dust of the battle we also rediscover the good in life, not the good life, but God's good in life. Life is not the highest value. But life is anchored in the good that is God. "Why do you call me good? There is only one who is good, God" (Matt. 19:17). Life is offered to us, as God's gift. We dare not gamble it away or destroy it. "Just to be is a blessing. Just to live is holy" (Abraham Heschel). Life is a loan from God, a loan to return.

How can we discover again that human values formed by humans are grounded in God as the Good? The road to the good in North American modernity has been covered up and needs to be uncovered from the debris.

Spirituality as Christian Formation: Formation of Jesus in Us

Before we join Bloom in deploring the downfall of the American spirit at our universities, we ought to remember that at many a university there is also something else to be discovered that is important for the life of our culture as a whole: a renewal movement. Seminaries (outside university settings) tell a similar story.

In Europe a professor told me this summer: "As a theology professor I'm a government employee. The spiritual life of my students is none of my business." So when I interpret Duke's covenant communities or prayer and contemplation communities in Europe it is not an easy task on these premises. The Continental backdrop makes clear by way of contrast what distinguishes us in our outlook, though often we take it too much for granted. We need to make it explicit

---

4. Oswald Spengler, *The Decline of the West* (New York: Knopf, 1962).

to others and ourselves how students among us are struggling for a *great new awakening* in spirituality. I already described the major dimensions of spirituality.

Covenant Communities

Theological education always effects at least some *Christian formation*, that is, Christian character as renewal of elementary relationships. Yet it seldom issues in structured community formation. Especially in concert with our sisters and brothers in Latin America, caught in poverty and distress, we learn that on account of God's own struggle for justice in history we are offered the power to shape history by the good and for the good even today. And thus by God's spirit-power we can have confidence in the future. Is this sinful presumption? I do not believe it is. Rather, it is the insight to be enabled in spite of the self-limitation of humankind to participate in God's work in history for the coming of God's kingdom. "Through the thick darkness thy kingdom is hastening," we sing. It is hastening into history.

In this situation the base communities of Third World countries, especially Latin America, appear to offer an attractive model of renewal. Not all of us have been equally enthusiastic. But most of us have been listening and watching.

There is no reason why we should be idealistic or romantic about them. But we can *learn* from a great historical movement. It is just that we as Protestants have to be very attentive to Catholics at this point. José Míguez Bonino wrote at the beginning of this decade:

> At the present time in Latin America, Christian communities of the common people — or base-level ecclesial communities, as they are wont to be called — are basically a Roman Catholic phenomenon. They are a pastoral experience of the Roman Catholic Church.

I think that this is what we carefully have to remember if we want to make use of the phenomenon in our setting. In some sense Protestantism in the States has already incorporated some of the features of the base communities a while back. Take the early Methodists. They had a kind of base community movement out of which grew the Methodist Church.

It is also the case that Míguez Bonino goes on to say something about Protestantism in Latin America. Obviously every generalization has its loophole, I am very aware of that. He had claimed, as indicated, that the base communities are a pastoral phenomenon of the Catholic Church. And he goes on:

> This does not mean we do not find an analogous experience in Latin American Protestantism. We do, particularly in some Pentecostal communities and in some indigenous communities (on the Bolivian altiplano, for example). But their historical process and their features differ. They are a minority phenomenon, and somewhat marginalized. They arise from a break-away experience, from a conversion that often is dramatic in character. For this reason they often represent a dialectical stance vis-à-vis populist sectors and movements to which the mem-

bers belong in terms of class. In some sense they have broken off their *natural* relationship with such movements, and they must recover it by a conscious option.[5]

Any kind of *general* conclusion from this for us is not helpful. There are many instances where we can learn from our Protestant sisters and brothers also in these special trials. What struck the imagination so widely in U.S. Christianity, however, was the change that had taken place in Roman Catholicism.

Major Aspects of Covenant Communities

The great fact of the Catholic base communities is that suddenly the Catholic Church also in Latin America has become "Protestant." It begins with the great lack of priests in most Latin American countries. In many places there is no one to pastor or celebrate the sacrament regularly. The major aspects of the communities are best summarized in four points:

1. Reading the Bible afresh (from below);

2. Celebrating the Eucharist more frequently;

3. Strong lay leadership; and

4. Social analysis in full awareness of social location.

Let me begin with the last point. 4. We often have heard the term "consciousness-raising." What is happening in Latin America takes place mainly because of the new impact of the Bible. People are waking up to the fact that they are free to live a life with God not bound by the ironclad laws of poverty and riches. Their abysmally dignity-less state is not something ordained by God forever. They do not need to be nonpersons. "For freedom Christ has set us free; stand fast therefore, and do not submit again to the yoke of slavery" (Gal. 5:1). The church has a responsibility to keep the door open all the time for people to break out of the straitjackets of poverty that keep them in bondage. But it is also clear right away that for the base community this is not a matter of privatistic self-correction. It implies rather that the people newly engaged in freedom and consequent dignity experience it only through community, for example, developing programs together in nutrition, health, education, etc., through social analysis.

3. In a sense, lay leadership means that everyone becomes a Christ to the other and forms *the body of Christ anew.* That is the first purpose. In the Apostles' Creed we confess that we believe in the Holy Spirit, the Holy Catholic Church, the Communion of Saints. The *ecclesia* we confess is initially and first of all the institution as a whole. The *koinonia,* the communion of saints, is always the joining together of the small groups of people God calls anew to reshape the institution into the body of Christ. It is just a fact of history that the institution always becomes ossified in its ways, and thus in need of the breath of God's

---

5. José Míguez Bonino, "Fundamental Questions in Ecclesiology," in *The Challenge of Basic Christian Communities,* ed. Sergio Torres and John Eagleson (Maryknoll, N.Y.: Orbis Books, 1982), 145.

spirit in the small community to make the body of Christ come alive again. Here is the contemporary reality of Messiah Jesus who brought God's future into the present and embodied God as the Good. The Christ exists here as community. This immediately implies in Latin American base communities the more frequent celebration of the Eucharist.

2. The point is that this whole "becoming Christ for each other" is a struggle over real-presence. Messiah Jesus is not something that is relegated to a remote past alone, but is the very core dynamics of the historical process as God's personal involvement in it. Messiah Jesus, that is the great name for what we sing: "Through the thick darkness thy kingdom is hastening." It is in the eucharistic meal that we meet this powerful engine of history under bread and wine. "Here would I touch and handle things unseen." Here would I touch and handle the solidarity of God with sinful and unjust men and women and especially with the victims of suffering: God personally involved in a justice struggle to set things right and to make all people acknowledge God's rights on them, so that all people can enjoy true human rights. Without bowing before God's rights (as embodied in the Eucharist) there can be no true humanity, no true personhood, and the nonperson remains. In this understanding the priesthood of all believers, and the layhood of all ministers as well, have their deepest roots in the Eucharist. Here is no king or vassal, no pope or mere "believer," no bossman or lackey.

1. Now the first point: Bible reading. There's always the chorus of objection to the significance of the notion of the nonperson as relevant for middle-class North American Christians and churches. We don't have them among us — these poor people, the saying goes. So we do not need to pay attention to this whole base community syndrome. This is a prideful and dumb denial of our real situation. It is primarily not a question of whether we are rich and others are poor, and that we now should identify with the poor and do good works *for* them. It is an issue of God's very own reality: God in Messiah Jesus becomes the despised and rejected one, a person of sorrows, and a person of grief, and we esteemed him not, as it says in Isaiah 53, and used in the Christian Scriptures to interpret the Messiah Jesus event. It is the case that only through the impact of reading the Bible from below do we arrive at that perspective. The base communities show it once again in the history of the church. But every time the Bible made a new impact throughout the history of the church there was conflict. In any case, it proves impossible to close one's eyes to God's own vulnerability and lowliness in Messiah Jesus in solidarity with the poor.

There is no spirituality in the base communities that has not principally happened time and time again in the history of the church. Guillermo Cook's *Expectation of the Poor: Latin American Basic Ecclesial Communities in Protestant Perspective* is an almost "unending" testimony to this fact, also covering Protestantism.[6]

---

6. Guillermo Cook, *Expectation of the Poor: Latin American Basic Ecclesial Communities in Protestant Perspective* (Maryknoll, N.Y.: Orbis Books, 1985), 173–229.

Covenant Discipleship and Theological Education

What impact will these reflections have on the assigned theme: "Christian Discipleship from a Third World Perspective: Some Questions for North American Theological Education?" We started out with the question: What is wrong with America? In the brief analysis of Bloom's book we did not touch on one crucial point: the elementary orientation point of the twentieth century is war. The First World War, the Second World War, the Korean War, the Vietnam War, the Contra War, an endless list that includes scores of bloody conflicts in addition to the big world conflagrations. Ultimately all our cultural and faith affirmations are tied into the value tentacles that the war economies produce.

We have spoken many words of peace during these decades but produced very little peace. The largest share of the U.S. tax dollar still goes for defense and its military hardware. There cannot be much community building in a military culture on which also the churches are piggybacking in financial and material success, whatever their professed concern for peace. One issue is whether the churches can recapture their essential dynamics in building the body of Christ. The question still is whether the church can be the church: both *ecclesia* and *koinonia*. This leads us to the first question about theological education.

Eucharist of the Poor

Is it at all possible to develop theological education apart from the dynamics between *ecclesia* and *koinonia* centered on the Eucharist of the poor? My answer is no. Theological education always becomes a separate head trip of all sorts of ideologies if it is not grounded in the growth dynamics of the church from *koinonia* to *ecclesia*. There are more times in history than we care to admit when theological students together with their professors had to break out of the sheer institutional shell of the intellectual rite and rote and begin from scratch with their whole Christian formation.

Here is where Charles Wesley's word is immensely to the point: "Let us unite what so long has been divided — knowledge and vital piety." This is not something that occurs perhaps once every five hundred years. It is a challenge for every generation. Søren Kierkegaard said, "Every generation has to be converted all over again to Christ." That has to happen also in the work of the mind, in theological education. There can be no theology for its own end. In fact, there can be no truthful theology as long as theology *is* its own end. Theology is always only a second step that grows out of vital piety. No one can deny that for the Wesley brothers vital piety was not some withdrawn mystical ecstasy in the closet of prayer, but first of all their own walk through the trials of the poor who did not experience the gospel shared. It was their having been claimed by the God of the poor that made the Wesleyan revival possible. And it was the genius of John Wesley that in classes (and bands) he made haste to offer himself to laypeople who for their day were reshaping the *ecclesia* through the *koinonia*, everyone watching over the other in love.

Instruments of God's Spirit. Just how one can introduce these dynamics into theological education is primarily not a "legal" administrative challenge (something done by fiat of the faculty), but the movement of God's spirit. There need to be the instruments of God's spirit present, students as well as faculty who open themselves to the leading of that spirit, blowing where it will. Somehow the insight has to break through that you cannot have theological education apart from the presence of Christ in the body of Christ also in the classroom. Theological education without the *praxis* of the body of Christ is dead. Obviously it takes a lot of doing to get our act together in this regard. We are saying Messiah Jesus is not accessible to theological education unless embodied in the classroom community as the one who stands in solidarity with the poor through the God of the poor. That is the cutting edge of theological education today.

God an American Idol. We have made God much too much an idol, a God who fits American success and pride. We constantly have to separate God and idol. "Religion," someone said not too long ago, and quite seriously reflecting on our cultural identification with God, "that's God and the free enterprise system." And the disentangling of God from our war economy is a perpetual challenge that can happen only if we tie together *didache* (teaching) and *koinonia*. No person can differentiate between God and idol all by herself or himself. It takes what Wesley called "watching over each other in love." But it is costly. It demands paying a price. You need to subject yourself to the community of *koinonia* in the larger *ecclesia* of the theological classroom. So there.

Koinonia *Formation*

Is it at all possible to have Christian character formation apart from the *koinonia?* No. Any theological education apart from character formation is not even half of the story of theological education. In fact, it isn't theological education at all. Character is that divine spirit which is shaped into our souls by God as the mark of our being human, being a person. Society in the West, the First World, realizes that there is no uniform *Weltanschauung* left, and so it doesn't even make the attempt to grasp for at least a *Lebensanschauung,* a lifeview, a vision of reality that is grounded in the source of value, and not just in merely human values. The personhood of human beings is, of course, widely talked about. And many realize that the world's poor do not have their personhood acknowledged and that they exist as nonpersons. But even those who consider themselves persons, in their very neglect of the poor and outcast, show that they too are nonpersons of sorts. The great task is to discover how we become persons again, children of God.

Here the small community is the crucible, related to the Eucharist. But that is not an easy road — because our whole history as Westerners, giants of conquest, comes into conflict at this point. Especially we Christians on these shores will need to remember that our personhood, in its core, our character, has been forged by conquest, Francisco Pizarro, Hernán Cortés, General George Custer, the American frontier. Our character has been shaped by exploitation: the exploitations of Indians and nature. *Divide et impera*, "divide and conquer," is not strange to any one of us in our character. We have to keep in mind the relationship between the image we have of God and our self-image. Widely we have managed to make God over in our image. So we have the idol. And ourselves as idol, too.

Challenge for the First World. There is an absolutely breathtaking challenge involved here for the church in the First World, insofar as the change to God from idol is not merely an American thing. "The problems that America poses were first occasioned by changes that took place in European thought, and must ultimately be faced and solved within the Old World as well as the New."[7] That is the main reason why I swung back so extensively at the beginning to the European continent. We are up against our whole Western conquest tradition in the present base community struggle. All our European roots are at stake at the same time. What we are basically up against is that from Europe we have inherited an image of God and an image of ourselves as humans that is now breaking to pieces under many pressures, the least of which is not Third World critique, of our American way of life. In the discipleship communities we are especially waking up to the fact that we have made God over in our own image, a powerful God of the powerful, and have not respected God's Otherness, God's alterity. We have knocked the real God down and gobbled up the pieces.

As a consequence we have also not respected the integrity of human beings, especially Native Americans. We have made the other human over in our own image. Tzvetan Todorov makes the point unmistakably direct and transparently clear:

> Since the period of the conquest, for almost three hundred and fifty years, Western Europe has tried to assimilate the other, to do away with an exterior alterity, and has in great part succeeded...as Columbus wished, the colonized peoples have adopted our customs and have put on clothes.[8]

It is my hypothesis that, in an elementary way, this is what we are ultimately struggling about in the small covenant communities of the Methodist Church in our seminaries. This is due to the impact of Third World base communities on our small community work. The "solutions" to such vast socioanthropological dilemmas, as John Wesley rightly sensed, can never come in sheer theory, but will come only, if at all, in bands and groups of people who *communally* seek to *embody* a new way of life. Therefore these groups put such hard questions to North American theological education. Now we come to the third and last question:

---

7. Lewis Mumford, *The Human Prospect* (Carbondale: Southern Illinois University Press, 1965), 200.

8. Tsvetan Todorov, *The Conquest of America: The Question of the Other* (New York: Harper and Row, 1984), 247f.

Accountability Factor

Is it possible at all to continue serious theological education in North America without the new accountability factor pressed on us by the communities? No. I am now supposed to move toward the end of my presentation. And we're just getting started. The point is that covenant communities, prayer and contemplation communities, the Order of St. Luke, and other groups have implications also at Duke that are as vast as the whole area of theological education. We can touch only on a few bases. The gist of it all is that in the *ecclesia-ecclesiola, ecclesia-koinonia* dynamics, and the character formation dynamics, we are praying for a new theological accountability. It is a very conflictual spiritual situation we are involved in. There are many voices who tell us that things are fine and we do not have to do more than keep the wheels of the church turning, use more contemporary language, be more relevant in Sunday school, etcetera, etcetera. It is the maintenance view of the church.

What we are calling attention to is that the new *ecclesia-koinonia* dynamics and Christian character formation are all tied into a new centering on the Eucharist as the real presence of the God of the poor (however faintly grasped as yet), who makes us accountable to each other and the world in new ways of vulnerability to the justice struggle. It involves the socioeconomic and sociopolitical structures in which we exist. It draws in ecology, animal rights, and many other new mandates for the church. It says very much the same as an early Christian: "My life and death are with my neighbor," or, as we sing, "Our mutual burdens bear."

Embodiment of the Eucharist. Accountability means that in the embodiment of the Eucharist, the mutual sharing of bread and wine, we give an account of our way of life to our sisters and brothers in Christ and we watch over each other in love. We are not under their thumb. But their conscience reflects for us the justice pressure of God. As it was put in Acts 2:42, only now focused in the *koinonia:* We are together in full communion (*koinonia*) in the Apostles' teaching, the breaking of the bread (the Eucharist), and the prayers. It is no longer possible to teach theology genuinely, seriously, apart from this praxis — what the Wesleys sensed long ago. Therefore, let us unite knowledge with the accountability of the Eucharist (vital piety).

I want to return briefly to the major introductory part. We in the small groups are relating in a new way to Western civilization as a whole. We are talking back, for example, to this European fear of the downfall of the United States: "We do not belong to those who shrink back and are destroyed, but to those who have the faith to make life our own" (Heb. 10:39).

It is clear to me that this kind of witness makes sense only to the extent that it grows out of the actual community experience in which we watch over each other in love. It is subject to the dynamics of accountability.

I have experienced the communities here at Duke for almost a decade as a "hands-on thing." We have, as already indicated, several types of communities, covenant, prayer and contemplation, the Order of St. Luke.

Now *you* are here, a greater multiplicity of approaches yet has become evident. The strength of the movement is that it is happening everywhere, however different the expression. We need only to nurture its spirit. The elementary structures will gradually emerge in greater commonality, just so we continue prayer and strengthen contemplation.

Need for a Network. There are great drawbacks still to cope with and to overcome. I find it extremely debilitating that we have not been able to bridge much of the gap between white and black on this score here at Duke. Traditions seem to be too different here to really mesh. We have always tried to steer away from a move that would make the small communities part of the curricular structure. *We have stressed the spontaneity of the spirit. What we need most right now in my limited view is a critical and self-critical stitching together of the experiences between the various Methodist seminaries, a network that with great intentionally will put itself to the task of uniting knowledge and vital piety in theological education.* We are very much in the beginnings. This is early years, as David Lowes Watson likes to put it. There have been mistakes. There will be more mistakes. I hope they will be the right mistakes: ones we can learn from.

Uniting knowledge and vital piety has been such a long-standing agenda that now it often seems like a cliché. I don't think it is a cliché. It's a very tough order. As I again walk through the small folder which was printed in the *Covenant Discipleship Quarterly*,[9] put together by some of our communities exactly four years ago, I find a few pointers. What you have here are just "buds," no final fruits. There is a long growth period, a maturing time, ahead. Probably some small community will want to do the folder all over again from scratch. But for the time being let me summarize where I think we might be going. There will be three major points already mentioned, each with two subheadings, always directed toward theological education.

The Ecclesia/Koinonia *Dynamics*

Big Church, Small Community History. There is always in theological education the *history* we orient ourselves in. In our Methodist seminaries the Christian tradition is refracted through the Methodist mode. Each time, however, we risk entering the discipleship community we also put history at risk. In taking the step to follow Christ anew, we experience what St. Paul says: "Behold, the old has passed away, the new has come" (2 Cor. 5:17). Our own theological history that we bring to discipleship is put at risk. We may have a liberal framework, an evangelical framework, a liberationist framework, an orthodox framework, whatever: Jesus molds it anew in our walk with him, so that new talk emerges time and again, new categories. That is perhaps the most forceful contribution of the base communities: walking with Jesus is always walking with the Bible in hand, as it were. The Bible time and again overrides our history(ies).

---

9. *Covenant Discipleship Quarterly* 1, no. 3 (April 1986): 5.

Public Dialogue. The divinity school or seminary with its structures cannot be anything but the *ecclesia* for us to begin with. We cannot help bearing public witness also within its walls. We do not throw down the gauntlet. We do not attack. But we try to crack the code. The academy always develops a code which wants to manage Jesus. It can't be helped. It is built into the nature of curricula. But Jesus, through disciples, breaks the code. "You have heard that it was said to the men of old...but I say to you..." (Matt. 5:21–22).

Christian Character Formation

In-Reach. Already in this process of putting our history at risk while walking together with Jesus, a new formation of soul and mind takes place where knowledge and vital piety fuse. It is an "in-reach" God evokes in our celebration of the Eucharist where personal growth is key together with Scripture meditation, relating to society and nature, sharing life experiences, burdens, and joys as opening up to God. And this in a sense turns the usual theological education flow upside down. We begin at the core with *ignorance (ignorantia)*: we see in a mirror dimly (1 Cor. 13:12). Only as character formation takes over does true knowledge build up: faith, hope, love, and the hard work of the intellect that goes along with it. And we learn speaking the truth in love (Eph. 4:15). Here I am already at the next stage.

Outreach. The love of Christ constrains us (2 Cor. 5:14) to become ambassadors in behalf of Christ (2 Cor. 5:20) in the world. What changes the soul reaches the world as goal, first in Durham (charity begins at home), but then also seeks to touch everyone in the global village. The global village is our social location now. Acting globally is thinking locally, and acting locally is thinking globally. God's got the whole wide world in God's hands. We share in that.

Accountability

Covenant Understandings. The small community is not a place of just warm feelings, emotional effusion, syrupy softheadedness. From the beginning in the communities of discipleship there were covenant understandings. "They were together devoting themselves to the Apostles' teaching as *full communion (koinonia)*, in the *Eucharist* and the *prayers*" (Acts 2:42). After the first Apostolic Council in Jerusalem, which decided on the relationship between Jewish and Gentile Christians, we hear: "It seemed good to the Holy Spirit and to us to lay upon you no greater burden than these necessary things: abstain from what has been sacrificed to idols and from blood and from what is strangled and from unchastity. If you keep yourself from these, you will do well" (Acts 15:28–29). We nail each other down on mutual commitments which change from generation to generation in some respects. That makes us accountable to each other in a non-chaotic, non-anarchic character formation. "Every athlete exercises self-control in all things. They do it to receive a perishable wreath, but we are imperishable. Well, I do not run aimlessly, I do not box as one beating the air; but I discipline my body — lest after preaching to others I myself should be disqualified" (1 Cor. 9:25–27).

Accountability Analysis. This ties again into the beginning, *ecclesia-koinonia* dynamics. We cannot begin theological education in this mode with some abstract Platonic truth pattern (a sheer theory); we begin with social analysis and personal analysis in our social location. That usually reverses theological education as a whole (as it has shaped up throughout almost fifteen hundred years of Western metaphysically and philosophically determined theology). In much theology Plato and Aristotle have much more to say than Jesus. That we are not aware of this hidden agenda most of the time makes us all the more culpable. We ought to know better. Knowledge and vital piety united in discipleship community makes for new theological education, a radical turning of tables. It is a tough Jesus we follow: "And he overturned the tables of the money-changers and the seats of those who sold pigeons. He said to them, 'It is written, My house shall be called a house of prayer; but you make it a den of robbers!' " (Matt. 21:12–13).

Solidarity of Suffering

In summary I need to stress that a tremendous solidarity emerges from this new dynamic Jesus brought, not the solidarity of wealth but of suffering and God's victory over suffering. New leadership is part of this solidarity. First of all, the Holy Spirit leads in this new mode of theological education. Which means that there is a tremendous freeing of gifts in all of us. "Each person has [her or his] special gift from God, one of one kind, and one of another" (1 Cor. 7:7). I do not have to remind you of St. Paul's great chapter on our gifts, 1 Corinthians 12. There are great diversities of gifts, but the same spirit (1 Cor. 12:4). All of this is for the upbuilding of the body of Christ, the discipleship community. "When one member suffers, all suffer together" (v. 26).

God calls for a new day in theological education. We will watch over each other in love — so the day might come soon. And God watches over me (Job 29:2). Verily, verily I say unto you: God watches over us — so that we might unite what so long has been divided, knowledge and vital piety. And full communion may result.

Endnote

Obviously in preparation of this piece I did not have before me our September 30–October 2, 1988, dialogue. It would be pound-foolish to try to engage the very fine exchanges in a further exchange on my part here on paper. It would turn into a pure afterthought, stifling the intention of the piece itself.

Yet I wish to call attention to some of the implications of our exchanges. (1) We cannot forget that we engage each other within the limiting walls of one denomination that is especially attuned, in terms of its tradition, to covenant discipleship. Our goal, or our ultimate horizon, cannot be limited to one denomination alone. We are much too much tied into the ecumenical dynamics.

Somehow we need to bring our wrestling to bear on the ATS [Association of Theological Schools] deliberations, to the say the least. But we might also consider tying in to one or two other denominations, as they too are struggling with the same issue in their seminaries. John W. Nevin used to think that our denominationalism was practically the Antichrist. That shows, I believe, especially in regard to Christian formation in this country. (2) This leads to the point of raising the question of how discipleship and witness relate to confession. *Katallagete* (Fall 1987) brought an entire issue on the contemporary relevance of the Barmen Declaration (1934) for North America. I do not see how we can even reflect on discipleship today without feeling the pressure of confession. But this means that besides *denomination* and its limitations the issue of *dogmatics* and its mandates looms on the horizon. (3) The bottom line here is that in my limited view (and I may be very wrong) we cannot deal with Christian formation as though it were a matter of one-issue politics. We are confronted with a "seamless robe." The sooner we understand this the better our grasp of the relationship of Christian formation to theological education.

31

FULL COMMUNION AND THE EUCHARIST: ON THE MEANING OF THE EUCHARISTIC PRAYER

Herzog was one of the architects of a union between the North American United Church of Christ and the German Evangelical Church of the Union. Building bridges between the two continents, he strongly emphasized not only new forms of mutual accountability but also the emerging mission of the church in a society more and more characterized by the phenomenon of globalization, a process driven mainly by economic forces.

In the search for alternative models of global relationships, Herzog develops a strong emphasis on God's counter economy as it grows out of the celebration of the Eucharist. This emphasis on the Eucharist is common in many of Herzog's writings from the mid-eighties on and is most powerfully expressed in his 1988 book God-Walk: Liberation Shaping Dogmatics.

In 1980, the Synod of the Evangelical Church of the Union (EKU) in Germany voted to enter into full communion (*Kirchengemeinschaft*) with the North American United Church of Christ (UCC). I was present. I would like to understand full communion in the first place as a listening to the needs and hopes of another church, but also as a duty to hold each other accountable, in radical identification with one's own situation, concerning a common preaching of the

---

Translation of "Kirchengemeinschaft und Eucharistie," first published in *Berliner Theologische Zeitschrift* 8, no. 1 (1991): 115–18; translated from the German by Mary Deasey Collins.

Professor Christof Gestrich, editor of this issue of the *Berliner Theologische Zeitschrift,* explains that this is the revised portion of a lecture presented on July 19, 1990, in Berlin at the Kirchliche Hochschule on the topic of the Christian understanding of freedom (see Herzog, "Freiheit ist anders," *Evangelische Kommentare* 23, no. 10 [1990]: 586–88). The first part of the lecture, which is not included in this publication, critically discusses an article published in *Newsweek* by the journalist George F. Will, who suggested that the incidents which are occurring in Europe involving freedom or liberation events (e.g., the dismantling of the Berlin Wall) meant a "second reformation." Herzog tried in his discussion also to revitalize the full communion between the Evangelical Church of the Union (in Germany) and the United Church of Christ by considering theologically the changed situation in Germany. He urged resistance to a religious transfiguration of the "victorious" free market economy, not to suppress the shadow side of capitalism and to take new, decisive steps toward the establishment of justice, especially in the North-South relationship.

gospel with its implied responsibility to the world.[1] To be sure, the churches in the United States and in Europe do not fulfill their duty by merely "going for politics." Rather, above all, they should be *prayed* in. Worship and the related celebration of communion present us with an excellent opportunity. Full communion between the EKU and the UCC should especially be practiced in the so-called sacraments. This is what our synods have decided. So far, however, we have recognized reciprocally baptism, Eucharist, and ordination, but we have not in any *binding* way identified with one another *theologically.*

As we cannot tackle everything concerning this desideratum all at once, I would like to begin with the Eucharist[2] as the summary of worship. Within the Eucharist, we start immediately with the heart of the matter, the eucharistic prayer, the prayer of thanksgiving, because this prayer is the engine that drives the whole: as goes the prayer, so goes the sermon, as goes the prayer, so goes the theology, as goes the prayer, so goes the church. It all begins with listening to God, to God serving us.

In this context, it is not possible for us to think from the standpoint of an individualistic anthropology. Our starting point is with the human being in community who is both the basis and the goal of full communion. This community person, this person who is capable of forming a covenant, is at heart an *animal orans,* a praying creature, a created being praying in relation to the creator and in community with other created beings. Two basic aspects are important here.

1. *God acts toward us in the Eucharistic prayer.* We cannot recognize one another reciprocally in sacrament and ministry without having God demonstrate to us through the Eucharist how God acts toward us in history. The whole theology of prayer is embedded in worship of word and sacrament in the history of the towns and countries of a nation.

2. *In the Eucharist, we are reminded of God's liberation history with the people of God.* Our progress in full communion has to happen much more consciously out of the worship experience, especially out of the eucharistic prayer, in which it becomes clear to us that the liberation from our ever new bondage is a part of God's covenant history with us, but in a very concrete way also a part of the history in which we live today.

At this point I would like to present a few more specific reflections on the

---

1. See *Kirchengemeinschaft im Schmelztiegel — Anfang einer neuen Ökumene? Anfragen und Dokumente aus der United Church of Christ (USA)*, ed. Frederick Herzog and Reinhard Groscurth (Neukirchen-Vluyn: Neukirchener Verlag, 1989). (The word *Schmelztiegel* should not be translated back into English as "melting pot." In English we would say "crucible," in order to express the idea of the crucible's refining fire.) It was not possible in this book to work up the rich discussion about full communion, especially concerning Roman Catholicism; see, for example, Heinz Schütte, *Ziel: Kirchengemeinschaft. Zur ökumenischen Orientierung,* 3d ed. (Paderborn: Bonifatius, 1985). Meanwhile has appeared — almost at the same time as our book — Eilert Herms, *Von der Glaubenseinheit zur Kirchengemeinschaft: Plädoyer für eine realistische Ökumene,* Marburger Theologische Studien 27 (Marburg: N. G. Elwert, 1989).

2. I shall use the word "Eucharist" or, as an adjective, "eucharistic," because for many of us in the United States preaching and communion cannot be separated from one another; the Eucharist is made up of both.

eucharistic prayer: it declares to us what all of worship wants to express. It has a trinitarian structure: the *praefatio* is directed to God, the creator, *die anamnesis* to God, the redeemer, and the *epiclesis* to the Spirit, who is the new creator.

God, the creator,[3] this means immediately both liberation and freedom. In the Book of Worship of the EKU, first of all there is the proclamation: "Truly, worthy and just, ... Holy Lord, Father Almighty, Eternal God ... " Next comes a remembrance of the forgiveness of sins and view of eternal salvation. However, in listening and in reciting in worship, I cannot forget a few different eucharistic prayers in the United States which attempt to express more content and which interpret the first article of the Apostles' Creed more correctly. This is how it is expressed in a prayer from the UCC: "We praise you for the beauty and fullness of the earth, where when all share none will be needy." Or, in a prayer from the United Methodist Church we hear: "You have made us in your image ... you have freed us from slavery and made a covenant with us to be our God."

Something important precedes the forgiveness of sins. This liberation through God remains a part of God's *covenant history* with us, which continues even today. In my opinion this should also be expressed in the eucharistic prayer so that it would tell more of salvation history. Indeed, it cannot tell enough of salvation history.

Liberation always precedes freedom. I do not know anymore how often I have heard at a confirmation in Germany the confirmands singing *before* the communion: "We long for freedom to find ourselves, freedom to do something with." Then the next verse says: "Lord, you are the judge! Only you can set us free ... " However, in the "official" eucharistic prayer *afterward*, nothing more of this appears. Why not? Basically we have here a piling up of awesome praises, even though communion is deeply rooted in the Jewish tradition of Passover, of liberation from Egypt. Why don't we hear a word about this in the prayer of the EKU?

There are certain liturgical matters which appear on the periphery of worship, matters which we do not centrally bring before God in prayer. Our liberation by God is among them. We presuppose it as a matter of course — a case of self-deception.

The problem is no longer that we might fall into the temptation to interpret inappropriately a portion of history with the aid of theological concepts in a nationalistic way. The temptation is that before God in worship, particularly in the Eucharist, we conduct ourselves and interpret ourselves completely ahistorically and forget that God still struggles in history in order to guide it toward the kingdom of God. Our own history becomes so uncannily pale that we hardly "exist" anymore. This blandness is a lack of reality. Neither world history nor church history is merely "a mishmash of error and violence" (Johann Wolfgang

---

3. On account of the necessary brevity, I will refer only to the first article of the Apostles' Creed. You can imagine for yourselves what would follow concerning the second and third articles.

von Goethe). We could present to God the truth of this interpretation of history in our current experience through the eucharistic prayer!

Then we would also be able to recognize in this prayer that we do not weave history by ourselves but rather, paraphrasing Martin Luther's words, are always "God-woven" as part of the world process.[4] At the same time also the following would be clear to us: we are so tightly woven into the fabric of the economic global power called "money" that we appear, as Anthony Sampson has pointed out, to be "money-woven" rather than "God-woven."[5] In the West-East dimension, but even more in the North-South dimension in contemporary history, it becomes evident how much we are entangled in "money" as the new world religion and how consequently as the church we must choose between God and idols. The Christian community to which we belong can bring the difficult problems of this situation before God in the eucharistic prayer!

When a few commentators in the United States refer to contemporary political events in Middle and Eastern Europe as evidence of a second reformation, then this is correct in that we recognize the *necessity for a new reformation:* our souls are in need of being freed once more — this time from the power which the new global power called money holds over us.

I look back upon four decades of resistance against anonymous powers in North America. We have experienced freedom within a particular freedom history. With the civil rights struggle of the 1960s, we could learn: we can do without racism, God takes responsibility for us. With the Vietnam War in the 1970s we could declare: we can do without neocolonialism, God takes responsibility for us. With the nuclear freeze of the 1980s we could witness: we can do without nuclear warheads, God takes responsibility for us.

Now in the 1990s we have perhaps the most difficult part before us: we can do without the global power called money. This is the challenge: to disempower the global power called money without giving up our economic resources, which are needed for the welfare of all people. This will not happen without rigorous analysis. However, at the Eucharist we can begin to identify our true situation in the eucharistic prayer and to obtain clarity about the power of the freedom of God's children. With communion we also experience the empowerment to live out our faith that with God all things are possible.[6]

---

4. Pointed out by Christof Gestrich, *Die Wiederkehr des Glanzes in der Welt: Die christliche Lehre von der Sünde und ihrer Vergebung in gegenwärtiger Verantwortung* (Tübingen: J. C. B. Mohr, 1989), 220, English translation: *The Return of Splendor in the World: The Christian Doctrine of Sin and Forgiveness* (Grand Rapids, Mich.: Eerdmans, 1997).

5. See Anthony Sampson, *The Midas Touch: Understanding the Dynamic New Money Societies around Us* (New York: Dutton, 1990).

6. The concluding portion of the lecture was concerned with the question of a "third way" "between capitalism and socialism as they really exist" and with the topic of a "theology of children."

– 32 –

DUAL CITIZENS

Still under the impression of the Persian Gulf War in early 1991, Herzog examines available theological paradigms for the relation of church and state. At a time when God-talk is often used in order to support the powers that be, and when the church has become a function of the state despite the principle of the separation of church and state, we need to rethink our concepts of idolatry as well as the objects of our solidarity. Going beyond the two major Protestant models of the Two-Kingdom Doctrine and the Lordship of Christ, Herzog suggests a new model. Christians as dual citizens need to understand that since God is lord of both realms, both church and state are held responsible by God in their own ways, but neither must put itself in God's place.

While Herzog was not able to develop these reflections further, the basic emphasis is clear: both church and state need to keep each other honest because the church can easily end up turning around itself in vicious circles, and the state is always tempted to overstep its limits and claim religious legitimation, thus becoming idolatrous. If God is indeed lord of both realms, what is their relation to the widows, the orphans, and the dying at the end of the war?

Recently events have transpired that have made deep inroads on the way we think in this country, and they have revealed some of the deepest springs of our action. I am referring to the Gulf War and its aftermath, as well as the parades and celebrations. It again raises the question of who we are as Christians still caught in nation-states as arbiters of human identity.

1

Are the old blueprints of the relationship between church and state still valid? The Gulf War seems like ancient history now as we watch the Soviet Union crumble. But in many tragic ways it is continuing and for some, in a sense, just beginning. One only needs to follow the media carefully to discover how the bad news piles up. Already at the end of May fairly conservative estimates

Unpublished, February 1992.

put the dead of the war at 200,000 with five to six million people displaced. Can we imagine that today there are an estimated eight hundred children dying every day in Iraq because of the poor health conditions caused by the Gulf War? There also have been reports that the Iraqi government will give men who marry widows $950 and lend them $1,250. Tens of thousands of widows are reportedly left from the Iran-Iraq war and the recent Gulf War.

On whose side does the biblical God take a stand? The widows? The orphans? The children in distress? And the dying?

A year ago, in January and February, it was said that the Gulf War had made a significant impact on established religion in the United States. Confronted with uncontrollable events, Americans turned to God. A Gallup poll reported on 44 percent of the adult population attending worship at the end of January — about 110 million people, the highest worship attendance in a quarter century. Fifty-seven percent of the North American public professed to be praying. Before the war the figure is supposed to have been 35 percent. In all this praying, who thought of the Iraqi widows and the dying children soon to come? Were the prayers only for our own people? And to *which* God were they offered?

In the crass drama of what happened so suddenly and in such a brief span of fire dropping from the sky, the Gulf War revealed a "new" framework for interpreting North American Christianity. In *The Restructuring of American Religion* (1988), Robert Wuthnow claims that the period of the Protestant-Catholic framework of American Christianity following the Second World War is over. We are now supposed to have entered the liberal-conservative period. Old rivalries are being laid to rest. New symbolic orders are being drawn. Denominations, while not obsolete, have become less important. To borrow a leaf from Karl Marx — much maligned these days — what if this "new" framework were simply a new ruling idea of the ruling classes in the religious establishment? They do seem to try to hurry us from one new idea to the next to keep us from thinking too much about the people's real plight.

What if the liberal-conservative grid had already been obsolete the minute it was "born"? What dynamics have now really taken over, perhaps ancient in history, and only new in expression? What did the war tell us — as we were helpless in trying to prevent it?

What some lay folk, some pastors and theologians, were ultimately playing out in their God-talk early in 1991 — was it not their Republican or Democratic ideology? Were we still justified by faith? No. We were justified by patriotism. A sign in front of a small North Carolina church during the Gulf War told it all in very plain terms: "Pray for victory, then for peace." It said nothing but: God justifies our war.

The mood expressed outside the churches also showed inside. The first Sunday after the war had begun, a vast congregation thronged a large North Carolina church. A color guard presented the colors. Congregants made the Pledge of Allegiance to the flag and sang "My Country 'Tis of Thee." The minister declared: "I'm so glad that tonight we've got God and that he is the captain of this great, great country. Aren't you?" The congregation responded in one voice: "Amen." The children's choir sang "This Is My Country."

This kind of sanctuary ambience makes it easy to believe that God legitimates our war and to conclude, as one person wrote to the newspaper of that city in a letter to the editor, "These people who oppose the war are anti-Christ and un-American."

In this atmosphere of patriotism prevailing in many churches, it becomes understandable that President George Bush could claim that the war the United States was fighting was a just war and that it had everything to do with what religion embodies, good versus evil, right versus wrong.

Would not Marx have had a heyday with the Bush theology? How could an intelligent man want to bring religion into this war that had been so very early announced as needful to sustain our way of life, that is, our oil supply? On the really important matters that counted we had not done our homework.

1. We had no concept of peace in Iraq. When the Kurds rebelled, they seemed to be following the invitation of President Bush to get rid of Saddam Hussein. When the uprising was in the process of being wiped out by Saddam, the United States had no idea of how to back up the rebels. Haynes Johnson of the *Washington Post* quipped that our leaders knew how to prepare for war but not how to prepare for peace. Obviously, meanwhile some new steps have been taken toward an overall peace process. But will we ever outlive the moral disaster of a war in which we seemed unable to prepare for peace?

2. We have no concept of peace at home. There is an awful sense of moral failure nationally. Neighborhoods are no longer safe. People get knifed, shot, mugged, and raped in the cities. Crimes of violence are rampant in smaller towns as well as in the larger metropolitan areas. In 1990, there were 23,000 homicides in the United States. I have no figures as yet for 1991. The growing complaint is that there is no moral leadership in this country — neither among church leaders nor the politicians.

Wuthnow's most telling comment on the liberal-conservative syndrome is that we are up against *two* civil religions. Two are by no means better than one. Both do not offer us any power of resistance against ourselves as warrior nation and a nation of more and more criminals. Both are as obsolete as war itself. They are co-responsible for the lie that turns God into an idol.

All this is to say that it is "Barmen time" in the United States. Just as in 1934 the Confessing Church in Germany rose against the idolatry of Nazism in the church through the Barmen Declaration, we today in the United States need to resist the present destruction of the rule of God. Here the major focus for understanding ourselves in our religious communities is no longer the liberal-conservative grid, but the idolatry–true worship grid. Idolatry is what St. Paul calls turning the truth into a lie (Rom. 1:25).

We need to apply social analysis to the idolatry. Its peculiarity is that we still use God as cover-up for our economic and political power moves to become reconciled. But because there is such a deep gap between what we will and what we actually do there is no way that we can make headway with just further "Barmen-talk." Today no one takes talk seriously on this score. Once upon a time it was dangerous to talk about God in the Soviet Union. It was also dangerous in Germany during "Barmen" days. No longer so.

There have been several attempts this past decade to nail down the present idolatry dilemma in statement form. I myself have been part of a few. One was published in 1987 by Clergy and Laity Concerned and in 1988 as a tract for the times by the United Church of Christ Wisconsin Synod under the title *Resistance Commitment as Commitment to Justice.* Yet all along I also knew that for our situation today Daniel Berrigan's argument was also right: "The church first undergoes the fires of persecution and disappearance, torment and death. Out of that experience comes a new and vital theology." It's just that as we undergo the "fires" we also have to speak. In a pluralistic society they are not usually persecutions, but it may mean being marginalized and made invisible.

Our situation is convolutedly difficult in its vast camouflage mechanism. Much of the verbal fireworks of Gulf War religion still keep us from the need of the hour: social analysis.

So we have an immense challenge: What is our response to the idolatry of our nation which in numerous instances, as we have seen, makes a forceful inroad into our churches? How do we come to terms with the nature of the church in view of the abomination?

2

One thing stands sure as bedrock: as church, we are no longer aliens in any shape or form. We are citizens, "no longer aliens in a foreign land, but fellow citizens with God's people" (Eph. 2:19). We have a right to walk upright in the common wealth of God, unafraid and of good courage. There is no nook and cranny of our nation where we could feel like foreigners. As full citizens of the household of God we have full responsibility for our country.

The time-honored Two-Kingdom Doctrine will fail us in our effort to understand what is going on, as will the notion of the Lordship of Christ. These doctrines are ideal (almost Platonic) blueprints that cannot guide us in our situation. What actually happens is that we find ourselves caught in a dual citizenship we cannot quite grasp as yet.

So when in a moment of national crisis as January a year ago, the national flag is paraded into church and religion is used to legitimate the secular, we act on the basis of false consciousness, as though the secular were not legitimate in itself and we had to consecrate it by the aura of the sanctuary. That can happen because in those instances the sanctuary seems radically distanced from the world as the real place of the holy. But we might also in our false consciousness do things the other way around: as Christian "aliens" making forays into the realm of the secular and thus the unholy, resisting the same in some overt act while forgetting our own involvement in the secular. In both instances we have been so doped by religion that we cannot discern the claim of the City of God in the midst of Bush City.

Thus we live out a dual citizenship in personal union. Caught in a false consciousness, we constantly try to play off one citizenship against the other, depending on the circumstances. Sometimes we seem more secular, sometimes more churchy, but we usually concentrate on one side and don't do much of anything in forthright Christian witness.

It is only as we throw our lives as fully into the state as into the church that we realize how in reality their basic turf is the same. The history of which the church is a part is the same history of which the state is a part. It is one history "under" two elements. As *our* history it sure is still two histories. But as God's history it is one history. It always has been. It is one realm, though still with dual citizenship in our half-blinded eyes. When, in terms of our continuing false consciousness, the state marches into the church with "the colors," it commits abomination: it claims the church as its own. In our false consciousness it comes to a seeming contradiction: as citizens of the church we had better turn around and throw ourselves into the conflict on state turf at the same time we take our stand on church turf, because in our kind of state the abomination cannot be done away with by concentrating on the one "turf" only. "Crush the abomination" — in both state and church at the same time and realize that both turfs are one in God's eyes.

In an essay titled "Building Communities from Within," the new president of the United Church of Christ, Paul H. Sherry, struggles with some of the implications of the dual citizenship dynamics: "The church is *not necessarily beholden to the empire and not lusting after domestication into the empire.* The claims of empire are enormous, at times overwhelming. The church as an alternative community resists these claims in faithfulness to its Lord and for the sake of empire, so that the empire may be reborn." Initially this seems to the point. Yet there is a catch-22 to it. We have to ask: who are these people who are supposed to build the alternate community? They are those who carry their Bush citizenship into the church. Church and state share in the same history of God. Yet in the church alone the idolatry cannot be smashed. To try to smash the idolatry we have to do it also on state turf. The Gulf War taught us a lesson. Being beholden to empire can happen in tricky ways. We can be out on the streets protesting and yet not be smashing the idolatry at all. We have to move beyond protest and destroy that part of the system itself that yields the power of being idolatrous. We not only have a right to do so, we have an obligation to do so. There is no place where we could be aliens. There is no place where we might hide as aliens, not in God's history.

What we have avoided too long in the United States is the hard-nosed social analysis many of our Latin American sisters and brothers have subjected themselves to for decades. If we church people want to stand by all people, which includes the starving millions on the southern part of the globe, we need to discover how beholden we still are to the overall sociopolitical ideologies that legitimate our church-state interplay: "In order to promote the interests of the poor in such circumstances it is necessary to accept the reality of the existing social ideology. And let us not be naive enough to think that to 'use' the system in this way does anything else except reinforce its strength and credibility" (Alistair Kee).

There are those who have not bowed their knees before Baal. A large number of United Church of Christ ministers, for example, signed a statement against the Gulf War or participated in demonstrations against it. Yet it was inside a United Church of Christ that I was offered the Stars and Stripes to buy — in support of our troops. Where in our churches was the really effective resistance to empire?

3

We cannot just put the church back into the church while the world gets back into the world. We cannot ever hope to build the "alternate" community. Most of the alternate communities I have seen being built these years all collapsed under the tragic weight of their Jim Jones leaders. They were too full of themselves. An alternate community exists only as Christians throw their lives into the conflicts of Bush City in passion for justice-love. The basic criterion is God's salvation relating us to the world's poor. How do we respond to them?

Paul H. Sherry recalls his '60s and '70s experience among the United Farm Workers "as they sought simple justice for migrant workers and their families." He speaks of it as a transforming experience as he watched them "take control of their lives and build community from within." Thus he himself shared in a bonding that was not immediately that of the church sanctuary. Renewal happened in solidarity with the world as a whole, standing by the poor. There is no other way today. Get out of the business of organizing new Jim Jones cadres! Trying to build alternative communities is faking it — opium of the people.

The church cannot be truly built from within. To become a church member is not like joining a holiness club. It is activating both citizenships to the point of giving one's life to both, making sure that the state does not usurp its power and the church deny its power. It is refusing to accept the existing social ideology. It is affirming God's presence among the poor.

In an article that appears in the October 1991 issue of the *Washington Monthly,* James David Barber shows how Bush circumvented Congress in preparing war against Iraq, lied to the American people about his intentions to go to war, and imperially decided the moment when the soldiers would begin fighting. Secretary of Defense Dick Cheney cynically claimed that "if the objectives were achieved at the lowest possible cost and casualty levels, it wouldn't matter what kind of debate or vote there had been in Congress." The president declared that the mission of our troops was wholly defensive and that they would not "initiate hostilities." Also Cheney declared that the troops were not there "in an offensive capacity." Says Barber, "Both men . . . lied." By the time Congress convened, "the president and his advisers had decided on war," so all Congress did was to rubber-stamp the president's imperial decision. And yet the president felt he needed to assure the people that the war represented all the good and right religion stands for.

Which brings us back to the North Carolina minister's statement that God is the captain of this great, great country: the theology of the president proves idolatrous. As citizens of this country, instead of giving religious legitimacy to the president's decision, we need to take away his power to lie and to use religion in idolatrous ways. We need to vote him out of office and curb the office of the presidency against the use of religion for state purposes.

Dual citizenship in the one realm of God cannot mean serving two masters. Being loyal to God, we will strive to make the secular state more honestly secular and the church more justly church. As George Bush shows, we still have lots of work cut out for us. We will not let him get away with murder.

What does all this say about theology? There are fewer and fewer people left in this turmoiled land who will think dialectically. They could, if they would. But they won't. Why not? Are they afraid? But of whom? There is a *coincidentia oppositorum* in regard to church and state that can only be expressed dialectically. Obviously church and state are not one and the same. And yet their history is one in God. They belong together in God's activity. They have to be acted upon together. They have to be thought together. Sounds self-contradictory? There is such a thing as dual citizenship. You need to think and live both at the same time. That's what the future will more and more demand of us theologians. Years ago Martin E. Marty used to quote F. Scott Fitzgerald: "The test of a first-rate intelligence is the ability to keep two things in mind at the same time, and still retain the ability to function."

HUMANKIND WITH A HUMAN FACE

In this paper, initially presented to the Council for Health and Human Services Ministries of the United Church of Christ, Herzog identifies another major part of the struggle for liberation, prefigured already in other contexts. European leaders like Jean-Frédéric Oberlin and their ways of connecting piety and the Christian faith with practical acts of transformation have provided some of the models on which Herzog built early on.[1]

In a world where thousands of children are dying every day of starvation or preventable diseases, the church, together with other communities of faith, needs to rethink its role in light of God's promise of healing. Nothing less than a new "world revolution" is at stake. This is diakonia *at the beginning of the twenty-first century.*

Recently there were reports in the newspapers about a Peruvian boy with virtually no face that a craniofacial surgeon from Scotland rebuilt over a period of several years. (Meanwhile there has also been a CBS *60 Minutes* report dedicated to it.) With this remarkable story in mind I wish to say a few words about giving *humankind a human face.*

Remembering this almost faceless two-year-old Peruvian boy, we might as well say that much of humankind today is without a human face.

When the Cold War was at its height and Alexander Dubček in the spring of 1968 took over the reins in Czechoslovakia, we heard about *communism* with a human face. Now the Cold War is a thing of the past. But there are still Somalia, the Sudan, Armenia, Bosnia, South Africa, Mozambique, Peru, and other places of "low-intensity" warfare — low intensity, however, only for those who do not live through it. There are also hunger, cold, and death. We sense that although the Cold War is over, the world has become a much more dangerous place in which to live. Now it is humankind as a whole, not just the communist bloc, that is without a human face. We recall from Los Angeles, this spring just a year ago, we too can be without a human face in our own country — very fast, overnight.

Unpublished, 1993.

1. See "Diakonia in Modern Times: Eighteenth-Twentieth Centuries," included as chapter 4 in this volume.

I do not have the time here to retell the story about the Peruvian boy David. My point is that, as in this doctor's rebuilding of this two-year-old's face, we are part of *God's rebuilding of the face of humankind*. That is your major assignment in the health services. I salute you for the work you have done. Part of the biblical and theological basis of this work is the need to broaden it more and more until it includes all of humankind.

1. The first biblico-theological point: The *human* face of humankind in the Bible is linked to the face of Jesus. "For it is the God who said, 'Let light shine out of darkness,' who has shone in our hearts to give the light of the knowledge of the glory of God in the *face* of Christ Jesus" (2 Cor. 4:6). That is the basic biblical foundation. Because this face has appeared on the human scene, not marred by sin, not defaced by self-distortion or self-disfiguration, the *human condition* has changed in principle. This is expressed in the gospel story when it reports that this person Jesus healed every disease and infirmity among the people, demoniacs, epileptics, and paralytics (Matt. 4:23). The disfigured face of humankind here and now is changed. For Christian faith, there is from the beginning this vast act of God to wipe the disfiguration of the human face off the face of the earth.

A church historian, Adolf von Harnack, said of Jesus of Nazareth: "The great English philosopher, John Stuart Mill, has somewhere observed that humankind cannot too often be reminded that there was once a man named Socrates. That is true; but still more important it is to remind humankind again and again that a person by the name of Jesus Christ stood in its midst." Why? Because humanity here has a new face, not a movie-star face, but a face of one with the *power of healing* that did not exist before in this magnitude among humankind.

2. The second biblico-theological point: The power of healing focuses first of all on *God's option for the poor*. "God chose what is lowly and despised in the world, God chose what is weak in the world to shame the strong" (1 Cor. 1:27). The option for the poor today frequently ends up a merely human option. But that is not the point of the Jesus story. Its point is that the *power of healing* is God's power. It is God who wants to heal the human face, beginning with the most threatened and the most lost. Jesus was sent to the lost sheep of the house of Israel (according to Matt. 10:6). In terms of biblical thought it is a basic faith reality that God is a tower of strength for the oppressed, that God has not forgotten the cry of the poor (Ps. 9:9, 12), that God is the Savior of the poor from those too strong for them (Ps. 35:10), and that God brings justice to the orphan and downtrodden (Ps. 10:18). The Christian healing ministries all have their fountainhead in this history of God struggling with threatened human life. There is a special *protection privilege* of the poor, as the Bible sees it. This whole debate about the *protection privilege* of the poor has become rather woolly lately on account of some misunderstood liberation theology claims about the poor. The next thing we hear is that the poor are supposed to know better than others what is right and wrong in the world and the church.

Yet some folks had better listen more carefully to what the real craftsmen and craftswomen of this theology are saying. I believe Gustavo Gutiérrez has always made the point very clearly: God is not on the side of the poor because they are good, but because God is good. We would be much further along in biblical and theological foundations of our work in the healing ministries if this observation were kept in mind. Which leads to the next point.

3. *Ultimately God is the doctor, the physician.* There is a passage in Exodus 15:26 which makes that point strongly. In the midst of the people of Israel gathering their wits, after having been able to walk on dry ground through the Red Sea, God tells them, "I am the Lord, your physician" or "I am the Lord, your healer." As we go back to the beginnings of the deaconess movement in the modern Protestant church, we always meet this strange power point of God's activity being appealed to as the effective agent of healing.

We do not have much time for remembering historical detail, but I need to mention Jean-Frédéric Oberlin (1740–1826). After graduating from the University of Strasbourg, in what is now Alsace-Lorraine, he took over what was something like a five-point charge in Waldersbach high in the Vosges Mountains, a backward collection of hamlets in stony and barren territory The backwoods farmers, uneducated, illiterate, speaking a patois, neither French nor German, said to Oberlin: things can't be changed. "Yes, they can," replied Oberlin, and started a new type of tree culture and agriculture and many other things too numerous to mention — above all the deaconess movement, with Luise Schepler as head deaconess. If you want to know where the kindergarten began, you have to go to Waldersbach in the Vosges Mountains. With the development of the kindergarten the deaconess movement started. From there it took off as a broader vision of women's special service in the church. This "can-do" notion of Oberlin's gave his followers strong confidence: "It is no secret what God can do."

By the time the movement arrived in Germany, it primarily concerned the sick, especially the poor sick, the handicapped, especially the poor handicapped, and the mentally retarded. You have to remember that much of Protestantism in Germany had been completely stripped of the Roman Catholic type of caring for the sick as practiced by Catholic orders. And as far as Protestant territories were concerned, especially big Protestant cities, there was no caring for the sick to speak of outside families, except poorhouses, where prostitutes occasionally were the only nurses available.

If the poorhouses got crowded, and they often did, two sick people would have to sleep in one bed. There are reports that in those days when sick people died during the night, there often was no one to carry the deceased out. So the other sick person would have to continue lying next to the dead body all night long until morning when some nurse reappeared.

It was in this situation that the deaconess movement heard the mandate: "I am the Lord, thy physician." "Ich bin der Herr, dein Arzt," as Luther translated it. Gradually Protestant hospitals were built, and there were institutions, and much of this was later translated to this country — you know the continuation of the story in the United States. Except for this tradition, we would not be assembling here this morning!

We need to add also that the deaconess movement by now almost has had its day in Germany, certainly also in the United States in most respects. Almost everything in the care of the sick and the old is being "professionalized." That may not be altogether such a bad thing, theologically speaking. It shows that secular society took note, copied what was good, and took over the major burdens. We need to live with this fact. It cannot be avoided. Where I wish to see our reflection turn for the moment is in the direction of another fact: the rejection of the church by many people today. They say: Look, the church is really not relevant. It has nothing to contribute anymore. So many bow out and leave the church altogether. To them I would like to say: the church has been a tremendous educator of Western civilization. And we had better work hard *that it becomes this educator once again, one more time.*

Some will tell me that part of the medical task we can leave up to Hillary Clinton: She's going to straighten the mess out. I myself doubt that our society in the future will be able to straighten itself out without the church. It will take a lot of liberation in the churches to live up to the great task. But that is where the action of the future will be. For that moment, your movement, the Christian health and human services, I believe, can make immensely important moves. Along which lines? Well, based on the theological point: God is the doctor. We need more humanly viable systems of health care, as God would have us promote them, not just in our country but the world over. For that task, we had better remember that the deaconess movement, while it did not change the *face* of the earth, gave part of humankind a much more human face. A great historic example.

4. Point four is a question: *Are we now almost exclusively rebuilding our own Western faces, but not the face of humankind as a whole?*

There are new "simple" cosmetic operation techniques for turning thin lips into pouting or sexy-looking lips. Surgeons can correct noses in numerous ways and smooth out wrinkles. But in countries of misery like Peru, beautiful women and men cannot afford to have even a substitute tooth if they lose one. I remember a young woman with a completely crooked head who probably was born with a closed suture in her skull and could not be operated on because there was no money and therefore no surgeon to do it.

God, the physician, is the God of all peoples, whether Christian or not. When I read your philosophy of human service organizations, I wondered, Is the "mission" there ultimately to the United States only? I quote from "We believe": "That the values of the Christian faith motivate our ministries of human service and must be central values of organizational life and mission. Through our participation in the church these values are interpreted and enriched." You hope "to devise programs which develop organizational leadership with an understanding of and a commitment to Christian service and the mission of the United Church of Christ." What is this mission? If you annually pour out 1.6 billion dollars for the actual work, and you maintain property valued in excess of 2.2 billion dollars — what if anything do we contribute to world health care? Ultimately, what does the United Church of Christ contribute to world health? I do not see our Protestant churches much involved in the health of the people of the world as a whole. The religious institutions are largely involved in trying to save their own skin as religious institutions. So the story of the Peruvian boy with virtually no face became important for me in two ways:

a. Would we have supported or tried to find ways of support, had we been approached to save the Peruvian child's *face*? What resources do we have for this sort of thing?

b. How do we see the task of world mission in health services to all the children of humankind? What will we do to galvanize our churches to that goal? Every day 40,000 children die of starvation or preventable diseases. That means 280,000 every week, 1,120,000 every month, over 13 million a year. The intriguing part of the Peruvian boy's story is that here was a doctor who did not give up.

It takes a *healing will* to carry through that type of work. And the question that faces us is whether we have the will — like Ian Jackson, the surgeon from Scotland — to go through with eighty operations of whatever kind to rebuild the face of humankind as a whole. That pertains to the Sudan as well as to Somalia, to Los Angeles as well as to Peru. One people, so to speak, does not have a nose; another people does not have a palate. My notion is that there are many people waiting for us healthy people to share our health on a much wider scale than imagined thus far. We need to think the unthinkable and to dream the impossible dream.

We as the UCC were the civil rights church of the '60s. What church are we today? We were the anti–Vietnam War church of the '70s. What church are we today? We were the just peace church of the '80s. What church are we today? The wall came down at the end of the '80s. What church are we today? What kind of church will we be for the '90s? The Council for Health and Human Services Ministries can become the headlight of our church in this decade and into the twenty-first century. It can give us all a new theme.

5. A last question: *And if we are almost exclusively rebuilding our Western faces, are we not often first of all rebuilding our white faces?* U.S. child poverty statistics for 1989 indicate that in North Carolina child poverty lies between 15 percent and 19 percent; in Mississippi it is 33.5 percent. The faces of the children caught in poverty are predominantly black faces. Black children are the most likely to live in poverty, with a 38.9 percent chance, almost two children out of five.

No one knows more than I the difficulties of changing these statistics. But what did Christ die for? And what did he live for?

The point I wish to make is that the situation in our country and throughout most parts of the world is such that only a gigantic new effort of the church and the other world religious communities can turn things around. We have no business continuing to live in our separate ways as Christians.

We are called upon to put our shoulders to the wheel of this new gigantic task, ecumenically. This is one of the reasons why we have full communion between the Evangelical Church of the Union in Germany and the United Church of Christ in the United States. We corporately can no longer disregard the 40,000 children dying every day. My theology becomes obscene if I do not begin my work with this basic fact of Christianity: "the children's crying" again like in Oberlin's day and "the children's dying" in our time. The task is too big for one denomination alone to tackle. Therefore I am glad that we are doing things together here ecumenically with the Reverend A. C. Oomen of Valore Medical College of India and Paul Gerhard Voget of the Neukirchener Erziehungsverein. We can think the unthinkable together. We can dream the impossible dream together.

This is Black History month. We were reminded that Martin Luther King, Jr., still had to say, "*I* have a dream." Well, today we can say, "*We* have a dream, *we* are not afraid, *we* will 'God-walk' hand in hand, black and white together. But *God* shall overcome, God the doctor, God the healer." This is the new thing after the Berlin Wall has come down. The man who, as it were, had to stay for a long forty years in Wittenberg behind this Wall isolated — the first Martin Luther — sang, "If we in our own strength confide, our striving would be losing...." And we have sung it hundreds of times. Therefore, finally: God shall overcome.

I am tempted to stop here and to say: "I have yet more things to tell you, but you cannot bear them now." Yet one thing still needs saying: I have been speaking all along, yes, of the old diakonia, but also of the new diakonia, of a political diakonia. I have been speaking of organizing a new world revolution.

Now, you'll say, he'll let the cat out of the bag and here comes Karl Marx with the *punch line*.

Before Karl Marx, and before G. W. F. Hegel, stands a giant of philosophy by the name of Immanuel Kant from the city of Königsberg, and both man and city were very much part of what is now the Evangelical Church of the Union. Modern Western philosophy still stands very much on Kant's shoulders. He was not only a giant metaphysician, or anti-metaphysician, but also a great lover of world community. One day, commenting on the things I have been stressing, he was saying that "the carrying out of these intentions is made difficult by the fact that the achievement of these purposes does not depend on the agreement of individuals, but on the progressive organization of world citizens into a system of cosmopolitan shape." That progressive organization today is the ecumenical movement. The Council for Health and Human Services Ministries can become its engine into the twenty-first century. It does not have to be its caboose. When God is the doctor, what kind of a face will the church give the human enterprise? "It is no secret what God can do."

– 34 –

LAS CASAS: CONSCIENCE OF THE POSTMODERN WORLD

Together with Rosemary Radford Ruether, Herzog organized a panel on Gustavo Gutiérrez's book Las Casas: In Search of the Poor of Jesus Christ *(Maryknoll, N.Y.: Orbis Books, 1993) at the annual meeting of the American Academy of Religion in 1994. Other presenters included Gutiérrez himself, Ada María Isasi-Díaz from a Hispanic mujerista perspective, George E. Tinker from a Native American perspective, and Kortright Davis from a Caribbean perspective.*

Herzog's presentation deals with the postmodern situation in the North American context. At a time when earlier histories of conquest and oppression are being dissolved into pluralistic indifference, what keeps North and South together? That millions of Native Americans on both continents were killed remains a fact that, shaping Christian identity consciously or unconsciously, still needs to be accounted for by theology. While North American theology never had a Las Casas who would have urged us to think through our theological commitments from the perspective of the Native American, we now have the chance to reshape history.

How to read Las Casas through the eyes of Gutiérrez in North America? I submit two angles. (1) North America is part of the North Atlantic community and we need to discern how Las Casas can function within its postmodern mentality. (2) The recent early November elections in the United States have shown that many people in this country are in a state of economic and political disillusionment, pointing to a search for a cultural alternative which would demand a new examination of colonial history.

In terms of the two angles I have two points:

1. Postmodernity notwithstanding, the geographic context of the Americas in their settlement by Europeans in the sixteenth century offers another foil for an understanding of how God relates in Jesus to all persons we have neglected.

2. We find ourselves compelled to reshape the money culture that we inherited as we listen to Las Casas as conscience of the West.

Unpublished presentation delivered at the annual meeting of the American Academy of Religion, 1994.

Understanding Jesus and Ourselves in New Ways

Gutiérrez makes the life of Bartolomé de Las Casas (1474–1566) a prism through which we can view the conquest of the two Americas. The evolution of Las Casas's thought intertwines here with the early history on these shores. Arriving as a twenty-eight-year-old in 1502 in the Indies, he is initially completely part of the *conquista*. Step by step he is forced to disengage himself from the prevalent outlook of his society. As a wide-awake person, from the beginning he lets his faith shed light on his life, and life on his faith. For a brief time he participates in the system that inflicted untimely and unjust death to the native populace of the Indies. The efforts of the first Dominican missionaries and his reading of the Scriptures bring about a change of life that abandons the initial *conquista* mentality.

Las Casas tried to view things in the New World from the natives' point of view. What is more, he is convinced that God wants their life to continue and does not will their death. So he tries to persuade people back home and the invaders themselves that there is a different perspective. His work turns around a very simple hinge of thought: "The grand theme of his life was the God of Jesus Christ, the God who dwells in history."[1]

The so-called evangelization of the Indies came at a gigantic expense of human life. Countless Indians were "stripped of their lives before their time" and had no chance for conversion.[2] That situation has not changed very much: "The same must be said of the poor today in Latin America, who continue to suffer a premature, unjust death."[3] What Gutiérrez finds he must do, therefore, is to show how the quest for liberation has to take into account "the complexity of the human person"[4] then and now. The historicity of human existence allows many influences to shape a human life. The vast apparatus of retelling the sordid story in great detail, the debates, the journeys to Spain in behalf of the Indians, his persistence to get a hearing in the courts of justice and to speak with the king himself: all this serves to prove Las Casas's view that there is no salvation without justice. And when for us at times the reading seems tedious and worrisome, each page of the book is a challenge to identify with the struggle of at least one person killed at the hands of murderers. We have a vague abstract notion of what happened. But we do not take the time to put ourselves into the shoes of those people who often died a slow and tortured death.

We live in an age when the appeal to the God of Jesus Christ, the God who dwells in history, seems somewhat naive and antiquated in the North American community. The basic questioning in this regard comes from postmodern thought — which is not just a North American phenomenon. Much of what ap-

---

1. Gustavo Gutiérrez, *Las Casas: In Search of the Poor of Jesus Christ* (Maryknoll, N.Y.: Orbis Books, 1993), 15.
2. Ibid., 4.
3. Ibid.
4. Ibid.

pears as postmodern in the United States comes from Europe. Michael Welker, a Heidelberg theologian, has just recently published in this country *God the Spirit* (1994). It is a theology of the Holy Spirit that takes into account liberation theologies while at the same time making sure that the postmodern situation in which these theologies are debated is understood. It is a brilliant book, but also an example of what I find lacking in many of the recent theologies within the North Atlantic community: the postmodern orientation does not worry about the history of the conquest.

What the new intellectual outlook is concerned with, for example, is the great impact of technology that has differentiated societies. Now there is "functional differentiation" of various dimensions. Economy, law, religion, education, and family "seek to become increasingly independent in relation to other subsystems."[5] In terms of their best intentions, they would all want to benefit the whole of society. But how? Society itself no longer has a center.

Society is now being "organized and perceived poly-centrically,"[6] says Welker. No central task can be discerned. Each subsystem faces challenges and develops problems of its own sufficient to keep its participants busy without them having to revert to other subsystems. So creating links between the various challenges and problems becomes "too abstract and too complex to continue to be institutionalized in the form of a common consciousness that knows itself as common."[7]

Although mass media communication is being used to counteract this diffusiveness, it turns out to be no more than a fiction. If we want a common consciousness that knows itself as common, we need to look for it somewhere else. Somehow the media keep up the fiction that there is a public sphere with some unity. But the way the postmodern pressures work, the mass media "cannot stop common sense and public moralities from becoming more and more powerless."[8] So Welker speaks of a systematically generated and intensified helplessness. There are just certain things that occur in natural and cultural destruction in modern society that we do not get a grip on.

Within the framework of helplessness the postmodern sensibility flourishes. This has been described in infinitely varied ways. Usually the mind here is trying to grasp all the countervailing forces which, while working in part against each other, at times also support each other. The result is the abandonment of the paradigm of modernity that is always looking for universally acknowledged "solutions." So the postmodern view rejects the assumption of "the unity of reality" or "a unity of experience." Reality is now "realities" that at times seem to connect and at other times not, "partially compatible and partially incompatible."[9]

---

5. Michael Welker, *God the Spirit* (Minneapolis: Fortress Press, 1994), 29.
6. Ibid., 30.
7. Ibid.
8. Ibid., 31.
9. Ibid., 38.

Postmodernity becomes difficult when directly imposed on the Christian walk, on what was initially called "the Way" (Acts 9:2). Apply the postmodern paradigm to the churches, especially the Protestant churches and their divinity schools and seminaries, and the result will usually be a trade-off game on the market of ideas. Our denominations have existed for a long time for the purpose of serving the whims of the religious "shoppers" walking toward churches as though they were shopping malls, looking for the more cultic, or the more free, or the locally autonomous, or the more emotional, more rationalist, more catholic — in any case, the more congenial.

It is quite clear that everyone sees reality from his or her own perspective. *That does not prevent us from having to own up to the context the churches are part of.* The dimension most radically shaping our churches in terms of context is that on these shores they are churches of the "new world." There is nothing more fundamental for them than this context. At least this is what the Gutiérrez book on Las Casas involves. It could only have been written in this ever-present context.

The methodological acknowledgment of this context is now what we need as basic presupposition of our theological work. I cannot speak for more than my own Protestant denominations. I hope that Roman Catholics can see it the same way. Other faiths have other terms in principle. I would hope that they could see a *kairos* here also.

It is important that Gutiérrez at the outset of the book underscores that facing the truth of our common heritage is inescapable now. The quincentennial, if nothing else, has brought it very much out into the open. Most of the leading countries of Europe that began the Protestant venture on these shores had some part in the conquest. None thus far has liked to be reminded of this history. But, as we know, those who do not understand their history are bound to repeat it.

We have a common responsibility here. We are compelled *to form a common consciousness that knows itself as common* (to hark back to the Welker argument). In a sense, we do not have to form it. It's there already, but we have been denying it. It stares us in the face in the Indian mounds and the ruins of the Indian cities and temples. There has been a tendency among us to regard these mounds as just so many historical dumping grounds or historical trash heaps. Although the denial of this history still happens, it is fast catching up with us, as in the legal battle of Native Americans to recover their burying grounds or their ritual objects which we turned into museum pieces.

They were Christians who invaded and settled these shores. All of it happened within a century, from South to North. Reality was envisioned on completely new premises the Indians never had heard of. For the Christians, contact with the New World "created a different, unprecedented situation."[10]

The unprecedented situation for Las Casas called for unprecedented thought. Before he began his work, church theology still claimed that apart from the

---

10. Gutiérrez, *Las Casas*, 243.

Christian faith there is no salvation. Yet the lot of the Indians was considered less ominous than that of Jews or Muslims who refused the Christian faith altogether.

Here Las Casas takes a bold step. Christ is head not only of those who believe in him but also of the unbelieving Indians.[11] God stands more believably on the side of those who suffer from the invaders than on the side of the invaders who deny their Christian faith by their walk.

All who come from outside these shores as Christians and now claim them as their possession are invited to view Christ in a new way and in the light thereof to relate to the Indian in a new way (as well as to history as a whole). Yet even in our day the churches are not struggling over a new understanding of Christology in terms of Matthew 25:31–46. There is a remnant thought of double predestination among the Presbyterians, and some notion of justification by faith among the Lutherans, and so on. Ecumenically we allow each other, with much humor, our little private faith turfs. We have little trade-offs in joking about each other's foibles or faith badges. Little do we understand that the power brokers of politics and economics are only too happy to let the whole show run in terms of "divide and conquer." No wonder Christianity comes across in culture in terms of impotence and mediocrity. The result is the widening credibility gap.

The weakness of the denominations is that they do not have a common Christology praxis in terms of Matthew 25:31–46, commensurate with their common context on these shores. It seems not to bother them at all that they have a common fate of theologically ignoring Jesus' presence in the hungry, the thirsty, the naked, and those in prison.[12]

The important point to realize here is that without a basic rethinking of what happened with the native population on both continents of the New World, nothing new in relating to other people today will be forthcoming in the Americas. It is part of our common history between North and South that the native populations were severely decimated in the Americas. That understanding needs to become part of the premises of our theologies whether they are postmodern, process, evangelical, or whatever.

What we need to learn ever anew is the vast destruction that was effected. On that background we then see how evangelization brought a gospel compared with which the actual life of the Christian community stood in flagrant contradiction. The population and genocide figures vary greatly among the various scholars. In 1939, the anthropologist Alfred L. Kroeber put the 1492 population figure at 8,400,000 for both continents, North America contributing not quite 1,000,000 of the total. Some twenty years after Kroeber's study the total figure according to research by Henry F. Dobyns was as high as 112,000,000 people before the arrival of Columbus. Others have by now gone even as far as suggesting that the total population was about 145,000,000, with 18,000,000 living in what are now the United States and Canada.

---

11. Ibid., 256.
12. Ibid., 255.

However one tallies these figures, it is the case that an immense genocide took place within the first hundred years, brought about by war and disease. The likelihood is that often up to 95 percent population loss was not unusual in most parts of the New World. Take Peru, where in 1492 most likely 9,000,000 Indians lived, perhaps even as many as 14,000,000. Before the close of the sixteenth century, barely 1,000,000 were still around. A few years later that was down to about 500,000. "At least 94 percent of the population was gone — somewhere between 8,500,000 and 13,500,000 people had been destroyed."[13]

If we turn to North America, the story in California, for example, is much the same. Between 1852 and 1860, the Indian population dropped from 85,000 to 35,000, which was a 60 percent drop in eight years. By 1890, there was a loss of 80 percent of the natives who had been alive when California became a state, with the number continuing to decrease. There had been gubernatorial demands to eliminate the California Indians, described as "ugly, filthy, and 'inhuman beasts,' 'swine,' 'dogs,' 'wolves,' 'snakes,' 'pigs,' 'baboons,' 'gorillas,' and 'orangutans.'" In summary, this "war of extermination against the aborigines, commenced in effect at the landing of Columbus," is "gradually and surely tending to the final and utter extinction of the race," as one Californian observer noted around 1850.[14]

This story needs to get a hearing in theological method, in the prolegomena of dogmatics co-determining the identity of the Christian and the Christian theologians. We need to own up to our responsibility for our history at this point. Only if we see that our history went wrong in completely neglecting the humanity of the "other," only if we see the shadow of our miscued anthropology (beasts, swine, dogs, wolves), will we have the grace to work on a new Christology. The wrenching aspect of this whole issue is that it will call for *shaping a common consciousness among churches which know what having in common means*. We cannot escape to some private methodological fancy about Native American esoteric idiosyncrasies. The mandate is whether the churches will want to break through to a new Christology or not.

Conscience of the West

In the present state of things a new Christology is hardly possible as yet. There is a search for an alternate society and an alternate human being. But the goal is

---

13. David S. Stannard, *American Holocaust: The Conquest of the New World* (New York: Oxford University Press, 1992), 87.

14. Ibid., 145. I need to call special attention to the great significance of this book in the context of reading Gutiérrez's *Las Casas* volume. We have here a vast array of data that link North America to the Spanish *conquista*, with clear stress on the lack of any debate about the morality of the New England conquest: "no such disputation took place among the Anglo-American colonists or ministers, however, because they had little doubt as to why God was killing off the Indians or to whom the land rightfully belonged. It is, in short, no accident that the British did not produce their own Las Casas" (237).

difficult to reach. Society seems more and more out of control. The recent election makes the difficulty manifest. A local newspaper quoted a young woman: "The country is so big and there are so many issues and everyone has a different point of view. It's hard to have a safe neighborhood any more."[15] Apparently people identify diversity of views with insecurity.

The one thing no one has a different point of view on is money. We have a money culture. We are moneyed beings. The genocide was all about money. Part V of the *Las Casas* book is titled by Gutiérrez "God or Gold?" Las Casas made quite clear that money was at the core of the human beings called *conquistadores:* "Gold is the real god of those who abuse the Indians."[16] Without the gold mines, "the gospel would not survive in the Indies."[17] "God is present because there is a king, and the king is here because there are mines. The strongest link in the chain is gold...incidentally triggering an evangelization."[18] "Were there no gold, no one would come to the Indies."[19]

This ultimately says a lot about the core of the human beings involved — what gold does to the fabric of their identities. "In view of all this, Las Casas's witness is particularly important for the self-discovery that the peoples of Latin America must make today. The sixteenth century was decisive in our history. Things happened and options were made then that marked the centuries to come."[20] Spaniards used the Indians as tools to acquire gold and wealth. "By contrast, Scripture makes us see persons as the end or purpose of life, and not mere tools for the acquisition of riches and power."[21] There is an inversion of values in the *conquista* outlook. Those who worship money are idolaters because they place themselves at the service of the product their own hands have made.[22]

The Las Casas witness is also important for the self-discovery the North American people will want to make. The gold obsession is no less a temptation today in any North American city, town, or farm than it was in 1492. What we now widely have as our North American self-image is Columbus. Said a high school senior in our local paper recently: "Money is everything to me. I want to be amazingly wealthy and have a job where I can step all over people for money."[23] That's who we are as "Americans." And the churches are legitimating (as they have most of the time) the money system we are part of. "Religion played an important role in legitimating this system of power. By defining the Spanish monarchs as 'defenders of the faith,' the church legitimated the military

---

15. *Durham Herald-Sun* (November 3, 1994): 1.
16. Gutiérrez, *Las Casas,* 439.
17. Ibid., 431.
18. Ibid., 432.
19. Ibid., 436.
20. Ibid., 456.
21. Ibid., 442.
22. Ibid., 442–43.
23. Frederick Herzog, "Athens, Berlin, and Lima" *Theology Today* 1, no. 2 (July 1994): 274.

and economic activities of the monarchs. Views of wealth and poverty are still connected with religious teachings."[24]

How do we break out of the iron grip that the legitimating dynamics of power have on us? Every day, 40,000 children die from hunger, disease, and other untoward events of Third World poverty. That is 280,000 a week, and over one million a month. During a year, that comes to almost 13,500,000. The German novelist Reinhold Schneider in 1938 wrote a book titled *Las Casas before Charles V*. Schneider used the Las Casas material to claim a measure of interference in behalf of the persecuted Jews in Hitler's Third Reich. Today we need to relate to the genocides of our time. The Holocaust figure of World War II has always been 6,000,000 persons. If Reinhold Schneider thought he could claim Las Casas for protesting the destruction of the Jews in Nazi Germany, and Edwin Maria Landau in the postscript to the 1990 edition of Schneider's work can speak of Las Casas as the "conscience of the West,"[25] we need to see the vast destruction of human life going on now on this globe, also in our midst, *and, reading our histories in a new way,* find a new starting point for the history of the Americas in the twenty-first century. This involves nothing less than reshaping our money culture.

We need to see this in the South on the foil of what was possible in the civil rights struggle of the '60s, later in the anti–Vietnam War protests of the '70s, and finally in the nuclear freeze challenge of the '80s. What we are facing right now is the globalization of the question, "God or gold?"[26] We can most effectively deal with this, of course, in terms of the Americas. It comes down to the concrete analysis of the IMF, the World Bank, and the General Agreement on Tariffs and Trade.[27] This often seems rather abstract, but the core of it can be explained to our whole generation, from teenagers to "Grey Panthers": "The third world war has already started. It is a silent war. Not, for that reason, any less sinister. This war is tearing down Brazil, Latin America and practically all the Third World. Instead of soldiers dying, there are children. It is a war over the Third World debt, one which has as its main weapon interest, a weapon more deadly than the atom bomb, more shattering than a laser beam."[28] History is not at an end. That it is ending is what some postmoderns perhaps would have us believe. We are probably facing the task of shaping the first globally humane history with the new century coming to us from the future with tremendous velocity. We are in the beginnings once more. We are harboring illusions. Perfectibility escapes us in an absolute sense. But we can choose the greater good and work for a more tolerable human life on this globe. That involves restructuring our

24. Robert Wuthnow, *God and Mammon in America* (New York: Maxwell Macmillan International, 1994), 14–15.

25. Reinhold Schneider, *Las Casas vor Karl V* (Frankfurt: Ullstein, 1990), 147–56.

26. Gutiérrez, *Las Casas,* 359.

27. *Columban Mission* (September–October 1994): 2–11.

28. Kevin Danaher, ed., *50 Years Is Enough: The Case against the World Bank and the International Monetary Fund* (Boston: South End Press, 1994), Frontispiece. See also Javier Iguíñez Echeverría, *Más pobreza, menos opresión* (Lima, 1993).

money culture. We will still need money to make human life more tolerable on this globe, but money need not be the measure of how we value ourselves and others; it need not be the basic vision of reality.

Liberation theology is often considered a *social moralism.* Nothing could be further from the truth. The struggle is indeed carried out in human conscience. But it is first of all a struggle over the more adequate vision of reality. We dare not be ashamed to ask as people of "the Way" whether Matthew 25:31–46 offers us this more adequate vision for the Americas. We make our moral decisions on grounds of such basic visions. For people of "the Way," conscience is trying to know together with God what reality is like.

There may well be "erroneous conscience,"[29] to use a term in Las Casas's theology, the conscience that could not do better under certain historical conditions. But it can always be appealed to — presupposing that the seeds of the greater good or the more adequate vision are already implanted into it for moving into a new stage of human development.

Much of the critical requestioning the Gutiérrez book invites us to has not been touched upon in these brief queries, for example, the relationship between Native Americans and African Americans or the place of women in the history of the conquest. I need to leave this and other requestioning issues to others.

The challenge in conclusion is to stress that there is much good to appeal to in normal folk on the street and in our churches. Doris Betts, one of our great Southern fiction writers, tells a story: as a twelve- or thirteen-year-old, she invited black children from the black school in town to meet with her and her friends in her home and to eat potato chips and drink "Co-Colas" with them. When she told her mother, "I could see her face stop. She'd never really had black people coming to her front door, sitting down on her living room couch, and having Co-Colas and potato chips. And then she said — and this is so elemental, but it's the basis of a good starting place beyond racism — she said, 'Well, I guess it won't be different in heaven.' She'd made that leap, perfectly. That's ultimately the leap that even uneducated Christians had to make if they believed in any kind of literal way. I don't see how they could prevent making that leap."[30] That is what my own thoughts on Gutiérrez's book are ultimately all about: making that leap.

Throughout these reflections two questions have been on my mind: (1) How in the postmodern West will Las Casas compete between compatible and incompatible realities? As a new reality offer, though bound to his time? And may the best reality vision win? (2) How can we understand the Las Casas appeal to conscience as different from an appeal to social moralism? Is the appeal to the "Christ of the Indies" an appeal to a new reality changing our view of life?

---

29. Gutiérrez, *Las Casas,* 359.

30. Quoted in Susan Ketchin, *The Christ-Haunted Landscape: Faith and Doubt in Southern Fiction* (Jackson: University Press of Mississippi, 1994), 245.

35

TRADICIÓN COMÚN
SHAPING CHRISTIAN THEOLOGY:
MUTUALIZATION IN
THEOLOGICAL EDUCATION

Sponsored by a grant from the Association of Theological Schools for research on issues of globalization and theological education, together with a group of other scholars and church leaders, Herzog explores new paradigms for theological encounters between North and South America. In the context of a relationship between Duke Divinity School and the Comunidad Bíblico-Teológica, a Methodist Seminary in Lima, Peru, which Herzog pioneered in the late eighties, key issues for new relationships on the global level are developed. In December 1992, four members of the Comunidad and the Peruvian Methodist Church came to Duke for ten days to finalize the following report, written by Herzog, which had been prepared on both sides during the previous year.

Trying to avoid earlier patronizing models and the dangers of contemporary globalization, central concepts of the new relationship include a new understanding of mission on grounds of God's mission, an understanding and further development of a common tradition of North and South which respects asymmetries and differences, starting with the trauma of the conquest, and an effort of "mutualization" of theological education, encouraging two-way traffic. A common tradition can only be developed "from the bottom up," where both sides take a closer look at their own specific histories and contexts, including the silences and repressions.

> In all these things we are more than conquerors.
> —ROMANS 8:37

Our report offers an analysis of globalization in theological education based on the cooperation between the Comunidad Bíblico-Teológica (CBT) in Lima, Peru, and the Duke University Divinity School since 1987. We developed our ap-

First published in *Working Paper Series 12*, Duke-UNC Program in Latin American Studies (April 1994): 1–39.

plication to the Association of Theological Schools (ATS) in the fall of 1991 to further the collaborative efforts between the two schools, and specifically to make possible reciprocal faculty visits, research, and dialogue. Within a year, life in Peru changed drastically. By the time summer 1992 arrived, the State Department had begun to advise against travel to Peru. By September the word was that "U.S. citizens should defer all travel to Peru until further notice."[1]

We therefore had to change our plan of a small team visit of the Duke Divinity faculty in mid-October. We had to limit ourselves to our Duke meeting and arranged to have as many of the Peruvians with us as possible.[2]

We began with the methodological presupposition that history has outrun our understanding. Our minds have not been able to keep up with events. During the time of preparing this report there was the week of car bombs in July and the week in September (just two months later) when the head of Sendero Luminoso (Shining Path), Abimael Guzmán, was captured. His trial also fell into this time. Seldom was an ATS report written under the pressure of such terror-filled process unrolling before the eyes of the investigators. There is no way as yet of doing justice to these fast-moving events.

Duke had been associated with the Comunidad Bíblico-Teológica of the Iglesia Metodista del Perú since 1987 for developing common research efforts and student-faculty exchange. In 1990 the CBT had outlined for us a way in which we might examine the significance of our common Methodist history since 1889. So when the ATS invitation came, we felt that here was a chance for a Third World school (more precisely a school of the hungry Two-Thirds World) to offer a hand in shaping our task as Duke University Divinity School into the twenty-first century while in Peru reshaping its own curriculum.

There are few efforts of mutuality where people from the Third World and the First World put their shoulders to the wheel of a joint labor of understanding the common theological task. As a consequence the actual learning process in theorizing about Third World theological education often has great limitations. Third World lecturers, if invited at all to participate in curriculum building in North America, can have a personal impact, but leave little of an imprint on corporate

---

1. The travel advisory was issued by the State Department on September 15, 1992.

2. During the months of July, September, and October 1992, Professor Frederick Herzog was in Lima at work with a Comunidad Bíblico-Teológica team of professors and students on the development of this report from the Peruvian side. The Peru team members of the CBT from the faculty were Oswaldo Fernandez (church history), Mirna Gaydou (dean), Siegfried Hösch (New Testament), Rosanna Panizo (rector), and Eric Torres (attorney and church liaison). Three of these — Fernandez, Panizo, and Torres — were able to make the trip to Durham. There were also students involved in an experimental class dealing with the history and doctrine dimension of our proposal. Present as guests at the Duke December meeting were others with experience in Peru and involvement in the collaborative efforts: Marigene Chamberlain (United Methodist Board of Discipleship), Luis Reinoso (Peruvian pastor), Leif Vaage (Biblical Studies, CBT, and Victoria University, Toronto), and Mark Wethington (United Methodist pastor and head of the Peru Task Force of the North Carolina United Methodist Conference). Throughout the past year all our efforts were centered on our ATS application, titled "Concrete Globalization Analysis for Core Course Development in a North American Divinity School."

change. We have come to the conclusion that theological faculties to a large extent have not as yet come under the scrutiny of the radically new situation.

Rationale

In this new situation the term "globalization" did not achieve very much for us. Initially, therefore, we began to use the word "mission" as an attempt to deal with globalization in terms of a more familiar word. We did not wish to evoke a long debate on missions — North American attempts to "plant" mission stations in what we now call the Third World. The fact is that the Methodist Church of Peru began as a "daughter" church of the United Methodist Church in 1889, and it has been autonomous since 1970. This relationship is still what brings us together today.

So in this context we use the term "mission" to focus on God's work already going on in the world (*missio dei*), a work that takes place ahead of us all the time. Yet it is imperative to view this work in concrete instances and not just in general terms. So we reflect on mission in the light of what have been the *achievements* and *failures* of our actual mission work. What should we know about the present condition of theological education in both our churches when it comes to mission?

What finally emerged in our work was a radical change in our concept of mission and the missionary situation. Today we need to work together in concert, in "joint ventures," as it were, to bring God's salvation, justice, and peace to bear upon North America as well as Latin America. Here is where we anchor the present ATS debate about globalization. In his sterling essay, "Globalization in the Teaching of Church History," Justo L. González makes the point that the notion that we could bring about change by "curricular reforms implies a gross underestimation."[3] If we want the asymmetry between Third World and First World theological education to disappear, we need to think of other solutions.

In our CBT-Duke attempt to work together across the miles, we learned that it is inescapable to stress the notion of mutuality. For González globalization comes down to exposing students and faculty "to alternative settings, alternative ways of being the church and of doing theology in such a way that each one of us may be better theologians in our own settings."[4]

Here we wish, however, to make a more specific theological point. Our task of mission is also to develop and to work with a *tradición común*, a common tradition in which we willingly acknowledge the importance of *our common heritage of the Americas.*

Most theological education in the United States is anchored in the imparting of a very specific tradition which is also very selective. In North America it is

---

3. Justo L. González, "Globalization in the Teaching of Church History," 3. Paper prepared for the ATS Consultation on Globalization and the Classical Theological Disciplines (March 13–16, 1992), Antiochian Village Conference Center, Ligonier, Pennsylvania.
   4. Ibid., 10.

largely the Mediterranean and Northern European cultures that provide us with data and clues, and, having wandered across the Atlantic, the combination still today ends up in most of our classrooms in the United States and Canada. It is this tradition that the United Methodist Church imparted also to the Peruvian Methodist Church. It impacts our Bible interpretation, our dogmatics, and our practical disciplines as much as church history itself. All this is thoroughly "Western." Thus far the basic tradition-framework of Christian theology for us both is a North Atlantic community product.

Yet *our most common tradition on these shores of two American continents is the past five hundred years.* There is a great lack of specifically injecting Latin American history into what thus far has been current as our "tradition." In Peru we have a view of mission and tradition that is nineteenth-century North American. Peruvian Methodist churches are without Latin American roots in our very common tradition. What is more, many of us have become accustomed to interpreting the early tradition of the Christian church as though it had been North European. But already at that time the tradition was much more encompassing than we have acknowledged.

Today we grasp a certain heritage that produces a wider, more encompassing tradition. In some respects the year 1492 (Columbus) turns out to be a more decisive factor for what our faith is in the Americas than the year 1517 (Luther). It contributes to shaping our humanity on these shores.

In Latin America human beings from Europe initially had to come to grips with their identity by seeing themselves as *conquistadores* or *invasores.* In the North, there soon was a nearly exclusive emphasis on Europeans being *immigrants* instead, as though the big chunk of real estate had been almost unpopulated: a wide empty space. The *conquista,* however, is not just a Latin American phenomenon. We discussed this point at many occasions. Insight was only gradually dawning, but then with considerable confidence. With more careful research we will be able to come to a more sharply focused agreement on the nature of the conquest.

In front of the Methodist seminary in Lima rises the famous Columbus statue that Sendero Luminoso might have blown to pieces October 12, 1992, had not Abimael Guzmán, its head, been captured September 12. In front of the Methodist Divinity School at Duke University stands the statue of James B. Duke, founder of Duke University. Thinking of the statue of Columbus, pressing the cross into the hand of the Indian maiden before him, we might remember the subterranean links drawn between the modern businessman and Jesus in the words of Bruce Barton: "He picked up twelve men from the bottom ranks of business and forged them into an organization that conquered the world." For Barton, Jesus is "the founder of modern business."[5]

---

5. Bruce Barton, *The Man Nobody Knows: The Discovery of the Real Jesus* (New York: Grosset & Dunlap, 1924), iv and v.

Is not since Columbus's day the *homo oeconomicus,* the modern "business-man," deep down in our souls shaping what constitutes our basic human self-image? In the harsh confrontation of the atheist Maoism of Sendero and Christianity in Peru, we begin to "appreciate" the tremendous erosion of "Christian values." What in the clash is really left of Christ as power of social and personal direction? Since Miami is the business and travel center of well-to-do Peruvians, an expression that occasionally appears in Peru is, "The values of Miami crowd out all other values." This is a core issue of theological education both in Peru and in the United States. Miami is not a city but a state of being, as an ad says.

Two very "Christian" continents have churned out immense human waste over five hundred years with an attendant immense environmental waste. The vast masses of the poor and the destruction of the environment on both continents have become an all-encompassing challenge for our interpretation of the Bible, of the whole Christian tradition, and of our modern human selfhood. Poverty here is a challenge for Christian justice as much as during the Reformation works-righteousness was a challenge in terms of divine justification.

The issue here is not to "run down" justification (or sanctification or any other focus of Christian interpretation of the Bible). The point is that the Bible in conjunction with God's activity in history has outrun our previous foci of biblical interpretation. We are here primarily not dealing with *our* "option for the poor." We are first of all confronted with the reality of God's own involvement with the poor: "for your sake Christ became poor" (2 Cor. 8:9). We are face-to-face with God's own mission in the world.

The whole point then becomes for us in both continents: "If you love those who love you, what reward have you?" (Matt. 5:46). So we remember that our societies and our churches are constituted by both the conquered and the conquerors (Native American/European, black/white). Here lies the deepest challenge of our work together. Perhaps St. Paul points a way into the future when he claims: "we are more than conquerors" (Rom. 8:37), a statement unfortunately often interpreted in a "triumphalist" way.

Comunidad and Church in Peru

The CBT views itself as an ecumenical school open to a variety of denominational expressions of the Christian faith. Taking into account the deep conflicts in which the church and theological education are involved in both countries and the need to move beyond them, the CBT team wrote a nine-page report titled "Theological Education and the Mission of the Church" specifically for our study. Three emphases stand out for consideration.

1. "To be able to harmonize the educational project with the mission of the church, a closer relationship of dialogue becomes necessary" (7). The need to grapple with the mission of the church is of foremost concern.

2. "Starting with ... the history of the mission ... the work of historical re-

covery of documentary sources must be complemented with the work of the local churches themselves. These, as a testimony, will gather the traditions which at the present time are scattered in the oral memory of the members and different attitudes and latitudes of the nation and therefore permit us to do a historical and theological reading" (5). The tradition point comes through very clearly, slowly growing from the local traditions into a wider framework of traditions.

3. "The area of theology has been able, from its beginning, to place emphasis on Latin American theology, giving it greater specific weight than Biblical thought and doctrinal theology. However, we consider it important to approach Latin American theology systematically and, within it, to begin to develop a Peruvian theology, understanding that to be specifically part of the national values and reality" (6). The doctrine-in-context point is equally strong.

The three points ultimately come down to the question of the tradition as catalyst: "How to appreciate the history of a church in a specific context without losing the global view? How to appreciate the historical development of the same tradition in different countries?" (p. 9)

The basic message the report conveys is that the Comunidad sees its situation and its future strongly in relationship to the Methodist Church of Peru: "The principal contribution of the CBT to the Methodist Church of Peru will be to provide it, through its graduates, with the ability to review itself and to respond to its total mission.... One of the elements to 'take off' from toward this goal would be the study of the history of Latin America and Peru in general and of the mission of the Methodist Church in that context" (7). As a consequence, there is the sharply profiled passion for *mission in the Peruvian society and culture:* "It becomes absolutely necessary for our purposes to study and analyze in historical perspective the model of Methodist mission in Peru from the Peruvian reality at the end of the twentieth century" (8).

References to historical studies, that is, to grasping the tradition, are frequent in the paper directly and indirectly. Thus far history had not played a key role in the CBT. But from now on Methodist history, Peruvian Methodist history, and Peruvian history besides Latin American history are to make an essential contribution in the educational process. There is, however, a finely woven networking necessary with *mission* and *doctrine in context*. It needs to become clear from the outset that the overall framework of the CBT report is a *challenge to the Methodist Church in Peru*. This is the truly creative aspect of the paper. Reference is also made to student field work, for example, as a place of close cooperation between Comunidad and church. But this is deemed by far to be insufficient to bring about a *closer relationship between the church and the Comunidad*.

What needs to be understood is that in March 1989 the Iglesia Metodista del Perú entered into a covenant with the North Carolina Conference of the United Methodist Church in conjunction with its Board of Global Ministries. The first priority of this covenant for the Peruvian Methodist Church was "the biblical-theological empowerment of the members of the Methodist Church of Peru."[6] The implication is that a solid framework of the mutuality of labor and dialogue with the church already exists as covenanted commitment for Methodists in Peru and in the United States. They have been working together for years.

The initiative at this moment is with the CBT, which needs to project a curriculum within the framework of the whole church's mission so that the local churches will again begin to see themselves in mission. "Reflection in our Methodist churches has not been nurtured sufficiently" thus far (1). This now needs to be done in great openness: "The academic and pastoral contribution of the CBT has been to maintain an open attitude of dialogue and pedagogical practice with the Methodist Church of Peru" (2).

The significance of focusing on the church as mission is very transparent: "Is the church doing any effective service in the place where it is located? The answer to this question should be, in our opinion, the kind of reflection around which the seminaries should orient their formative task" (5). In other words, concern for the tradition in the recovery of church history and focus on doctrine in context are not ends in themselves, but want to evoke the *caminar en el camino divino* (walking in God's way) in church and society. It becomes the question of the faithfulness of the church to God, who is at work in history.

One way of going about this is for the Comunidad to provide the church "with dynamic leaders, not with bureaucrats" (7). What the present curriculum of the CBT provides is a pastoral model that is almost exclusively directed "to the formation in the ministry of worship, teaching and pastoral care," but "unrelated to the social problems in which we should be immersed and still containing elements of a pastor-centered church" (6). In the finely tuned summary of what is happening in Bible studies (with much New Testament, and leaving the Old Testament "in second place"), practical theology, and sociological studies, there is already a strong self-critique, stressing the lack of a Peruvian theology wrestling with national values and reality.

All this leads up to the point of permitting "the church to act consciously in the global context" (3). This might happen in a twofold way: (*a*) By putting into practice the Discipleship Covenant between the Methodist Church of Peru and the North Carolina Conference of the United Methodist Church" (1); and (*b*) by developing a Documentation and Investigation Center that contains the historical archives of the Methodist Church of Peru (5). Here the work of the *tradición* will find its concrete laboratory. This takes the peculiar mode of working on a common tradition.[7]

---

6. *Iglesia Metodista del Perú, Pacto de Discipulado,* Acta de la reunión de consulta, 17–18 de Marzo 1989 (General Board of Global Ministries, The United Methodist Church), 22.

7. When we come to unpack the point, it is very important to remember that the detail of the Discipleship Covenant describes the areas with which those sharing in the covenant need to be concerned and which they will carefully develop if they wish to involve themselves in *biblical-theological empowerment* — its fundamental premise (ibid., 22–34). The Working Document on the Covenant describes nine areas: 1. Evangelism, 2. Social Action, 3. Human Rights, 4. Christian Education, 5. Missions, 6. Stewardship, 7. Ecumenism, 8. Educational Work, and 9. Liturgy and Worship.

The one really "new" angle that is added by the intellectual struggle of the CBT is that of the *tradición común*. The struggle of the Methodist Church in Peru during the past few years in the midst of a vast societal conflict has been compelling the people of God to inquire seriously about its roots.

One cannot understand the troubled conscience of the CBT about the church unless one sees how wide the net was cast by the church itself in its aspirations. Will those aspirations forever remain sketched on paper without being pursued in hands-on mode? Yet in order to reach the hands-on mode effectively, one has to do historical archaeology on one's roots simultaneously.

The general importance of tradition is widely sensed in the United States today. In some respects what is happening in the Methodist Church in Peru is nothing but what is also happening in many places in the United States: recovery of the past. In order to make the similarity sharply clear, reference to Robert Bellah et al., *Habits of the Heart* (1985) aids us in understanding:

> Communities, in the sense in which we are using the term, have a history — in an important sense they are constituted by their past — and for this reason we can speak of a real community as a "community of memory," one that does not forget its past. In order not to forget that past, a community is involved in retelling its story, its constitutive narrative, and in so doing, it offers examples of men and women who have embodied and exemplified the meaning of the community. These stories of collective history and exemplary individuals are an important part of the tradition that is so central to a community of history.[8]

The complexity of the context we are viewing historically calls for a peculiar wakefulness. It keeps us from being complacent.

It is here that the preparatory work of Oswaldo Fernandez (CBT, church history) for the CBT report has offered crucial guidance.[9] He prepared his paper for use in the Comunidad and at Duke. The point is that in the Methodist tradition in Peru some work has been done already, but it still is a very limited approach.[10]

---

8. Robert N. Bellah et al., *Habits of the Heart* (New York: Harper and Row, 1985), 153.

9. Oswaldo Fernandez, "La historia en la formación teológica, en la perspectiva de globalización" (CBT Paper), October 20, 1992.

10. Wenceslao Bahamonde wrote his doctoral dissertation at Hartford Seminary in 1952: "The Establishment of Evangelical Christianity in Peru (1822–1900)." It offers a description of Methodist progress in Peru. But it lacks an explanation of the Methodist presence within the sociohistorical context, though it deals with primary sources and contributes valuable information from missionary archives. The work of the Commission on History of the Methodist Church, organized at the celebration of the First Centennial of the Methodist Church in Peru headed by Armando Marull, in 1989 offered a document titled "One Hundred Years of Methodism in Peru." It presents a minimum history addressed to Peruvian churches, reflecting the vision of a pioneer church of Protestant heritage able to forge a mission for the whole country. Hugo Barreto wrote a 1989 thesis for his licentiate called "The Methodist Presence in the Ecclesiastical District of Lima and Callao," a work focusing the influence of different aspects of the Wesleyan tradition in a geographically limited area. In 1988, a Peruvian encounter of the churches of the Wesleyan tradition took place in which José Míguez Bonino participated. It established the need for developing local Methodist history and integrating it into Latin American history as a whole within the framework of salvation history. At the conference Rosanna Panizo developed the theme of "Women in the Methodist Mission in Peru." Oswaldo

From this account very basic questions arise. Who are the Methodists in Peru? From where do they come? From which Methodist current? Where is Peruvian Methodism going? In the absence of researched answers we run the risk of assuming answers to fill in the gap ideologically, playing a guessing game without a critical approach to the historical sources. The global perspective (part of the present CBT-Duke study) demands that we give a scholarly account of the data of place, persons, events, and the life of Peruvian society as a whole. In the process the CBT curriculum (hitherto pastoral without being missional) needs to *completar la oferta educativa* (round out the curricular offerings).

Oswaldo Fernandez begins his observations on church history at the CBT with some important reflections on the basic uses or "nonuses" of history in the North-South context of both Americas. Whatever reflections we engage in with the study of Methodism in North America, in our framework it has the potential of immediately beginning with the *tradición común*, that is, Methodism in both Americas.[11] What benefit do we find in considering Latin America as part of the picture? There are few opportunities that compel us to see ourselves in the mirror of our mission history, much of which has not been used for seeing the *consequences* of our Christian global action. It can be a very creative moment when all of us begin to work together, those who still in their flesh bear the marks of formation and deformation through this mission and now are becoming more and more the subjects of their history, and those who are the heirs of the missionary-sending agency. It is partly a growing search for intersubjectivity. In other words, it is not an issue of just studying an obscure past in documents. The past in part is still alive in oral traditions. There are still Christians who embody the history of missions. To tie together our histories: this is *a job that needs to be done in mutuality.* A new paradigm for grasping modern church history and Christian theology is being shaped in the process.

Fernandez stresses the "ahistoricity" of traditional theology in North America and Latin America, its lack of relationship to the "here and now," which includes a reading of the past. There are events from the past of large parts of humanity that theology excludes from its own history. How do we teach the history of a church in a particular context without losing sight of the global church? The study of the mission of the church compels us to take note of global demands. Thus the North-South relationship emerges as an inescapable responsibility of the church historian. Fernandez's first step here is calling attention to God's mission. It is God's mission that compels us to acknowledge the "wisdom of

---

Fernandez presented the first steps in his research on the Methodist background of the Holiness churches and their relationship to the Social Gospel. Just recently we discovered that there is also a thesis on Methodism in Peru after the 1930s written by James Carlton Stanford at the University of North Carolina. The most widely known publication about Methodism in Peru is Rosa del Carmen Bruno-Jofré, *Methodist Education in Peru: Social Gospel, Politics, and American Ideological and Economic Penetration,* 1888–1930 (Waterloo, Ont.: Canadian Corporation for Studies in Religion, 1988).

11. A pioneering attempt is found in David Martin, *Tongues of Fire: The Explosion of Protestantism in Latin America* (Oxford: Blackwell, 1990), especially in the chapter called "The Methodist Model: Anglo-American Cultural Production Reproduced in Latin America," 27–46.

those who were defeated by domination and the consequent dependency." In focusing on God's mission, the "other" human being appears, demanding "a just treatment and an integration of the theological reading of the data."

In this very moment we are already beginning to work through our North-South history together so that we understand what a *tradición común* is. In broad terms, the future work together has already been outlined on those grounds. It starts with the Wesley heritage. There are specific understandings of our common task.

1. In trying to do things together, the development of a Documentation and Research Center as part of the Comunidad becomes crucial. Such a center will be a concrete opportunity for the Wesley heritage to be explored in Methodism and other church communities. In the words of Oswaldo Fernandez:

> A church historical archive will be imperative. This approach to the sources needs to be a joint effort and will help to find answers to questions like: to what extent was the common Wesleyan tradition rooted and to what extent "contextualized" [in Peru]? In case it was not rooted, which explanations do we find in the primary documents? How do new data reflect a theology in different periods that needs to be studied from a global perspective?

2. Considering together the challenge of a documentation and research center at the Comunidad, we discover links with Duke Divinity School concerns where, for example, the proposed Lilly Foundation study "United Methodism and American Culture" will be lodged. In its project-outline also the United Methodist link to Peru appears: "Has mission philosophy, including current issues generated by the new Mission Society but also past missiological policy and practice reflected distinctively a U.S. 'establishment' agenda? Might case studies of missions to Peru . . . shed helpful light on the evolution of Methodist views of culture?"[12]

3. At the beginning of walking together we have an *ida y vuelta* situation — two-way ticket, or, to change the metaphor, a two-way traffic. Our task is to set up the conditions for doing research together. We need to develop the relationships and invest the kind of money the theological enterprise requires in this case. At Duke part of that framework will also be a deepening of efforts in three courses: Church History (Modern Christianity), Christian Theology, and the Church's Ministry, to attend to the global reality of the church using Peru as a case study.

When we point to the *tradición común*, we are speaking of selecting anew a wide framework of mutual reference in Christian discipleship.[13] Those who do

---

12. "United Methodism and American Culture: Foci of Research and Policy" (Duke Divinity School paper, December 1992): 2.

13. In this context we need to note the ecumenical range of church backgrounds which shape this project and this report. Present from the Peruvian side were members of the Iglesia Metodista del Perú and the Iglesia Evangélica de los Peregrinos del Perú, the latter a Peruvian Holiness denomination with roots in the (former) Pilgrim Holiness Church in the United States. From the North American side there were members of the United Methodist Church, the United Holy Church of America (an African American Holiness-Pentecostal denomination), the Presbyterian Church

not understand their histories are bound to repeat them also in the church. Those who do understand will find the joy and cost of discipleship in full communion.

La Tradición Común

In our discussions of a "common tradition" we have recognized at least two specific senses in which representatives from the CBT and Duke Divinity School share common roots. The first is the sense of our experience in the Americas, with the ambiguity about European roots in new contexts, and perhaps our reckoning with ourselves as part of a tradition of *conquistadores* or invaders (both in the North and in the South). Here a new paradigm is evolving, a new self-understanding, with no guilt trip involved. It is simply an issue of the "grid" through which we see reality.

The second specific sense of *tradición común* lies in the Wesley heritage of our churches, a heritage that has often been obscured by later developments, but whose contemporary recovery we perceive to be critical for the renewal of Methodist Churches in Peru and in the United States, and also for the sense of "connectedness" between Methodist and Evangelical churches who share these Wesleyan roots, such as Holiness and Pentecostal churches, and even "indigenous" churches (such as the Iglesia Evangélica Peruana, founded in 1908) who share aspects of the Wesley heritage (such as hymnody).

There is obviously also a third way of working with the *tradición común:* our Catholic and Protestant heritage. But we knew we were not able to cover everything at the same time. So we focused mainly on the first two aspects.

Justo L. González had objected to curricular reforms as an answer to the challenge of globalization. In the light of our discussions with our Peruvian colleagues, we said to each other over and over again that at stake for us in the North was a paradigm shift in the mind of the teacher. It involves the instructor's social location, basic historical heritage, and interpretative key or angle. Thus far North American instructors do not broadly "factor in" Latin American reality when it comes to church history, North American Christianity, or Christian theology.

We will describe here in brief our North American effort to overcome this lack. Incorporation of Peruvian studies into our required ministry sequence, the Church's Ministry 10 and Church's Ministry 100, was projected for summer 1993. Professors Richey, Fulkerson, and Turner participated in the junior level Church's Ministry 10; Wethington participated in the senior course, Church's Ministry 100. Both Ted Campbell (in Church History) and Frederick Herzog (in Christian Theology) introduced material from Peruvian church history in the

---

U.S.A., the United Church of Christ (through one of its branches deeply rooted in Methodist spirituality), and the Evangelical Lutheran Church of America. So there was also a strong Evangelical presence.

spring semester 1992. We had agreed especially on the hundred years of the
United Methodist mission in Peru (1889–1989) for orientation.[14]

In Christian Theology, the effort, for example, for three days was focused on
how the understanding of the church as God's mission is christologically rooted
in God's own historical mission in the world. How seriously did our churches
take Christology as they developed a mission in Latin America? Today we are
confronted with the consequences of our mission (attrition of our mission work,
etc.), which we also need to take seriously. Before the class sessions, the students
had been given Peruvian material. After three sessions they had to write a ten–
minute evaluation, answering specific questions.

The student papers from Duke were the first materials we began to work with
in Peru later in July. It made us focus on the specific Peruvian history of the
Methodist Church and the wider history of the church in Latin America. Here
Oswaldo Fernandez introduced the notion of the *tradición común* that unites
us on both continents. The experimental course Herzog taught at the CBT in
September and October soon underscored this dimension.

An observation made by Sydney Ahlstrom suddenly made eminent sense. "It
is important to see that the impulses which led Luther to the Wittenberg church
door were integrally related to those which sent Spanish caravels out across the
Western sea."[15] In Europe the Protestant Reformation impulses were connected
also with business interests of the princes so that later *cuius regio eius religio* was
as much a Reformation principle as justification by faith. Since 1492 in New
Spain, Columbus's business interests and the evangelization drive went hand in
hand. The *conquistadores* were driven by gold as well as the cross. In any case,
since Columbus's day the business drive plays an important role in shaping the
human self-image in this hemisphere. The earliest settlers already had to see
themselves as business folk.

Has not the time come self-critically to make that self-image the basic anthropological point for theology? We have a tremendous common tradition between
North America and Latin America, and it is imperative that we now shape it
theologically.

What Tradición Común *Dare Not Be*

How can we honestly do things and say things together when both schools are
on an incommensurable footing financially and thus also in terms of size of staff,
library resources, and learning space? Siegfried Hösch, New Testament professor
at the CBT, shared with us part of his reflections on these matters in regard to
the usual reaction of foreigners to a Third World situation. He suggested that we

---

14. See the names of all the participants at the end of the chapter. Ted Campbell and Herzog
agreed initially to start with material from Rosa del Carmen Bruno-Jofré, *Methodist Education in Peru:
Social Gospel, Politics, and American Ideological and Economic Penetration, 1888–1930* (Waterloo, Ont.:
Canadian Corporation for Studies in Religion, 1988).

15. Sydney Ahlstrom, *A Religious History of the American People* (New Haven: Yale University
Press, 1972), 25.

from the North would do well to research the effects of "colonialization" in all its dimensions on the persons who missionized the "natives" in Peru. Instead of focusing on the impact of Protestant "colonization" within the Andean context, the challenge is not to dissect the victims but to analyze the victimizers and to heal them. Offering a longer quote from Hösch is the best way to show what dare not happen in our context:

> There are different kinds of tourism: adventure tourism, culture tourism, sex tourism. A relatively new variety is religious tourism to Third World countries. A brief stay, impressions, photos, souvenirs. The motive usually is the visit of some relief project. Part of the idea is personal encounter instead of mere money support and a few thank you notes, something that is important for both sides. The foreign visitors are received and hosted warmly. It's part of the culture of the hosts. But it's not only that. Money is also at stake: donations are supposed to continue to flow.
>
> When people take a trip, they afterwards have lots of show and tell opportunities: photos, *artesanías*, souvenirs. One highly valued souvenir of religious tourists is *the hope of the poor*. We discover it often in travel accounts or in quickly produced books with provoking titles like "God in the Garbage." Ranking at the top right now is the hope of *women*. At present it has the best marketing appeal. The reading public excitedly inquires about it. The worse the situation of the women, the more the praise of their heroic courage, their meekness, their kindness, and their organizational talent.
>
> While the heroines overseas drop exhausted and desperate on their beds at night, the visitors sit at their desks again at home and splash the hope of the poor on paper. Price: DM 12,80.[16]

The point is that there is also a literary exploitation of the poor. Globalization that itself falls prey to the exploitation syndrome ends up on the ash heap of history.

In the light of these reflections we examined in Lima the Duke students' comments in Christian Theology. Among the thirty-one student responses (photocopied, distributed, and read in Peru), there were comments like: "There was a tendency for missions to try to superimpose their own social location on the ones they were trying to help." Or: "When spirituality is separated from social movement and vice versa, the Social Gospel becomes a divinized political agenda, a means of exporting North American and European social values and systems."

There was severe criticism of the limited mission focus in this matter. On the one hand, one can ask whether the student assessment did justice to the actual conditions of the Methodist Church of Peru. The Social Gospel may not have been that influential all around. On the other hand, there is the question whether the criticism deals sufficiently with the colonizer's mentality itself. What it comes down to is the sober challenge for church history and Christian theology instruction in the North to take into account a historical grid that is different from the one by which we were trained.

---

16. Siegfried Hösch, Mission Letter (CBT material, 1992), 26.

The Way to Go?

While in some sense the word "globalization" occasionally seems to suggest that we are on the verge of discovering a new dimension of theology, it becomes clearer every day that practically all the crucial issues we were locking horns over in the civil rights struggle are still with us today, though partly with new labels or terms, and are continued in the globalization debate. Because of the present global challenges, we understand better today that the major mandates of globalization are not those of ethics but of Christian theology. Or, rather, in the new context the distinction between ethics and systematic theology here turns out to be a false one. In the globalization focus the main bone of contention is now Christian anthropology — the human self-image (with ecclesiology following a close second). Related to the self-image mandates of today are issues of pluralism or ecumenical tolerance. But ecumenical tolerance as such is not the key to globalization.

In this context we discussed parts of the recent book by Harold J. Recinos, *Jesus Weeps*, a superb globalization argument among theological publications at this point in time. He dedicates the book also to "all persons committed to understanding human diversity." That plays itself out in a particular view of anthropology: "Pastoral anthropology seeks to enable local church communities to enter into an authentic examination of the cultural other."[17] The result of the approach is a deep appreciation of cultural difference, especially of ethnic minorities, Asians, Latinos, Blacks, and Native Americans, for example, as we are forced more and more to live together in one global environment. The lasting merit of the book is to have brought globalization "back home" to our own backyards, our own doorsteps, and our own homes.

In the chapter called "Globalization: Encountering Some City Voices," Recinos is moving and deeply committed to all the right things. The issue is whether or not there is another dimension to this segment of reality that we can disregard only at our own peril. Are these encounters with the other no more than pluralist challenges that require equal attention in a vast sea of diversity?

Could it be that, if we do not grapple with the challenge of the other also christologically, we miss the global mandate of the church? What if there were already a christological shift taking place in the experience of the poor from the so-called unipersonality of the Christ of the creeds to the multipersonality of the Christ of the deeds? At one point Recinos says, "Christ was in the experience of utter abandonment I came to know so well in the streets."[18] What if this first of all would have to be fleshed out christologically so that we see the vast diversity Recinos appeals to on the foil of God's global activity among all humankind? What if the issue were first of all to understand the divine diversity?

Might there perhaps be an identity in all the diversity we see? What if it were God-identity that makes globalization in mutualization work? And God-

---

17. Harold J. Recinos, *Jesus Weeps* (Nashville: Abingdon, 1992), 130.
18. Ibid., 33.

identity in God-diversity? This is not a place to develop a doctrine of the Trinity. But is not the Trinity the place to look for divine diversity as the basis of the multipersonality of Christ impacting human diversity?

Sometimes we have to take a bold step. There is a memorable passage in Albert Schweitzer's *The Philosophy of Civilization:* "I am undertaking what has never been attempted before, namely, so to pose the problem of Western philosophy as to make the Western search for a world-view come to a halt and take account of itself."[19] We are trying to make the ATS's search for a global view come to a halt and take account of itself.

From a more liberal Enlightenment perspective, a big push is needed to be more and more open on the humanistic level. So we get an avalanche of pluralism. But humanly nothing is gained. In snowballing pluralism the humanistic self-image inadvertently stays the same — the *homo oeconomicus.* Extremes begin to touch each other: the conservatives are safe with their image of *homo oeconomicus* because the pluralism syndrome does not seem to touch them. The liberals in so much diversity find a good rationale not to change either, and thus are also safe as *homo oeconomicus.* So all the talk about change cancels itself out. It partly (however minimally) explains the increasing erosion of ethical criteria and standards in society.

So we stew around in pluralism and diversity and do not have to change our humanistic self-image. It issues in a bifurcation between theological God-determination and cultural self-appreciation, the divinely formed self-image and the cultural self-image. Which way to go? While not negating the need to discover the "other" in the vast cultural panorama, mutuality in the plight of poverty changes the self-image of the *homo oeconomicus* on grounds of the God-image. The human self-image change depends on the christological image change described above. It comes about only when we immerse ourselves in God's struggle against human suffering. The temptation for theologians is always to see the change necessary "out there" through mere perception, tied to the practical fields of parish and ministry, and not "in here" in the theologian's own self-space of creativity. The challenge is to embody God in mutuality as we go through the historical process together. That takes worshiping together, celebrating the Eucharist together, and bearing our "mutual burdens." As long as that does not happen, the "classical disciplines" of theological education go begging in our globalization attempts. The basic construct is wrong.

Advocacy *or* Tradición Común

We remember at this point our original objective we had proposed to the ATS. We wanted to find out how church history data from the "Two-Thirds World" might shape certain dimensions of systematic theology in new ways. We have tried to tackle the task in mutuality, walking together through a history thus far not worked through corporately.

---

19. Albert Schweitzer, *The Philosophy of Civilization* (New York: Macmillan, 1949), 73.

What becomes important in this context is the person of the theology teacher in regard to the classical theological disciplines. Robert A. Evans in his Preface to Recinos, *Jesus Weeps,* speaks of him as empowered in "advocacy," for example, for systemic justice in Peru or South Africa.[20] Evans's argument for Harold Recinos is very believable. But in regard to the framework of globalization within theological education there is also the question of the character of the reality referred to. That reality can be perceived only in a common endeavor that seeks to understand in it the working of God within a common tradition.

The complexity at this point needs further discussion among us. The hard choice comes about because of our commitment to God's mission as central to our work. An illustration might aid understanding. Asked to recant his views about the motion of the earth, Galileo is supposed to have said under his breath, "And yet it moves." In the face of all the callousness toward the vast masses of the world's poor from Somalia to Peru, we might be tempted to cry out, "And yet they suffer." The reality-truth in God's mission is that God personally is in the midst of suffering humankind and that this God's reality is our real business. God is doing something to us in the suffering mode. What are we doing about it together with God — as theological instructors?

God is the one who is involved in real advocacy. That is why God as Holy Spirit is called the Paraclete, the advocate. It is the common tradition that makes us aware of God's advocacy in different ways:

1. This tradition makes us pay attention to our *social location* in which professors with their students in relationship to the church see the light in truly seeing themselves. In being aware of their ties to a "foreign history," theologians are compelled to describe every thought of theirs in terms of walking along with God's walk through history. They can no longer afford to stand at a distance.

2. Part of the "grid" of the new social location is a strong grasp of the *interdependency of poverty.* In Peru, only 15 percent of the people live above the poverty line, with an unbelievable attrition of poverty among the children. In July 1992, the statistics of child poverty in the United States for 1989 came out. In North Carolina, child poverty is said to have been between 15 percent and 19 percent; in Mississippi it was 33.5 percent. Black children are the most likely to live in poverty — with a 38.9 percent chance — almost two children out of five. The same causes that make for poor children in the United States make for poor children in Peru.

3. The concretion of the *tradición común* in the interdependency of poverty is focused in the black theology/Andean theology challenge that needs immediate exploration in church history and Christian theology. Books like James H. Cone, *Martin and Malcolm in America,* and Frans Damen and Esteban Judd Zanon, *Cristo Crucificado en los Pueblos de América Latina,* will here be helpful in defining the framework.[21]

---

20. Recinos, *Jesus Weeps,* 12.

21. James H. Cone, *Martin and Malcolm in America* (Maryknoll, N.Y.: Orbis Books, 1991); Frans

4. Nothing of our thought process will appear very effective in the end un-less our emerging *tradición común* is anchored in a common praxis. While this may seem hard to bring off across the many miles, Dean Mirna Gaydou tried to express the possibility in a brief note of October 23, 1992:

> We have worked together now with a number of faculty for many weeks on the CBT/Duke report for the Association of Theological Schools in January 1993. In the process three areas have opened up where important work can be done to-gether in the long run (for many years, that is). (1) The research center for the Iglesia Metodista del Perú archives, something like a Centro de Documentación e Investigación. (2) The project "100 years Theological Education in Peru" (The Thomas Wood Centennial) 1893–1993. (3) The praxis task of developing a new praxis-theory relationship in theological education centered, for example, in the Aldea Cieneguilla [village for orphans of the guerrilla war].

Mirna Gaydou's *first* point has become the centerpiece of several steps of our thought process along the way. So there is no need to underscore previous com-ments. The second point, emphasizing *research,* follows from the first point. The *third* point is the one now needing major attention as we wind up our reflec-tion in regard to specific courses. The issue is, in the end, which praxis we are anchored in together as faculty and students. There is no instant solution to it all. But it needs to be clear that here we touch the main nerve of our common venture.

Appendix

We append here our reflections on the specific areas of our study, church history and Christian theology.

Church History: Modern European Christianity

At the 1988 annual faculty retreat for Duke Divinity School, focused on global-ization in theological education, Ted Campbell commented that most instructors in the traditional theological disciplines (including himself in church history) had not been trained in such a way as to be able to teach from a significantly global perspective. Any furtherance of the project of globalization would depend on a serious "retooling" of theological faculty.

Damen and Esteban Judd Zanon, *Cristo Crucificado en los Pueblos de América Latina* (Cusco, Peru: Instituto de Pastoral Andina, 1992). The whole ATS report was written in constant "inner conver-sation" with our Black Church Studies effort, and off and on in direct conversation with William C. Turner as director of Black Church Affairs at Duke University (who also participated in the May 1991 faculty trip to Peru). There were also early conversations with James H. Cone, reaching back over a period of more than two decades to 1970–71. For a long time I have been thinking that black theology challenges and Third World mandates interface. It is an infinite task, as I see it. We will not be through with meeting the theological demands in our generation. I need to express my thanks to Daniel M. Bell, Jr., who over the past months developed for me tentative "Conclusions and Obser-vations" in researching our Duke documents on Black Church Affairs. I hope that this ATS report will also further our Duke Divinity School growth in Black Church Affairs mandates.

The present curriculum at Duke has been structured in such a way as to reflect the strengths and interests of our history faculty, but not in a way that would stress the global character of the church's historical experience. The required sequence in church history — Early and Medieval Christianity, Modern European Church History, and American Christianity — can be read as a narrowing projectile whose very tip is contemporary North American Christianity.

As a first step in developing the global perspective on Modern European Christianity during the 1992 spring semester, Campbell replaced two weeks of materials with new material on European Mission activities. The two weeks dropped were: (a) a second week of material on the Enlightenment (basically all material on the Enlightenment was reduced to one week), and (b) a concluding week on the Ecumenical Movement (in the hope that in required introductory courses — "The Church's Ministry," "Christian Theology," and "American Christianity" — students may gain some exposure to the Ecumenical Movement). Added were: (1) a week's study of Catholic missions in the sixteenth and seventeenth centuries, and (2) a week's study of Protestant missions in the nineteenth century.

Our ATS-sponsored project with the CBT added considerable depth to these two weeks' study. The week on Catholic missions focused on the missions to Peru in the sixteenth century and the conversion of the Inca peoples. Of particular interest were the sixteenth-century "Councils of Peru," a series of church councils led by reform-minded Catholics which stressed the centrality of catechesis, the development of native clergy, and the importance of utilizing Native American languages. Although subsequently ignored, these councils served as catalysts for class discussions of indigenization in missions.

The week on Protestant missions focused on the development of Methodist churches in Peru, especially because of our connection with the CBT. Course descriptions had to be fudged a bit at this point, because Protestant missions were sponsored both by North American as well as European churches in this period.

Our December discussions with faculty members of the CBT have been greatly illuminating on both of these points. One of Campbell's criticisms of the literature of Mission History has been that it has a tendency to read like a "telephone book" with endless lists of names and dates and acronyms of mission-sending agencies who dispatched people here and there. But encountering members of the CBT directly and hearing the same history from the perspective of some of its "recipients" shed a radically different light on the narrative. Campbell reports that he could sense (even in facial expressions and gestures) the points at which this history is of vital contemporary meaning for Christians of Peru.

Our December conversation over the *tradición común* revealed, on the one hand, a common search for roots (*raizes*) both in our American experience and in our particular Wesleyan heritage, a quest that (as both sides see it) is critical in the development of our present self-understanding. On the other hand, it also revealed points at which we dare not be too hasty in asserting a commonality of northern and southern experience of the Christian faith in the Americas.

To change the basic "grid" through which church history instructors assess historical realities will take considerable effort. Campbell offers at least the following three points for critical self-evaluation. (1) By introducing new historical materials concerning global missions, we can become more aware of significant aspects of our Christian identity that we have consistently blocked out in conventional North Atlantic readings of Christian history. (2) By continuing to work on the selection of materials (especially primary sources when they can be made available in English), we can broaden and deepen our basis for historical judgment. (This happened in Campbell's spring 1993 offering of this course.) (3) By continuing active research in collaboration with those who still bear marks of mission history in their flesh, we can better understand the need to root contemporary historical reflection in a situation of praxis in living Christian communities.

Christian Theology

The ATS grant for globalization assessment relative to the classical theological disciplines made a first step realizable. Yet globalization for Christian theology here turns out to be a code word. Our first speech act needs to be a call to a moment of silence for forty thousand children dying each day throughout our globe and of the need for Christian theology in its starting point to take such a fact into consideration.

Christian Theology, choosing books for a required course, aligns itself with a certain tradition. Does this tradition leave out important data of the past that would then also logically compel it to leave out significant data of the present?

Christian Theology in the Duke environment, if the books selected are any indication, is a Protestant phenomenon with the Reformation at its core. Duke's Methodist background makes Luther and Wesley natural reference points. In terms of the Aldersgate experience, Wesley felt his heart strangely warmed on hearing the preface of Luther's commentary on Romans. Accordingly, justification and sanctification constitute the major hermeneutical framework of Christian doctrine. There are also references to the wider church, Roman Catholicism, Eastern Orthodoxy, and so on. But these concerns, as a rule, are viewed through the glasses of the Protestant principle.

As we began to reflect on the task at hand it became clear that the mandate was twofold: (1) to examine historically and self-critically the notion of the tradition we had grown up with; (2) to discover the "second language of commitment" (Robert N. Bellah)[22] ensconced in the conventional classroom language of Christian theology.

---

22. Bellah, *Habits of the Heart*, 175. The actual phrase used in the book is "second language of *social* commitment." Our task was to discover a second language of *any* commitment, social commitment included.

In regard to facing the fact of forty thousand children dying each day, we real-ize in pondering the tradition that Protestant doctrine so far has concentrated heavily on "religious" issues. There are various ways of describing it. A common reference point is the abuse of the Christian faith in Roman Catholic customs of Luther's day. There was the practice of so-called indulgences. An enterprising monk by the name of Tetzel coined the sales pitch:

> As soon as the money clinks in the chest,
> The soul flies up to heavenly rest.

Luther countered the mercenary *do ut des* faith of cheap grace with the teaching of justification by faith.

In most founding moments of new expressions of the Christian faith there is first a negative phenomenon, a distortion; then comes a counterpoint. Thus we first have Tetzel, then Luther. At the beginning of the American experience we have Christopher Columbus:

> Let us in the name of the Holy Trinity go on sending all the slaves that can be sold.

Then comes the counterpoint, Bartolomé de Las Casas, speaking up in behalf of the native people to be sold into slavery to Europe.[23]

While Luther's stand has become the hinge of Protestant faith history and most of Protestantism circles around it, the Las Casas witness has been blocked off. What are the implications of this witness today as it is being uncovered more and more?

We had begun with the question of how church history with new data from the churches of the "Two-Thirds World" might expect to shape certain dimen-sions of Christian theology in new ways. The still very tentative answer is multifaceted and reflects the difficulties that need to be worked through in a long process of reorientation. Colleagues in the field have different backgrounds and will want to see evidence of how a hitherto hidden tradition can become creatively useful. We can offer here only a few first steps.

1. Only in embodying mutuality in the present theological task together with colleagues from the "Two-Thirds World" will we discover new data that can be used creatively for concrete globalization.

2. The Duke student evaluations showed that with new data we basically begin to see ourselves in a mirror not available before. It can easily happen that with the new mirror view of ourselves we sit in judgment on predecessors from the North. There was something wrong, for example, with the way the Social Gospel invaded the self-image of Peruvians. Yet our new self-image does not

---

23. This fact alone almost calls for a course by itself. If divinity schools or seminaries have a course on Augustine, Martin Luther, or Karl Barth, why has Bartolomé de Las Casas not found a similar "slot"? Initially we can begin at least in a small way to introduce Las Casas material. I myself will be using George Sanderlin, ed., *Witness: Writings of Bartolomé de Las Casas* (Maryknoll, N.Y.: Orbis Books, 1992), and Gustavo Gutiérrez, *Las Casas: In Search of the Poor of Jesus Christ* (Maryknoll, N.Y.: Orbis Books, 1993), in the readings of the basic course in Christian theology.

automatically read the data accurately. It needs to subject itself to ever renewed self-critique in the light of further new data. The immediate task is open-ended. We need to adduce more data in hard research.

3. The experimental CBT seminar led by Frederick Herzog sharply focused the clash between the "values of Miami" and the "values of the Andes." It turned out that the premises North American Christian theology usually is built upon did not figure helpfully in the shaping of a "Peruvian" theology. Since Karl Barth's *Dogmatics in Outline* (1949) had been used at Duke for a long time as basic textbook in Christian theology classes across the board, it appeared advisable to examine, for example, how the Spanish edition (Karl Barth, *Bosquejo de Dogmática,* 1954) would fare in the Peruvian classroom. It seemed rather abstract, but offered a solid introduction to European Protestant thought. More meaningful to the Peruvian students was their discovery that they had a praxis of their own in their Peruvian setting, in this case a village for abandoned and orphaned children of the guerrilla war.

4. We constantly returned to the self-image issue developing in the Peruvian poverty situation. Obviously the self-image of the North American instructor did not fit. Here was a starting point for new research, part of which was reading historical theology once more in a self-critical light, for example, also the neo-orthodox impact of Barth in the past forty years on Latin America. Like Barth's work itself, it had not directly evolved from a new praxis.

5. What turns out to be crucial now is the introduction of further data into the basic Christian theology course as presently taught. It cannot be done all at once. This past year Luis Reinoso, formerly of Lima and now working in North Carolina, in consultation with Frederick Herzog developed a bibliography of some six hundred Latin American titles that step by step needs to be worked into the class process. A further title in North American black/white encounter had been introduced into the course this 1993 spring semester. It shows that the widening impact of the study is not only in the North-South dimension. We are not allowed to think that parts of our own cities are unlivable and have to be left to the drug lords while we theologians concentrate our energies on field trips to the Third World.

6. No globalization without mutualization. No mutualization without justice. We need to see the interdependency of poverty between Lima and Durham. North Americans cannot afford to involve themselves in year-long studies with millions of dollars for supporting the improvement of theological education when it takes only a split second to repent, that is, to change one's mind. Of course that needs data. A few of the data we discovered relate to the fact that usually foundations which will provide money for improving theological education in the North will not offer money for supporting Third World schools in the same effort. When Duke Divinity School runs on a budget of $6,000,000 a year, the CBT is overjoyed when it gets $60,000 a year from the North through various channels. It will be easy for the reader to figure the percentage. The asymmetry runs through our entire report as "silent partner." We cannot go on

that way. Here is where much hard thinking needs to be done in the future. "The persisting question is, does our organizational structure continue to serve our missional responsibilities?"[24] That includes our money structure. We need to learn to speak to power without fear, that is, to the money managers who often do not understand the actual *theological* issues of poorly implemented globalization. If we do not make clear to them their truly creative possibilities in the Third World church, North American theological educators may soon be shackled in a Babylonian captivity not even a Martin Luther could handle. We need a new "theology of money" in globalization. We need to develop it not *for* our sisters and brothers in the Third World, but in mutuality together with them.

7. The common work between the CBT and Duke Divinity School continues. Rector Rosanna Panizo has taught at Duke in February and March of 1993. As soon as the political situation in Peru changes, there will again be student involvement.[25]

---

24. *Grace upon Grace: The Mission Statement of the United Methodist Church* (Nashville: Graded Press, 1990), 37. Though I quote only one sentence from the statement, it has been all along the basic sounding board of our ATS report. Since my colleague in the field, Thomas A. Langford, had much to do with the writing of the United Methodist mission statement, I wish to thank him also for his part in the shaping of this *opusculum*. Of all the support I received on our side of the project over the years, his is the most sustained and thus presents the "largest share."

25. It remains to thank the Reverend Mr. Luis Reinoso for his sterling labors in bibliography and translation and Ms. Sarah Freedman for her unstinting secretarial help in typing up many versions of what in the end still stays a "draft of a draft," especially since the common effort of a group stands behind it. Globalization as mutualization is an infinite task. The Duke people who at the December 1992 Duke consultation contributed to this project, together with the Peruvian colleagues and others involved with the CBT, are Ted Campbell, Mary McClintock Fulkerson, Russell Richey, and William C. Turner. Here I need to underscore the work of our Peruvian colleagues once more without whom this project would not even exist. So I "salute" Oswaldo Fernandez, Rosanna Panizo, and Eric Torres for coming to Duke. In Lima it was Mirna Gaydou as dean who made sure even under the most trying circumstances that the work could go on in great regularity and who contributed a major portion of the CBT report. (In spite of societal pressures to write off feminism as a bourgeois Western or leftist-Marxist phenomenon, Rosanna Panizo and Mirna Gaydou have been offering a constant feminist witness at the CBT. They have insisted on providing courses on women's issues for students and workshops for church members. The Latin American situation has a long way to go to come to terms with its patriarchal past and present. But Peru has excellent feminist centers. Rosanna Panizo is in constant contact with them as well as with feminist theologians in other South American countries. There is a far-flung network growing. Duke faculty and students can learn from the CBT what feminism in the "Two-Thirds World" can achieve.) A special note of thanks must go to Ted Campbell, who put himself on the "firing line" here, especially with his efforts in the church history course. That part of the Appendix is from his pen. Teresa Berger, chair of the International Studies Committee, was in Germany at that time. We are grateful for her enthusiastic assistance and guidance. Dean Dennis M. Campbell's foresight made the project possible, and his patient oversight carried us through to the final sentence.

36

For Stan, Who Also Reads
Karl Barth

*Members of the same faculty, Frederick Herzog and Stanley Hauerwas picked
up the habit of corresponding through notes in the years before Herzog's death.
This letter is an example of the fairly open tone of conversation.*

*In light of Barth's critique of liberal theology, Herzog raises the question of
how the liberal focus, which leaves modern humanity in control in theological
matters, is best overcome. In this letter he develops a different way out of the
dilemma by focusing once more on God in light of the poor, those who are not in
control, with whom God freely identifies.*

In your just published book *After Christendom?* (1991) you articulate, or begin
to articulate, a project to replace the Enlightenment project or at least to stand
against the Enlightenment project, as best I understand it. You usually speak of
it as the liberal project.

Just like you, I reject "systematic theology" (see my essay "Vom Ende der
systematischen Theologie," in Hermann Deuser et al., *Gottes Zukunft der Welt:
Festschrift für Jürgen Moltmann*, 1986 [chapter 24 in this volume]). Just as I do,
you state that it makes no sense to say that "theology can be done as if our social
and political considerations are an afterthought" (19).

Following up on that you also claim that "the very idea of systematic theology
was a result of a church with hegemonic power that belied the very substance
that made the church to begin with" (19). I do not have the time here to show
where we then begin to differ on the shape or character of what ought to come
in the place of systematic theology. I usually, for want of a better word, speak
of dogmatics, as you know.

Right now there are developing, at least in intention, vast new (let me not
call them "systems," since their authors disclaim the term) *projects*. Your project
wants to "reshape the understanding of salvation that so many share" (19). Almost immediately you make this an *ecclesiological* point: "I try to show how our

Unpublished letter, January 6, 1992.

understanding of salvation is shaped by the social status of the church" (19). And your project seeks to prove (like the project of others today) that we are struggling over the character of ecclesiology (as I often said of Gutiérrez whom I mention since his name appears later on in your book; obviously there are others of whom I have said the same).

You "use" the church in your logic (as I read it) as concrete tradition (28). Here the rubber hits the road. But which tradition? Which concrete tradition? Which concrete church? My predecessor and esteemed colleague Robert E. Cushman (whose heritage I have tried, besides another heritage, determinedly to uphold) asked a similar question years ago: *Which church?* Obviously the context was different. But I mention Cushman because at Duke we were used to asking these kinds of nosy questions.

I need to inject just one other point. You were present in one of our faculty committee meetings where I (in order to make a point of the discussion "stick") recently was compelled to make a distinction between ideological ecclesiology and Barmen ecclesiology. Let me just push this, for clarification's sake, one step further and say: in the present furious debate I see a vast difference between ideological ecclesiology and martyr ecclesiology. I'll get back to the point presently.

You emphasize, I guess just as I do, that you want social location to play a crucial role: "These awkward times give us the opportunity to recover the locality of Christian salvation called the church. Without the recovery of such locality, such particularity," the whole project makes no sense (35), as best I understand it. Now what?

So I start looking for the concrete church, the particularity. Is it a denomination, a group of denominations, the ecumenical movement of churches, or the North Carolina Council of Churches, a local church council, Durham Congregations in Action (DCIA) in our town, Methodist classes, or a Wesley band? I do not know. Am I not supposed to know? Or am I asking an unfair question? I have read chapter 4.

I read on, continuing my query. You claim: "Salvation is a political alternative that the world cannot know apart from the existence of a concrete people called church" (35). Which concrete people? Some of the more profiled liberation theologians, by and large, make no bones about their specific church affiliation, whether they speak of the poor church or base communities or the Roman Catholic Church. From your text, the question arises: Is your project ultimately to be slated for what I can only regard as a head-on confrontation with liberation themes? But why then do you not offer us an equally concrete church? What I am getting at is, Which of the real conflicts of a concrete church are you taking on?

In the committee meeting I referred to above I also appealed to Karl Marx. We both know his limitations. But his insights in terms of his nineteenth-century environment are not gainsaid by his limitations. I'll append a German cartoon (from his homeland; serves him right!) which will inject the proper humor apropos to my point. My question to you is, Is Hauerwas's church ultimately the church in the ideal realm, the ideal church?

We both have studied enough of Marx to know that in German idealism my true religious existence is my existence in the *philosophy* of religion (see Erich Fromm, *Marx's Concept of Man,* 187). So is my true religious existence, in terms of Stan in the philosophy of the church, or theology of the church?

How do I gird myself "from" your remarks against the notion that in you the actual pains of labor, and its attendant suffering in any conflict, are sublated and even sublimated? Do I here exist first of all in the *idea* of the church? Obviously, there is with you debate about the "concrete" church. But is it not debated first of all, that is, on the primal level, in terms of books we respond to?

So can you be very surprised that I am not sure whether at some point there isn't a certain misidentification going on in your recent book?

You refer a lot to human beings and Christians in this first chapter and to what Christians think. But what about what God thinks? And how else might you bring that off unless you would say something about the function of the *Bible* in all of this? Did not Barth make it "lesson number 1"?

Therewhile didn't Barth make it clear that this was not a matter of proof-texting, that is, of quoting the Bible, but of learning to reason together with the Bible, falling in line with its "God-logic"? Somewhat along the "Come let us reason together" of Isaiah 1:18? Didn't he also make it abundantly clear that over against your Enlightenment counterpart he already fought so effectively, we would want to shun biblicism like the plague and yet let dogmatics become *also* (besides a few other things) an inquiry of "what we ourselves must say 'on the basis of the Apostles and prophets'"? (*Church Dogmatics,* I/1, 16).

I believe I have a fairly adequate view of the Hauerwas position on the Bible. Where I am wrong I'll stand corrected. But the question that interests me now is, What does Stan actually *do* with the Bible? There are lots of interesting points I might want to discuss with you. But they are all rooted in one basic issue: What function does the Bible have for you? What is its specific authority?

I

What about the biblical salvation reasoning? We both would like to say — like Walter Cronkite of "ancient days": This is the way it is Monday, January 6, 1992.

But which way is salvation January 6, 1992? At an early point you claim: "I think that the church always exists, if it is faithful, on foreign or alien ground" (18). Yet is not the church biblically keyed into "the earth is the Lord's, and the fullness thereof" (Ps. 24:1)? If the church is faithful to God, will the ground on which it exists ever be foreign or alien? Is it not rather the case that the church might alienate *itself* from this ground of the Lord, and thus from God, too? What about our alienated churches? So, what is the function of God in your salvation logic? Is the Hauerwas logic contained in the sentence "The church's main task is to be what we are: God's salvation"? (44)

Why should I not be thrown for a loop when I also read (same page) that in our societies "there is literally nothing for which it is worth dying.... If, as Christians, the church saves us from this emptiness, surely the world may see that it is God's salvation indeed"? (44)

Had I wrongly thought with Luther, Calvin, and Barth, and in some sense with the ancient church, too, that God's *salvation is Jesus Christ*, is God personally? Still, always as God's right hand?

What is the difference between the liberal stress on humanity as salvation and the stress on the church as salvation? Aren't we still with humanity as salvation when we move to the church? Only that now it would be "liberalism in sheep's clothes"?

Hadn't Barth always warned of those who insisted on the *ecclesiam habemus*, "we are the church, we are the church together"?

II

What about the biblical justice reasoning? It was difficult for me to plunge into the second chapter because I found little linkage between the two: chapter one and the next chapter. I longed to know more about Jesus Christ as God's salvation before delving into the "Politics of Justice" (45).

Why not begin the second chapter with the Bible's reasoning about justice? But is there little more than a general criticism of the way justice generally seems to be used in (which concrete?) churches? I do not need to quote back to you what is not only on paper but also in your mind. That is, you have the whole picture in mind anyway.

The gist of it in a few of your sentences: "If there is anything Christians agree about today it is that our faith is one that does justice.... We are told that justice demands that we must reshape and restructure society so that the structural injustices are eradicated forever..." (45). But who really talks that way? The real craftsmen and craftswomen of our trade?

Yet even if they did, does this eliminate our struggle with *God's* justice? The abuse does not x-out the right use (*abusus non tollit usum*). I would have thought you might have said something like, Our faith is one that believes in *God's* justice.... Obviously it is not biblical to say that justice demands that we must reshape society. But does that allow us to hide the truth that God's justice *is* already reshaping society?

Obviously with your premises set up it is (then) easy to knock down John Rawls's liberal account of justice (on four or five pages). I know you needed that "in," so that later (50–58) you could make Gutiérrez look very much like Rawls and thus attack him. Why not in the future instead of all this negativity about Rawls start with Barth's great 1938 essay "Justification and Justice"?

Of course, *authors* choose their dialogue partners, and not the readers. The question is not whether people are yearning to hear God's Word on God's justice.

The question is what they need to hear. That is what dogmatics seeks to make clear, I believe.

III

What is the biblical view of the poor? There's somehow a contradiction in my mind between what you do with Gutiérrez and Latin America (50–58) and your account of Latin America in the last chapter (via Todorov's book that I had offered you to read several years ago), 136–40. Gutiérrez appears somewhat like a Jim Jones, in any case, a sect leader, quite out of the blue. There was at least the Second Vatican Council that went before, and Medellín 1968. Medellín sought to reflect the rootedness of Latin American theology for the first time — on its own soil among its own people.

You too like a good story. Why can't you let the Latin American story enter in along with Gutiérrez? Why does he have to appear on the foil of Rawls almost like a North American liberal? So it is easy to administer your major blow against liberation. Why do you need "*our* recent intellectual and political history" (54) to make liberation theology look bad in general and Gutiérrez in particular?

As regards your last chapter, there is a tone — a whole octave deeper. I can say together with David Toole, "I detect something new here" (153). It's just that David too gets stuck in the end on practically the same horns of the dilemma you're caught on all along. You want to break out of the hammerlock of liberal theology and do it in real hard. But do you really rid yourself of its anthropocentricity?

Might the biblical view of poverty and the poor offer a way out? Toole starts with somewhat the same intuition, but leaves the Bible out of the picture. Why not wade into the last chapter of Gustavo's *Theology of Liberation* (1988 ed., 162–73)? Why not argue with him about the biblical view of the poor rather than his view of the new man? I do not mean at all to exempt Gustavo from "mistakes" (54). My point is that there might be some closure between you two on a common way "in" on the biblical truth that you touch on in your last chapter: "The challenge is how, as Christians, we can find a way to witness to the God of Abraham, Isaac, Jacob, and Jesus without that witness becoming an ideology for the powers that would subvert that witness" (148). Well, how can we find a way to witness to this God? My notion is: by yielding to God's self-witness.

That brings us back to the "authority" of the Bible. I went through this long "wilderness wandering" of thought for almost four pages to make clear to myself, in tracking your steps of thought, where you take me up Mount Nebo, so that I might see the Holy Land. To make one point quite clear: the wilderness wandering is no fault of yours. It's just my awkward tracking.

The whole struggle we are into right now in North American theology, is it not ultimately about the character of God? And isn't it the case that in the Bible God shows God's self as poor God also among the poor — not only, but *also?* And isn't this the cutting edge of the whole marvel and mystery of the character of this God we need to begin with, a "Thou" that will not let us go?

Isn't this the Bible, not of biblicism, not of inerrantism, but of dynamism, the power of the Holy Spirit through whom God gives a self-witness exactly at the one vulnerable point of history called Jesus Christ and at the many other vulnerable points Jesus names in Matthew 25?

IV

The speck of spice from Karl Barth. If you hadn't said about a month ago in some meeting that you were reading Karl Barth I would probably not have thought of ending my search for understanding Stan Hauerwas the way I'm doing it now. But Barth might come to our assistance in clarifying the core challenge. I need to say this (practically *again* now) in closing my wanderings: I was much moved by your last five pages or so. And I was moved by what Toole comes up with, as it were, in response in his last two pages.

And yet there is, or part of it is, grave doubt. By the time I got through reading I felt like Atlas. I ask myself: Do I have to carry all this weight on my shoulders? All this much Christian world? All the right words are there. But in which order of priorities? Are the martyrs (real witnesses) so lost in witness that they aren't even conscious of it?

As for Toole, he ends up with Deleuze, Nietzsche, and MacIntyre. And with notions such as: "I am forced to judge in such a way that I cannot...but lie" (160). "I am forced...I cannot but lie..."? I am entirely involved in this. It is very moving. If only I could hear a note of: "They exchanged the truth about God for a lie" (Rom. 1:25). The whole thing here is, I have no other word for it, anthropocentric. Where is there any struggle to ascertain God's truth?

I am not now arguing for the theo*centric.* And certainly not implying a Tillichian tension of theonomy versus autonomy. Rather, here is where *Barth* helpfully comes in. Since you can read the relevant passages yourself, I'll lift out only the absolutely necessary, hoping, though, that you aren't shortchanged in the process. I'm still in *Church Dogmatics, I/1.*

It is touching the way you quote "I love to tell the story." I can only work with it if I preface it by "Jesus loves me, this I know, for the *Bible* tells me so."

Two fellow theologians had "gotten to" Barth, E. Schaeder and G. Wobbermin. Barth explains that between those two and him there was a very fine line, and yet this line stood for a world of difference. He clarifies the difference by introducing two "new" terms, ego-bound Word, and Word-bound ego.

Schaeder/Wobbermin seem to admit that the way of faith is always from God to humanity and not the other way around. But they apparently qualify this by suggesting that, once God comes, then there comes about not only a Word-bound ego, but also an ego-bound Word. Suddenly Barth sees the specter of *human control* of the Word rising up (242). *Homo capax verbi dei!*

Barth wants to say, God's Word cannot be "stuck" on the ego like the fly on flypaper. The reality of the church and the believer's faith are always a creation of God, time and again. There needs to be the *shock of recognition:* never can God's word pass from God's hand into control of human hands. Never can the church be salvation. No ego-bound Word!

So Barth returns to drawing conclusions in regard to Schaeder/Wobbermin: "Tell them this and at once you stir up angry irreconcilable strife" (244). The bottom line: when we say this "we have the crushing majority of leaders and led in the Protestant church today against us" (244). We still have — on both sides, left *and* right.

I am not claiming that you aren't at all with Barth at any point. I see you both valiantly struggling against the same disease. But when it comes to the antidote as I turn to you I am helpless. Do you let Jesus "cast out" the demons of liberalism? Or do you let these demons still hide under the guise of unreconstructed language? There isn't just the question of the violence of language, but also the problem of the poisoning of language. If you do let Jesus cast out the demons, why don't you tell this story — in new language?

The most beautiful point (for me) of your book is the "reminder that the way of nonviolence is never easy and that our language can embody that violence in ways that we hardly knew"(152). But see: there is also this *poisoning* of language by liberalism that gets into the ways we shape our basic method-blueprints and the way we talk. With you, lots of language has changed. But in what way have you really changed the liberal pattern of *formulating* the theological argument? I am grateful for your book because it makes me ask that question.

I gave the logical shape of your discourse a lot of thought. I tried to compare it with Barth's. I might not be seeing things that *are* there. It's happened to me before. To the extent that I am fair in what I see I find really no parallel in the logic of the basic blueprint. To have changed the great "grid" of thought, the basic filter through which we pour all our reflection theologically — that was Barth's great achievement. Has it already touched you? If not, when will you let it touch you? If it has, where do I look?

A brief switch in thought for a moment. What do I miss most in Stan's thought? Angels. And angel stories. It's not just Gabriel at the Annunciation, the heavenly host of angels at the birth, the angels after the temptation ministering, and the angels at the open tomb, it's also "He will give his angels charge over you to guard you in all your ways" (Ps. 91:11). And countless other witnesses to angels.

There is so much going on all around you, and in front of my nose, and behind your back: "Unresting, unhasting, and silent as light, nor wanting nor wasting thou rulest in might. Thy justice like mountains, high soaring above...." Isn't it God's activity and that of angels?... There is so much to unpack. *All* of that needs unpacking,

Yet so much is being excluded from the wonder of the narrative...that could make me forget the identity MacIntyre seeks.... O, but for this divine self-forgetfulness...let go and let God!

Aren't the really interesting things those North American theology no longer really touches upon? Not how many angels can sit on a pinpoint... but how many angels it takes to keep you from sitting on a pinpoint — for example, the one that I seem to have put there.

After Christendom? Angels. Isn't that the first square inch of what Barth developed as the "new" grid?

Fred

January 6
Epiphany 1992

37

LETTER TO GABRIEL FACKRE

This letter is a response to a survey by theologian Gabriel Fackre on the state of systematic theology, sent out to 219 graduate school systematic theologians, the results of which were presented in a presidential address to the American Theological Society, published in the Christian Century *(June 28–July 3, 1991) and in* Dialog *(January 1992).*

Developing a new vision of the future of theology, Herzog suggests another look at the content of the Christian faith on the one hand, and a self-critical encounter with those who have fallen through the cracks of mainline American history on the other. Both focal points are rooted in the theological efforts of recent decades in which Herzog himself was deeply involved: the 1978 document Toward the Task of Sound Teaching in the United Church of Christ, *published by the United Church of Christ Office for Church Life and Leadership, and a letter of thirty-nine United Church of Christ seminary professors in 1983, arguing for the importance of theological reflection.*

Dear Gabe,

Your letter invites us to state where we think systematics "should be going." I sat down on your "assignment" an unconscionably long time. You wanted brevity. I wrote already more than four pages. Let me try again and study brevity. This is my third try.

As background of my comments you want to keep your work in the United Church of Christ in mind, reflected in your good Craigville efforts. You know where to get a handle on work of mine. My last piece is in the fall 1990 *Prism*. — I admire you for your courage to do this "survey."

There are two framework premises of my answer. (1) As years go by, I believe we will realize that on account of liberation theology we will have to develop completely new perceptions of the *content* of theology, certainly of God, Christ, and the Holy Spirit. For example, much of previous theology did not conceptualize what it means that we Christians worship a "poor God" and a "poor Christ." (2) I am increasingly sensitive to our status as "aliens" on these two continents of the Americas. There's a little over two hundred years of United States of

---

Unpublished, January 6, 1991.

America. But there go two thousand years of Native American history before, in fact, practically twenty thousand years on these shores.

In Lima, Peru, on the median of the Paseo Colón, just across from the Methodist Seminary, stands a statue of Christopher Columbus (I guess some thirty-five or forty feet up). On the pedestal before him kneels an Indian maid (the "symbol" of the Americas). She has thrown the arrow at Columbus's feet. The admiral of the seas does not look at her, but into the distance (for new conquests?). Yet what does he press into one of the maiden's hands? The cross.

Next year, 1992, we'll have five-hundred-year Christopher Columbus celebrations and commemorations on our two continents. I know, the National Council of Churches has expressed misgivings. But there is much more at stake than misgivings. I do not have to tell you. You know all that. There is the *prior question.* Who of us really thinks out of this historical well of two thousand or twenty thousand years of American history when it comes to theology?

A few days ago on TV we could see the Native Americans on their horses trotting back through cold and snow to Wounded Knee: 1890–1990. They have to look at our history from the outside. Can we do it too? Our *money* sure owns this land: "This land is your land, this land is my land . . . " But our *soul* does not own this land — yet.

This issue of the prior question is not one of bad conscience. God forbid! It's also not a matter of sentimentality. It's a mandate of spiritual sanity. When will we take the step beyond European-American theology to American-American theology? Not developing American-American theology *instead* of European-American theology! But *prior to!*

The cross in the hand of Christopher Columbus is still the symbol of conquest. Is it not in our theological hands the same symbol of conquest, too? *In hoc signo vinces!*

a. So where should systematics be going? It needs to begin with a radical self-critical examination of the systematic theologian in his/her social location. Too often we systematicians start our theology developing methodologies with their criteria, warrants and evidence, etc., without asking a single question about whose interest we are legitimating (in our methodologies) and whom we serve.

b. Self-critical examination of the theologian compels attention to discipleship: sharing in the realpresence of God in Christ in the human struggle for justice and dignity, represented by the Eucharist. Here the theologian is inescapably confronted with the poor and oppressed as well as the sin-sick and sorrow-worn, the losers as well as the lost. Theology here turns out to be the second step only. It is reflection on discipleship, which is intimately tied to the truth/untruth struggle of the church. In the process, theology discovers that church doctrine ultimately is all about God's justice struggle for the dignity of the human person.

Just two notes to illumine the points a bit in the light of what another theologian is suggesting.

1. I certainly do not wish to exclude the conventional methodological considerations. I agree with David Tracy (in *The Analogical Imagination,* 1981): Without demand for publicness, "for criteria, evidence, warrants, disciplinary status — serious academic theology is dead" (21). Yet there is the *prior question:* methodological criteria and warrants of *what?*

In a recent book you also would be interested in, John Milbank, *Theology and Social Theory* (1991), the same point is made about public education: "Education especially reveals the concealed public dimension of political life which even liberalism cannot suppress: in deciding *what* to teach, what to pass on, any society expresses its view about what is really self-fulfilling" (197). I'm quoting this point here merely to say that we're sure not as theologians, in grappling with the *what,* so very unusual. Our whole society has a problem with *what* it is that it ought to pass on, if it still even knows what the issue of the *what* is.

In any case, systematic theology in North America is not at all clear about the *content* it wants to methodologize about. That content has to be settled first. If I understand you, that's your Craigville concern. That was our *Sound Teaching* concern in 1978. That was the concern of the letter of the "39" in 1983. If systematic theology in North America were clear on that score it would, I believe, see its primary task as *dogmatics* (the way I outline that in *God-Walk*). It would also begin worrying about the relationship of the now much hailed megachurches to megacrime and megadrugs. Why is it that with 426 persons of every 100,000 of the U.S. population behind bars we are the leading crime country of the world followed by South Africa and next by the Soviet Union? Are we systematicians still influencing culture and society or simply assisting in trivializing Christianity — the Sophists of our day I wrote about in *Prism?*

2. David Tracy goes on to suggest on the same page that "the theologians must speak explicitly to a third public, the church" (21). Must speak *to the church* — a third public? That's not the first question. The prior question rather is, are we theologians involved at all in the struggle of the church at the lowest point of God's entry into the world? Are we theologians developing our theological thought in that context? And in a truth/untruth struggle?

By now you probably regret that you wrote me the postcard reminding me of your August 16, 1990, invitation. As you might have surmised, I find it very difficult to respond to these invitations to surveys in our field. I am not saying, there is no will to address the hard issues. I'm not tired. And I'm not cynical. I just find that people do not even want someone to sound the tocsin. Often I think had the young Luther lived in this county in our time we would have crucified him on a cross of gold. I know, this is not a nice letter. Forgive. But you asked for it.

Sincerely,
Fred

– 38 –

A Tongue Completely New

While in his work Herzog paid close attention to oppression along the lines of race and class, he gradually also came to understand the struggles of women and introduced feminist issues in his teaching. Hammering out the project of liberation theology in a North American context, Herzog begins to realize the importance of the feminist perspective in the seventies: "Many a white male theologian will gladly acknowledge the processes of liberation going on here, the determined witness to freedom, and the valiant battle for human dignity. He cannot but align himself with these processes as a sign of hope."[1] In his book Justice Church: The New Function of the Church in North American Christianity, *Herzog not only shifts to inclusive language, he has become more deeply aware of feminist issues. In the Liberation Theology Group and the Euroamerican Theology Group of the American Academy of Religion, he worked closely together with feminist theologians Letty M. Russell, Susan Brooks Thistlethwaite, and Marjorie Hewitt Suchocki.*

This poem shows his growing openness to the voices of women, the search for a common journey which is able to acknowledge otherness and difference.

Perplexed
and even vexed
I listen.

You speak to me a tongue
completely new,
you glisten —

Your word, it cuts,
it breaks the old
to pieces,
our self releases.

First published in *Sojourner,* Women's Center, Duke Divinity School (March 1994), 16.

1. Frederick Herzog, "Which Liberation Theology?" *Religion in Life* 44, no. 4 (Winter 1975): 448.

No more the
gushing romance
lauding woman,
no more the knight
who courts his lady —
that deal was shady.

The deal with truth
makes us companions:
so much alike
and yet wondrously
other.
Am I a brother
of our new earth's mother?

And have I ever sung
in my real mother tongue?

– 39 –

Eucharist: Our Identity
Mission: Our Character
Discipleship: Our Purpose

In this address to a faculty forum at Duke Divinity School, Herzog challenges theological education in North America to deal with those parts of American history that are still repressed. Becoming aware of tensions close to home, we need to develop a sense for the broader global tensions of today. Gathering around the eucharistic table, theology might be led to a new sense of unity which respects diversity.

At the end Herzog raises three questions which bear promise for new theological formation in the twenty-first century. Theology will only continue to make sense if we come up with the courage to "ask questions we have never asked before." At stake is not only the future of theological education but also the future of the church.

Three score and nine years ago our fathers brought forth on this continent a new divinity school, conceived in liberty, and yet not dedicated to the proposition that all persons are created equal.

Now we are engaged in a great crisis of will, testing whether that school, or any school so conceived, can survive and meet the needs of the twenty-first century. The evil of segregation was officially terminated nearly four decades after the founding of the school. Yet did it mean that all theological demons of schizophrenic segregation were cast out immediately? Some burden of the past remains. There is still some inherited doublethink and doublespeak around in our theological mentality. It is ultimately rooted not just in the reality of slavery on these shores, but in the way this big chunk of real estate was conquered theologically. In this land, what is gone is the segregation, what has remained is the reservation.

My hypothesis: Duke University Divinity School's moment of destiny today is to settle its account with American history. North American theological education has widely become the spit and image of our culture of conquest and

Unpublished, January 3, 1995.

domination. In order to face the women's challenge, we need to let the history of the conquest enter our theological reflection. Rooted in history, we can inject the implications of our Theology-in-Context courses into our basic Christian ministry courses and eventually into all other courses as well. If we do it well, perhaps other schools will pay attention.

Right now we do not need new courses or a new curriculum. What we do need is a cooperative research project of the faculty to compact the basic findings of the required Theology-in-Context courses in order to let them permeate our basic ministry instruction in basic Christian ministry courses as well as in the other courses.

One of the most crucial sentences regarding the *tasks we can no longer evade* is an observation by Sydney Ahlstrom: "It is important to see that the impulses which led Luther to the Wittenberg church door were integrally related to those which sent Spanish caravels out across the Western sea."[1] There were not just theological results of what happened at that Wittenberg church door, but there were practically a hundred years of war after Luther's death (1546) until the Westphalian Peace of 1648, first in the so-called Wars of Religion and then in the Thirty Years War. The Reformation as well as the invasion of America triggered an immense shadow side of human life because of the mighty secular power impulses driving both — besides the religious impulses that fill theology books.

My hypothesis implies no guilt trip. It is an invitation to make scholarship more scholarly yet. Theologically we have been hiding much of our history on these shores. George E. Tinker, a North American Indian theologian pondering the situation, brings the matter down to a simple question:

> What is our blindness today? With the best of intentions and with the full support of our best theologies and intellectual capabilities, do we continue to fall into the same sorts of traps and participate in unintended evils?

With a fine sense of brevity he states:

> My presupposition is that without confronting and owning our past, as white Americans, as Europeans, as American Indians, as African Americans, and so forth, we cannot hope to overcome that past and generate a constructive, healing process, leading to a world of genuine, mutual respect among peoples, communities, and nations.[2]

With this introduction behind me, a few *content* considerations are in order to put flesh on these bones. In terms of a few categories we have used before: identity, character, and the purpose of theological education at Duke are at stake.

---

1. Sydney Ahlstrom, *A Religious History of the American People* (New Haven: Yale University Press, 1972), 25.

2. George E. Tinker, *Missionary Conquest: The Gospel and Native American Cultural Genocide* (Minneapolis: Fortress Press, 1993), viii.

Eucharist: Our Identity

According to Russell Richey, in the fall/winter 1994 *Divinity News and Notes*, we are in the third faculty generation:

> This third faculty generation is in as strong a reaction against neoorthodoxy as neo-orthodoxy was against liberalism. Its post-neoorthodox, or as it likes to style itself, "post-liberal character," is most noticeable in methodology, now pluriform. Narrative, hermeneutics, liturgy, spirituality, character, and liberation theology (black, feminist, Third World) — all receive emphasis by one or more faculty members. (4)

My commitment is not pluriform, but I agree with Russ that we proceed at the moment with the idea that pluriform is right. Principally there is no mutual accountability built into a situation where "all receive emphasis by one or more faculty members." The dynamic of our Duke history moves us — also in methodology — toward unity, though not uniformity. The story of our first years as the second-generation faculty contains the struggle over desegregation. In the body of Christ you cannot have a segregated table. If you do, you have a table of injustice. Ephesians 4:5 is written, so to speak, in big letters across the walls of this school: "One Lord, one faith, one baptism." In terms of identity, I have made the Ephesians tenet my own by underlining: *one* Eucharist, *one* mission, *one* discipleship. If the Divinity School lives this way as God's school, it will have tremendous implications for theological studies. If the York Chapel communion table is not the ultimate identity of the faculty conference table, we might as well close shop. How does each course organize itself around Jesus' realpresence? I do not mean to suggest that we should feel our religious pulse, but that we might develop a common research project that is in keeping with the mutual accountability heritage of the church.

Mission: Our Character

God's presence in the Eucharist in Jesus is the center of God's own mission to the world. We find the *character* of theological education right here. Mission begins at home, with God's justice making toward all people etching itself into our very being. The present rethinking of missions, for example, in the Board of Global Ministries, needs at least an equally committed effort on the part of theological faculties, who should not wait until they are asked to do the same.

The issue is uniquely focused in the challenge which women students are offering us. The mission of the church toward women and the mission of women themselves are crucially at stake in the character of theological education. The mandate here is the true equality of all persons before God and before fellow humans — when absent mindedly many assume that equality already exists. In the late '80s students like Judah Jones, Debbie Luther, and Fran Moody were singing themselves into our hearts with the song, "Weave, Weave, Weave Us Together *in Unity* and Love." At times they asked that the end of classes would be celebrated as a Eucharist. We were not without conflicts then, but by now conflict has reached the public eye, as the women's voices in the December 14–20 issue of the *Independent* prove.

Our greater awareness of tensions among us between men and women can open our eyes to other injustices, often conveniently overlooked in our efforts at pluralism and globalization which might hide more sophisticated forms of colonialization. I am thinking, for example, of Third World women, of the many negative globalization effects of IMF, World Bank, and GATT which we are concerned about in the Peru Initiative, and of the homosexuality issue, never yet fully faced by us in our own situation.

Discipleship: Our Purpose

Putting Eucharist and God's mission together is discipleship: we can do it only in the Christian walk. We often also refer to it as *Christian formation*. The painful thing is that at Duke we consider Christian formation as optional. It is up to the students to form themselves — we seem to have nothing to do with it. So some students end up in Covenant Discipleship, Prayer and Contemplation, or the Order of St. Luke. A lot of thought needs to go into the reason why discipleship or Christian formation, melding the Eucharist and God's mission, is not optional. There are more than enough spirituality studies by now, but I do not know of any Christian formation research that integrates spirituality with the classical theological disciplines and relates our present issues to our conquest history.

What I am asking for is hard-nosed common research, making our own teaching efforts its object, and asking:

1. What is the shape of mutual accountability, self-critically/eucharistically rooted in our own conquest history?

2. How can we, in view of our conquest history, share in God's mission in the teaching task?

3. How do we shape Christian formation in mutuality among ourselves *and with our students* instead of perpetuating a pattern of domination?

We have to ask questions we have never asked before.

Afterword

THE IMPORTANCE OF THE LIFE AND WORK OF FREDERICK HERZOG: A PASTOR'S PERSPECTIVE

by Peter R. McGuire

In the spring semester of 1995, months before Frederick Herzog's death, I was a student in his introductory theology course at Duke Divinity School. Like most of his students at the time, I was unaware we were being taught from a perspective outside the mainstream of theology. There was little realization of the uniqueness of Herzog's approach to theology and what it could mean for ministry.

In many ways, I did not begin to appreciate Herzog until I worked as a student chaplain in the terminal unit at Rex Hospital in Raleigh, North Carolina, the following academic year. When confronted with death and suffering, I realized the inadequacy of much of my own theology. In those moments of counseling patients and families in the midst of grief, the inherent strength of Herzog's theology became clear. Herzog did not teach theology from the perspective of conventional theological scholarship, because his life was not merely focused on his academic career.

Herzog was born to German parents in Ashley, North Dakota, who returned to Germany when he was ten years old. From 1947 on, Herzog was a student in Basel, Switzerland, where he was an assistant to Karl Barth. In 1949 he went back to the United States to attend Princeton University. While enrolled in the doctoral program, writing a dissertation on Friedrich Schleiermacher under the guidance of Paul Lehmann, he pastored a multichurch Reformed charge in Ashley, North Dakota. This was the same charge his father, who died in 1949, served from 1922 to 1935. In June of 1953, Herzog received his Ph.D. from Princeton.

In July of 1953, he went to the Mission House Seminary in Wisconsin, which later became the United Theological Seminary of the Twin Cities, where he taught until 1960. While at Mission House, Herzog was a moving force in the school's effort to infuse the old German Reformation tradition with a spirit of ecumenicity and social responsibility. In January of 1960, he joined the faculty of Duke Divinity School at Duke University in Durham, North Carolina. At first he declined the invitation to come to Duke because the university was not as yet integrated. When he realized that some faculty members were trying hard to have black students admitted, he decided to join the struggle.

Throughout his life, Herzog was intimately involved in the life of the church from the local to the international level. Beginning in 1961, and continuing until his death, he and his wife, Kristin, were active together in their local church, Pilgrim United Church of Christ in Durham. Much of their work focused on adult Christian education. On the international level, he was a delegate from the Evangelical and Reformed Churches to the World Council of Churches in Evanston, Illinois, in 1954. He served on theological commissions of the various conferences of the World Council and contributed to the theological boards of the United Church of Christ. Beginning in the 1980s, he was a motivating force in the development of "full communion" between his own United Church of Christ (UCC) and the Evangelical Church of the Union in Germany (EKU), one of the churches to which the UCC can trace its origin.

From his earliest professional days, Herzog expressed concern for social issues. In the 1950s, while at Mission House, he stood in solidarity with the striking workers at the Kohler Company as they demanded better pay and working conditions. After moving to North Carolina in 1960, he became passionately involved in issues surrounding racial integration, both in the university and in the community surrounding it. In 1964 he participated in a sit-in and was arrested with several other professors while peacefully protesting segregation at a restaurant in Chapel Hill.

Herzog was active in the Durham community and worked to involve the Divinity School in the community as well. Through his example, Divinity School students were inspired to take part in local issues. One way in which he involved students during the 1960s was through his work with a Durham community organization called Operation Breakthrough, an attempt by citizens and organizations to combat the pervasive effects of poverty. Several of Herzog's students participated in Operation Breakthrough by tutoring children, repairing dilapidated residences, and trying to help a poor neighborhood community create a playground.

Throughout his life he maintained an interest in the issues of the poor in his local community. He attempted to raise citizens' awareness of social issues through letters to the local newspapers. Realizing that African Americans and the poor did not have a voice, he tried to raise the consciousness of his own white community to stand in solidarity with them.

In 1969, Herzog wrote about a paraplegic worker named William Edwards, who became his friend. In reflecting on his experiences with Mr. Edwards, he concluded, "You don't understand what theology is until you have looked in the face of suffering."[1] This powerful truth fundamentally challenges the complacency of modern mainline Protestant churches.

---

1. Frederick Herzog, "Let Us Still Praise Famous Men," *Hannavee* 1 (April 1969): 4–6 included in this volume as chapter 6.

Herzog's particular approach to liberation theology questions our efforts to make the church a "spiritual beauty parlor" or a successful "enterprise." Beginning in the late 1960s, but especially with the book *Liberation Theology: Liberation in Light of the Fourth Gospel*, Herzog raised the question whether the modern Protestant church was taking seriously the Messiah Jesus of Scripture. Were we "taking up our cross," as the disciples were called to do, or had we shifted the focus of Christianity to the more comfortable subject of the middle class and its problems? In other words, had we rewritten the challenges of Matthew 25 in a manner better suited to our perceived needs?

In a letter to United Methodist Bishop C. P. Minnick Herzog shared what he believed to be one reason why mainline churches like the United Methodist Church continued to suffer dramatic membership losses. He said, "There is very little left in the churches that 'really' grips people, so that they 'really' would want to 'lay down their life for Christ.' "[2] He believed the church would only become relevant again by rediscovering the meaning of discipleship, a living faith shaping the totality of our existence. From the pastor to the layperson, we all must examine our faith regarding its impact in the world beyond the church. Whether the issue is toxic waste, equitable salaries, or the effects of globalization, Herzog's life and work show that the church is not fulfilling its call to discipleship by simply talking about God on Sunday morning. Discipleship is walking with God at all times and at all places.

Herzog's book *Justice Church* points out that, as denominations become increasingly intertwined with the culture at large, they fail to realize that they live in "apostasy."[3] This is because the church fails to realize that each congregation is part of the power struggle going on in the global village as a whole. So what will it require for pastors and laypersons to incorporate into ministry the theological approach Herzog offers in his works? The growing tide of marketing solutions to church problems, for instance, must be reversed in order to return to the reality that God was not a silent witness in the life of Jesus of Nazareth. God chose the poor, the oppressed, and the underprivileged whom we can join to take a stand in history.

As leaders in the church, pastors need to examine their own theology and ask whether they are endorsing a Jesus not reflected in Scripture. In *God-Walk*, Herzog asks, "Are we using our commitment to Christ merely to legitimate our life politically and economically? Or does Christ open a way for a critical spirituality?"[4] In the local church parishioners and pastors are called to an awareness of the struggles of all persons so that society will begin to perceive the commonality of the justice struggle. If God is taken seriously, the church is called to move be-

---

2. Letter to Bishop C. P. Minnick, dated January 13, 1991. The quote is from a handwritten note that was attached to the letter.

3. Frederick Herzog, *Justice Church: The New Function of the Church in North American Christianity* (Maryknoll, N.Y.: Orbis Books, 1980), 96.

4. Frederick Herzog, *God-Walk: Liberation Shaping Dogmatics* (Maryknoll, N.Y.: Orbis Books, 1988), 46.

yond the framework of its own history. In the coming decades, the growing tide of human suffering will challenge the church to realize its corporateness within a "globally humane history." Will it choose the "greater good and work for a more tolerable human life on this globe"?[5]

Since the brokenness of humanity is diverse, God's justice struggle is multi-faceted. It is waged on many fronts, economic, racial, and environmental. Within these broad categories, we find issues of class, gender, and theology. But for laity, clergy, and academic theologians alike, the justice struggle begins with the concrete witness in our own social location. Authentic theology begins in gutters, hospitals, farms, and roads, as much as in classrooms or places of quiet contemplation. Authentic theology is found in one's "walk."

In the current literature diagnosing the decline of the mainline Protestant churches, it is often argued that churches are too top-heavy. In *Justice Church* and later in *God-Walk* Herzog observed this problem as well, noting that both theological education and ministry tend to originate from the top down, rather than the bottom up. The result has been a laity-clergy duality, with local congregations centered on the minister's "whims and needs," rather than being engaged in the justice struggle at the grassroots.[6] So what is the solution?

It is necessary for the church to remember that it is God who establishes its agenda and mission. Contemporary society, culture, and theological fads do not determine the identity of the church, Herzog argued:

> Theology does not become significant again because of a changed scene. Christian thought is always significant as the idea-framework that grows out of praxis. The church is significant at the point where we see the world in all its facets, gripped by the God who is struggling for justice.[7]

In reading the present edition of Herzog's works, pastors, laypersons, and theologians will realize that we are not ultimately measured by the number of volumes written, the size of the congregation's budget, or the "programs" offered to market the church. Rather, what matters is the number of people finding God at work in their lives. Does the family losing their home to foreclosure believe God is way out there in "Beulah Land," or do they believe the same Messiah Jesus who "had no place to lay his head" struggles with them? For Herzog the question is, What is Jesus doing right now?[8] Jesus is risen and actively struggles with all who seek justice.

Herzog's theology challenges Christians to reexamine their priorities and ask the question, "To whom is our theology accountable?" For him, theology is accountable to all humanity and beyond it to all creation, because all creatures are intimately related. Through the presence of the Holy Spirit, God is actively at

---

5. Frederick Herzog, previously unpublished essay, "Las Casas: Conscience of the Postmodern World," included in this volume as chapter 34.

6. Herzog, *God-Walk*, 127.

7. Ibid., 151.

8. This question is raised once again in *God-Walk*. Almost forty years earlier Herzog had already brought up this question in a letter to Dr. Elmer J. F. Arndt of May 7, 1959.

work in creation. And when one part of it, be it the environment or an individual, suffers from the sin of another, God suffers with it. The church is then called to be a part of God's rebuilding of the face of humankind.[9]

Such thoughts led Herzog to become involved in relationships with churches and academic institutions in Peru, from 1987 until the end of his life. He led the way for countless members of United Methodist churches in North Carolina to visit Peru and for representatives of the Peruvian Methodist Church and the Methodist Seminary in Lima to visit North Carolina and Duke University. Together with the Reverend Dr. Mark Wethington, he worked toward an official covenant between the Methodist churches of Peru and of North Carolina which is still active. His purpose was to help people become aware of missions as an exercise in "mutuality" and to raise awareness of how economic and political practices in North America affect the lives of others. Herzog's theology challenges Christians to think and act globally as well as locally.

In "Dual Citizens," he wrote that it is necessary to make "the church more justly church" and the state more honest. In an effort to accomplish this, he sought to broaden the emphasis on education on both the grassroots and the academic level. In the 1960s and 1970s, Herzog attempted several times to create a degree program which intertwined theological education, politics, sociology, and economics. He described his vision of theological education in *Understanding God: The Key Issue in Present-Day Protestant Thought*, when he wrote, "'Clinics' in social change would have to be established, in which the student could become directly involved in relating his theoretical reflection in systematic theology to concrete findings in society."[10]

Christian discipleship is about giving one's whole self to both realms of life, the secular and the holy, completely. With this in mind, Herzog recognized the importance of small groups in the formation of Christian discipleship. He emphasized that with a focus on the Eucharist we would grow to realize our accountability to each other and the world, both socioeconomically and sociopolitically. Our discipleship would compel us then to ask, for example, How do these economic policies impact our community, our state, our nation, and the world around us? Herzog knew that real Christian living is struggle *and* contemplation.

Between 1981 and 1982, Herzog wrote what turned out to be an early draft of *God-Walk* called "Sound Teaching." He used it in class and asked his students to consider the impossibility of separating a pastor's spiritual responsibilities and the concern for the political world outside the church. On the last day of class in 1982, he wrote this statement:

---

9. Frederick Herzog, previously unpublished essay, "Humankind with a Human Face," included in this volume as chapter 33.

10. Frederick Herzog, *Understanding God: The Key Issue in Present-Day Protestant Thought* (New York: Charles Scribner's Sons, 1966), 128.

What we need to learn is that God is already at work in such situations. There's a melding of warfare and soulfare in Ephesians.... The political and the spiritual are of one piece there.... We need to learn our facts and figures in whatever situation God puts us in.... Before long (and some of you are already in a parish setting) all of you will have to make decisions about the very fabric of existence. You don't have to be afraid. Use your head. Think. Don't close your eyes.[11]

During the semester I studied under Dr. Herzog, I struggled a great deal with what he said and with what was going on in my own life. In almost every class, I openly debated with him about issues in his lectures. However, my own problems compelled me silently to bow out of my classes, and I struggled over whether or not to continue at the Divinity School. After two weeks, Dr. Herzog called me at 7 a.m. one morning and told me he needed me in class, "because it wasn't complete without you." Only one other person had called during those two weeks. I was stunned that a professor would take the time to inquire as to where I had been. Because of his concern, I remained in school and graduated.

The work of Frederick Herzog is important for Christians in all positions, because it reminds us that living faith emerges in the context of joining God's justice struggle. A church not engaged in the struggle faces the prospect of irrelevance. Living faith obliges us to pursue truth in the midst of the untruths of the world, breaking down the barriers between church and society.

What Herzog's Christian witness taught me is that all persons matter. Even if unable to see eye to eye at the moment, we are all interrelated in the eyes of God. In my own ministry that has become a focal point. From Herzog I learned of the Christ who actively compels us all to come to the table together, helping one another to struggle with the everyday burdens of life. Herzog's vision of the church depends on individuals taking up their cross and joining with "the broken body of our Lord uniting us in the world, healing the broken body of humanity."[12]

---

11. Unpublished class notes, "Sound Teaching," Fall 1982, 84.
12. Frederick Herzog, previously unpublished sermon, "The Eating and the Glory," included in this volume as chapter 10.

The Works of Frederick Herzog

Books

Understanding God: The Key Issue in Present-Day Protestant Thought. New York: Charles Scribner's Sons, 1966.

Ed. *The Future of Hope: Theology as Eschatology.* New York: Herder and Herder, 1970.

Ed. *Theology of the Liberating Word.* Nashville: Abingdon Press, 1971.

Liberation Theology: Liberation in the Light of the Fourth Gospel. New York: Seabury Press, 1972.

Justice Church: The New Function of the Church in North American Christianity. Maryknoll, N.Y.: Orbis Books, 1980.

God-Walk: Liberation Shaping Dogmatics. Maryknoll, N.Y.: Orbis Books, 1988.

With Reinhard Groscurth, eds. *Kirchengemeinschaft im Schmelztiegel — Anfang einer neuen Ökumene? Anfragen und Dokumente aus der United Church of Christ (USA).* Neukirchen-Vluyn: Neukirchener Verlag, 1989.

Dissertation

"The Possibility of Theological Understanding: An Inquiry into the Presuppositions of Hermeneutics in Theology." Th.D. Dissertation, Princeton Theological Seminary, 1953.

Articles

"The Nature of the Church." *Mission House Seminary Bulletin* 1, no. 1 (May 1954): 8–11.

"What Is Theology?" *Mission House Seminary Bulletin* 1, no. 2 (November 1954): 16–33.

"Exploring the Pending Merger." *Mission House Seminary Bulletin* 2, no. 1 (May 1955): 16–30.

"Jesus Christ and Church Union." *Messenger* (November 1, 1955): 9–12.

"The Place of the Bible in the Church." *Mission House Seminary Bulletin* 2, no. 2 (November 1955): 7–33.

"Critical Queries Plus Retorts." *Mission House Seminary Bulletin* 3, no. 1 (May 1956): 18–28.

"The Kerygma and the Peripheral." *Mission House Seminary Bulletin* 3, no. 1 (May 1956): 15–17.

"Theologian of the Word of God." *Theology Today* 13, no. 3 (October 1956): 315–31.

"Perils of Ecumenicity?" *Mission House Seminary Bulletin* 3, no. 2 (December 1956): 7–9.

"Philip Schaff — Ecumenical Prophet." *Mission House Seminary Bulletin* 4, no. 1 (May 1957): 11–16.

"Theological Issues in the Barmen Statement." *Mission House Seminary Bulletin* 4, no. 2 (July 1958): 14–19.

"Theologian on Tillich." *Christian Century* (December 10, 1958): 1432–33.

"A Christian Approach to Decency in the Social Order." *Social Action* 26, no. 3 (November 1959): 4–9.

"Man's Suffering and the Suffering of Jesus Christ." *Theology and Life* 2, no. 4 (November 1959): 288–97.

"Theological Faculty Member in a Religious University." *Duke Divinity School Review* 25 (November 1960): 73–75.

"Local Ecumenicity: An Introduction to the New Delhi Study Booklet." *Duke Divinity School Review* 26 (November 1961): 95–101.

"Focus on Faculty: Frederick Herzog." *Duke Divinity School Review* 27 (November 1962): 146–48.

"Possibilities and Limits of the New Quest." *Journal of Religion* 43, no. 3 (July 1963): 218–33.

"Montreal — An Image of Things to Come." *United Church Herald* (September 1963): 21–23.

"Honest before God." *Duke Divinity School Review* 28 (November 1963): 206–9.

"The Present-Day Authority of the Heidelberg Catechism." *United Church Herald* (December 1, 1963): 12–14.

"The Montreal 'Crisis' of Faith and Order." *Theology and Life* 6, no. 4 (Winter 1963): 309–20.

"The Norm and Freedom of Christian Worship." In *Worship in Scripture and Tradition*, 98–133. Ed. Massey H. Shepherd. New York: Oxford University Press, 1963.

With A. M. Pennybacker. "The Community of Freedom and Compassion." *Mid-Stream* 3, no. 3 (March 1964): 4–31.

"The Church as Stewardship and Mission." In *Stewardship in Mission*, 51–67. Ed. Winburn T. Thomas. Englewood Cliffs, N.J.: Prentice-Hall, 1964.

"Diakonia in Modern Times: Eighteenth–Twentieth Centuries." In *Service in Christ: Essays Presented to Karl Barth on His Eightieth Birthday*, 135–50. Ed. James I. McCord and T. H. L. Parker. London: Epworth Press, 1966.

"After Civil Rights — What?" *Duke Divinity School Review* 32 (Fall 1967): 230–36.

"Riots, Rats, and Forgiveness." *Pulpit* 39 (February 1968): 10–12.

"Die Gottesfrage in der heutigen amerikanischen Theologie." *Evangelische Theologie* 28, nos. 2–3 (February–March 1968): 129–53.

"God, Evil, and Revolution." *Journal of Religious Thought* 25, no. 2 (Autumn–Winter 1968–69): 5–28.

"August Hermann Francke." *Mid-Stream* 8, no. 3 (Spring 1969): 41–49.

"Black and White Together?" *Duke Divinity School Review* 34 (Spring 1969): 115–20.

"Political Theology." *Christian Century* (July 23, 1969): 975–78.

"Theology and the Politicized University." *Christian Advocate* 13, no. 17 (September 4, 1969): 7–8. German translation: "Die Theologie und die politisch gewordene Universität." *Evangelische Theologie* 30, no. 5 (May 1970): 274–79.

"The Political Function of Church Architecture." *Studia Liturgica* 6, no. 4 (1969): 130–46.

"'Politische Theologie' und die christliche Hoffnung." Trans. Karen Brühl. In *Diskussion zur "politischen Theologie,"* 121–44. Ed. Helmut Peukert. Munich: Kaiser, Grünewald, 1969.

"Let Us Still Praise Famous Men." *Hannavee* 1 (April 1970): 4–6.

"God: Black or White? The Upshot of the Debate about God in the Sixties." *Review and Expositor* 67, no. 3 (Summer 1970): 299–313. German translation: "Gott: Schwarz oder Weiß? Die Herausforderung des christlichen Glaubens durch die schwarze Theologie." Epilogue to James Cone, *Schwarze Theologie: Eine christliche Interpretation der Black-Power-Bewegung,* 165–85. Munich: Kaiser, Grünewald, 1970: 165–85.

"The Political Gospel." *Christian Century* (November 1, 1970): 1380–83.

"Theology of Liberation." *Continuum* 7, no. 4 (Winter 1970): 515–24.

"Towards the Waiting God." In *The Future of Hope: Theology as Eschatology,* 51–71. Ed. Frederick Herzog. New York: Herder and Herder, 1970.

"Political Theology in the American Context." *Theological Markings* 1, no. 1 (Spring 1971): 28–42.

"Between Ignorance and Arrogance." *Theological Education* 7, no. 1 (Autumn 1971): 73–74.

"Die Kirche als Befreiungskirche." *Evangelische Kommentare* 5, no. 2 (February 1972): 68–72.

"Ein neuer Kirchenkonflikt in den USA?" *Evangelische Theologie* 32, no. 2 (March–April 1972): 161–85. English translation in Herzog, ed. *Theology of the Liberating Word,* 11–24.

"Befreiung zu einem neuen Menschenbild?" *Evangelische Kommentare* 5, no. 9 (September 1972): 516–20.

"Response to Paul Lehmann." *Union Seminary Quarterly Review* 28, no. 1 (Fall 1972): 83–85.

"Political Theology as New Hermeneutical Focus." *Theological Markings* 3, no. 1 (Spring 1973): 27–34.

"Theology Post-Vietnam." *Christian Century* (June 13–20, 1973): 677–80.

"Gibt es ein Leben vor dem Tode?" *Evangelische Kommentare* 6, no. 9 (September 1973): 516–20.

"The Burden of Southern Theology: A Response." *Duke Divinity School Review* 38, no. 3 (Fall 1973): 151–70.

"Origins of *Liberation Theology*." *Duke University School Review* 38, no. 3 (Fall 1973): 126–28.

"Why Do You Think I Knelt Down among the Words of the Fourth Gospel?" *Duke Divinity School Review* 38, no. 3 (Fall 1973): 127.

"Future Shock after Vietnam." *Frontier* 16, no. 4 (Winter 1973): 218–20.

"Theologie am Scheideweg." *Evangelische Theologie* 34, no. 1 (January–February 1974): 70–80. English translation: "Theology at the Crossroads." *Union Seminary Quarterly Review* 31, no. 1 (Fall 1975): 59–68.

"The Liberation of White Theology." *Christian Century* (March 20, 1974): 316–19.

"Liberation Theology Begins at Home." *Christianity and Crisis* 34 (May 13, 1974): 94–98.

"Liberation Theology or Culture-Religion?" *Union Seminary Quarterly Review* 29, nos. 3–4 (Spring–Summer 1974): 233–44.

"Amerikas Theologie vor einem Neuanfang?" *Evangelische Kommentare* 7, no. 9 (September 1974): 528–32.

"United Methodism in Agony." *Perkins Journal* 28, no. 1 (Fall 1974): 1–10. Republished in *Doctrine and Theology in the United Methodist Church*, 26–38. Ed. Thomas A. Langford. Nashville: Kingswood Books, 1991.

"Commentary on the Bishops' Call." *Perkins Journal* 28, no. 1 (Fall 1974): 5–12.

"Liberation Hermeneutic as Ideology Critique?" *Interpretation* 28, no. 4 (October 1974): 387–403.

"Liberation Theology: Continuing the Discussion." *Christianity and Crisis* 34, no. 17 (October 1974): 226–29.

"Reorientation in Theology: Listening to Black Theology." In *The Context of Contemporary Theology: Essays in Honor of Paul Lehmann*, 225–41. Ed. Alexander J. McKelway and E. David Willis. Atlanta: John Knox Press, 1974.

"Responsible Theology?" In *Philosophy of Religion and Theology: 1974 Proceedings*. American Academy of Religion Section Papers, 159–73. Ed. James Wm. McClendon, Jr. Missoula, Mont.: Scholars Press, 1974.

"Interdependence of Spaceship Earth." *Christian Century* (March 26, 1975): 304–7.

"Whatever Happened to Theology?" *Christianity and Crisis* 35, no. 8 (May 12, 1975): 115–17.

"Wenn Supermacht zum Götzen wird." *Evangelische Kommentare* 8, no. 8 (August 1975): 456–59.

"Which Liberation Theology?" *Religion in Life* 44, no. 4 (Winter 1975): 448–53.

"Jesus and Power." In *Philosophy of Religion and Theology: 1975 Proceedings*. American Academy of Religion Section Papers, 197–211. Ed. James Wm. McClendon, Jr. Missoula, Mont.: Scholars Press, 1975. See also *Justice Church: The New Function of the Church in North American Christianity*, chapter 2.

"Solidarität mit den Schwachen." In *Öffentlichkeit als Gemeinde: Eberhard Stammler zum 60. Geburtstag*, 73–83. Ed. Rudolf Weeber and Robert Geisendörfer. Stuttgart, 1975.

"Doing Liberation Theology in the South." *National Institute for Campus Ministries: Southern Regional Newsletter* 1, no. 2 (January 1976): 6–7.

"Liberals versus Liberationists." *Christian Century* (July 21–28, 1976): 666–67.

"Theologisches Gewissen im Zwiespalt: Hartford-Aufruf und Boston-Erklärung in ihrer Wirkung." *Evangelische Kommentare* 9, no. 8 (August 1976): 451–54.

"How Do I Know What I Think until I See What God Does?" *Perkins Journal* 29, no. 4 (Summer 1976): 12–18.

"Birth Pangs: Liberation Theology in North America." *Christian Century* (December 15, 1976): 1120–25. Also in *Mission Trends No. 4: Liberation Theologies in North America and Europe*, 25–36. Ed. Gerald H. Anderson and Thomas F. Stransky, C.S.P. New York: Paulist Press, and Grand Rapids, Mich.: Eerdmans, 1979.

"Introduction: On Liberating Liberation Theology." Introduction to Hugo Assmann, *Theology for a Nomad Church*, 1–23. Maryknoll, N.Y.: Orbis Books, 1976.

"Pre-Bicentennial U.S.A. in the Liberation Process." In *Theology in the Americas*, 139–74. Ed. Sergio Torres and John Eagleson. Maryknoll, N.Y.: Orbis Books, 1976.

"Schleiermacher and the Problem of Power." In *Philosophy of Religion and Theology: 1976 Proceedings*. American Academy of Religion Section Papers, 285–99. Ed. Peter Slater. Missoula, Mont.: Scholars Press, 1976. See also *Justice Church: The New Function of the Church in North American Christianity*, chapter 3.

"Voting for a Violent Society." *Durham Morning Herald* (February 8, 1977): 4.

"What Do These Stones Mean?" *Hannavee* 1, no. 4 (April 1977): 15–16.

"From Good Friday to Labor Day." *Journal of Religious Thought* 34, no. 2 (Fall–Winter 1977–78): 15–22.

"The Bible and the Marxist Revolution." *Theological Markings* 1–2 (Winter 1977): 7–15. Also in *Justice Church: The New Function of the Church in North American Christianity*, chapter 4.

"Christian Revolution." *Theological Markings* 1–2 (Winter 1977): 16–26.

"Liberation and Imagination." *Interpretation* 32, no. 3 (July 1978): 227–41. Also in *Justice Church: The New Function of the Church in North American Christianity*, chapter 5.

"Theologie unterwegs zur Kirche." *Evangelische Kommentare* 11, no. 9 (September 1978): 515–17.

With J. Deotis Roberts. "Contextualization of Theology in the New South." *Journal of Religious Thought* 36, no. 1 (Spring–Summer 1979): 54–60.

"Am Ende der Nachreformation." *Evangelische Kommentare* 12, no. 9 (September 1979): 503–5.

With Thomas Ambrogi et al. "Theological Education and Liberation Theology: An Invitation to Respond." *Theological Education* 16, no. 1 (Autumn 1979): 7–11.

"Hat die reiche Kirche ein Gewissen?" *Evangelische Kommentare* 13, no. 10 (October 1980): 568–71.

"Luther and Liberation." *Christian Century* (October 29, 1980): 1035–38.

"What Does Full Communion Mean?" *EKU/UCC Newsletter* 1, no. 4 (November 1980): 1–5.

"Was Justice Done in Greensboro?" *Christian Century* (December 17, 1980): 1236–37.

"What Does It Mean to Be a Disciple in the Global Village?" *EKU/UCC Newsletter* 2, no. 1 (April 1981): 4–6.

"1984 hat schon begonnen." *Evangelische Kommentare* 14, no. 10 (October 1981): 572–75.

"Seeking to Identify EKU/UCC Global Covenant in Mission/Faith." United Church Board of World Ministries Paper (New York: 1981): 8 pages.

"North Atlantic Peace Witness?" *Christianity and Crisis* (March 1, 1982): 47–49.

"Authority and the UCC Statement of Faith." *Penn Central News* 21, no. 2 (Summer 1982): 8.

"Where Is the Church Going in the '80's?" *Occasional Papers of the Wisconsin Conference* 1, no. 1 (Autumn 1982): 11 pages. Also in *God-Walk: Liberation Shaping Dogmatics*, 150–67.

"Pfarrer als Laien Gottes." *Evangelische Kommentare* 15, no. 10 (October 1982): 535–38.

"Reformation Today." *Christian Century* (October 27, 1982): 1078–81.

"Who Speaks for the Animals?" *No Other Foundation* 3, no. 4 (Winter 1982): 14–18.

"Dogmatik IV." In *Theologische Realenzyklopädie*, 9:104–16. Ed. Gerhard Krause and Gerhard Müller. Berlin and New York: Walter de Gruyter, 1982.

"The German Reformed Churches' Unconditional No to Nuclear Weapons." *Sojourners* (June–July 1983): 10–11.

"Kings Traum lebt." *Evangelische Kommentare* 16, no. 10 (October 1983): 533–34.

"Wenn die Bombe nicht fällt: Die amerikanische Diskussion über eine neue Lebensgestaltung." *Evangelische Kommentare* 16, no. 10 (October 1983): 536–38.

"Thesen zum Zusammenführen der Ströme der Reformation." *Evangelische Theologie* 43, no. 6 (November–December 1983): 548–56.

"Passion Week." *Social Themes of the Christian Year*, 159–64. Ed. Dieter T. Hessel. Philadelphia: Geneva Press, 1983.

"A Contemporary Statement of Christian Doctrine." *Interpretation* 38, no. 1 (January 1984): 73–76.

"Kritische Spiritualität." *Evangelische Kommentare* 17, no. 10 (October 1984): 541–43.

"*Praxis Passionis Divini.*" *Evangelische Theologie* 44, no. 6 (November–December 1984): 563–75.

With Gustavo Gutiérrez. "Dealing with the True Problems." *Books and Religion: A Monthly Review* 13 (March 1985): 7–8.

"Our Tradition as Justice Power." Conversation with Susan Thistlethwaite. *New Conversations* 8, no. 1 (Spring 1985): 4–7.

"Why We Can't Wait." *New Conversations* 8, no. 1 (Spring 1985): 26–30.

"God-Walk and Class Struggle." *Circuit Rider* 9, no. 6 (June 1985): 4–6.

"Vernunft der Weisheit: Amerikanische Aufklärung im Licht kritischer Spiritualität." *Evangelische Kommentare* 18, no. 10 (October 1985): 551–53.

"Laying the Groundwork at Duke Divinity School." *Covenant Discipleship Quarterly* 1, no. 3 (April 1986): 4–5.

"A New Spirituality: Shaping Doctrine at the Grass Roots." *Christian Century* (July 30–August 6, 1986): 680–81.

"Die Quelle der christlichen Lehre." *Evangelische Kommentare* (October 1986): 570–73.

"Der Schrei der Sprachlosen." *Gottesdienst und Predigt* 4, no. 6 (December 1986): 2–6.

"Vom Ende der systematischen Theologie." In *Gottes Zukunft, Zukunft der Welt: Festschrift für Jürgen Moltmann,* 502–10. Ed. Hermann Deuser, Gerhard Marcel Martin, Konrad Stock, and Michael Welker. Munich: Chr. Kaiser, 1986.

"Ökumene am Scheideweg." *Evangelische Kommentare* 20, no. 10 (October 1987): 563–65.

"Resistance: A Justice Project." *Koinonia: Issues of Church and Society* (Summer 1988): 10–14.

"In der Solidarität des Lebens: Der Untergang des Abendlandes in den USA?" *Evangelische Kommentare* 20, no. 10 (October 1988): 563–65.

"Liberation Theology on the Front Burner." *Good News* 22, no. 3 (November–December 1988): 12, 14.

"Zukunftsschock aus dem Coca-Feld: Die Lage in Peru." *Evangelische Kommentare* 22, no. 10 (October 1989): 6–8.

"Camino Divino." *Encuentros* 1 (1989): 9–12.

"Kirchengemeinschaft im Schmelztiegel — Anfang einer neuen Ökumene?" in *Kirchengemeinschaft im Schmelztiegel — Anfang einer neuen Ökumene? Anfragen und Dokumente aus der United Church of Christ (USA),* 28–70. Ed. Frederick Herzog and Reinhard Groscurth. Neukirchen-Vluyn: Neukirchener Verlag, 1989.

"Full Communion Training." *Covenant Discipleship Quarterly* 5, no. 5 (May 1990): 9–16.

"Moses in Contemporary Theology." *Interpretation* 44 (July 1990): 253–64.

"Liberation and Process Theologies in the Church." *Prism* 5, no. 2 (Fall 1990): 57–68.

"Freiheit ist anders." *Evangelische Kommentare* 23, no. 10 (October 1990): 586–88.

"Kirchengemeinschaft und Eucharistie." *Berliner Theologische Zeitschrift* 8, no. 1 (1991): 115–18.

"Poor." In *Dictionary of the Ecumenical Movement,* 804–5. Ed. Nicholas Lossky et al. Geneva and Grand Rapids, Mich.: WCC Publications, Eerdmans, 1991.

"*Status Confessionis.*" In *Dictionary of the Ecumenical Movement,* 956–57. Ed. Nicholas Lossky et al. Geneva and Grand Rapids, Mich.: WCC Publications, Eerdmans, 1991.

"Theology, North American." In *Dictionary of the Ecumenical Movement*, 1001–2. Ed. Nicholas Lossky et al. Geneva and Grand Rapids, Mich.: WCC Publications, Eerdmans, 1991.

"Das andere Amerika entdecken: Es geht um mehr als um die Kolumbus-Debatte." *Evangelische Kommentare* 25, no. 1 (January 1992): 9–11.

"Freedom." In *A New Handbook of Christian Theology*, 191–94. Ed. Donald W. Musser and Joseph L. Price. Nashville: Abingdon Press, 1992.

"Amerika Wiedererfinden?" *Evangelische Kommentare* 26, no. 2 (February 1993): 69–71.

"Gottes Gerechtigkeit in der Liturgie." *Thema: Gottesdienst* 7 (1993): 48–57.

"Deal der Wahrheit. Mit christlicher Verbindlichkeit gegen die Gewalt." *Evangelische Kommentare* 27, no. 1 (January 1994): 33–34.

"*Tradición Común* Shaping Christian Theology: Mutualization in Theological Education." *Working Paper Series* 12. Duke-UNC Program in Latin American Studies (April 1994): 1–39.

"A Theology for the Americas." Review essay of *Las Casas: In Search of the Poor of Jesus Christ* by Gustavo Gutiérrez. *Christian Century* (July 13–20, 1994): 687–88.

"Athens, Berlin, and Lima." Review essay of *To Understand God Truly* by David Kelsey. *Theology Today* 51, no. 2 (July 1994): 270–76.

"Toward a Twenty-first Century Catechism?" *Prism* 10, no. 1 (Spring 1995): 19–30.

"Die Zeit drängt..." *Evangelische Kommentare* 28, no. 8 (August 1995): 448–49.

"Auf neuem Kurs?" Conversation with Gustavo Gutiérrez. *Evangelische Kommentare* 28, no. 9 (September 1995): 536.

"Das Gewissen steht auf." *Evangelische Kommentare* 28, no. 9 (September 1995): 533–38.

"New Birth of Conscience." *Theology Today* 53, no. 4 (January 1997): 477–84. Reprinted in *Liberating the Future: God, Mammon, and Theology*, 142–49. Ed. Joerg Rieger. Minneapolis: Fortress Press, 1998.

"Methodism, Missions, and Money." In *Doctrines and Discipline*. Ed. Dennis M. Campbell, William B. Lawrence, and Russell E. Richey. Nashville: Abingdon Press, 1999.

Index of Subjects

action/reflection, 30, 150
activism, 138, 184–86, 204
  political, 73
  social, 16, 73
advocacy, 330
African Americans, 2, 3, 5n, 6n, 11, 22,
  48, 54, 100, 146, 224, 351
ahistoricity, 323
alienation, 135
alms, 35, 36
angels, 343, 344
animals, 255–59
anthropocentrism, 258, 342
anthropology, theological, 112, 147, 167n,
  171, 238, 243, 244, 248, 250, 290,
  311, 328
apologetics, 64, 191, 246
apostles, 29
Apostles' Creed, 279, 291
Asian American, 207
atheism, 72, 101
atheists, 211n
Auschwitz, 67
authority
  biblical, 63, 85, 239, 339, 341
  secular, 61
  theological, 8, 62, 64, 127–29

baptism, 209–11, 241, 290
Barmen Declaration, 7, 204, 210, 252,
  288, 295
base communities, 267, 275, 276, 278–80,
  285
Bible, 22, 61, 86n, 107, 128, 129, 144,
  147, 159, 230, 339, 342
  as empowerment, 149, 163
  encounter with, 9
  as a handbook of liberation, 160
  interpretation of, 48, 318, 319
  new impact of, 279
  reading, 15, 135, 280

  as starting point, 231, 271
  walking with, 285
  see also Scripture
Bible Belt, 135
Bible-in-hand approach, 22, 100
biblicism, 339, 342
black
  becoming, 100, 194, 195
  bourgeoisie, 130, 132
  church, 2n, 207, 228, 229, 269
  community, 74, 76, 80, 127
Black Muslims, 59, 84
Black Power, 50, 66, 67, 71, 83, 126, 130,
  131, 163, 170

Calvinism, 238
capitalism, 37n, 61, 150, 158n, 160, 164,
  167, 173–76, 253, 261, 289n, 292n
Chalcedon, Council of, 248
charity, 8n, 15, 16, 37, 41, 44, 52, 54, 96
children, 261, 292, 300, 304, 305, 313,
  330, 333–35
  black, 304, 330
Christ, 14
  black, 68, 69
  body of, 235, 275, 279, 281, 282
  life of, 15, 250; *see also* Jesus, life of
  Lordship of, 293, 296
  mystery of, 29
  poor, 271, 345
  presence of, 91
  prophetic office of, 158
  servanthood of, 34, 56
  see also Jesus; Jesus Christ; Jesus of
    Nazareth; Christology; Christopraxis
Christendom, 189
Christ-event, 104, 112, 119, 145
Christian community, 15, 19, 60–62, 64,
  65, 67, 68, 72, 103, 200, 227, 228
  reality of God in, 61, 62

Index of Names

Abernathy, Ralph, 130
Agee, James, 54
Ahlstrom, Sydney E., 4n, 326, 351
Alves, Rubem A., 134n
Anderson, Ray S., 184n
Anselm of Canterbury, 101
Aristotle, 214, 287
Arius, 64
Arndt, Elmer J. F., 357n
Asbury, Bishop Francis, 197
Assmann, Hugo, 134, 151, 152–55, 159, 164, 167
Athanasius, 64
Augustine, 249, 334n

Bachmann, E. Theodore, 42n, 43n
Bahamonde, Wenceslao, 322n
Baldwin, James, 59, 82, 84, 87
Barber, James David, 298
Barreto, Hugo, 322n
Barrett, C. K., 106
Barth, Karl, 7, 8n, 64, 75, 88, 95, 102, 169, 170, 173, 211n, 245, 334n, 335, 337–44, 354
Barton, Bruce, 318
Baum, Gregory, 146n
Beaumont, Francis, 178
Becker, Ernest, 223
Becker, William H., 171
Bell, Daniel M., Jr., 331n
Bellah, Robert N., 89n, 136n, 322, 333
Bengel, Johann Albrecht, 105
Bennett, Lerone, Jr., 121
Benoit, Jean Paul, 35n
Berger, Peter L., 189n, 190, 203
Berger, Teresa, 336n
Berrigan, Daniel, 107, 296
Berryman, Phillip E., 134n
Bethea, Joseph B., 146n, 167
Betts, Doris, 314

Beyer, Hermann Wolfgang, 34n
Beyreuther, Erich, 34n, 36n, 37n, 38n, 39n, 44n
Blake, Eugene C., 46n
Blank, Joseph, 116n
Bloch, Ernst, 131n, 160
Bloesch, Donald, 245
Bloom, Allan, 276, 277, 281
Boch, Karl Eduard, 35n
Bodelschwingh, Fritz von, 44
Boff, Leonardo, 217
Bohren, Rudolf, 214, 215, 216
Bonhoeffer, Dietrich, 7n, 31, 32, 92, 206
Borch, Herbert von, 231n
Brandes, Volkhard, 131n, 164n
Brewster, Charles E., 193n
Brown, Delwin, 272n
Brown, John Pairman, 88n
Brown, Raymond, 106, 115, 116
Brown, Robert McAfee, 168, 266
Brown, William Adams, 237, 240, 241n
Brueggemann, Walter, 252
Bruno-Jofré, Rosa del Carmen, 323n, 326n
Bultmann, Rudolf, 100, 106
Burke, Joyce, 131n, 164n
Bush, George, 295, 298, 299
Bushnell, Horace, 239, 240

Callahan, Daniel, 117n
Calvin, John, 340
Campbell, Dennis M., 7n, 336n
Campbell, Ted, 325, 326n, 331–33, 336nn
Camus, Albert, 103, 170
Carmichael, Stokely, 66, 83n
Carretto, Carlo, 220
Carson, Rachel, 256
Cavaliere, Felix, 120
Celier, Léonce, 37n
Chamberlain, Marigene, 316n
Channing, William Ellery, 239, 240